TESTING

TESTING

TESTING

TESTING

SOCIAL CONSEQUENCES

OF THE EXAMINED LIFE

F. ALLAN HANSON

UNIVERSITY OF CALIFORNIA PRESS

BERKELEY LOS ANGELES OXFORD

University of California Press
Berkeley and Los Angeles, California
University of California Press
Oxford, England
© 1993
by The Regents of the University of California

Library of Congress Cataloging-in-Publication Data

Hanson, F. Allan, 1939–
    Testing testing : social consequences of the examined life /
F. Allan Hanson.
        p.   cm.
    Includes bibliographical references and index.
    ISBN 0-520-08060-2 (alk. paper)
    1. Self-perception—Social aspects—United States.
    2. Examinations—United States—Psychological aspects.
    3. Examinations—Social aspects—United States.   4. Examinations—
History.   5. Social control.   I. Title.
    BF697.5.S43H365   1993
    150′.28′7—dc20   92-32639
                                                                    CIP

Printed in the United States of America
1   2   3   4   5   6   7   8   9

The paper used in this publication meets the minimum
requirements of American National Standard for
Information Sciences—Permanence of Paper for Printed
Library Materials, ANSI Z39.48-1984 ∞

To Louise

We are entering the age of the infinite examination and of compulsory objectification.

Michel Foucault,
Discipline and Punish

CONTENTS

ACKNOWLEDGMENTS

For financial support connected with this project, I thank the University of Kansas for sabbatical leave, an intrauniversity visiting professorship, and grants from the General Research Fund. I am also grateful for a grant from the Spencer Foundation. I conducted research on testing in New York and Paris during the 1988–89 academic year, and I would like to thank Columbia University's Department of Anthropology and the UFR-CIS at the University of Paris-Val de Marne for extending every hospitality and courtesy to me.

In various stages of its development, parts or all of the manuscript have been read and commented on by Robert Antonio, Daniel Batson, E. F. Corwin, Jr., Helen Dee, George Hanson, Katherine Hanson, Mary Catherine Keslar, Richard King, Fransje Knops, Harvey Molotch, Jane Olsen, Michelle Tullier, and Carol Warren. To all of them, I wish to express my gratitude for criticism and helpful suggestions.

Louise Hanson has been at the heart of every project over the last three decades, sometimes as joint author and sometimes as silent partner. For this study, she carried out research in the folklore of testing, medieval judicial procedures, tests in popular magazines, and the history of the university. She read widely in the pertinent theory, and all aspects of the analysis have been regular topics of discussion between us for nearly five years. Her constant love, fierce loyalty, ebullient humor, and uncompromising criticism inform every facet of my life and thought. She also plays a mean game of tennis.

1

INTRODUCTION:

INFINITE EXAMINATION

The unexamined life is not worth living.

Socrates

America is awash in tests. Some nursery schools require the toddlers who would attend them to pass an entrance examination. That is just the beginning of an endless torrent of tests that will probe every corner of their nature and behavior for the rest of their lives. A faculty member at Columbia University spoke of a friend who was planning to begin graduate studies after having been out of school for several years. The professor asked whether she was anxious about the Graduate Record Examination, a standardized test required for admission to graduate school. "Well," was the response, "I'm an American. I was born to be tested."

This book is about how our addiction to testing influences both society and ourselves as socially defined persons. The analysis focuses on tests of people, particularly tests in schools, intelligence tests, vocational interest tests, lie detection, integrity tests, and drug tests. Diagnostic psychiatric tests and medical tests are included only tangentially.[1] A good deal of the descriptive material will be familiar to readers from their personal experience as takers and/or givers of tests. But testing, as with much of ordinary life, has implications that we seldom pause to ponder and often do not even notice. My aim is to uncover in the everyday operation of testing a series of well-concealed and mostly unintended consequences that exercise far deeper and more pervasive influence in social life than is commonly recognized.

This is an anthropological study, and it proceeds by the method that I term "institutional analysis." In this method, social institutions—the ways of organizing people into networks, relationships, and groups and the modes of behaving, thinking, and believing that are shared and customary in a society—are viewed as things in their own right. They may be analyzed in terms of their own histories, patterns of development, structures, and meanings. Although social institutions exist only in what the people who make up a society think and do, those people are often unable to say what the institutions are, how they are organized, how they work, or what consequences they have. They know them by using them and living them, not by discoursing on them. This is anything but surprising, for people no more ponder the peculiar implications of the social institutions they participate in as they go about the business of daily living than they reflect on the grammatical structure of their language as they engage in ordinary conversation, and that applies with special force to the vast numbers who have little awareness of cultures (or languages) other than their own. The anthropologist or sociologist, however, seeks to achieve some distance on social institutions, viewing them analytically and comparatively as constituting one way of life among many. That perspective enables the scholar to recognize and evaluate the far-reaching consequences of particular social institutions on the people whose lives are organized by them.[2]

Traditionally, anthropologists have focused their attention on small, tribal societies in faraway places. But these propositions about social institutions apply equally to all societies. We are no less products of our social institutions, and no more aware of their structure and consequences, than are the Nuer or the Maori of theirs. In recent years, anthropologists have increasingly joined sociologists in the investigation of how social institutions work at home. The analysis of one's own society is particularly interesting because it reveals extensive (and occasionally disturbing) consequences of behaviors that one had previously taken for granted as the "natural" way of doing things. This study explores the place of testing in the structure of contemporary American social institutions and its consequences for us as persons who live in terms of them.

Production and Domination

The two most important consequences of tests, I will argue, is that they are mechanisms for defining or producing the concept of the person in contemporary society and that they maintain the person under surveillance and domination. In *Stories in an Almost Classical Mode*, Harold Brodkey writes of his childhood: "But I did well in school and seemed to be peculiarly able to learn what the teacher said—I never mastered a subject, though—and there was the idiotic testimony of those peculiar witnesses, IQ tests: *those scores invented me.* Those scores were a decisive piece of destiny in that they affected the way people treated you and regarded you; they determined your authority; and if you spoke oddly, they argued in favor of your sanity" (my emphasis).[3] Even more than Brodkey, Victor Serbriakoff was invented by intelligence tests. Told by a teacher at age fifteen that he was a moron, he quit school and worked for years as an unskilled laborer. At age thirty-two he happened to take an intelligence test, which indicated that his IQ (intelligence quotient) was a towering 161. His life changed totally. He tried his hand at inventing and received patents, he wrote books on his favorite topic (not surprisingly, intelligence), and he became chairman of the International Mensa Society, an organization with membership restricted to individuals with IQs over 140.[4]

The other side of the coin is less publicized, but surely the humiliation and sickening sense of inadequacy brought on by poor performance on tests is a painful memory that millions carry for years. Virtually everyone recalls good or bad experiences with tests—standardized or classroom tests in school or aptitude, lie detector, or drug tests in the armed forces or in connection with a job—and can trace the effect of those experiences on their lives. In a very real sense, tests have invented all of us. They play an important role in determining what opportunities are offered to or withheld from us, they mold the expectations and evaluations that others form of us (and we form of them), and they heavily influence our assessments of our own abilities and worth. Therefore, although testing is usually considered to be a means of measuring qualities that are already present in a person, one of my two central theses is that tests to a significant degree *produce* the personal characteristics they purport to measure. The social person in contemporary society is not so much described or evaluated by tests as constructed by them.

In addition to constructing social persons, tests (and this is my second major thesis) function to control and dominate them. There was a time when people in the West considered themselves to be cradled in the hand of a caring God. Divine love and grace were believed to be such that people could count on forgiveness when they contritely acknowledged, as the Book of Common Prayer puts it,

> We have left undone those things which we ought to have done; And we have done those things which we ought not to have done; And there is no health in us. But thou, O Lord, have mercy upon us, miserable offenders. Spare thou those, O God, who confess their faults.

Today those things which we have done and have not done are monitored by human rather than divine agencies. Information about them is no longer offered in voluntary confessions but is extracted from us "miserable offenders" by tests: tests to determine if we have done our homework, if we can drive an automobile competently, if we have taken drugs, if we have lied, if we were at the scene of a crime, if we have contracted a sexually transmitted disease, and so on ad infinitum. If the conviction of living under God's ever-present gaze served to temper people's behavior previously, we are more perfectly controlled and dominated now because the human agencies that administer the tests are less forgiving than God. They offer or withhold rewards, opportunities, and punishments on the basis of test results. And this pertains not only to offenses we may have committed but even more important, to educational and other accomplishments that we may have achieved or wish to achieve. This is the basis for a remarkable advance made by testing in the field of social control: it enlists people as willing accomplices in their own surveillance and domination. The system is set up in such a way that if people hope to reach their goals, they must actively strive to comply with expectations embedded in tests regarding what they should and should not do.

It is not news that persons are defined, conditioned, and controlled by social institutions. This happens in all societies and is routinely accomplished everywhere by child-rearing practices and various techniques of education and behavior regulation. All societies also have techniques for generating knowledge about people. The conduct of social life necessitates that people know something of each other, if for no other reason than to know who can be trusted with confidences and who cannot, or whom to charge with specialized tasks of healing, religion, political leadership, or defense. What is unique about testing is that it has brought knowledge, control, and the social definition of the person to a new level of perfection and totality. Never before has any society deployed such a rich and ingenious panoply of dedicated techniques to scan, weigh, peruse, probe, and record the minutiae of its members' personal traits and life experiences. Never before has science, with all the power and prestige that have come to be associated with it, been brought so fully to bear on the problem of generating, storing, and retrieving precise knowledge about so many facets of the human individual. As a result of so much testing, it is certainly fair to say that more knowledge has been accumulated about individuals in contemporary society than at any previous time in history. This knowledge is used to control the behavior of individuals and also to characterize them in terms of their achievements and talents, their physical and mental characteristics, their normalities and abnormalities as measured along innumerable dimensions, many of which were not even recognized a century ago. And, as concrete individuals have been characterized in new and enriched ways, the general definition of what a person is—the social concept of the person—has likewise been transformed.

Most tests are intended to contribute to social ends that are generally reckoned as beneficial, such as equal opportunity, honesty, law-abiding behavior, acquisition of knowledge and skills, identification and development of individual interests and talents, and optimal vocational placement on the basis of such interests, talents, knowledge, and skills for the mutual benefit of the individual and society. But tests do not always serve the purposes for which they were designed. Often they have other, less desirable consequences. For example, serious doubts have been raised about the ability of lie detector and written integrity tests to measure honesty accurately. If these doubts are justified (and I think they are), the use of such tests results in the misclassification of many individuals, with severe damage to their reputations and opportunities to secure employment. Drug tests are only partially effective at identifying drug abusers, but many of the circumstances in which they are used assault the privacy and dignity of those who are forced to undergo them. Intelligence tests are designed in part to promote equal opportunity, but it happens that test scores are perfectly correlated with mean family income: those who score highest on tests have the highest average family income, and those who score lowest come from families with the lowest average income.[5] Thus instruments that aim to promote equal opportunity in fact systematically favor the advantaged to the detriment of the disadvantaged. In addition, intelligence tests feed a temptation to assess self-worth by comparing one's performance with that of others. This produces an unhealthy sense of inadequacy among those who do not do well on tests and an equally unhealthy exultation at the expense of others among those who excel.

The reason tests often have detrimental consequences for human beings is that they furnish a field where a fundamental contradiction among institutions and values in contemporary society is played out. On the one hand, social institutions have a logical structure and dynamic of their own, and much of history can be read as the development of more perfect manipulation and subordination of human beings and human activities to their (the institutions') ends. This general point of view has been richly developed in social theory by Marxist, structuralist, and post-structuralist thinkers—most notably, for the purposes of this study, Michel Foucault. On the other hand, the liberal, democratic ideals of individual autonomy, dignity, and the opportunity for self-actualization rank high among the values of contemporary society. Quite frequently, I will argue, tests are instruments of the evolving system of dominating institutions that act to curtail individual freedom and dignity. Therefore, it is almost inevitable for a study that seeks to explore the human consequences of testing to include a critique and some proposals for how its more destructive effects might be restrained.

The most important contribution that a book such as this one can make to that cause is to analyze just what the deleterious aspects of testing are and how they operate. After all, it will scarcely be possible to regulate testing effectively unless its workings and consequences are well understood. In addition to such analysis, at various points in the discussion, more practical short- and long-range solutions will be suggested which might be effective in harnessing some of the more harmful elements of testing. In some cases, testing should simply be stopped. Trial by ordeal, a legal test that required an accused individual to undergo an excruciatingly painful experience such as holding or walking on red-hot iron or plunging an arm into boiling water, had its heyday and was ended. Some contemporary tests are no less destructive than ordeals in the anxiety and suffering (now psychological rather than physical) that they provoke. It is high time to bring this to an end. A significant step in this direction was taken in 1988, when lie detector tests by polygraph and other mechanical devices were outlawed in the private sector. I will argue that similar action can and should be taken against additional kinds of testing, including most drug tests, integrity tests, and intelligence tests. Other uses of testing—for example, for assessment in the schools and for vocational placement—also have their detrimental consequences, but they are so inextricably woven into the fabric of society as currently organized that no simple prohibition of them is feasible. The solutions that I will suggest in these cases require long-range adjustments in a variety of social institutions as well as in testing practices.

INTRODUCTION

Testing in America

To say that tests are with us from the cradle to the grave conveys a sense of their ubiquity, but it is an understatement. Prenatal tests such as amniocentesis are used to ascertain some of a person's characteristics (gender, the presence of various defects) prior to birth, and, before that, pregnancy tests are used to determine if somebody is there in the first place. (The chain can be traced back even farther: fertility tests indicate the possibility that somebody *might* be there in the future.) At the other end, the testing persists beyond death. Autopsies include tests to answer questions such as cause of death, and cadavers are used for a variety of anatomical tests. Human remains are subject to testing almost eternally: archaeologists and their allies test bone, teeth, stomach contents, and anything else they can scrape up in their quest for information about human beings and our evolutionary predecessors from hundreds to literally millions of years after they died.

Tests tell us who we are when we are not quite sure. A few months before their nine-year-old daughter Arlena died of congenital heart disease, Ernest and Regina Twigg ordered genetic tests, which proved that she could not be their biological offspring. Suspecting a switch of infants, they requested that similar tests be conducted on Kimberly Mays, the only other white female who was delivered in the same period in 1978 in the rural Florida hospital where Arlena was born. The tests indicated that the infants had indeed been switched, and Kimberly's father, whose wife died in 1981, was left with the problem of how to inform his daughter of her true identity.[6]

We test when we already know what the test is designed to tell us, and if the test results differ from what we already know, we believe the test. Robert Sternberg tells the story of a young woman who was admitted to a college on the basis of other credentials even though her score on the Miller Analogies Test, an intelligence test used to predict the likelihood that applicants will succeed in college, was below the cutoff point. She went through the program with distinction, but when it came time to graduate, the college withheld her diploma until she retook and achieved an acceptable score on the admissions intelligence test.[7] Again, at major international athletic competitions between 1968 and 1991, several women have been disqualified because, contrary to the appearance of their genitals and their lifelong perceptions of themselves, a genetic test of cells taken from the mouth indicated that they are actually male.[8]

Like God or opportunity, tests descend when and where they are least expected. In a replay of "The Rape of the Lock" suited to the conditions of contemporary society, Ninni Burgel's estranged husband fished strands of her hair from the drains of a sink and bathtub she had used and had them tested for drugs. The results indicated "high, off-scale readings of cocaine or cocaine-related substances." Burgel submitted this evidence of drug abuse to support his claim for child custody in their divorce case. Not enough hair was retrieved from the drains for confirming tests, however. Two further samples, each the diameter of a pencil, would be required. A court order prevented Mrs. Burgel from cutting or chemically treating her hair while an appeals court deliberated whether she should be constrained to provide the additional material for testing. Eventually the court decreed, in a 3–2 decision, that she must allow a physician to cut the samples.[9] "But the locks were never shorn: three days later, Mrs. Burgel settled out of court."[10]

As Mrs. Burgel discovered to her dismay, one may be confronted with a test almost anywhere, any time. The elaboration of testing in America at the end of the twentieth century, both in terms of the number of tests and the variety of issues that they measure, is simply staggering. One effort to enumerate mental tests currently in use—Richard Sweetland and David Keyser's *Tests: A Comprehensive Reference for Assessment in Psychology, Education, and Business*—contains over 3,000 entries.[11] In addition to the well-known personality and aptitude tests, these include instruments such as the Seeking of Noetic Goals Test (SONG, a test that measures the strength of motivation to find meaning in life), the Thanometer (which measures awareness and acceptance of death; another test by the same author is called Coitometer), the Bank Personnel Selection Inventory, and the awesome Megatest (which measures very high levels of intelligence in adults when "ordinary intelligence tests lack sufficient ceilings"). Testing has imploded as well as exploded. Turning inward on itself like Lewis Carroll's smiling Cheshire cat, the testing enterprise includes tests that measure how people react to taking tests, such as the Swinn Test Anxiety Behavior Scale.[12] In addition to mental tests, more than 3,000 laboratory tests are available for medical diagnosis. Any effort to reach a grand total of ways in which human beings are tested would require enumerating, in addition to what has been mentioned already, vision tests, hearing tests, radiological tests, and tests of competency to operate various kinds of machinery. And certainly the end of the list is still not in sight.

Tests are found everywhere in the process of education. They punctuate progress through the grades, with quizzes, hourly tests, midterms, and final examinations serving as the staple measures for certifying that courses have been successfully completed (or not) and at what level. Recent legislation requiring that all students be given education appropriate to their ability has ignited an explosion of testing to identify those students who require special education, of either a remedial or enriched variety. Then there are the standardized tests that measure students' psychological profiles, interests, and intelligence levels. These are given in enormous quantities: from 100 million to 200 million of them are administered in the American school system each year, an average of from two and a half to five standardized tests per pupil per year.[13] These tests are used to evaluate the schools as well as the students. By comparing the profiles of scores attained on standardized intelligence tests, judgments are made as to the quality of education offered in different school districts, cities, or regions of the country. The trend is gathering momentum for states to require further standardized tests to determine if students have attained the minimum competency necessary to be promoted at certain grade levels and to receive a high school diploma. The system of higher education pours out its own alphabet soup of further standardized tests: PSAT, SAT, and ACT for college admissions and scholarship competitions; GRE, LSAT, MCAT, GMAT, and numerous others for admission to graduate or professional schools.

One does not escape testing on leaving school. Certain professions have certification tests required of all who would practice them, such as the bar examination for lawyers, medical boards for physicians, and licensing examinations for accountants, engineers, real estate agents, and many others. The National Teachers Examination is part of the certification process for teachers in many states. Many public and private employers require vocational preference and aptitude tests as part of their application procedures, plus more specific tests tailored to particular jobs: manual dexterity tests and competency tests pertaining to various bodies of knowledge or the ability to operate certain kinds of machinery. Often these tests are given not only at the moment of application but also at regular intervals throughout employment with the company. Such is also the case with physical examinations, which many companies require of their employees. In recent years, the war on drugs has opened a front in the workplace, where drug tests by urinalysis are increasingly deployed in a variety of circumstances. Until prohibited by federal law in 1988, lie detector tests by polygraph and other mechanical devices were required of applicants and current employees in numerous private sector companies. They are still regularly required in various segments of the armed forces as well as in connection with employment by governmental agencies such as municipal and state police, the CIA, and the FBI. The vacuum left by the prohibition of polygraph tests in the private sector is rapidly being filled by paper-and-pencil integrity tests and even handwriting analysis to assess the honesty of applicants and employees.

Several recent scandals—the most spectacular being the stripping of Canadian sprinter Ben Johnson of an Olympic gold medal in 1988—have drawn attention to the use of steroids by athletes. Among efforts to control steroid use is an agreement between the United States and the (former) Soviet Union whereby each conducts spot tests for drug use by its athletes who engage in international competition and informs the other of the results. The agreement also authorizes officials of one country to visit the other and conduct unannounced drug tests of, in 1991, up to one hundred athletes.[14]

In the medical context, a recent cartoon depicting a physician telling a patient, "It looks like a simple paper cut, but let's run a battery of tests to be sure" is only too true of what comes of visits to the doctor. Dr. Donald Young of the Mayo Clinic has called many diagnostic tests unjustified "fishing trips,"[15] but in today's litigious climate, it is difficult to escape the impression that they are ordered as much to protect the physician from subsequent complaints and malpractice suits as they are to assist in the diagnosis and decisions for treatment. Testing has a long tradition in American medicine. In 1912, an American physician, reporting on a tour of hospitals in the United States after practicing in France for nearly three decades, stated,

> I was simply thunderstruck with the number of . . . tests I saw being made; . . . tests seemed to me, like the Lord's rain, to descend from Heaven on the just and on the unjust in the most impartial fashion. . . . The final impression left on me by all this was that the diagnosis and treatment of a given patient depended more on the result of these various tests than on the symptoms present in the case.[16]

Possibly, the prevalence of medical testing stems from patient expectations as well as from physicians' predilections. Laboratory tests seem more scientific, and therefore more reliable in American minds, than diagnoses that physicians make on the basis of their own experience, knowledge, and skill.

The ethical and social implications of present and future biomedical tests are immense. As mapping of the human genome proceeds, new tests will be designed to determine genetic characteristics more precisely, and techniques will be developed to alter them by genetic engineering. Thus it is likely that the future holds the potential, through testing and other procedures, for society to intervene in the genetic makeup of its members. This is usually discussed in terms of how it will then be possible to eradicate genetic defects and diseases. Promising as that may sound, the prospects are not wholly auspicious. Already parents of children born with defects are filing wrongful birth suits against physicians who, it is claimed, should have identified the problem by prenatal testing and informed the parents in time for them to have considered the option of abortion. In addition to the psychological damage done to children who learn that their parents consider them to be "wrongful births," Myra Christopher (executive director of the Midwest Bioethics Center in Kansas City) reckons that the cost of performing prenatal tests for every diagnosable disability "would be so exorbitant that it would bankrupt the country."[17]

It is not difficult to imagine, furthermore, that increasingly refined prenatal testing technologies and genetic engineering could be used to produce infants with physical attributes, behavioral propensities, and other qualities that are socially approved or parentally desired. This is already happening in a relatively crude form when parents determine the gender of their offspring by means of selective abortion on the basis of prenatal tests such as amniocentesis or chorionic villus sampling (CVS). And what goes now for sex might in the future go for sexual preference. No sooner did news break of research findings suggesting a possible link between homosexuality and a certain condition of the brain than the prospect was raised "that the new discovery could lead to . . . a test that would detect a budding homosexual in the womb early enough for the fetus to be either whisked out in an abortion, or somehow changed with the proper cocktail of hormones."[18]

Testing and Positivism

Modern testing has its roots in the unbridled optimism of positivism: the point of view that all nature (including human nature) is governed by invariable laws and that these laws can be discovered and unerringly applied by means of science. Positivists embrace the idea of progress and express boundless confidence that rational, scientific understanding of human affairs will inaugurate a new era of peace, prosperity, and social justice. Many of these ideas had been enunciated earlier in one form or another by Bacon, Hobbes, Locke, and Hume, but for our purposes, a particularly apt expression of the positivist perspective on science was articulated by Henri de Saint-Simon, who wrote at the dawn of the nineteenth century. He argued that the last vestiges of the decadent old order—based on feudalism in the social, political, and economic sphere and on Catholic dogma in the intellectual sphere—had finally been swept away by the French Revolution. The challenge facing European civilization as it entered the nineteenth century was to erect a new social order, based on the principles of industrialism and science. The following passage catches Saint-Simon's enthusiastic vision of the new social order:

> Here it is not the strongest who control but those most capable in science or industry. They are not summoned to office because they have the power to exercise their will but because they know more than others, and consequently their functions do not consist in saying what they want, but what they know. They do not dictate orders, they only declare what conforms to the nature of things. The scholars show what the laws of social hygiene [!] are; then, from among the measures they propose as a result of these laws, the industrials choose those which experience has proved most practicable. The first will say what is healthful and what is not, what is normal and abnormal; the second will execute. . . . Things will occur as they are now occurring in industry, where, for example, chemists can tell us of the laws of combination of bodies, physicists of their resistance, and engineers deduce their applications, without any place provided in all this for the play of capricious . . . wishes.[19]

The positivist program embraced a new, scientific view of the human being. Previously, the knowledge that had been accumulated about the natural world was thought to bear little relevance to questions about the human condition, because human beings were not considered to be natural objects. Created in the image of God, and little lower than angels in the order of things, humans were thought to exist on a more elevated plane of being than the plants, animals, and inanimate objects that made up nature. All this began to change in the sixteenth and seventeenth centuries when, with the growth of a scientific world view, human beings lost their patina of divinity and were placed squarely within the realm of nature. Expanding on this view, positivists anticipated a science and engineering of human behavior. Thus Auguste Comte (a major positivist thinker who was Saint-Simon's secretary, disciple, and, later, bitter enemy) took it as a special goal of his course in positive philosophy (offered in Paris beginning in 1826) to contribute to the development of the human sciences. Testing would eventually play a central role in these sciences, because it was to emerge as the preeminent technique for gathering scientific knowledge about human beings.

Although the basic agenda of positivism had been set near the beginning of the nineteenth century, it required another century for testing to come of age in the West. Different types of tests matured, of course, at different times. But in general, testing has experienced its most massive proliferation during the twentieth century as an expanding and increasingly technical division of labor required the identification of competent personnel to fill various specialized positions, and, simultaneously, social scientists developed new techniques to measure a wide variety of human traits. Furthermore, recent testing has become more refined in its capacity to measure differences between individuals. A century and more ago, most testing was intended to make rather gross discriminations, primarily between normal individuals and those with mental deficiencies or other abnormalities. As techniques have improved, tests have differentiated among normal individuals on the basis of increasingly minute distinctions. They have multiplied in number and diversified in jurisdiction to the point that their power now touches virtually everyone, not once but often, not incidentally but crucially. The chapters that follow explore the impact of this on social and personal life. To set the stage, it will be helpful first to develop a general definition of testing and to distinguish among a few of its basic types.

What Is a Test?

All tests are means of gathering information. A glance at the usage of the term in ordinary language, however, is sufficient to establish that not all means of gathering information are tests. If a demographer asks how old you are and you tell her, information has been gathered, but that process is not called a test. Again, when Robinson Crusoe saw a footprint on the beach, he acquired the information that another human being was on his island, but we do not refer to that event as a test either. Nevertheless, it is possible to vary the conditions of both of these examples so that they become tests. It is a useful exercise because it enables us to identify the distinctive features of tests.

Begin with Robinson Crusoe and his footprint. Assume that certain hints had led him to suspect the presence of another human being on the island. Nothing conclusive, but suggestive bits of evidence such as broken twigs or matted down grass where a person or some other large animal might have passed or slept. Assume further that the island's only source of fresh water was a pool surrounded by a border of sand ten feet wide or more at all points. Robinson could well decide to test his suspicion that the island contained another human by carefully smoothing the sand around the pool and then returning two or three days later to see whether any human footprints were visible in it. The process would not necessarily provide conclusive proof. Friday, for example, might have divined Robinson's purpose, wished to remain undiscovered, and so smoothed over his footprints behind him as he left the pool. Nevertheless, it is entirely appropriate to refer to Robinson's effort to gather the information as a test. But why should this be a test, while his discovery of Friday's footprint on the beach was not? The salient difference between the two events is intention: Robinson stumbled across the evidence in the first instance, while in the second, he carefully planned and arranged a set of conditions that would bring it out.

All tests contain the condition of intent: they are planned, arranged, given, or conducted by someone with some purpose in mind. It is important to recognize, however, that while intent often involves the orchestration or manipulation of the events that are to constitute a test, this is not always possible or necessary. The chemist can bring certain substances together in a laboratory so as to observe how they interact, but the astronomer cannot change the movements or positions of heavenly bodies for experimental purposes. Ethical and political considerations limit the experiments that can be done by psychologists, sociologists, and anthropologists, while it is impossible in principle to create experiments in history because one cannot set up circumstances and manipulate events that have already happened. It is entirely possible, however, to seize on already-occurring conditions and events and use them as experimental tests. This is commonly done in astronomy and may happen in history and social science as well. For example, historical developments on the island of Rarotonga have been used as an experimental test of whether different courses of political change in Samoa and Tahiti during the nineteenth century are better explained in terms of varying effects of the conversion to Christianity or of different European colonial policies.[20] It is important to recognize, however, that such "ready-made" constellations of events would not be called tests until someone uses them for the purpose of acquiring knowledge. This stands as further support for the proposition that intent is a necessary condition of tests.

Although it is necessary, intent alone is not a sufficient condition for there to be a test. If it were, our other example (a demographer asks your age, and you tell her) would qualify because it obviously involves an intentional effort to gather information. Yet no one would call that a test. Again, it is possible to vary the circumstances of the example until it becomes a test, and that process will reveal another distinctive feature of tests.

Assume that you refuse to reveal your age to the demographer. She might decide to use torture, and this procedure may ultimately produce a confession of your age. But such torture would not be called a test, at least, not a test of your *age*. (It is, in fact, a test of something else, as will become clear in a moment.) Assume further that you come from Rapa, an island in French Polynesia where a person's exact age is of very little social interest. You might not be able to tell a demographer your age, as was the case with many of the Rapans I asked when I did fieldwork there in the 1960s, because you do not know it.[21] Yet Rapans do know their own names, where they were born, and who their parents are, and the French government requires that each birth be officially registered. Therefore, it would not be difficult for the demographer to ascertain your age, even if you do not know it, by checking the birth records. But no one would say in that event that she had determined your age by means of a test.

Finally, assume that you are (or were) someone who had lived long ago, whose skeleton archaeologists had unearthed. To determine your approximate age at the time of death, they might submit your remains to a laboratory for analysis. And this procedure, at last, would in ordinary language be called a test of your age. Why here but not in our other examples? The critical point is that in the last case, a *difference* exists between what we may call the "test result" (the facts that are directly collected; in this case, certain characteristics of bone) and the "target information" (the point or purpose of the inquiry; in this case, the age of the individual at death). This difference is not found in those examples that are not tests. When a demographer asks you your age, and you tell her, the information she receives (your age, as told to her by you) is the same as the target information she seeks. If she resorts to torture to loosen your tongue, it is still the case that the confession she wrings out of you is the very information that it has been her purpose to obtain. And if, meeting a blank wall of ignorance when she asks your age, she discovers it in the birth records, the facts she has unearthed are precisely what she wanted to know.

This indicates that a test is a special sort of investigation in which the information that is collected is not itself the information that one seeks but is instead a *representation* of it. Thus one does not give a screen test to see how well an aspiring actress will do in a screen test but to ascertain how she might come across in motion pictures; a standardized intelligence test is not given because one wants to know if a person can answer the particular questions on the test but to use that information to predict how well the individual would do at answering any number of questions of a similar kind and, therefore, to say something about that person's general intelligence. Now it should be clear why use of torture to force someone to reveal one's age is indeed a test, although not a test of age. It is a test of the strength of one's determination to conceal the information and/or of one's ability to withstand pain—matters that are different from, although ascertainable on the basis of, test results such as the length of time the subject remains silent and the severity of the punishment.

The final distinctive feature of tests has to do with the difference between test givers and test takers. In nearly all cases, test givers are (or represent) organizations, while test takers are individuals. Moreover, test-giving agencies use tests for the purpose of making decisions or taking action with reference to test takers—if they are to pass a course, receive a driver's license, be admitted to college, receive a fellowship, get a job or promotion, and so on.[22] That, together with the fact that organizations are more powerful than individuals, means that the testing situation nearly always places test givers in a position of power over test takers. As will become clear later, this is a fact of great importance for any analysis of the social consequences of testing.

Now we are in a position to define a test. As the term is used in this book, *a test is a representational technique applied by an agency to an individual with the intention of gathering information.* Beyond its value for deciding what is and is not a test, this definition will serve as a guide in the chapters that follow, for a good way to analyze any use of testing is to examine the power it vests in test givers over test takers and to ask how it satisfies the criteria of intent and representation. Raising these questions will assist our investigation of the nature of the individual as objectified, dominated, and made transparent by testing, as well as of the sort of society, composed of such selves, that we live in now.

The tests to be analyzed here may be divided into two broad types. *Authenticity* tests are designed to identify some qualitative state of being about a person, often a state of being with moral or legal significance. Usually the results of an authenticity test are reported simply as positive or negative: is this individual innocent or guilty, honest or false, noble or commoner, drunk or sober, a drug user or not? The most important examples of authenticity tests in current use are honesty tests and drug tests. *Qualifying* tests are concerned to measure the person's ability or inclination to perform certain activities. Qualifying tests may be general (e.g., intelligence or personality tests) or specific (e.g., tests of small motor skills necessary for certain occupations); they may test one's aptitude or potential, or one's achieved ability. Results of some qualifying tests are expressed simply as positive or negative (normally one either passes or fails a driver's license test, for example), but more commonly, they are reported on a graduated scale that enables a quantitative judgment of, say, the extent of an individual's verbal aptitude, or knowledge of seventeenth-century British history, or skill at repairing carburetors.

Both authenticity and qualifying tests may be found in most places and historical periods. Nonetheless, authenticity testing was stressed in preindustrial society. It remains important in industrial and postindustrial society, but the wide variety of specialized activities characteristic of these social forms has created a greatly increased demand for qualifying tests.[23] Part I is devoted to authenticity testing, first in its preindustrial, pre-scientific forms and then as it exists today in lie detection, integrity tests, and drug testing. Part II treats qualifying tests, again beginning with some of their earlier forms but reserving the most extended discussion for the various forms of qualifying tests in common use now. The last chapter will draw together many of the conclusions about the several kinds of testing reached in the earlier chapters. It will present my final analysis and critique of testing as a mechanism for fabricating and dominating the person, and it will advance proposals for bringing some of the most harmful consequences of testing to an end.

I

AUTHENTICITY TESTS

2

BEFORE SCIENCE:

THE EARLY HISTORY OF

AUTHENTICITY TESTING

God knew the truth—and could be asked

Robert Bartlett,

Trial by Fire and Water

Appearances may deceive. People often have reasons to present themselves as something other than what they are. To foil the human tendency to dissimulate, techniques have been devised everywhere to bypass what people say and tap the underlying truth by other means. Foremost among these techniques are authenticity tests. Although qualifying tests are more prominent today, in preindustrial society, authenticity tests were the primary form of testing. This chapter, a historical review of authenticity tests, provides a context for the subsequent discussion of their contemporary usage. Moreover, analysis of their early forms allows further insights into the distinctive features of tests in general.

As already explained, tests are representational devices. The ultimate purpose of a test is to discover target information, of which the test result is a sign or representation. While deceptions may be artful, the truths beneath tend to be simple and stark. Therefore, the information sought in authenticity tests is usually of an either/or form: genuine or impostor, honest or deceitful, faithful or heretic, innocent or guilty. Folklore provides a rich source for the variety of ingenious tests that might be used to answer such questions.

Identity

Tests frequently appear in folklore as means to determine someone's true identity: long-lost kinsman, heir to the throne, fugitive criminal, and so on. The testable sign of this target information may be some telltale capacity, as when a stranger is accepted as brother because he can accurately recount an event that occurred in childhood or when, as in an Indian tale (reminiscent of Latter Day Saint prophet Joseph Smith), a man's identity is certified because he is the only one who can read a magic book.[1] The future King Arthur, Wagner's Sigmund, and Odysseus were similarly identified by the unique ability to withdraw a sword embedded in a stone or tree or to bend a certain bow. Conversely, the inability to accomplish a task may unmask an impostor, as when, again in a story from India, a false bride was undone when she was unable to finish the true bride's weaving.[2]

Characteristics of the body are commonly used as signs in tests of identity. Fitting a slipper was the means of identifying Cinderella, and similar tests are found in many other folktales.[3] In the Ozark tale, "The Soot on Somebody's Back," a pretty girl is repeatedly raped in the darkness, perhaps by one of her brothers. On the third night, she places a dish with soot and grease beside her bed and smears some of it on the back of her unknown assailant. The next day, at the invitation of the eldest (whom the sister had taken into her confidence), the six brothers go swimming, and one of them never comes back.[4] Distinctive scars, birthmarks, and other permanent body characteristics frequently serve in folklore as the basis of tests for identifying kin, friend, or foe. A New Zealand Maori marked for vengeance was known to have overlapping front teeth. A suspect was tested by having a woman perform a lascivious dance in front of him, causing him to laugh. This enabled his enemies to see the telltale sign, and he was soon in their hands.[5]

Tests of identity may pertain to class membership as well as to specific individuals. One test for vampires is to check for their lack of a reflection in a mirror, and Japanese folktales relate how it is sometimes possible to determine if certain individuals are mischievous foxes who have taken human form by looking for the tips of their tails peeping out from under their clothing. Strangers who claim to be of noble blood may be tested to determine if they possess the requisite sensitivity, as happens in the story of the princess and the pea. A male version describes a prince who said he thought he was sleeping on a heavy beam, which turned out to be a hair in his lower bedding.[6]

Character

Many tests in folk literature are designed to ascertain if an individual merits trust or some great benefit, such as a king's daughter as bride and/or a kingdom (or half of one, anyway). Cleverness or judiciousness may be tested by asking candidates to solve riddles or answer questions; courage and ingenuity are signified by enduring frightening ordeals or fulfilling assignments that require perilous quests or impossible tasks. To determine his successor, William the Conqueror is said to have asked his sons what kind of bird they would prefer to be. The first said a hawk, because it resembles a knight; the second said an eagle, because all other birds fear it; and the third said a starling, because it makes its living without injury to anyone. The third was chosen.[7] Cinderlad, the hero in the folktale, "The Princess on the Glass Hill," was tested on several occasions. First he demonstrated his courage by spending several nights in a barn despite terrifying manifestations that had driven his older brothers away, for which he was rewarded with three magic horses and suits of armor. Later those magical accoutrements enabled him to accomplish the impossible task of riding up a glass mountain and thus to claim the princess seated atop it as his bride, together with half her father's kingdom. Numerous European and Arab folk traditions include the tale of the peasant girl who helped her father win a dispute by solving riddles. Her cleverness caught the attention of the king, who resolved to test her further by setting her to impossible tasks, which she succeeded in accomplishing. This sufficiently impressed the king that he married her and made her his trusted adviser.[8]

Chastity, an issue on which folktales indicate that a woman's word is not invariably reliable, is a common subject for testing. Italian stories describe several devices. One is to lead a woman of questionable virtue to a place where there are two fountains. In the presence of a chaste woman, the fountain that produces clear water flows, but if she is unchaste, the other, muddy, fountain gushes forth. A litmus test of the issue was to set her before a picture that would change color depending on her condition.[9]

Tests that may be classed under the general heading of loyalty are extremely common. The fidelity of spouses is a common subject of tests, the wife nearly always being the one whose behavior is scrutinized. The Bible establishes a ritual procedure whereby a wife suspected of adultery must drink consecrated water, which will cause her to miscarry if she has been unfaithful.[10] The representational structure of the test is clear: the test result (whether or not she miscarries) differs from but signifies the target information (whether or not she has committed adultery). The British tale, "The Loving Wife," recounts how a husband pretends to be dead in order to test his wife. True to his suspicion, he had hardly been laid out before the wife entertained a young man in her bedroom. The "corpse" jumped up and attacked the pair with a stick.[11]

Feigning dire circumstances also occurs in folktales when the fidelity of friends is to be tested. A ruse that usually succeeds in unmasking false friends is to inform them that all one's money is gone. Another test is to carry a slaughtered animal in a bloody sack to one's friends, telling them that one has killed a man and asking them to help get rid of the body.[12]

As King Lear learned to his undoing, the true feelings of relatives may also be other than they appear. A test in such circumstances was devised when three sons disputed the inheritance from their father. The father's corpse was exhumed, and the sons were told that the one who could shoot an arrow closest to the heart would have the estate. The two older brothers let their arrows fly, but the youngest could not bring himself to shoot. The estate was awarded to him, for he alone had demonstrated true love for his father.[13] Similar is King Solomon's trenchant test for determining which of two claimants was a baby's true mother.[14]

Biblical precedent (this time the temptation of Adam and Eve in the Garden of Eden) is also visible in stories of how the obedience of servants might be tested. The master ushers the servant into the dining room and invites him to partake of anything of the sumptuous feast that is spread before him, save one covered dish. The master then leaves, and eventually, the servant, unable to contain his curiosity, raises the lid of the forbidden dish. A mouse jumps out and runs away. When the master returns and checks the dish, the absence of the mouse is taken as evidence of the servant's disobedience.[15]

Honesty, Guilt, and Innocence

Tests of various sorts have always been used to help decide law cases, especially in the absence of more direct forms of evidence such as the testimony of unbiased eyewitnesses. Perhaps the simplest test in judicial procedures is the testimony of biased noneyewitnesses, or compurgation. Compurgators were character witnesses who swore not to the facts of the case but to the integrity of the person they supported, who was usually their kinsman.[16] The number of supporters varied with the nature of the crime and the circumstances. In medieval Wales, a woman accused of infidelity could disprove the charge with seven compurgators, but fourteen were necessary to answer a second charge, and a third charge would be dismissed only on the oaths of fifty.[17] To rebut a charge of murder by savage violence or poisoning, Welsh law demanded no less than 600 compurgators.[18]

Compurgation qualifies as a test by our definition, in that it is an intentional and indirect effort by an organization (in this case, a court) to gain knowledge about an individual. It is not a very complex or instructive sort of test, however, because the gap between the information derived from the test and the target information is narrow indeed. For the Welshman accused of murder by savage violence, for example, it is merely the difference between 600 of his relatives swearing that he would not do such a thing and the court's judgment that he did not do it. From our perspective, medieval legal tests become much more interesting when they move from seeking evidence from human witnesses to soliciting it from God. Divine judgment was sought primarily through trial by battle and by ordeal. As with compurgation—perhaps even more so—battle and ordeal were intended to be used only when more direct forms of evidence were lacking. In thirteenth-century Catalonia, for example, "if the accuser can prove his charge through authentic charters or through trustworthy witness, then that proof should be admitted and battle should not be adjudged . . . [for] men may have recourse to the judgment of God only when human proof fails."[19] And the twelfth-century charter of Tournai specifies that an assault to which there are witnesses will be judged according to the accounts of the witnesses. If there are no witnesses and the assault occurred during the day, the accused may clear himself by a "sevenfold compurgation," but if it occurred at night without witnesses, the trial is to be by ordeal.[20] As Bartlett explains, "In the case of an attack in the dark with no witnesses, there really might be the temptation to wonder who could know the truth of the matter. The ordeal offered a solution at just this point. God knew the truth—and could be asked."[21] But since God could not be expected to answer in plain language, the question was posed by orchestrating a situation in which the either/or outcome could be read as a message from God.

Trial by Battle

Framing the test in the form of trial by battle (also known as the wager of battle) amounts to letting rival claimants fight, with the assumption that victory represents God's judgment in favor of the combatant who is in the right. The main biblical precedent is found in the story of David, the shepherd boy who challenged the huge, well-armed, and battle-experienced Philistine champion Goliath in full confidence that, with God's help, he would prevail.[22]

Trial by battle was widespread in the early Christian era in Europe. In Ireland, "so general was it, indeed, that St. Patrick, in a council held in 456, was obliged to forbid his clergy from appealing to the sword, under a threat of expulsion from the church."[23] "No legal procedure was more closely connected with feudalism, or embodied its spirit more thoroughly than the wager of battle."[24] By the thirteenth century, however, French kings were attempting to abolish it as they strove to centralize power in their own hands and courts, while nobles clamored to retain it as a means of maintaining their privileges and independence vis-à-vis the crown.[25] Eventually, the monarchy prevailed and the wager of battle dwindled, at different rates in different places, until by the fifteenth century, it was an oddity.[26]

English law adopted trial by battle late (it was introduced by William the Conqueror) and was also late in abolishing it. One of the more common circumstances in which it might occur was in connection with the "appeal of death." This provision of English law held that within a year and a day after an individual had been acquitted of murder in a jury trial, the widow or next of kin of the deceased individual might demand a second trial. As a private suit, this second trial normally took the form of trial by battle. In 1774, an effort was made in the House of Commons to terminate the right of appeal of death in the colony of Massachusetts Bay (as part of a bill to punish rebellious colonists for the Boston Tea Party). This occasioned considerable protest that the erosion of fundamental rights, beginning in America, might soon come home to England itself, and the offending provision was struck before the bill could be passed. In 1818, more than two and a half centuries after trial by battle had ended in France, an Englishman named Thornton was acquitted of murdering a girl. Her brother claimed the appeal of death, and Thornton maintained his innocence and readiness to prove it by combat. The court certified the validity of the proceedings, and a trial by battle was scheduled. A crowd gathered, and the duel was precluded only by the failure of Thornton's challenger to show up. It was only the following year, 1819, that the right of appeal of death was finally abolished in England, and it may have been abolished as late as 1837 in South Carolina.[27]

When in full flower, wager by battle spilled well beyond combat between the principals to a controversy. It was common for a suitor to accuse one of the witnesses against him of perjury and demand to have the truth of the matter revealed by battle between them. In thirteenth-century England, a litigant might even challenge his own witness to battle if the latter's testimony was not to his liking. And in both English and French courts of that time, the loser of the case might appeal the verdict by challenging the judge.[28]

It was generally considered inappropriate for women, the physically disabled, and ecclesiastics to engage in combat personally, so they were usually represented in trial by battle by champions. For example,

> When Gundeberga, the Frankish wife of the Lombard king Charoald (626-636), was accused of treason, a deputation from her relatives suggested, "Order the man who brought this charge to arm himself and let another man of Queen Gundeberga's party proceed to single combat with him. By the conflict of these two the judgement of God will be made known, whether Gundeberga is innocent or guilty of this charge."[29]

Although in principle they should be represented by champions, in actuality, priests and monks were not always of pacific personality, and many accounts tell of churchmen avidly pursuing their interests by means of the wager of battle.[30] Women too might occasionally represent themselves in combat. German law lay down certain procedures to be followed when a woman faced a male opponent:

> The chances between such unequal adversaries were adjusted by burying the man to his waist, tying his left hand behind his back, and arming him only with a mace, while his fair opponent had the free use of her limbs and was provided with a heavy stone securely fastened in a piece of stuff.[31]

One might puzzle over such niceties. After all, David's encounter with Goliath proved that the support of the Lord is sufficient to overcome any disadvantage. Nevertheless, the men of the Middle Ages went to great lengths to ensure that when they placed their fate in God's hands, the odds as calculated in this world were not against them. Doubtless this was because the logic of trial by battle did not conform fully to the precedent of David and Goliath, where the human odds were so heavily on one side that divine intervention was credible only if it favored the other. One could scarcely attribute a victory by Goliath, that is to say, to an act of God. Trial by battle, however, aimed to create a circumstance rather like casting lots (a procedure that was also used in medieval trials and disputes), wherein the odds were so even that no human prediction of the outcome was possible. Then the result, regardless of the side it favored, could be attributed to God's intervention.[32]

Thirteenth-century English law made fine distinctions as to what disabilities would excuse an individual from trial by battle. The loss of molar teeth was not adequate for disqualification but the lack of incisors was, for the latter were held to be important weapons.[33] If the adversaries were unevenly matched, measures might be taken prior to the battle to equalize them. "Thus the knight who demanded that his antagonist should undergo the destruction of an eye to equalize the loss of his own . . . was strictly within the privileges accorded him by law."[34]

These refinements make Welsh rules pertaining to twins appear all the more remarkable. Under Welsh law, twins were considered to be a single person; they received, for example, but a single share of the family inheritance. But the legal status that spelled disadvantage in one arena worked an advantage in another, for if a twin became involved in wager by battle, he and his brother would take the field as one man.[35]

The scruples about equal odds operated only between social equals; when adversaries of different rank met in trial by battle, it was often a different story. If noble met commoner in judicial combat in France, the noble might enjoy the right of fighting on horseback with knightly weapons while the commoner would meet him on foot, armed with shield and staff. Such would be the case, at any rate, if the commoner had the audacity to be the challenger; if the noble condescended to challenge the commoner they would meet on equal terms.[36] While interclass duels did occur on occasion, for the most part, the wager of battle was very much the province of the aristocracy. In thirteenth-century Germany, a superior need not deign to fight anyone below his social station. A Jew could not decline the challenge of a Christian, but presumably the Christian was immune from challenge by a Jew.[37] More fundamentally, in a sharply stratified social system consisting of an armed nobility and an unarmed peasantry, the lower stratum of society lacked the training and, it was doubtless thought, the fineness of mind and sense of honor to engage meaningfully in the wager of battle. Another sort of test was deemed to be more appropriate to judicial needs pertaining to the lower classes: the ordeal.[38]

Trial by Ordeal

Ordeals of various forms are found all over the world. In medieval Europe, the three most popular were the ordeals of hot and cold water and of hot iron. The oldest of these—of Frankish origin and the only form to be mentioned from the earliest reference to trial by ordeal in about A.D. 500 until about 800—is hot water. The procedure required that the individual reach into a boiling caldron to retrieve some object, normally a ring or a stone.[39] During the reign of Charlemagne, 768–814, several other forms of ordeal came into being, and for the next four centuries, ordeal was a major judicial instrument. The ordeal of cold water called for the individual to be cast into a stream or pond. The ordeal of hot iron initially required the person to walk over nine red-hot plowshares; somewhat later, carrying a red-hot iron for three paces increased in popularity.[40]

As with trial by battle, the ordeal was a test that established conditions where, in the absence of witnesses or other sufficient human evidence, the decision of innocence or guilt was referred to God. In the case of cold water, God would signify his judgment by causing the innocent to sink and the guilty to float. This was thought to be so because water, a pure substance, rejects evil. Hincmar, Archbishop of Rheims (845–882) and major advocate for the ordeal, explained that the guilty party "is unable to sink into the waters over which the voice of the majesty of the Lord has thundered, because the pure nature of water does not receive a human nature which has been cleansed of all deceit by the water of baptism but has subsequently been reinfected by lies."[41] In the ordeals of hot water and hot iron, the innocent emerge unharmed, while the guilty suffer grievously. The rationale for this is, variously, that with the help of God, Shadrach, Meshach, and Abed'nego walked unscathed through Nebuchadnezzar's fiery furnace,[42] that the burning bush through which God communicated with Moses was not consumed by the flames,[43] that Lot was not harmed by the fire that destroyed Sodom,[44] that the faithful will not be harmed by the flames on judgment day, and that fire seeks and burns out wickedness, to which it has a natural antipathy.[45]

Precisely what qualified as not being harmed by the hot water or hot iron is not, however, entirely clear. The suspect's hand was bandaged after carrying the hot iron and was inspected three days later. Bartlett states that if the hand "was 'clean'—that is, healing without suppuration or discoloration—he was innocent or vindicated; if the wound was unclean, he was guilty."[46] This is a clear indication that the innocent were anticipated to be burned. On the very next page, however, he refers to expectations that innocent suspects would not be burned at all by hot iron or hot water. Perhaps these matters varied with time and place and with the prejudices of those who officiated at the ordeal.

Most important, ordeals by their very design traded in miracles, and miracles tend to become increasingly miraculous with time and retelling. Hence the most memorable accounts of ordeals seldom concern themselves with nuances in how well a wound is healing. A favorite motif is the queen who, accused of adultery, vindicates herself by the ordeal. A prototype is the case of the barren Queen Teutberga of Lotharingia. In 858, King Lothar, her husband, wished to marry his mistress and legitimize their children in order to have an heir to his throne, so he accused Teutberga of a variety of sexual crimes. Her innocence was proven by the ordeal of hot water, undergone on her behalf, however, by one of her retainers.[47] The embellishment of the theme is apparent in the

account of the ordeal undergone by Queen Emma, Edward the Confessor's mother, [which] is certainly fictional. . . . Emma was

33

accused by the villain of the piece, Robert of Jumieges, the Norman archbishop of Canterbury, of adultery with a bishop (a not uncommon conjunction). The queen offered to undergo the ordeal of hot iron; Robert of Jumieges unwillingly agreed, but only if he could specify particularly rigorous conditions: "let the illfamed woman walk nine paces, with bare feet, on nine red-hot ploughshares— four to clear herself, five to clear the bishop. If she falters, if she does not press one of the ploughshares fully with her feet, if she is harmed the one least bit, then let her be judged a fornicator." The queen, resting her hopes on her innocence and on the help of St Swithun, walked over the ploughshares "and did not see the fire nor feel the burning." In gratitude she gave to St Swithun nine manors, one for each ploughshare, and the bishop accused with her did likewise.[48]

Events that brought down the guilty were no less miraculous than those that uplifted the innocent. Brother France Maria Guazzo recounts the sad tale of a man convicted of heresy by the ordeal of hot iron in Strasbourg. While he was being conveyed to the stake to be executed, he was exhorted to confess his sin and repent, so that he might not suffer the eternal fire of Gehenna. He did so, and immediately his hand was healed. When the judge presiding at the execution saw no trace of a burn on the hand, he concluded that the man must be innocent and released him. Then the complications began:

> This man had a wife not far from the city, who had heard nothing of what we have just told. When he came to her rejoicing, and saying: "Blessed be God, who has today delivered me from the death of my body and my soul!" and told her how it had been, she answered: "What have you done, most unhappy one, what have you done? Have you recanted your true and holy faith because of a moment's pain? It would have been better for you if your body could have been burned a hundred times, than that you should once draw back from the true faith." Alas! who is not seduced by the voice of the serpent? Forgetting the great goodness of God to him, forgetting that undoubted miracle, he listened to his wife's advice and again embraced his former heresy. But God did not forget to avenge Himself for so great ingratitude, and wounded the hand of each of them. The burn re-appeared upon the heretic's

hand, and since his wife was the cause of his returning to his error she was made a partaker in the backslider's pain. The burn was so severe that it penetrated to the bones of their hands: and because they dared not in the town give vent to the cries which the pain wrung from them, they fled to a neighbouring wood where they howled like wolves. What need I say more? They were taken and led back to the city and together cast upon the fire which was not yet quite extinguished, and were burned to ashes. What, I ask, is the truth of the matter? Does the flame follow heresy, even as a shadow follows the body?[49]

Although, in general, the ordeal was considered to be appropriate to lower classes while the nobility had more frequent recourse to compurgation and trial by battle, certain rank and other distinctions may also be drawn between types of ordeals. If a person of quality was to be tried by ordeal, hot iron was the means of choice, hot water and cold water being suitable for plebeians.[50] Another distinction, this time between hot iron and cold water, had to do with speed of result. Trial by hot iron demanded a three-day waiting period before the verdict could be determined by the condition of the bandaged hand, while the result of the cold water ordeal was immediate: the individual either sank or floated. There was, therefore,

no neutral period of waiting in which crowds would disperse and emotions calm, and the cold water trial of heretics was thus particularly susceptible to crowd influence and mob justice. At Soissons in 1114, for instance, the condemned heretics were lynched by the crowd while the bishop's court was still discussing the sentence.[51]

One might be tempted to imagine that trial by ordeal waned as the European mind lost its confidence in miracles in the face of advancing rationalism and naturalism. Such, however, was far from the case. The heyday of the ordeal came to a close in the twelfth century, long before such new modes of thinking had taken root.[52] Ordeal was done in not by protoscientists who doubted miracles but by scholastic theologians who accepted them implicitly. Their main argument (which applied to trial by battle as well as to trial by ordeal) was that these techniques tempted God. They set up situations that invited—even presumed to guarantee—a miracle to be performed by God in the interest of justice. But, the scholastics argued, a miracle is a free act of God; it may or may not occur for God's own good reasons. Therefore, ordeal and combat are unreliable as judicial tests, and those who promote them are impious in their belief that human connivances can force the hand of God. Such arguments had been advanced, even by popes, as early as the ninth century. However, they had effect only as the centralized church grew in power and influence. By the early thirteenth century, that process had reached the point that an official condemnation of trial by ordeal by the Lateran Council of 1215, under the papacy of Innocent III, was sufficient to bring the practice essentially to an end.[53]

Tests of Witches

Well after its suppression in the thirteenth century, trial by ordeal reemerged in the great persecutions of witches in the fifteenth, sixteenth, and seventeenth centuries. In many ways, witchcraft was the ideal crime for detection by ordeal: its secrecy made more empirical forms of evidence hard to come by, while its alliance with the devil made it particularly loathsome to everything pure and to God, who might therefore be expected to be more than a little willing to signal the truth through the outcome of the ordeal. In 1594, Jacob Rickius, a judge from Bonn, addressed the problems of evidence in witchcraft trials and the importance of the ordeal. He wrote to the effect that

> the offense is so difficult of proof that there is no other certain evidence than the ordeal; that without it we should be destitute of absolute proof, which would be an admission of the superiority of the Devil over God, and that anything would be preferable to such a conclusion.[54]

The most popular ordeal for witches in this period was cold water, in the procedure known as "swimming a witch" (fig. 1). As the famous witch-hunter, Matthew Hopkins, practiced it in sev-

Figure 1.
The witch swims! Illustration from Montague Summers's
The Discovery of Witches: A Study of Master Matthew Hopkins.
Commonly Call'd Witch Finder Generall.
Published by Cayme Press, London, 1928.

enteenth-century England, the suspect would be tied, right thumb
to left big toe and left thumb to right big toe, and then lowered into
the water by means of a rope tied around the waist. The test was
repeated three times, and if the individual floated, it was proof of
witchcraft.[55] Rationales offered for swimming witches in this
period stressed the witch's satanic connections. For example,

> In 1583, a certain Scribonius, on a visit to Lemgow [Lemgo, in
> northern Germany], saw three unfortunates burnt as witches, and
> three other women, the same day, exposed to the ordeal on the
> accusation of those executed. He describes them as stripped naked,
> hands and feet bound together, right to left, and then cast upon the
> river, where they floated like logs of wood. Profoundly impressed
> with the miracle, in a letter to the magistrates of Lemgow he ex-

presses his warm approbation of the proceeding, and endeavors to explain its rationale, and to defend it against unbelievers. Sorcerers, from their intercourse with Satan, partake of his nature; he resides within them, and their human attributes become altered to his; he is an imponderable spirit of air, and therefore they likewise become lighter than water.[56]

Curiously, in southwest Germany of the 1640s, the contrary notion, that the *innocent* would float and the guilty sink, prevailed. Before using it in earnest, the Bavarian army resolved to test the test and so offered twelve thalers to any innocent citizen who would volunteer to undergo it. A man came forward and validated the test by floating on three trials. Then the army swam a number of suspected witches (soldiers' wives, for the most part) and executed several of those who sank.[57]

Swimming witches in the sixteenth and seventeenth centuries never commanded the official legitimacy that the ordeal had enjoyed during the medieval period. It was done primarily by peasants and viewed scornfully by the educated elite.[58] Even some of the most ardent witch-hunters viewed the ordeal with skepticism. Dominicans Kraemer and Sprenger, authors of the famous fifteenth-century manual on witchcraft, *Malleus Maleficarum*, surmised that witches might come through the ordeal of hot iron unscathed because the devil would intervene to protect them. They even opined that persons who offered to undergo trial by ordeal should for that very reason be suspected all the more of being witches.[59]

Another test for witches was to search for certain telltale marks on their bodies, which might have been placed there by the devil during their initiation ceremony.[60] They were often red or blue in color and might take the form of the footprint of a hare, toad, dog, spider, and so on. A distinctive feature of devil's marks was that they do not bleed and are impervious to pain. Witch-hunters would arm themselves with long needles for pricking suspicious marks to determine if they could draw forth blood or a reaction of pain.[61]

Other bodily features such as warts, boils, and even hemorrhoids or the clitoris were sometimes identified as special marks of the devil. These were taken to be teats at which the devil himself or imps would suck blood from the witch. (Imps were spirit familiars that the witch would send out to do mischief.) Such teats tended to be found on the eyelids, armpits, lips, shoulder, or posterior of men and on the breasts or genitals of women. The bodies of suspects were minutely examined for these unnatural teats, and candidate growths were probed and jabbed with needles to ascertain if they would bleed or produce pain.[62] John Taylor reports how in colonial America the body of executed witch Goodwife Knapp was examined for devil's marks after it was taken down from the scaffold.[63] An argument broke out among several women concerning whether certain appendages (of the genitals, certainly) were witches' teats. One of the women claimed that they were not, on the grounds that she had them herself. The other women rebuked her, and (perhaps realizing the possible consequences of what she had been saying) she finally yielded.[64]

Goodwife Knapp was but one of many suspected witches subjected to postmortem examinations. Although this seems not to have been the case in the West, some cultures contain the belief that individuals might be witches without being aware of it. The sure test to identify them is autopsy. Among the Azande of the Sudan, after death, the intestines of a suspected witch would be removed and carefully examined for witchcraft substance: a blackish, oval swelling. If found, that constituted proof that the deceased was indeed a witch.[65] The Kaluli of Papua New Guinea believe that virtually all deaths are caused by witchcraft. In vengeance, an individual suspected of being the witch responsible for a death might be killed in a surprise nocturnal raid on his longhouse. The body would be dragged outside, opened, and an individual holding a position neutral between the relatives of the suspected witch and his killers would examine the condition of the heart. If it was firm and dark in color, the individual was not a witch, but a yellowish heart soft in texture identified the person as a witch.[66] These testing procedures by autopsy have a number of factors in common with trial by ordeal. They share the assumption that a determinate, either/or condition actually exists: the individual in question either is or is not a witch. In each case, the avowed purpose of the test is to ascertain the true answer to that question. A test, with its indirect or representational mode of knowing, is necessary because direct knowledge of the matter is impossible. In the European case, this stems from the inability to look at the contents of people's hearts (figuratively speaking) and minds, while for the Kaluli, a test is required because one cannot look at the hearts (literally speaking) of the living. One procedural difference is whether the victim is killed before the test (as the Kaluli do) or after it (the European way).

Torture

After the suppression of trial by ordeal in the thirteenth century, torture became an important means of determining innocence or guilt in European courts.[67] As with ordeal and combat, torture was used particularly for those "invisible" crimes for which witnesses or other tangible evidence tended to be lacking: adultery, heresy, witchcraft, and so on.[68] Torture, however, relied for its result directly on the suspect rather than on asking God to produce a miracle. It was applied with great alacrity in the persecution of witches during the fifteenth, sixteenth, and seventeenth centuries. For one thing, it was believed that witches could be induced to remove their spells by beating or working other violence on them. It was necessary to pursue this tactic with diligence, however, because a witch would probably persist in the denial of being the author of the spell in question. If one hurt them badly enough, they would usually confess and undo their mischief.[69]

Torture was also used as a means of releasing the witch from bondage to the devil. The limitations that normally constrained torture were often disregarded in the case of suspected witches because the devil was believed either to prevent the witch from feeling the pain or at least to encourage the witch to endure it. The ultimate breakdown and confession was conceived as the witch being finally wrenched from the power of the devil and liberated to speak the truth.[70]

It was an impossible situation for the victim, who was considered either to be an unrepentant witch, in which case torture continued and intensified, or a penitent witch, in which case execution followed shortly. Johannes Junius, burgomaster of Bamberg, was caught in this snare in 1628:

> Junius had been accused of witchcraft and tortured until he confessed. His letter, written in a hand shaky from his sufferings, and smuggled from prison to his daughter, begins, "Many hundred thousand good nights, dearly beloved daughter Veronica. Innocent have I come into prison, innocent have I been tortured, innocent must I die. For whoever comes into the witch prison must become a witch or else be tortured until he invents something out of his head."[71]

Many people of the time were blinded to such (to us) obvious injustice by the conviction that confession was a blessed victory for everyone concerned, including the witch, because the grip of the Evil One on a human soul had been broken. As Guazzo put it, rapturously,

> The Divine Shepherd in His unspeakable mercy and loving kindness again and again recalls to the fold His sheep that have been carried away by the wolf and again He feeds them in the celestial pastures; and so when witches have been cast into prison and have confessed their sins, not grudgingly and under the stress of torture, but willingly and with penitential joy, it may well be said that they obtain the opportunity to avert so great and eternal a calamity from themselves at the small expense of their most wretched lives.[72]

Torture differs from ordeal because, as a direct means of wringing confession out of a suffering prisoner, torture is not a test. Probably many pitiable souls, quailing before the impending agony of the boiling caldron or the hot iron, were also moved to confess. But such fear was in principle only a by-product of the ordeal; the expectation was that the possibility of pain should be a matter of no consequence to the faithful. The point of the ordeal was to read the ability of the suspect to go through with it, or the condition of wounds resulting from it, as a sign of something else: God's pronouncement of the individual's innocence or guilt. Ordeal was in that sense an indirect means of acquiring knowledge, and thus it satisfies one of the defining features of a test. Torture, however, applied pain not as an appeal to God or in quest of a sign of anything. It was simply a technique of raising the stakes to the point that suspects—particularly slaves and lower-class people, whose word was not considered to be very reliable—would finally abandon their lies and reveal the truth. Therefore, torture is no test because, for all its paraphernalia and horror, it is merely a form of the direct means of gaining information by getting someone who knows to reveal it.

Analysis

We have defined a test as a representational technique applied by an agency to an individual with the intention of gathering information. Unpacking that definition with respect to tests from preindustrial society will clarify some of the fundamental elements of the logic of testing and will indicate certain consequences of testing—both intended and unintended—that will reappear in various guises in later chapters.

A Test Is a Representational Technique . . .

Test results are important not in themselves but as indicators of some other, "target" information. It is therefore essential in the analysis or critique of any test to know how representation operates in it. In considering cases of representation, it is convenient to distinguish between the "signifier" and the "signified." In testing, the signifier is the test result, while the signified is the target information—what the test is designed to reveal. So in one test for witchcraft, the teats found on a suspect's body are signifiers, and the signified is the (presumed) fact that the individual is a witch.

Signifiers may be related to signifieds in different ways. Two of the most important ones are "metaphor" and "metonymy." Metaphor is the relation of resemblance or replaceability. The sign of the cross that a Roman Catholic traces on the forehead and torso resembles the shape of the cross on which Jesus was crucified and is therefore a metaphoric signifier of it. Occasionally, in circumstances where the religion of the Dinka (a tribe of the Sudan) calls for the sacrifice of an ox and one is not available, a cucumber will be substituted with the promise that a beast will be sacrificed as soon as possible.[73] Although the cucumber bears no resemblance to an ox, it nevertheless signifies it metaphorically because it replaces or "stands in" for the ox.

Metonymy refers to the relationship of contiguity, or co-occurrence. Cause and effect, given their co-occurrence, constitute one type of metonymy. "Where there's smoke, there's fire" is a case in point, the effect (smoke) being a metonymic signifier of the cause (fire). Metonymy may also be noncausal. For example, a neon sign depicting a martini glass signifies a cocktail lounge by metonymy, because that vessel is (in our society) conventionally found in cocktail lounges.[74]

Tests rely on both metaphor and metonymy, and examples of each are visible in the tests that have been discussed above. Teats and devil's marks are metonymic signifiers of witches: such appendages and marks were thought to be found in association with witches, in the same way (logically at least) as martini glasses are found in association with cocktail lounges. The test in the story of the princess and the pea likewise relies on metonymy. It is assumed that a property invariably found in association with princesses is inordinate sensitivity. A test is conducted to determine whether a particular young woman has that property; if so, she must be a princess. Finally, metonymy underpins the logic of ordeal and trial by battle. God favors the righteous, the truthful, and the innocent; he abandons the heretic, the false, and the guilty. Therefore, victory in trial by battle, absence of pain or wounds in the ordeals of hot iron and hot water, and sinking in the ordeal of cold water metonymically accompany—are associated with—truth and innocence, while the opposite results are metonymic signifiers of dishonesty and guilt.

Some examples of trial by battle and ordeal also contain metaphor. Occasionally the test is undergone by a proxy, a champion for a woman or an infirm man in trial by battle or a servant who undergoes the ordeal in place of the accused (as happened when Queen Teutberga was tried for sexual misconduct). The proxy is a metaphoric representation or signifier of the principal in the case. In its logic, if not in all particulars, the situation is similar to the Dinka sacrifice of a cucumber as a stand-in for an ox.

Another way that metaphor operates in testing is that the subject's behavior in the test is taken to be similar to—and therefore representative of—that person's behavior in many other situations. Examples are the ersatz mother who accepted Solomon's proposal to cut a disputed infant in half, the young man who could not bring himself to shoot arrows at the heart of his father's corpse, and the servant who opened the forbidden dish. In each, the assumption is that the subject will behave in the future (or has behaved in the past) in a manner similar to the behavior demonstrated in the test. This assumption underwrites the extension of the test result to the broader conclusion as to whether the subject is a true mother, a loving son, or an obedient servant. The test, that is to say, stands as a metaphoric signifier of the subject's more general conduct or character. This type of logic may be the most common to be found in all testing.

Nearly all tests achieve their representational character by the principles of metaphor or metonymy. Which of them is in play, and how, will be one topic of analysis for the various, more modern tests that will be discussed in later chapters. For the moment, it is crucial to recognize that metaphor and metonymy are not part of the nature of things but are rooted in culture. No intrinsic, invariable connection exists, for example, between the signifier "Omaha" and any particular signified. In Siouan languages, it refers to a tribe; in contemporary American English, it most commonly signifies a Midwestern city (but also a Siouan tribe and a beach in Normandy); and in Tahitian, it means "to urinate." A cucumber may stand in metaphorically for an ox, or a champion for a damsel, only because the conventions of the time and place provide for it. Similarly, cultural conventions alone certify that where there are teats there are witches, that victory in combat signals the favor of God, and that a loving son cannot bear to shoot arrows at the corpse of his father.[75]

This point takes on great significance when we remember that the ostensible purpose of testing, preindustrial and since, is to reveal the truth about some purely objective, independently existing state of affairs. But what has just been said proves that this cannot be the case. Because representation is an essential component of any test, and because what counts as representation is a matter of social convention, tests provide information about reality *as construed by culture*. On the basis of certain bodily appendages or blackish swellings on the intestines, empirical evidence visible to anyone, fifteenth-century Europeans and African Azande made unequivocal decisions about who was a witch and who was not. But it does not follow that there objectively were witches in Europe of that time or in Zandeland. That conclusion depends on what the evidence means or signifies, and *that* is a product of the cultural understandings prevailing at a particular time and place. This is the nature of all testing, including the tests of honesty, vocational interests, and intelligence that prevail in contemporary America. No less than the Kaluli determination that a person is or is not a witch on the basis of the color and texture of the heart, these too rely on the cultural construal of what certain facts mean.

. . . Applied by an Agency to an Individual. . .

The design of the test and its administration are in hands other than those of the test taker. They decide if the circumstances merit a test, they oversee its application, they interpret its results, they determine what action (reward, punishment, whatever) is to be taken. It is, very simply, a matter of power.

The control of the situation by someone other than the subject of the test is obvious in the case of the master who told his servant to eat of anything spread on the feasting table save for one covered dish, or in the story of the princess and the pea. In these examples, the subject is not even aware that a test is being conducted. Someone else unilaterally establishes the conditions of the test, observes the subject in those conditions, and reaches a conclusion. The power differential is still more vivid and overwhelming in judicial tests. They demand the accused ones to gather compurgators to testify to their innocence, to fight or find a champion, to thrust arms into boiling water, to carry red-hot iron in the hands or walk on it with bare feet. And through all the prayer and pleading, protesting, promising, and pain, they dispassionately watch, inspect, evaluate, and decide. They swarm over the body of a suspected witch, meticulously inspecting it for birthmarks, boils, and sundry appendages (genital and otherwise), pinching and probing with fingers, pricking with needles. They strip the person naked, tie toes to thumbs, cast the wretch into the water, and clinically calculate the buoyancy while the suspect suffers the agony of near-drowning.

It does not end here. Those accused of evildoing are reduced to the point not only of enduring the ordeal but even of *asking* for it, perceiving it to be the only avenue available to prove their innocence. And when they do, that indispensable fifteenth-century guidebook to witch-hunters, the *Malleus Maleficarum*, cautions in an exquisitely heartless twist that those who offer to undergo ordeal to clear themselves probably do so out of confidence that the devil will bring them through successfully. Therefore, they should be all the more suspected of witchcraft.[76] And finally, those who are disfigured by ordeal, broken by torture, and sentenced to burning at the stake are expected to be grateful to their inquisitors and tormentors for having set them free from the grip of evil and having restored their candidacy for God's saving grace at the negligible price of their miserable lives.

Who are the "they" that exercise such power over those unfortunate enough to be accused of criminal activities? It is not really the executioners, torturers, and witch-hunters, for these are only agents. The same, ultimately, may be said of the accusers who begin the process and the judges who preside over the end of it, pronouncing the sentence. As with the "they" who control prices, decree the rate of unemployment, set the need for higher taxes, and establish vital national interests in today's world, the "they" who exerted power over the individual by means of the tests of pre-industrial society are much greater, diffuse, and pervasive than any human individual or even any group. It is ultimately the total sociocultural system that dominates, inexorably expressing itself and evolving by working out the implications of its structure and fundamental principles.

However, as Foucault has so perceptively noted, the power exercised by ordeal, torture, and public execution was limited.[77]

The measure of power is not how much pain and suffering it can produce but how efficiently it can achieve its ends. Witch-hunting, for example, died out in Europe after the middle of the seventeenth century because developments in education, preaching, and pastoral care among the common people proved to be a more effective (if less dramatic) means of establishing religious discipline and containing heresy than burning witches.[78] Judged by the results, power applied through the boiling caldron, the hot iron, the torture chamber, and the executioner's scaffold was comparatively feeble. It has since been replaced with subtler but more pervasive and effective expressions of power. Among these, as will become apparent, are the tests of industrial and postindustrial society.

. . . with the Intention of Gathering Information

The authenticity tests of preindustrial society are aimed at getting at the truth of matters such as a person's identity, fidelity, feelings, innocence, or guilt. They rest on the assumptions that a true or authentic state of affairs does exist and that testing is a means of ascertaining what that truth is when it is concealed from direct observation. This holds for contemporary tests as much as for those of preindustrial society.

These assumptions are mistaken. Because of their representational quality, tests measure truth as culturally construed rather than as independently existing. This has already been demonstrated. But there is more. By their very existence, tests modify or even create that which they purport to measure. Consider first the tests of royal blood in the tales of the princess and the pea and the prince who was unable to sleep because a hair buried in his bedding felt to him like a large beam.[79] The logic of these tests, as presented in the stories, begins with the assumption that people of royal blood have inordinately fine sensitivities. This assumption validates the following test situation: if this stranger is of royal blood, then she or he will be able to perceive something as insignificant as a pea or a hair in the bedding. What is being tested is the status of a specific individual, on the basis of a general proposition about a class of people. But in the effect of their telling, the logic of testing in these stories runs in the opposite direction. It conveys the message that because this prince or that princess was disturbed by a hair or a pea concealed in the bedding, persons of royal blood must have inordinate sensitivities. That is, a general proposition about a class of people is being promulgated on the basis of stories about the experience of some individuals of that class. Therefore, these tests in folklore help create the circumstance they purport to measure: they are among the devices that ingrain in people's minds the belief that aristocrats are by their nature refined and superior to commoners.[80]

These tests with peas and hairs are so fanciful that they certainly never actually took place, although that does not detract from their indoctrinating function. A test from folklore that could conceivably occur with the reported result is the master who tested his servant's obedience by inviting him to partake of any dish in a sumptuous feast save one covered dish, which contained a mouse that would escape if the lid were lifted. This test also fabricates what it purports to measure. Imagine that the test were actually conducted. It is entirely possible that an utterly loyal and obedient servant would raise the lid, not with any intention of taking what is inside but simply out of curiosity to see what it is. Nonetheless, he is dismissed as disobedient, and, insofar as his reputation is affected by the episode, he is treated accordingly by others. Hence the test literally made him, at least in the eyes of the world, into something that he had not been prior to it.

This test has another, more general fabricating capacity that has nothing to do with actually applying it. As with the princess and the pea or the prince and the hair, this story conveys a message. This time it is a message about the proper relation between master and servant. The good servant, it states, is blindly obedient to any command of the master, no matter how irrational, inconsequential, or unjust it may appear. Moreover, the message continues, the servant who deviates from this ideal is liable to summary punishment. In this way, the story about the test perpetuates the power of the dominant class.[81]

The capacity of tests to fabricate that which they are presumed to measure works not only through folktales about tests but also—probably more so—through tests actually conducted. Consider tests for witchcraft. The Kaluli of Papua New Guinea really would remove and examine the heart of an individual killed on the suspicion of witchcraft, and if it was soft in texture and yellowish in color (as some hearts really are), they took that as physical evidence that the individual was indeed a witch. In this way, the test bolstered and verified the proposition that there are witches, a proposition that, in our time and place, is false. In precisely the same way, Europeans a few centuries ago really did tie unfortunates' toes and thumbs together and cast them in the water to observe whether they would sink or float. The outcome in the case of the more buoyant was taken as proof that the particular individual was a witch. And, of course, nothing could stand as better evidence for the general proposition that witches exist than proof that certain individuals are witches. Again, the reversal of logic is apparent. Ostensibly, the testing situation moves deductively from general to specific: there are witches, they have certain properties, this individual has those properties, therefore this individual is a witch. But so far as the proclamation of a message is concerned, the logic moves in the reverse, inductive direction: this individual has certain properties, those properties are characteristic of witches, therefore this individual is a witch, therefore witches exist. As with the capacity of stories such as the princess and the pea to promote attitudes about intrinsic differences between the classes, this is another example of the capacity of testing to create what it purports to measure.

It was, of course, too late in the case of the proven Kaluli witch, but in Europe, those who had tested positive as witches were invited to discourse on their black arts, to describe their intercourse with Satan, imps, and other denizens of evil, and to implicate others who had joined in witches' rides and participated with them in the obscene sabbat. Some of the confessions were remarkably detailed and vivid. Matthew Hopkins, the seventeenth-century English witch-hunter, records the revelations of a witch from Maningtree, in Essex, and even claims to have been an eyewitness to certain events (see fig. 2).

Figure 2.
Frontispiece from Matthew Hopkins's
The Discovery of Witches.

So upon command from the *Justice* they were to keep her from sleep two or three nights, expecting in that time to see her *familiars*, which the fourth night she called in by their severall names, and told them what shapes, a quarter of an houre before they came in, there being ten of us in the roome; the first she called was

1. *Holt*, who came in like a white kitling.
2. *Jarmara*, who came in like a fat Spaniel without any legs at all, she said she kept him fat, for she clapt her hand on her belly, and said he suckt good blood from her body.
3. *Vinegar Tom*, who was like a long-legg'd Greyhound, with an head like an Oxe, with a long taile and broad eyes, who when this discoverer spoke to, and bade him goe to the place provided for him and his Angels, immediately transformed himselfe into the shape of a child of foure yeeres old without a head, and gave halfe a dozen turnes about the house, and vanished at the doore.
4. *Sack and Sugar*, like a black Rabbet.
5. *Newes*, like a Polcat. All these vanished away in a little time. Immediately after this Witch confessed severall other Witches, from whom she had her *Imps*, and named to divers women where their marks were, the number of their *Marks*, and *Imps*, and *Imps* names, as *Elemanzer, Pyewacket, Peckin the Crown, Grizzel, Greedigut* etc.[82]

Hopkins would swim accused witches, search, probe, and prick them for teats and devil's marks, prevent them from sitting down or sleeping, and force them to walk incessantly as part of his confession-provoking procedures.[83] He went on, curiously, to deny the use of "any torture or violence whatsoever,"[84] but torture was generally a favored technique for loosening the tongues of suspected witches. In circumstances where torture would intensify until a confession was obtained, a great many victims certainly fabricated stories they knew to be entirely false just to stop the pain.[85] And yet these confessions must have acquired tremendous existential import for those who made them. They terminated the agony of torture, and they were the basis for the subsequent sentence of death. While being led to execution, often by the terrible means of burning at the stake, confessed witches were earnestly exhorted to repent of the deeds they had described, for the salvation of their eternal souls. With such ultimate meanings in play, it would be anything but surprising if many of those accused, convicted, and executed as witches came to believe their own confessions, no matter how fabricated they may have been at the beginning, with desperate sincerity.[86] In that event, tests for witches, especially when seconded by torture, contributed to the creation of a reality devoutly affirmed not only by zealous inquisitors and a credulous populace but also by at least some of those convicted of the crime.

Conclusion

Several important generalizations have emerged from this analysis of the tests of preindustrial society.

1. The testing situation entails the application of power over the subjects of tests. Such power is to a degree in the hands of the persons who order and administer the tests, but it inheres more importantly in the organizations they represent and especially in the total social system.

2. Given the intrinsic representational character of all tests, and given further that what counts as representation is a matter of social convention, tests are not and cannot be measures or indicators of some purely objective, independently existing state of affairs or reality. They are concerned instead with reality as constructed by culture.

3. Related to and expanding the second generalization is the third generalization that tests are important in the array of mechanisms whereby culturally constructed realities are formed. Tests, that is to say, act to transform, mold, and even to create what they supposedly measure.

While it is possible to draw these generalizations with special clarity from an analysis of the tests found in preindustrial society, they are not limited to those tests. Indeed, the major objective of the following chapters is to demonstrate that they hold as strongly (if, occasionally, more subtly) for testing as it is currently practiced.

3

LIE DETECTION

A fluttering Heart, and unequal Pulse, a sudden

Palpitation shall evidently confess he is the Man, in spite of

a bold Countenance or a false Tongue.

Daniel Defoe,

An Effectual Scheme for the Immediate Preventing of

Street Robberies and Suppressing all other

Disorders of the Night

Our exploration of contemporary authenticity testing begins with lie detection. It may appear to be a curious beginning, for lie detection occupies the less-reputable neighborhoods in the city of testing. German courts have held that lie detection's aim to bypass the conscious mind (which may wish to conceal certain information) so as to dredge facts directly from the unconscious compromises the right to avoid self-incrimination and erodes the basic human quality of free will.[1] No less august a personage than Pope Pius XII was moved to condemn lie detection for its capacity to "intrude into man's interior domain."[2] Subjects I have interviewed often reported feeling demeaned by the suspicion of wrongdoing implicit in the request or insistence that they submit to a lie detector test and violated by the prospect of machine-enhanced snooping into their private affairs. Attitudes such as these have given lie detection an unsavory enough reputation in official circles that a federal law greatly curtailing its use in the private sector took effect at the end of 1988.

These foibles notwithstanding, lie detection is of great interest for our analysis because it brings certain common characteristics of testing into peculiarly interesting and instructive focus. Most important, because the whole purpose of lie detection is to reveal information that subjects wish to conceal, the power that test givers typically exercise over test takers is particularly prominent here. After analyzing certain exaggerated—occasionally even caricatured—features of testing as they appear in lie detection, it will be easier for us to identify the subtler versions of those same features that lurk in more respectable forms of testing.

The Ghost in the Machine

In tracing the context of assumptions within which lie detection operates, it is helpful to begin over three hundred years ago with French philosopher René Descartes. Standing at the source of modern philosophy, Descartes distinguished sharply between the body and the mind. His theory, now known as Cartesian dualism, holds that while activities of the body take place openly in the physical world, where they can be observed by anyone, the thoughts and emotions that constitute mental activities occur in some metaphorical "place" deeply buried within a person. The doings of the mental "ghost in the machine" (as Ryle termed it)[3] are hidden from public view. Observation of them is the exclusive prerogative of the self, who (until Freud and others muddied the waters with the concept of an unconscious mind) has immediate and total access to them by introspection.

People have long cherished the prospect of intruding on the private precincts of other minds, and no society has lacked shamans or psychics who lay claim to the pertinent preternatural powers. In our own society and century, the strongest bid for direct communication with ghosts in other machines comes from a persuasion that claims to have solved the problem by the judicious application of modern science and technology in a family of procedures known generally as lie detection or (a somewhat more genteel designation often used by proponents) the detection of deception. In essence, lie detection operates on the premise that a mind-body connection exists such that it is possible to know something about what a person is thinking on the basis of certain measurable physiological responses. Lying—or, more precisely, anxiety about being discovered in a lie—is thought to produce bodily perturbations. These may be no more than slight fluctuations in blood pressure or subtle changes in the voice, however, so liars are often able to conceal their prevarication-provoked physiological responses from the ordinary scrutiny of human observers.

One scheme for unmasking callous deceivers was advanced by Daniel Defoe. Although he proposed it in 1731, the tactic of scrutinizing subtle bodily signs for evidence of a guilty ghost lurking within is totally in accordance with the assumptions that underwrite contemporary lie detection:

> Guilt carries Fear always about with it; there is a Tremor in the Blood of a Thief, that, if attended to, would effectually discover him; and if charged as suspicious Fellow, on that Suspicion only I would always feel his Pulse, and I would recommend it to Practice. . . . It is true some are so hardened in Crime that they will boldly hold their Faces to it, carry it off with an Air of Contempt, and outface even a Pursuer; but take hold of his Wrist and feel his Pulse, and there you will find his Guilt; a fluttering Heart, an unequal Pulse, a sudden Palpitation shall evidently confess he is the Man, in spite of a bold Countenance or a false Tongue.[4]

Today, thanks to the ultrasensitive instruments of modern technology, the imperceptible quickenings of the most accomplished, cold-blooded liar are now susceptible to precise measurement, recording, and scientific analysis. This points, incidentally, to another way in which the analysis of lie detection reveals a general characteristic of testing in a special light. Testing has a tendency to fragment or decenter the subject, to characterize the person in terms of one or a very few dimensions rather than as a fully rounded, integrated human being. This appears in the case of lie detection in a peculiar, extreme, and (from the suspect's point of view) threatening form. Not only is the subject divided but the parts are actually set against each other, so that the mental ghost is betrayed when the blabbermouth bodily machine spills the beans. But bad news for the subject may be good news for the community, especially for that branch of it devoted to law enforcement. As one interrogator happily described the distinctive achievement of lie detector tests, "the criminal can no longer hide in the deepest recesses of his mind."[5]

Many of the medieval tests described in chapter 2 sought to plumb the deepest recesses of criminals' minds by putting questions to God, who would answer through the outcome of ordeal or combat. As part of an overall secularization of society, one of the most salient transformations in assumptions about tests in general as we pass from these antecedents to their modern forms is the renouncing of all reliance on God's omniscience in favor of purely human knowledge, as enhanced by the methods and mechanisms of science. This is especially visible in lie detection, where issues that would previously have been put to trial by ordeal or battle are addressed from a putatively scientific perspective and with heavy reliance on technological devices. Lie detector tests deal with human qualities in terms of things. The polygraph itself is a thing, a machine. Its job is to measure the activities of other concrete things: the heart, the lungs, and the skin. The ultimate purpose is to detect truth and deception, but these too are understood as correlates of physical things and events rather than purely as subjective qualities of mind or morality. The aura of science is further fortified by a tendency to classify subjects according to their physical responses in polygraph tests. To examiners, people become objectified as "spot responders," "reactors," "nonreactors," "respiratory reactors," or "diminishing reactors."[6]

As we have seen, modern testing has its roots in positivism. Lie detection's redefinition of human qualities in terms of things is an outstanding example of the agenda charted for positivism by Saint-Simon. He argued that human misery, strife, and war stem from decisions and actions in the realm of human affairs that are taken on the basis of opinions. If they could instead be based on things, as scientifically determined and understood, then human affairs would be regulated according to positive facts rather than ephemeral, uncertain opinion.

It is no longer men controlling men. It is truth alone which speaks; it is impersonal, and nothing is less capricious. In short it is things themselves—through the mediation of those who understand them—that indicate the manner in which they should be handled.[7]

Advocates of lie detection have anticipated similar happy results from the extended application of polygraph technology to, say, the legal system. Unlike the capricious, opinion-laden decisions of judges and jurors, the scientific lie detector test is not subject to bias.[8] Robert Ferguson, Jr., provides example after example where polygraph tests have rectified the errors of juries, proving the innocence and securing the release of falsely convicted defendants.[9] In one case, a judge had his doubts about a jury's conviction of a man tried for robbery and assault with a deadly weapon. He delayed sentencing and ordered a polygraph test. The results indicated that the convicted man was in fact innocent. Refusing to allow a man to be convicted under these circumstances, the judge vacated the jury's verdict.[10]

The results of polygraph tests are grounded in concrete things as known systematically by scientific methods of measurement and are therefore objective and certain. The polygraph speaks truth as a matter of principle. Therefore, if the results of a particular polygraph test are manifestly mistaken, the problem lies not with the nature of the test but with how it was conducted or, perhaps, with the person who was being tested. On the analogy that one does not lose confidence in fingerprinting because particular prints are occasionally smudged, "there is no reason, therefore, why any derogatory implication should be attached to the lie-detector technique because of the occasional unfitness of the person upon whom a deception diagnosis has been attempted."[11]

The situation is fascinating: a testing technique that has been touted as being so thoroughly saturated with science as to be nearly infallible has been so widely perceived as fundamentally flawed that a law has been passed against it. Arguments on both sides of the issue will be reviewed here and in chapter 4, as we examine more closely what lie detector tests are, how they work, and what social consequences they have.

Lie Detector Machines

Modern lie detection boils down to a machine-enhanced capacity to detect minute bodily perturbations, together with the professional skill to interpret their mental correlations. The machine most commonly used in lie detection is the polygraph. Quickly reviewing some of the highlights of its development, the polygraph was foreshadowed in the mid-nineteenth century when Italian criminologist Cesare Lombroso utilized measures of pulse and blood pressure in the interrogation of suspects. By 1908, the well-known psychologist, Hugo Munsterberg, was advocating the use of blood pressure for detecting deception in the law courts. William M. Marston, one of Munsterberg's Harvard students, claimed to have discovered a specific physiological response that accompanied lying. An avid publicity hound, he made several unsuccessful efforts to apply his technique in the investigation of the kidnapping of the Lindbergh baby. Ultimately, Marston went on to other pursuits and, under the pseudonym of Charles Moulton, created the comic strip character "Wonder Woman."[12]

Marston's claim that a specific physiological response exists for deception did not survive, but exploration into more general links continued. John A. Larson developed a large and unwieldy machine capable of providing continuous measures of blood pressure, pulse, and respiration rates. Working closely with the criminologist and police chief, August Vollmer, he used the instrument for investigations in the Berkeley Police Department. His most famous success was a shoplifting case in the early 1920s. The culprit was known only to be one of thirty-eight women living in a certain dormitory. Larson interrogated all of them with the assistance of his machine and found that one reacted much more strongly to questions about the thefts than the other thirty-seven. Confronted with the findings, she made a full confession.[13]

A high school student named Leonarde Keeler, fascinated by police work, used to spend his spare time around the Berkeley Police Department in those days. He took a keen interest in Larson's and Vollmer's experiments, and in 1926, Keeler developed the first compact, portable polygraph machine. It remains the

"hits" on a question, in the parlance of the trade) may be inter-preted as signifying deception.

The type of signification that operates in polygraph tests is metonymy. The presence of an observable effect metonymically signifies the co-presence of its cause, even if the cause is not observed directly. Precisely in the same way as smoke signifies fire, in the logic of the polygraph, certain physiological pertur-bations, properly analyzed, signify deception.

Stanley Abrams sets out to provide a more detailed account of the rationale behind polygraph examinations.[15] In an apparent effort to drench his discussion in as much science as possible, he even includes information on the human cell and the operation of neurons, although, alas, no relation between these particular matters and the operation of the polygraph is identified. In the more pertinent part of his account, Abrams keys polygraph to the "fight or flight" reaction that has been indelibly imprinted in human beings and other animals over eons of evolution as an adaptive response to situations of danger. The threat of being discovered in a lie provokes this reaction, which consists of a set of physiological changes that prepare the individual to fight or to run away. "Vasoconstriction takes place in the peripheral blood vessels and causes an increased flow of blood to the skin, thereby allowing for a dissipation of the heat engendered by muscular effort and fostering a reduction of blood loss should injury occur."[16] Moreover, sweat appears on the palms and hands "to aid in locomotion or grasping. . . . Stronger contractions of the heart send more oxygenated blood through the body and an additional blood supply is directed to the skeletal muscles allowing for a more effective utilization of the arms and legs."[17] These devel-opments are monitored by the various measuring devices of the polygraph. Therefore, lie detection by the polygraph, as Abrams cogently points out, produces an interesting twist on evolutionary patterns of self-preservation: "ironically, those same responses that typically serve to get the individual out of trouble get him into difficulty if he is deceptive during a polygraph test situation."[18]

Although this polygraph machine is the one in general use today, technological elaborations have been tried from time to time. The Darrow Behavior Research Photopolygraph (fig. 3), mar-

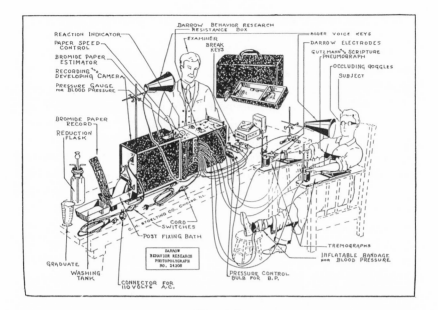

Figure 3.
Darrow Behavior Research Photopolygraph. From Paul V. Trovillo.
"A History of Lie Detection." *Journal of the American Institute of Criminal Law and Criminology* 29 (1939):874.

keted half a century ago, seems to have been attached to the subject's body in every way imaginable. Apparently, the apparatus used by the CIA, which makes frequent use of instrumental lie detection, is similar. An informant said that it expands the number of physiological characteristics monitored from three or four to twenty-eight and that an individual wired up to it "looks like an astronaut." At the other extreme, Israel's Weizmann Institute has developed a machine that does not touch the subject's body at all. It measures palpitations of the stomach remotely, by microwaves, on the theory that such movements increase in frequency when an individual is lying. The device is in use at border checkpoints, where individuals may be subjected to lie detection without their being aware of it.[19]

Lie detection by remote sensing, of course, obviates the necessity to hook the subject up to clips, tubes, and wires. These attachments frequently provoke a good deal of consternation.

Several polygraph examiners told me that it is frequently necessary to assure subjects that the machine will not give them electric shocks; occasionally, people observe with apprehensive humor that they feel like they are going to the electric chair.

The psychological stress evaluator (PSE) is a type of lie detector machine that attaches nothing to the subject's body. It is
designed to analyze stress in the voice. As its history was explained to me by a PSE examiner, the device was invented by two
army officers, Charles McQuiston and Allan Bell. They wanted to
give lie detector tests to suspected double agents and others in the
jungles of Vietnam and found that the polygraph was not suitable
for such use in the field. With the PSE, one asks the same sort of
questions as would be used in a polygraph test, but the subject
answers (yes or no) into a tape recorder microphone. The tape is
then run, at one-quarter speed, through a special analyzer that
produces a chart composed of closely packed lines of varying
heights and positions on a narrow strip of paper similar to that
used in cash registers. The expert studies the chart for points of
vocal stress or tension, not audible to the ear, that may be found
in the answers to certain questions on the test.

The general theory behind the PSE is identical to that informing the polygraph: anxiety about being caught out in a lie produces certain physiological responses (this time in the voice),
and these can be detected and recorded by the machine. In an
interview, a PSE examiner provided a more detailed rationale that
(in contrast to Abrams's reliance on the fight or flight reaction)
trades on the relation between the subconscious and conscious
sectors of mind. It is an outstanding example of the tendency of
lie detection to disarticulate the person into fragments that are
then set against each other. The subconscious mind, he explained, is like a computer data bank with no discriminating
controls. In response to any question, the subconscious simply
dumps everything it has on that topic. The conscious mind, which
is a highly discriminating gate-keeping device, reviews what the
subconscious has produced and decides what to reveal. The verbal answer to any question is what the conscious mind lets pass.
Even if a question has potentially damaging implications for the
self, such as whether one stole something (when one in fact did

steal it), the subconscious foolishly churns out the correct answer: yes. The conscious mind, however, in effect says (and this is a quotation from the PSE examiner), "You dummy, I'm not going to say that. It will get me in trouble." Hence the subject gives a false answer to the question: no. Whenever one lies, then, there is a difference between the responses of the unconscious and conscious components of the mind. That difference produces psychological tension, or stress, and that in turn affects the voice in a way that is measurable by the psychological stress evaluator. The logic of signification is the same as for the polygraph, operating on the assumption that perceptible effects signify, by metonymy, concealed causes. The word "stress," incidentally, was frequently used both as a noun and as a verb by the two PSE examiners I interviewed. Whereas polygraph examiners tend to say the subject "hit" on a certain question, the PSE examiners would say the subject "stressed" on it.

As with the Israeli remote sensor, it is possible to give PSE tests without the subject being aware of it. A polygraph examiner told me that some insurance companies record telephone conversations with policyholders concerning loss claims so as to subject them to analysis by the PSE. Another pointed to a PSE tape prominently displayed on the wall of his office. It was, he said, the voice of Patty Hearst as recorded from a telephone conversation while she was with the Symbionese Liberation Army, and he indicated several points on the chart where she stressed.

The lie detection profession itself has stressed on the question of the PSE. PSE examiners argue that their newer and simpler technique is as accurate as the polygraph. Polygraph examiners, who are much more numerous and whose technique is more common, tend to dismiss the claim, often with expressions of contempt not unlike those that critics of the whole idea of lie detection level against the polygraph. Thus an unfriendly schism has emerged between PSE and polygraph examiners.

Uses of Lie Detection

The U.S. Congress Office of Technology Assessment has estimated that as of 1987, some two million polygraph tests were given annually in the United States.[20] Lie detector tests are regularly employed by the CIA and the National Security Agency to detect spies or double agents in their midst. Police departments test criminal suspects and their own personnel in various internal investigations. In 1972, Imperial Wizard Robert Shelton ordered Ku Klux Klansmen to take lie detector tests in an effort to root out informers and FBI plants in their midst.[21] George Steinbrenner had lie detector tests administered on several occasions to New York Yankees executives when he was angered that news of trades leaked out before the official announcements.[22] In 1985, the Reagan administration was planning to plug leaks by demanding lie detector tests of high government officials, including Cabinet members, until Secretary of State George Shultz shot the plan down by saying he would resign rather than submit to such a demeaning and ineffective procedure.[23] One examiner told me that he was engaged by the church to test a Catholic priest who was accused of having an affair with a female parishioner. The church fathers decided they would take the opportunity to also look into the state of the priest's faith. In addition to questions about his relationship with the woman, while the priest was hooked up to the machine, he was asked if he assented to the various propositions of the Nicene Creed. It seems that he passed that part of the test with flying colors, although he did not do so well on the morals charge.

Prior to the 1988 legislation banning it in the private sector, by far the most common users of lie detector tests, accounting for 90 percent of the two million annual tests estimated by the Office of Technology Assessment, were private businesses whose employees regularly handle cash or items of value, such as retail firms, pawn shops, and banks. Businesses using the polygraph included over 30 percent of the Fortune 500 companies and at least half of the retail trade firms.[24]

Business turned to lie detection in an effort to control employee theft. Not many years ago, retail firms chalked up most of their unaccounted losses to external factors such as shoplifting. Now they attribute the lion's share to internal theft. Not that the reality has changed. Instead, managers have reluctantly come to the conclusion that their employees simply do not (and never did) deserve the trust that was once placed in them. Although internal disciplinary measures or termination are much more common responses to employee theft than legal action, in 1982, some 335,000 American workers were arrested for stealing from their employers. When employees who are not prosecuted and those who are never caught are added, the totals become impossible to verify. Estimates vary widely; among the more pessimistic are that 70 percent of all workers steal something during their employment, that employee theft is responsible for some one-third of all business bankruptcies, and that annual losses suffered by American business due to employee theft total $40 billion or more.[25] Staggering as this total is, some perspective is provided by a National Institute of Justice estimate that corporate management steals three times that amount through securities fraud, corporate kickbacks, embezzlement, and insurance fraud. This moves critics of the business use of lie detection to ask why hourly employees have been forced to submit to lie detector tests while executives are rarely tested.[26]

However they may answer that question, employers have sought to combat employee pilfering and other problems by applying lie detector tests in four main circumstances: *preemployment* screening represents an effort to avoid hiring untrustworthy employees; current employees may be kept under surveillance and deterred from unacceptable behavior by *periodic* tests (given at regular intervals) or *random* tests (given unannounced at any time); and *specific* tests are given in the course of investigations into thefts or other particular acts of wrongdoing that have occurred. (Tests of the last sort are also used by law enforcement agencies in criminal investigations.)

Until very recently the use of polygraph tests by American business was dramatically on the rise, having tripled in the decade prior to 1987.[27] Lie detection expanded in this period not only because of the growing perception that employee theft was more common than had been previously suspected but also because legislation protecting employee interests made it extremely difficult to learn about applicants from previous employers. To protect themselves from possible legal action, employers will often divulge no more about former employees than the period of their employment and the position they held. Potential employers are interested in knowing more about their work history: their reliability, congeniality, honesty, and habits that may have adverse consequences for the company, whether they are likely to agitate for a union or make other trouble, why they left earlier jobs, and so on. Two issues of special interest are drugs and homosexuality. Drug use may have an impact on job performance and place the employer in serious legal jeopardy if the employee is in a job that affects the safety of others. Moreover, drug addiction is extremely expensive, and addicts frequently steal to support their habit, often from their employers. Intravenous drug users and homosexuals represent high-risk categories for AIDS, and this disease is so expensive to treat that one or two cases have serious repercussions for a company's health insurance program. Unable to ascertain information of these sorts from previous employers, many companies resorted to lie detection as a means to discover it for themselves.

If the experience of the Vermont State Police is any guide, what they discover may be startling. A preemployment lie detector test was used in the screening of the 203 individuals who applied for positions in 1983. Nineteen applicants did not even show up for their scheduled tests, and only 75 were retained for further consideration after the test. The other 109 admitted, under the scrutiny of the polygraph, to a total of 238 kinds of disqualifying offenses. These included drug use, larceny, lying on their application forms, abnormal sexual practices, and "immature acts." Sixty-five of the 75 who "passed" the lie detector examination made admissions of misdeeds that were not considered serious enough to drop them from further consideration.[28] One wonders, incidentally, if any of those who did not show up for the test or were disqualified by it had a record as distinguished as a former police officer who (unsuccessfully) applied for a job in the Washoe County (Nevada) Sheriff's Department. In the course of the preemployment lie detector test, that worthy "admitted accepting bribes on two occasions, 'rolling' a homosexual and beating him to a point that required hospitalization, stealing property while answering an alarm at a burglary scene, and ransacking the apartment at a death scene and stealing the property of the deceased."[29]

Some employers use lie detection to weed out not only applicants who have engaged in criminal behavior on previous jobs but also persons who are thought to be potential troublemakers or union agitators. The following assessment of the polygraph was made in 1984 by a uniform dry cleaning chain in Buffalo, New York.

> The polygraph very definitely has improved industrial relations at our facility and every other non-union facility where it is used properly. The simple reason is that with polygraph an employer tends to eliminate bad employees, those who are deep into drugs, dishonest, troublemakers, etc. . . . In a union facility, usually the bad employees are protected by the union bosses because they are strong union supporters and when there is polygraph involved these bad employees will do everything in their power to fight it. . . . Trade unions and civil rights organisations continually complain about polygraph, apparently because it promotes good relations between employer and employee and when you have these good relations you likely will not have employees voting a union in. . . . A refusal to take a polygraph test is taken into consideration along with other information at hand in making a decision to promote or to hire. Polygraph is the most valid aid in selecting staff known to man. . . . The polygraph, properly utilized, prevents labor disputes.[30]

It has even been possible to exert the force of lie detection in the absence of actual tests. The application forms used by many companies included a question about whether the applicant would be willing to take lie detector tests prior to being hired or as an employee with the firm. Often companies did not actually give tests to job applicants because they are too expensive. But a fast-food chain proprietor told me that if a person answered "no" to that question, "unless the application is *incredible*, there is no way that we would consider that applicant further." The reason she gave is that "philosophical" problems with taking a lie detector test can signal an overly independent turn of mind that might lead to noncompliance with other company policies down the line.

The Test

Because the polygraph is a portable machine, a lie detector test can take place in almost any surroundings. Sometimes subjects are directed to go to the examiner's office for the test. Other examiners may visit the company or other locale where people are to be tested and set up shop in any available room or office. Some examiners prefer to bring their own office with them and work out of a trailer or camper in the parking lot. In general, the room in which the test is given should be reasonably plain so as not to distract the subject. Some polygraph examiners, in an effort to heighten subjects' perception of the test as a professional procedure, go so far as to wear a white coat, stethoscope dangling from the neck, and to spray the air of the examining room with ethyl alcohol.[31] About the only piece of furniture specifically designed for lie detection is a straight-backed chair with concave armrests long enough to provide support for the subject's hands, where the fingertip clips are attached. This is not essential, however, for the test can be effectively conducted with the subject's arm resting on a table or on chair arms of normal length.

The typical lie detector test begins with a pretest interview. The examiner explains how the polygraph machine works and reviews the questions to be asked. While most polygraph examiners agree that the pretest interview is an extremely important part of the overall process because it sets the general ambience for the test, they are not of one mind as to precisely what that ambience should be. Some attempt to set the subject at ease, while others strive to increase nervous tension. In the latter case, the examiner's goal is often not so much to conduct a reliable polygraph test as it is to extract a confession. A police officer told me that occasionally the polygraph is used in this manner as a last resort in cases where the evidence against a suspect is not conclusive and the likelihood of a conviction is small. The suspect is told that things look very bad but that it might be possible to clear the record by means of a polygraph test. If the person can be induced to confess during the course of the test, charges will be filed (on the basis of the confession, not the polygraph test). If not, the suspect will be released regardless of what the polygraph chart shows about innocence or guilt (the evidence of polygraph tests rarely being accepted in court).

The polygraph is an effective tool in the hands of a skilled interrogator, who can use it to help convince suspects that their lies are not fooling anyone. When the aim is confession, other interrogation techniques may be used in the pretest interview, such as the suggestion of one polygraph instructor that the questioner sit close to the subject and that there be no table or other obstacle between them. Any kind of obstacle gives the person being questioned a certain degree of relief and confidence. The questioner may start with his chair two or three feet away and move closer as the questioning proceeds, so that ultimately the knees are in close proximity. This physical invasion of the subject's territory by the questioner, the crowding in as he is questioned, has been found in practice to be extremely useful in breaking down a subject's resistance. When a person's territorial defenses are weakened or intruded on, his self-assurance tends to grow weaker.[32]

Whether or not the examiner wishes to intimidate the subject, a ubiquitous aim of the pretest interview is to convince the subject that the polygraph really works. "The polygraphist . . . ," writes Abrams, "must engender enough of a feeling of confidence in the subject to relieve the anxiety of the innocent and at the same time increase the fear of the guilty."[33] Fred Inbau and John Reid suggest that the examiner tell the subject quite emphatically, "if you're telling the truth this machine will show it; if you're not, the machine will show that, too."[34] An examiner I interviewed habitually tells subjects just prior to the test, "Every story has three sides—your side, his side, and the truth. This machine is going to get the truth."

Lie detector tests are used not only to ascertain the subject's own improprieties but also to learn what one may know, or suspect, about the wrongdoings of others. The stage is often set for this during the pretest interview by convincing the subject that "divulgence of the suspicions is necessary for the subject's own test purposes."[35] The polygraph, that is to say, is presented as a machine with rather mysterious properties that necessitate that a person betray any suspicions about other employees or suspects to be found innocent oneself.

One common means of instilling respect for the machine is to run a "stim" (stimulation) test prior to the actual test.[36] The examiner, saying that he is going to demonstrate the accuracy of the polygraph, hooks the subject up to the machine and directs her, in one type of stim test, to draw a card from a deck. The subject is told to sit still, look straight ahead, and, for the purposes of the stim test, answer "no" to all questions. The examiner proceeds to ask if it is any of a number of possible cards and then identifies the correct card on the basis of the polygraph chart readings. (Some polygraph examiners, it seems, cover their bets on the stim test by using a trick deck of cards.)[37]

Actual examinations vary according to whether they are concerned with the subject's general honesty and history of wrongdoing (as in applicant screenings and periodic and random tests of current employees) or are part of the investigation of a specific crime. In general, however, the test consists of some ten to fifteen questions of three basic types. *Irrelevant* questions have to do with nonthreatening matters regarding which the subject can fully be expected to give honest answers: questions such as "Is today Thursday?" or "Do you live in Chicago?" or "Were you born in 1946?" The chart readings for these questions depict the subject's physiological profile when responding truthfully. *Control* questions are designed to be threatening and to evoke an untruthful response from anyone. These may vary a good deal with the particular sort of wrongdoing one is interested in uncovering and the particular history of the subject. For a person with a criminal record, a control question might be, "Did you ever commit a crime that was not found out by the police?" A person being investigated for assault might be asked, "Did you ever desire to hurt anyone?" An applicant in a preemployment screening might be asked, "Did you ever steal anything?" The chart readings for control questions show the physiological signs of anxiety connected with deception. Finally, the *relevant* questions (or "hot" questions, as they are often called in the trade) pertain to the particular issue under investigation. If this is a specific crime, the question focuses directly on it, such as, "Did you rape Judy Barnes on July 17?" or "Do you know who stole $500 from the cash register two weeks ago?" Relevant questions in periodic tests of current employees or applicant screenings are perforce somewhat more general, such as, "Have you stolen any money from the company during the last six months?" or "Did you steal any merchandise from your previous employer?" or "Have you ever been fired for reasons of dishonesty?"

Analysis of the chart is basically a matter of comparing responses to the relevant questions with those to the irrelevant and control questions. If the subject is lying in responding to the relevant questions, the readings for them will resemble those for the control questions; if the subject is telling the truth, they will resemble the readings for the irrelevant questions. Or, phrased somewhat differently, a deceptive subject will show greater perturbations for the relevant questions than for the control questions, while a nondeceptive subject will react more strongly to the control questions. The reason is that the guilty individual is more threatened by the relevant questions than the control questions, while the innocent individual, having nothing to fear from the relevant questions, is more threatened by the control questions.[38] Test results are usually reported as "DI" (deception indicated), "NDI" (no deception indicated), or "Inconclusive." The last is used when no clear pattern is discernible on the charts.

Polygraph examiners are interested in creating conditions in which the charts will be as "good" as possible; charts, that is to say, that lend themselves most unequivocally to an interpretation of either DI or NDI. Examiners may differ, however, on how to bring about these optimal conditions. According to Phillip Davis and Pamela McKenzie-Rundle (herself a former polygraph examiner), the subject who has been "pumped up" during the pretest interview is most likely to produce the sharply different responses to relevant, irrelevant, and control questions that are essential for "good" charts.[39] However, a polygraph instructor told me that his main goal is to put subjects at ease during the pretest interview, partly to facilitate the production of "good" charts. An overly nervous subject, he explained, is likely to give erratic responses even to the irrelevant questions. This makes the chart as a whole much more difficult to interpret and produces a result of Inconclusive. Moreover, the subject who has been "pumped up" by the test situation may even be driven by the pressure to make a false confession.

A careful polygraph test involves running several charts, that is, going through the same set of questions three or more times, with periods of interview/interrogation in between. This provides additional opportunities for the subject to make a confession, or, conversely, for areas of apparent deception or guilt that showed up on the first chart to be resolved in the subject's favor. In either event, the charts and the overall result of the test are clarified with repetition.

One technique for such clarification, which seldom works to the benefit of the subject, is the following:

> Once a test has been administered to a guilty individual it is extremely effective to display the records to him and point out the deception criteria—at the same time reminding the subject that the recordings represent his own heart beats, his own blood pressure changes, etc., and not those picked up by the machine out of thin air or placed there by the examiner.[40]

A particularly powerful technique is to go through the test two or three more times, pointing out to the suspect how, with each successive chart, the indications of deception become more pronounced. Eventually the evidence from the polygraph becomes so self-evident that only the most intransigent subject can avoid confessing.

But, of course, the alternative explanation is not difficult to imagine. Subjects "hit" more and more decisively on the relevant question with repeated testing not necessarily because of guilt but because they are distressed about how the response to it appears on the previous chart and are increasingly apprehensive about it when the test is run again.[41] This, incidentally, sheds additional light on the practice of reviewing the questions with subjects prior to administering the test. This is done, they are told, as an assurance that no surprise questions will be sprung while the chart is running. That is true enough, but the practice also has certain advantages for the test itself which are not so immediately apparent. For one, a subject might be surprised by an unexpected question, and even if the person has nothing to hide on that question, the surprise itself could produce physiological responses that might be difficult to distinguish from those associated with deception.[42] For another, to review all questions in advance alerts deceptive subjects to just when in the test a relevant question is coming. Their attention focuses on it, and they become increasingly apprehensive as it approaches and then relax after it has passed. This produces a characteristic response pattern known as "peak of tension," which is taken as particularly damning.

Is is possible, however, that the peak of tension might also characterize the responses of innocent individuals who go into lie detector tests knowing full well that they are suspected of certain misdeeds and who therefore are apprehensive about the relevant questions. This is obviated in another testing format, known as the Guilty Knowledge Test.[43] Suitable only for investigations into specific acts of wrongdoing and not for general preemployment or periodical checkups, the Guilty Knowledge Test trades on information that only the guilty individual would know. The precise location of a rape, for example, or some characteristic of the clothes the victim was wearing might not have been made public. One could then construct a polygraph test with a series of alternatives, for example, she was wearing a red blouse, a blue blouse, a sweatshirt, a woolen sweater, and so on. Regardless of how much anxiety an innocent suspect might have about the test, he would not be likely to "hit" on the correct alternative because he simply does not know it. The guilty suspect, however, is much more likely to react. And if the possibilities and the order in which questions would be asked were reviewed in advance, it is reasonable to expect that the responses would manifest the typical peak of tension pattern.

Polygraph examiners I have interviewed enjoy telling stories of their most interesting cases, including their greatest triumphs. One of these was a classic use of the Guilty Knowledge Test and is interesting in addition because it demonstrates that the verbal answers given by the subject are really not an essential part of the test. A murder suspect agreed to be hooked up to a polygraph but refused to answer any questions. "That's all right," said the examiner, "all you have to do is to sit there." He informed the subject that they were going to find out just where the body was hidden. He produced a map of the city, divided it into quadrants, and, pointing to each in turn, asked, "Did you hide the body in this section? In this section?" and so on. Although the subject sat mute, the chart showed a larger response for one of the quadrants than for the other three. The examiner divided that section into quadrants and repeated the questions. The narrowing process continued with, it can be imagined, the subject becoming increasingly apprehensive. Finally, a bit of territory the size of a house lot was specified. The police dug there and discovered the body.

Polygraph examiners may use ingenious—if on occasion remarkably simple—techniques to ascertain if someone is lying. Keeler, who also tried the technique of identifying the location of a body by means of pointing to quadrants on a map,[44] was once asked to use the polygraph to determine if an individual who claimed to be blind was in fact so. Keeler did not find it necessary to ask any questions of the individual at all. He simply hooked him up to the polygraph and then held a picture of a nude pinup girl in front of him. The needles went wild, and they had their answer.[45]

Polygraph subjects too have developed a set of techniques—some simple and some more ingenious—to "beat" lie detector tests. The technique that usually first springs to mind, especially among persons with little experience of the polygraph, is to maintain such rigid control over one's physiology that no telltale perturbations will disturb the polygraph when one lies. This is extremely difficult to accomplish, although in one case an enterprising individual may have made it work. A highly experienced examiner told me about a subject whom he had tested before and whose previous tests had indicated a great deal of deception. This time, however, the charts indicated no deception at all; they looked, indeed, too perfect. The examiner said to the subject, "This is too good to be true. What are you doing?" The subject, apparently prouder of his ruse than apprehensive about being discovered in an effort to beat the test, unbuttoned his shirt and displayed his torso, completely wrapped in aluminum foil. In principle, this should have no effect whatsoever on the polygraph readings, but the examiner surmised that the trick gave the subject such confidence that he succeeded in muting the physiological responses that normally accompany deception.

Another technique is to use some substance prior to the test in an effort to mask one's responses. Typewriter correction fluid such as White-Out is believed by some to be effective for this purpose. (Does the rationale have to do with some supposed generic capacity of the liquid to cover things up?) Subjects have been known to paint their fingertips with it to thwart the galvanic skin response measure—surely a ruse that would not be difficult to detect. Alternatively, the subject can drink it. One individual who was told by a friend that he could beat the test with correction fluid "drank five bottles of White-Out, threw up during the pretest interview, and confessed."[46]

The most effective way to thwart a lie detector test, however, is not to attempt to minimize one's reactions to the relevant questions but to maximize them on the irrelevant and control questions. Chart analysis rests on identifying differences among these three types of question. The assumptions are that all subjects will show little reaction to irrelevant questions, that an innocent individual will react more strongly to control questions than relevant questions, and that a guilty subject will show the reverse profile. Thus, a conclusive finding of deceptiveness is not possible if the responses to control questions are stronger than to relevant questions,[47] while the entire test is thwarted if responses to irrelevant questions are stronger than those to relevant or control questions.

Subjects may resort to a variety of techniques if they wish to intensify their responses to irrelevant or control questions. Pain is effective for this, and one practice is to come into the examination room with a tack in one's shoe and to press the foot down on it when one wants to provide a heightened response. Somewhat simpler is to bite one's tongue; easier still is to tighten the sphincter muscle, which produces a minor perturbation in the blood pressure. Finally, it is easy for any subject to confound a lie detector test simply by refusing to sit still. Wriggling, coughing, and intentionally varying the rate of one's breathing all have the effect of defeating the polygraph's physiological measures. A common method to distort the readings produced by the psychological stress evaluator, which measures voice patterns, is to wear a necktie and to press one's throat against its large Windsor knot while answering irrelevant or control questions.

Many countermeasures are not difficult for the examiner to detect. People with tacks in their shoes often limp painfully into the examination room. Some examiners have subjects sit on an air-inflated pillow that is connected to the polygraph machine in order to detect sphincter tensing. And, of course, subjects who deliberately cough and squirm are often not even trying to hide their refusal to cooperate.

A deceptive subject who uses subtle techniques that escape the notice of the examiner may achieve the false negative test result of NDI (no deception indicated). The examiner who detects efforts to defeat the test is likely to attempt by cajoling or by threats to convince the subject to desist from them and to cooperate fully with the test. If the subject will not do so, it will be impossible for the examiner to reach a conclusion of DI (deception indicated) on the basis of the charts. The only option is to report an inconclusive test result, although very possibly with a notation on the report that the subject's refusal to cooperate might in itself indicate deception.

The Examiner

Examiners vary greatly in their interest in and skill at detecting efforts to beat the test and in all other aspects of polygraph tests. Therefore, many experts in lie detection strongly advance the opinion that the examiner is the single most important factor in any lie detector test. Professional quality of examiners is a sore point in lie detection, for licensing regulations vary widely among states (and are completely absent in some), so it has been possible in many places for a high school graduate with less than six weeks of specialized training to hang out a shingle as a professional lie detector examiner.[48] There is, moreover, considerable incentive to do just that, for lie detection can be a fairly lucrative profession. The fee for preemployment and periodic tests varies from about $25 to $75 or more, while tests in specific criminal investigations, done in more elaborate circumstances with attorneys present, may cost more than $200. Businesses are understandably concerned to keep their costs down, so many of them opt for lie detector tests at the cheaper end of the scale. Some examiners accommodate this by offering low-cost tests, but then they attempt to maximize their income by increasing their volume. In 1972, for example, one examiner in Alexandria, Virginia, earned a handsome living by giving more than 2,000 lie detector tests annually (an average of 8 per day for 50 five-day weeks), although he was scarcely at the lower end of the cost scale because even at that time he charged $75 per test.[49]

Examiners I interviewed frequently stated that the greatest threat to their profession is the presence of incompetent and/or unscrupulous individuals in their midst. They call them "chart rollers," and they accuse them of producing highly unreliable results through sloppy testing. It is essential for valid results, examiners told me, to ascertain whether the anxiety that accompanies the response to certain questions is produced by deception or by some other circumstance. This often involves running several charts and long interviews, in a process that may require two or more hours. The process is so mentally demanding on the conscientious examiner, one told me, that he is utterly exhausted if he does two tests in a day. Chart rollers, whose primary concern is to maximize the number of tests they give, are unwilling to devote the necessary time and care to this imperative. They do a perfunctory pretest interview, run a single chart, simply report "deception indicated" for the questions where stress is recorded, and move on without exploring the issue. Thus their rate of "false positives" (erroneous conclusions that the subject is lying) is high. A grocery store manager recounted an experience with a chart roller who polygraphed two cashiers for "sweetheart checking"—a procedure whereby the cashier charges the customer (a relative or friend) far less than the actual price, such as ringing up a ham as a pack of chewing gum. The polygraph results indicated deception by one of the checkers, and the examiner reported that she had been giving merchandise to her brother, John. She was fired but then sued for wrongful termination, pointing out that she did not have a brother named John. The store settled out of court and decided it was time to get someone else to do their polygraph testing. One examiner said that the most unscrupulous chart rollers will run people through in about ten minutes, sometimes without even hooking them up to the machine, and then provide a fabricated report and charge the fee for a completed test.

The PSE has perhaps been especially attractive to would-be chart rollers because the training program is shorter still—only two weeks, as one PSE examiner told me. The PSE is also appealing to business because it often costs less than the polygraph. The cheapest rate I have come across is from a policeman trained as a PSE examiner, who told me that he used to moonlight by doing PSE tests for $8 each. Under his system, the employer would ask the questions, tape record the subject's responses, and send the tape to the examiner. He would analyze the tape on the PSE machine, identify the questions on which deception was indicated, and mail his report to the employer. The report would recommend that the employer discuss those questions with the applicant to determine if the stress that showed up on the chart stemmed from deception or some other cause, but he does not know if employers actually followed up on the recommendation. Certainly the PSE examiner did not do it because he never set eyes on the applicants. This seems to be a highly evolved form of chart rolling. When I asked him why he did it, he replied, "If some fool pays some other fool to do that, why not?"

Partly in an effort to achieve a more respectable image and to work toward establishing self-policing ethical and professional standards, polygraph examiners formed a professional society, the American Polygraph Association (APA). The APA publishes the journal, *Polygraph*, and attempts to present polygraph tests and polygraph examiners in the most favorable light possible to the outside world. The seal of the association is the blindfolded figure of Justice, holding a balance scale in her left hand. But in her right hand, instead of a sword, she holds a long polygraph chart, one end of which trails on the ground near her feet. The motto "Dedicated to Truth" is printed beside her.

Another effort to police the profession was through state licensing of polygraph examiners. While this did not exist in all states, the concept came to be supported by many polygraph examiners as a means of rooting out chart rollers, giving them the aura of true professionals and fending off moves to curtail lie detection by legislation. The importance placed on state licensing is clear from the following passage by two polygraph practitioners.

> State polygraph licensing boards began to crop up [in the early and middle 1960s] and make purposeful headway in the investigation of public complaints that alleged personal, embarrassing, or sexually oriented questions associated with polygraphy. The word spread quickly. A good number of examiners had their license to practice suspended or revoked. It was not long before that kind of complaint became a rarity. By the end of 1982, polygraph licensing boards were tougher than boot leather. As a result, strict licensing administration and regulation became a blessing to ethical examiners.[50]

Legal Control of Lie Detection

The salutory promise of a professional association and state licensing turned out, however, to be wishful thinking. Public suspicion of lie detection persisted, and by the end of the 1970s, at least sixteen states had enacted laws designed to control or prohibit lie detector tests in the workplace.[51] According to polygraph proponent Ferguson, who welcomes tough state licensing of polygraph examiners, such legislation was really a grotesque aberration of a dark time in the nation's history. It was because of the liberal-dominated 1960s, he explained, that several states "let witch hunts initiated by Mob controlled labor unions, and other rotten-stinking sources, cause 'elected' state representatives to enact ridiculous antipolygraph statutes of the flimsiest sort."[52] But legislative threats to the polygraph were also emerging on the federal level. Polygraph control bills were proposed by Senator Sam Ervin (North Carolina) in 1971 and 1973 and by Senator Birch Bayh (Indiana) in 1977.[53] These bills were not adopted, but in 1987, Representative Pat Williams (Montana) introduced another bill that successfully passed through the entire legislative process and became law. The Employee Polygraph Protection Act, which took effect on December 28, 1988, drastically curtailed the use of lie detection in the United States. In essence, this law prohibits most private sector employers from requiring prospective or current employees to submit to preemployment or periodic lie detector tests. An employer may still request an employee to submit to a lie detector test by polygraph (but not by PSE or other devices) if there is reason to suspect the employee of some specific wrongdoing. All local, state, and federal governmental agencies are exempt from the law and may therefore continue to use any form of lie detection for employment or any other purpose. A number of private firms are also exempt from the provisions of the law, notably those under contract for sensitive work for the Department of Defense, CIA, or FBI; those involved in the manufacture or distribution of controlled substances; and those in the security guard, armored car, or security alarm fields. These exemptions mean that lie detection will certainly not disappear from the American scene. Nevertheless, it will be dramatically reduced: some 80 percent of the two million lie detector tests given annually in the United States fall under the law's ban.[54]

Those who supported the bill argued that lie detection violates constitutional and legal rights to privacy, to due process of law, and to be presumed innocent until proven guilty.[55] But perhaps the most important concern that led to the legislation had to do with the accuracy of lie detector tests. Especially disquieting is the problem of false positives: that lie detector tests label as dishonest some people who in fact are honest. The particular circumstances of lie detection in the employment setting produce a magnification effect with reference to false positives, such that even with an accuracy rate of 85 percent, the tests generate some alarming results. Representatives of the American Psychological Association explained it in testimony before the

House Subcommittee on Employment Opportunities in the following way:

> Assume that polygraph tests are 85 percent accurate, a fair assumption based on the 1983 OTA report [on the validity of lie detector tests]. Consider, under such circumstances, what would happen in the case of screening 1,000 employees, 100 of whom (10 percent) were dishonest. In that situation, one would identify 85 of the dishonest employees, but at the cost of misidentifying 135 (15 percent) of the honest employees. As you can see, in this situation the polygraph tester identifies 220 "suspects," of whom 61 percent are completely innocent. It can be shown mathematically that if the validity of the test drops below 85 percent, then the misidentification rate increases. Similarly, if the base rate of dishonesty is less than 10 percent, and it most likely is, the misidentification rate increases. It is obvious that in the employment screening situation it is a mathematical given that the majority of identified "suspects" are in fact innocent![56]

Congress found it to be intolerable that preemployment screening by lie detector tests would reject more honest than dishonest applicants, especially when the stakes involve people's reputations, self-esteem, and opportunity to earn a living.

If lie detection is so drastically flawed, one wonders why the Employee Polygraph Protection Act has so many exceptions. Is it not hypocritical, as some members of the House Committee on Education and Labor registered in their dissenting views on the bill,[57] to marshal such powerful arguments for outlawing lie detection in the private sector but then to place no impediment whatsoever on its continued use for any purpose in the public sector? Indeed, one journalist reports that lie detection has actually increased in the federal government since the bill went into effect late in the Reagan administration: "The Reagan and Bush administrations have vastly expanded the use of polygraphs in recent years, routinely administering them in the course of 'leak' and national security investigations."[58] In the Conference Report that adjusted differences between the Senate and House versions of the bill, the exemption of public sector employees was explained as a matter of legislative committee jurisdiction:

By exempting public sector employers and private contractors engaged in intelligence and counterintelligence functions, the conferees recognize the functions performed by these employers are not within the jurisdiction of the committees which reported the legislation, and the policy decisions as to the proper or improper use of such tests are left to the committees of jurisdiction and expertise.[59]

The Conference Report does not explain, however, why exemptions from the bill are also granted to private companies that operate armored cars, other security service firms, and companies that manufacture or dispense controlled drugs.[60] Contradicting the arguments about polygraph inaccuracy on which the bill is supposedly based, continued use by the government and these private sector exemptions seem to betray a belief that lie detection really is an effective tool for identifying dishonest employees and applicants, even if certain excesses and imperfections compromise their civil rights. But, the thinking seems to go, that is justified for people charged with keeping political secrets or with special responsibilities in the war on drugs or the custody of money.

A similar ambivalence surfaced during the Senate Judiciary Committee hearings on the sexual harassment charge raised against Supreme Court nominee Clarence Thomas in October 1991. Polygraph tests seem to have a special appeal in cases of sexual harassment, which by their nature tend to occur in private, with no disinterested witnesses available. If in past centuries disputes that came down to the word of one litigant against another recommended soliciting the opinion of God via trial by ordeal or battle, in our own time, a lie detector test promises to cut through efforts at dissimulation and get the answer directly from the principals themselves. Judge Thomas's accuser, Anita Hill, did in fact take, and pass, a polygraph test. Although all parties acknowledged difficulties with polygraph tests and their inadmissibility as legal evidence, this was perceived by some as speaking in her favor. Senator Paul Simon (Illinois) noted, "I don't find generally that people who are not telling the truth volunteer to take lie-detector tests,"[61] while Senator Patrick Leahy (Vermont) said that the test result supported her credibility.[62]

Curiously, although the test was mentioned by senators and members of the media many times during those tension-filled days of October (and roundly scorned by avid supporters of Judge Thomas such as Utah Senator Orrin Hatch), hardly anyone thought to point out that Congress itself had passed a law against lie detector tests just three years before.[63]

Written Integrity Tests

Also not covered by the Employee Polygraph Protection Act are paper-and-pencil tests that purport to measure honesty, such as the Reid Report, the Personnel Selection Inventory, the Stanton Survey, and the Wilkerson Pre-Employment Audit. R. Michael O'Bannon, Linda Goldinger, and Gavis Appleby identify forty-six of these so-called honesty or integrity tests currently on the market.[64] Most of them are designed for preemployment screening, although a few are for use with current employees. Many employers seem to be turning to them as a replacement for the now-banned polygraph. Test publishers report dramatic increases in sales since the antipolygraph act was passed. Approximately 2.5 million such tests are administered annually by an estimated 5,000 to 6,000 companies.[65] This is already a considerable increase above the two million polygraph tests administered in the United States in 1987, well before the antipolygraph law went into effect.[66] Budget-conscious employers might have reason to prefer them to polygraph tests because they are considerably cheaper. They cost from $4 to $35, with most tests clustering in the $6 to $15 range.[67]

Questions are of two basic types. Some solicit outright admission of previous wrongdoings, while others explore attitudes and personality characteristics that may be correlated with honesty or dishonesty. The former ask whether, during the last few years, the subject has shoplifted, broken into a home or business, stolen from an employer, used an alias, driven while intoxicated, written a bad check, had a friend who steals, and so on. Attitude-probing questions might ask the subject to respond with "agree," "disagree," or "undecided" to a broad series of propositions, such as that it is acceptable to break unjust laws, that people are usually not what they seem to be, that a store employee should not be fired for taking pens and pencils, that it is necessary to have laws governing morals, that smoking a marijuana cigarette is no worse than drinking a Coca-Cola, that employers should not be concerned about drug or alcohol use so long as the employee performs well on the job, that a thief deserves a second chance, that most people cheat on their income tax, that the subject has occasionally felt like breaking something, would never lie, sometimes feels sorry for oneself, has wild daydreams, likes to create excitement, has not had many lucky breaks, would prefer to talk to an interesting person at a social gathering, sometimes goes to places where it would not be good to be seen by an acquaintance.

Integrity tests and scoring techniques come in a variety of formats. In some cases, an answer key and instructions for scoring are included with the packet of tests. In others, written answer sheets may be mailed to the test publishing company for scoring, or the employer may have the result immediately by calling the company and reading the answers over the telephone. Still other tests are taken on a computer and scored automatically.[68] Telescreen, Inc., markets a test that is taken by means of a touch-tone telephone. The subject listens to questions on the telephone and has three seconds to punch keys signifying "yes," "no," or "not applicable."[69]

Integrity tests have been developed outside the mainstream of psychological testing, often by polygraphers and always by companies interested in marketing them. Nearly all research on their validity and reliability has been conducted by persons associated with those companies rather than by independent scholars and is unpublished or appears in reports issued by the test publishers rather than in peer-reviewed journals.[70] Although most of that research reflects favorably on integrity tests, one reviewer has been quoted as saying, "As an analogy, would we consider it good science to publish a review of research on the effects of smoking on health when almost every study was supported by the Tobacco Institute?"[71]

Even the research on integrity tests conducted by interested parties raises grave suspicion as to their value. The Office of

TABLE 1

Predictive Validity Studies of Overty Integrity Tests

Study	Sample Size	Number Passed (% of total)	Number Failed (% of total)	Number found Engaging in Dishonest Behavior (% of total)
1	479	241 (50%)	238 (50%)	17 (3.5%)
2	3,790	1,570 (41.4%)	2,220 (58.6%)	91 (2.4%)
3	527	173 (32.8%)	354 (67.2%)	33 (6.3%)
4	61	50 (82%)	11 (18%)	6 (9.8%)
5	801	472 (58.9%)	329 (41.1%)	21 (2.6%)

Source: Office of Technology Assessment (1990), p. 55.

Technology Assessment identified five studies, all conducted by the publishers of the tests under study, where applicants in retail enterprises were tested and hired regardless of the test result. Their work records were scrutinized to determine how many of those identified as dishonest by the test were found to engage in theft or other dishonest behavior on the job. Study results are summarized in table 1. The briefest examination of these figures indicates that something is seriously wrong with integrity testing. It is, of course, unlikely that all dishonest employees will be apprehended, but it is alarming that (except for Study 4, with its small sample size) those labeled dishonest by integrity tests outnumber those who are actually caught in dishonest behavior by between ten and twenty to one. In four of the five studies (again Study 4 is the odd one out), over 40 percent of those who took integrity tests failed them, and in two of the studies (including Study 2, with by far the largest sample), the dishonest ones represent large majorities. If we are to believe the testimony from representatives of the American Psychological Association that

10 percent or less of workers are dishonest, it is obvious that staggering numbers of honest individuals are branded as dishonest by integrity tests. Reversing the principle of the American justice system that it is better to acquit several guilty individuals than to convict a single innocent one, integrity tests seem to be more akin to the philosophy that "if you hang 'em all, you'll be sure to get the guilty ones."

The Office of Technology Assessment report is a carefully researched document that finds inadequate evidence to confirm or deny the claim that integrity tests predict dishonest behavior[72] but nevertheless identifies sufficient problems with them to reach the final conclusion that "the potentially harmful effects of systematic misclassification, possible impacts on protected groups, and privacy implications of integrity tests combine to warrant further governmental attention."[73] Another report on integrity testing, prepared by a special task force of the American Psychological Association, is also critical of integrity tests at numerous points. Many tests have cutoff scores that mark the point between passing and failing or that define zones such as high, medium, and low risk. But information about how test publishers have determined the proper location of cutoff points is insufficient or absent. (The data in table 1 concerning how many pass and fail integrity tests dramatize the cogency of this criticism.) The report also chides some publishers for promoting their tests with fraudulent claims and complains that research and evaluation of test reliability and validity are seriously hampered by the fact that test publishers often conceal the necessary information under a cloak of proprietary interests. Test results could well be affected by insufficient attention to linguistic and cultural variables when tests are translated into other languages such as Spanish.[74] Curiously, however, and especially in light of the strongly negative testimony from representatives of the American Psychological Association in the congressional hearings on polygraph tests, this report is equivocal. In tenor, it tilts toward employers' needs to curtail theft and promote productivity as against the interests of employees in privacy and personal dignity. Among the assumptions that guided the investigation, the one they identify as "perhaps of the greatest importance" is the highly pragmatic consideration that if integrity tests were not available, employees would subjected to something worse.[75] Hence the bottom line:

> Despite all our reservations about honesty tests, however, we do not believe that there is any sound basis for prohibiting their development and use; indeed, to do so would only invite alternative forms of preemployment screening that would be less open, scientific, and controllable.[76]

The OTA report was commissioned by the House Committee on Education and Labor. It is likely that the request was made as a step toward considering legislation to control integrity testing. A similar OTA report on the polygraph was requested and used as an important basis for the development of the Employee Polygraph Protection Act. In earlier forms, the bill that eventually became that law included written and oral as well as mechanical tests, although references to the written and oral forms were deleted in committee pending further study.[77] Those inclined toward legal control may find integrity testing to be more elusive than polygraph testing. For one thing, the OTA report representing the further study on integrity testing desired by Congress is not nearly so decisively negative as the earlier report concerning the polygraph. Thus Rep. Pat Williams, the Democrat of Montana who requested the OTA report, indicated that he would not sponsor legislation until still more research has been completed. Moreover, efforts to establish legal control of integrity tests might encounter problems in stating exactly what they are. This is relatively straightforward with the polygraph because such a test may be unambiguously defined in terms of the use of a machine that measures physiological responses. To define a written or oral integrity test is much more difficult.[78] It could scarcely be by label, because publishers could (and often already do) call them "inventories" or "surveys" rather than "tests." Nor would it seem prudent or practical to forbid all employer inquiries into applicants' theft, vandalism, absenteeism, or other problematic behavior in previous jobs. Therefore, potential legislation controlling integrity tests might prove to be considerably more complicated to write and to enforce than was the case with poly-graph and other mechanical tests.[79]

These issues aside, it is nevertheless possible to criticize the sheer logic that grounds the concept, design, and scoring of hon-esty tests. In the first place, these tests are intended to measure "honesty," but a single character trait corresponding to that des-ignation may not exist. In a classic study in social psychology, Hugh Hartshorne and Mark May conducted experimental tests of lying, cheating, and stealing among 11,000 children aged 8 to 16 and found little evidence that these behaviors clustered in the same individuals. Someone who might lie is not particularly disposed to steal, a child who might steal could not therefore be expected to cheat, and those who might cheat on one kind of test might not cheat on another. Their conclusion:

> Neither deceit nor its opposite, "honesty," are unified character traits, but rather specific functions of life situations. . . . There is no evidence for supposing that children who are more likely to resort to deceptive methods than others would not use honorable methods with equal satisfaction if the situation in which dishon-esty is practiced were sufficiently controlled by those who are responsible for their behavior.[80]

Hartshorne and May's conclusions are not unequivocally ac-cepted. J. Philippe Rushton argues forcefully that their own data, when examined from a different statistical perspective, suggest that lying, cheating, and stealing do tend to cluster (together with selfishness and a few other qualities) in certain people. He con-cludes that a general personality trait of morality does exist and is more characteristic of some individuals than others.[81] The issue is not finally resolved, but no one seems to question that one important determinant of whether people will behave honestly or not is the specific situation in which they are placed. This would imply that employers should pay at least as much attention to creating conditions in the workplace that discourage stealing and other undesirable activities and to rewarding honest behavior as they do to tests that claim to categorize some people as honest and others as dishonest in any and all situations.

Again, questions on integrity tests that pertain to past activities are based on the assumption that people who have stolen from employers or engaged in other dishonest behavior in the past are likely to do so again in the future. This is probably correct (within the limits of the situational considerations mentioned above), and about 25 percent of those who take integrity tests do admit to delinquencies of various kinds.[82] But, of course, it does not follow that *only* those who admit to past misdeeds have performed them. Surely the group of those who deny previous dishonest behavior contains some wrongdoers who perpetuate their dishonesty by concealing it on the test. These people would be at least as likely to be dishonest employees as those who made admissions on the test. Following the convention of considering a positive result to be an indication of dishonesty and a negative result to be no such indication, these questions are susceptible to false negative results. That is, they may well identify certain persons as not being dishonest who in fact are.

Certainly it is a primary purpose of the attitude-probing questions to smoke out those false negatives, but again there are logical problems. It is not always possible to know precisely how the tests are scored because testing companies often protect this information as proprietary.[83] This is another factor that complicates research on the tests. Nevertheless, David Lykken reports that highest marks on attitudinal questions go to those who favor harsh punishment for infractions (e.g., that an employee who steals a few dollars each week should be fired) and who assume a high degree of honesty in everyone (e.g., a belief that very few people cheat on their income tax). "The rationale for such scoring," he writes "is that a thief will be unlikely to recommend harsh punishment for acts he might himself commit and he will probably contend that most people are as dishonest as he is."[84] True enough, but this net catches many more than moral degenerates because, as Lykken points out, "the logic does not work in both directions."[85] Even if all thieves oppose harsh punishment, it is likely that many who are not thieves also oppose it. Even if all scoundrels believe that people in general are not much good, many who are not themselves scoundrels may share that dark assessment of human nature. Therefore, these questions have the reverse flaw of those that inquire into past wrongdoing. Now the problem is false *positive* results: attitudinal questions are likely to label as dishonest a number of people who in fact are honest.

Given these difficulties, the most effective strategy when confronting an honesty test may be to throw honesty to the winds—to learn the kinds of considerations that go into the scoring and to answer the questions accordingly, without regard for truth. One experiment with college students found that a group told to fake the most honest results they could on an integrity test scored a full standard deviation higher on attitudinal questions and half a standard deviation higher on admissions of past misdeeds than a group that was instructed to answer all questions completely honestly.[86] As for the alternative: "If the questions are to be answered honestly, then what is required [to score well on the test] is a punitive, authoritarian personality combined with a worldview like that of the three monkeys who hear-no-evil, see-no-evil, speak-no-evil."[87] Or, as I was told in earthier language by the proprietor of a fast-food chain in Texas, "We used written honesty tests for a while, but quit when we found that the people we were hiring were just *too weird.*"

A strategy of beating the test by giving the preferred answers may not always work, because on occasion the rationale behind preferring one answer to another may not be possible to perceive. It may, in fact, not exist. Consider the following two questions, from a Stanton honesty test:

1. Do you think people who steal do it because they always have?

2. Do you agree with this: once a thief . . . always a thief?

According to scoring expectations, honest people will answer "yes" to the first of these questions and "no" to the second.[88] It is possible, however, that many people—some of them honest and true—may be able to discern little, if any, difference between the questions. While this scoring strategy might foil efforts to beat the test, it is scarcely conducive to confidence in its validity.

To end on an ironic note, honesty tests are not always entirely honest themselves.[89] In some tests, the questions about previous wrongdoings are labeled optional, and the directions state that they may be left blank if the subject does not wish to answer. But the instructions to the test administrator advise that anyone who does not answer them should be viewed as probably having something to hide. Again, interviewers may be encouraged to lure test subjects into making damning revelations. In one test, a section to be completed by interview includes a question about the applicant's attendance in school. The instructions to the interviewer, stressing that school attendance record is a highly significant indicator of the likelihood of success at work, recommend minimizing its importance by posing the issue with a wink and a smile, such as, "John, when I was in school I often found that going to class was a waste of time. How about you?"

4

NO SANCTUARY

O Lord, thou has searched me and known me!
. . . .
thou discernest my thoughts from afar.
Thou searchest out my path and my lying down,
and are acquainted with all my ways.
Even before a word is on my tongue,
lo, O Lord, thou knowest it altogether.
Thou dost beset me behind and before,
and layest thy hand upon me.
. . . .
Search me, oh God, and know my heart!
Try me and know my thoughts!
And see if there be any wicked way in me,
and lead me in the way everlasting!

Psalm 139

Of the two main theses this book aims to establish—that tests frequently create the personal characteristics they purport to measure and that testing is a means of exercising power—lie detection, a technique for surveillance and control, is obviously most relevant to the second. Using the largely descriptive account of chapter 3 as a foundation, here we investigate how lie detector tests exert power and domination over those who take them. The analysis leads to the conclusion that lie detection represents an important advance in what Foucault has called the "disciplinary technology of power."[1]

Communing/Communicating with the Polygraph

When administered with care by experienced and proficient interrogator-examiners, polygraph tests are potent instruments for bringing information to light which people wish to keep hidden. Their power to elicit confessions and revelations may be analyzed in terms of the framework of communication established by the test. A polygraph test replaces the normal pattern of dialogue between two persons with a matrix of communication involving four parties: the polygraph machine, the examiner, and the subject, who is bisected, Cartesian-like, into physical and mental substance, body and mind. The synapse of information transfer occurs between the two physical objects or machines: on the one side, the polygraph, and on the other, the subject as body, a bundle of physiological functions. Standing somewhat to the side are the two mental objects or persons: the polygraph examiner and the subject again, but this time as a volitional and moral agent.

The two machines commune together as the polygraph reaches out to embrace the subject's body with bands, tubes, and clips. The body responds loverlike to the touch, whispering secrets to the polygraph in tiny squeezes, twinges, thrills, and nudges. But both machines are treacherous. The body, seduced by the polygraph's embrace, thoughtlessly prattles the confidences it shares with the subject's mind. The polygraph, a false and uncaring confidant, publishes the secrets it has learned on a chart for all to read. The subject as mind, powerless to chaperone the affair, watches helplessly as the carnal entwining of machines produces its undoing.

Even as he sat in the polygraph examining room chair and watched Dee Wheeler secure the instrument's attachments to his body, he joked and laughed, confident he would leave the room a free man. But his smile faded when the instrument's slender recording pens spelled out the killer's escape route and pinpointed the spot where he buried the murder weapon.[2]

But when his brain and autonomic nervous system put deception criteria on the polygrams, Abrose broke down and confessed.[3]

C. B. Hanscom bore down. His question formulations became exacting and precise. Aaron's autonomic nervous system, in a manner of speaking, blew its control fuse. Hanscom backed off, then began a delicate and deliberate interrogation. It wasn't long before Aaron had confessed not only to the burglary in question but also to the murder.[4]

Advocates of the psychological stress evaluator (a machine that produces a sound wave chart from a tape recording of the subject's voice) point to the absence of physical connections as an advantage, but in fact the reverse is true. The physical grip of the polygraph contributes to the subject's sense of impotence before the machine, and this is one reason why the polygraph is more effective than the PSE and other lie detection devices in breaking through subject resistance to provoke confessions.

We will return to the subject as mind in a moment, but first we need to acknowledge the fourth figure in the communication matrix: the polygraph examiner. If this person is an incompetent amateur or an unscrupulous chart roller, the test does not approach its potential. The full power of the polygraph is realized only when manipulated by a determined and skilled examiner. Profiles of such individuals are uncommon; it is conceivable that Ferguson, who on occasion refers to them as "champions of justice," goes a little overboard with his:

Who and what may be termed a "competent polygraph examiner"? We might simply describe him as a rare breed, dedicated to the welfare of his country, confident of his ability, well trained and educated; he is an experienced interrogator with a profound knowledge of the psychology of human behavior, thoroughly versed in law and physiology, compassionate and understanding, fair and impartial, ethically oriented. He has been around. He has lived.[5]

The effective examiner plays two distinct roles in a polygraph test. First he[6] is the expert technician. He affixes the polygraph's sensors to various parts of the subject's body, calibrates the machine before the test begins in earnest, carefully instructs the subject to relax and to sit completely still while the machine is running, asks the questions in an even monotone, and interprets the charts. In this role, he umpires the tryst between the two machines; he is detached and objective, the consummate scientist. "The primary function of the polygraphist," explains examiner and polygraph theoretician Sylvestro F. Reali, "is to allow the subject to physiologically show the polygraphist the truth from within the subject himself. Allowing for no input to that end from the examiner."[7]

The second role reveals the human side of the examiner. He seems genuinely to like the subject, to be pulling for the subject to "pass" the test. If deception is indicated on some of the questions, the examiner spares no effort to identify extraneous issues that might be responsible for it, and his greatest satisfaction is to prove the subject not guilty. He seems to understand the feeling of helplessness experienced by the subject in the face of a lie detector test and to sympathize. He wants to assist in any way he can. But the examiner is frustrated in these benevolent intentions unless the subject allows him to help. It is necessary that the subject place complete confidence in the examiner and cooperate fully so that, together, they might bring the test to a happy conclusion.

This, of course, is a role that examiners sometimes adopt treacherously, with the intention of cajoling the subject into a confession. But many examiners are sincere in this posture, and their most satisfying cases are those where they managed, after hard and creative effort, to clear an innocent individual suspected of a crime. One examiner told me of a young man he was called to test, who was accused of stealing stereo equipment from the store where he worked. On the first polygraph chart, the subject's responses to the relevant questions about the theft indicated deception. The polygraph examiner, however, was not convinced of the suspect's guilt. Following the first chart, he interviewed the subject at great length to ascertain whether some extraneous issue might be causing the anxiety that appeared on the chart. Finally, taking the examiner into his confidence, the young man confessed that some ten years before he had been involved in a homosexual encounter. He was afraid that if his employer ever found out, it would cost him his job. The examiner assured him that this matter was irrelevant to the issue of the stolen equipment and that the secret was safe with him. This reassured the subject, and the examiner then turned on the polygraph and ran a second chart. No deception was indicated on the relevant questions about the theft, and the young man was cleared.

Polygraph examiners frequently report that "spillover" from anxiety about extraneous issues, as in this case, is a major cause of "false positives" (charts that indicate deception although the subject is actually innocent) in lie detector tests. Efforts are made to minimize this possibility by trying to put the subject at ease during a pretest interview, a process that normally includes reviewing all the questions that will be asked on the test. Often an "outside issue" question—one that asks if the subject is afraid that the examiner might probe into some issue that has not been discussed previously—is included on the test. The rationale is that a subject who is convinced that such outside issues will not be raised will be more relaxed during the test. Alternatively, as happened in the case of the homosexual encounter described above, the catharsis of confessing to an outside issue may relieve tension that could produce a false positive result. In either event, so the theory goes, anxiety stemming from extraneous matters is reduced and is therefore unlikely to produce charts that falsely indicate deception.

One method that helpful examiners use to avoid false positive results is through further inquiry into the control question (to which any subject is expected to respond deceptively and which is used as a point for comparison with responses to the relevant questions). If the initial chart indicates deception on a relevant question, Inbau and Reid recommend that the examiner pursue the source of deception by telling the subject that the charts indicate lies but that probably the deception is spilling over from the response to the control question (which in their system is, "Did you ever steal anything in your life?").[8] The examiner goes on to say that to clear the charts, it is necessary to be entirely honest on the control question. This is presented as a minor inconvenience to satisfy the peculiarities of the polygraph but of no real consequence because past thefts are not relevant to the present investigation. The subject is then invited to confess all past thefts, after which another chart is run, this time with the control question rephrased as, "Other than what you have already told me, have you stolen anything in your life?" This process may continue through several more charts, the examiner explaining that deception is still indicated and urging the subject to reveal any additional past wrongdoings. Ultimately, the subject is utterly purged of secrets about the past, the charts are clear of any indication of deception, and the polygraph examiner has fulfilled the professional obligation to preserve the innocent from false accusations.

A well-conducted polygraph test has an uncanny capacity to convince the subject that one's most private thoughts cannot be defended against intrusion. One is maneuvered into a position where the only option available seems to be confession. A young woman explained it this way:

> You come in feeling like an honest, decent person and then he starts telling you that you're showing a reaction to some question about drugs or stealing and you try to think of a reason, things you've done, maybe years ago. You get to feeling as if the all-important thing is to get the machine to say that you're all right. You feel as if the thing can almost read your mind but not really accurately, it exaggerates, gets things mixed up. And you feel that if you tell the man everything you can think of, everything you've ever done that you might feel guilty about, why then finally it might come out with a clean record.[9]

An examiner told me that one of his subjects marveled, "You know more about me than my husband does," and polygraph specialist John Reid claimed, "We get better results than a priest does."[10] The lengths people go to bare their souls before the polygraph would be funny if so much pathos were not involved. Among employees polygraphed in a fast-food restaurant in Florida, one neatly wrote on the consent form, "I owe 99 cents for soft drinks.

I also owe 30 cents or more for small sundae," and appended her initials. Another confessed, "I have taken coffee and the inside of onion rings without paying," and a third divulged, that "Since I have been employed, I have given ice away with water."

Confessions, of course, are not always innocuous. It may be that the subject really is guilty of the malfeasance under investigation—a circumstance that the thorough polygraph test is, of course, designed to ascertain. And occasionally the extraneous information that is revealed is of much weightier import than the matter being investigated. One examiner told me that he has even gotten confessions of murder in routine preemployment screenings.

The impotence of the subject as mind in the lie detector situation sometimes impels people to lose confidence in their own convictions and to become abjectly dependent on the examiner. Then they may offer to confess to the delict under investigation even if they are innocent. Examiners I have interviewed report that it has sometimes been necessary to tell subjects, very carefully, not to confess unless they actually committed the crime. Working on the basis of a strong police presumption that a woman was guilty of a certain crime, an examiner succeeded in extracting a confession after about forty-five minutes of work with the polygraph. He then discovered, however, that she was unable to supply certain factual details about the case that the perpetrator would surely know. He concluded that she was in fact innocent, but it took him hours to convince her of that and to persuade her to retract the confession.

The experience of confessing before the lie detector may remain an uncomfortable memory for years. During a preemployment polygraph screening, a meat cutter I interviewed was asked if he had done anything for which he could be sent to jail. Although the examiner assured him he was only interested in the previous six or seven years, the urge to confess stimulated by the test resulted in an admission of something he had done some fifteen years before. He got the job, but his experience with the polygraph has rankled ever since. "They've got something that's mine," he told me. He worries that this information, which he considers to have been stolen from him, appears on his employment record.

Nor is such a concern necessarily misplaced. I asked several polygraph and PSE examiners what they do with confessions that are unrelated to the matter they have been charged to investigate. One said he never passes it on, but others answered that they write the information down and include it in their reports. Therefore, it is not always in the subject's interest to extend the trust that the accomplished polygraph examiner courts so ardently. It has been explained how police might encourage a suspect to submit to a polygraph test when their evidence is not strong enough for an indictment. The suspect is told that the test represents the best chance to clear oneself, but in reality, it is a last-ditch effort to obtain a confession, without which the case will be dropped. The police officer who explained this is convinced that when the department uses lie detector tests on its own personnel in internal investigations, the same game is being played. "They tell you they want to clear you of this," he said, "but really they're trying to hang it on you."

Asymmetry and the Power of Lie Detection

Our definition of a test includes the notion that it is an information-obtaining device applied by an agency to an individual. It is obvious that the individual to whom a lie detector test is applied enters the test situation alone and essentially defenseless. The test giver, in contrast, is an agent who comes to the test armed with technological apparatus and the official authority of the sponsoring organization. It is an utterly asymmetrical situation that pits the solitary subject against the full weight and resources of the organization. Even when the purpose of the test has to do with some possible benefit for the subject, such as screening for a job, the asymmetry of the situation is in the forefront. The test giver asks the questions, and the subject answers them, with full recognition by everyone concerned that the organization will evaluate the answers and use the resulting information to decide what to do about the subject. These observations apply to written integrity tests as well as polygraph tests. In fact, they apply to essentially *all* types of tests, and they highlight an important aspect of the power that characterizes testing in general. Information still flows essentially one way from subject to test givers, that information is extracted and processed according to an agenda and technological apparatus controlled by the test givers, and it is still used by the test-giving organization to make decisions about the individual test taker. The sense of impotence may be exaggerated in the case of a polygraph test, when the subject is literally in the clutches of the machine's sensing apparatus, but takers of other kinds of tests are also held in the grasp—now metaphorical but no less meaningful—of test-giving organizations. As with preindustrial authenticity tests such as trial by ordeal, the asymmetry that places a scrutinizing organization on one side and a scrutinized individual on the other is a relation of power. If we are to understand the social consequences of lie detection, it is essential to know how that power works.

On occasion, it works so well that it literally *creates* what it purports to measure rather than identifying something that was previously there. I am referring to cases where people, disoriented by the circumstances of a polygraph test, come to distrust their own memories and confess to crimes they did not commit. Confessions can be created in the crucible of polygraph tests with much less expenditure of violence and energy than was visited on those unfortunates of four or five centuries ago who, utterly broken by torture, would come to believe that they were, indeed, witches. A particularly effective technique is for the polygraph examiner to run a chart and pin it to the wall. He then points to the response monitored for the relevant or "hot" question and asks why the subject "hit" on it. (In fact, the response may indicate deception only very slightly, if at all. But subjects normally have no knowledge of how to read polygraph charts and so have no way to interpret what they are shown apart from what the examiner says.) The examiner then leaves the room, allowing the subject to study the chart and stew about the response. The examiner returns and runs another chart, asking the same questions in the same order. The subject knows full well when the hot question is coming and is worried that the chart might again indicate deception on it, a worry that subsides after the question has been asked and answered. The new chart is pinned on the wall, and, sure enough, the subject did "hit" on the relevant question again, even more this time, and a distinctive "peak of tension" pattern (responses building up over a few questions prior to the hot one, climaxing on it, and then relaxing on subsequent questions) starts to appear. The subject is again left alone to ponder the chart, after which the examiner returns and runs yet another chart—same questions, same order. The subject is increasingly nervous about the course that events are taking, and when this chart is pinned on the wall, the peak of tension pattern is unmistakable, even to untrained eyes. Confused and bewildered by a pattern of physiological responses that objective, scientific measures make obvious, ultimately the subject concludes that his or her own memory must be blotted out or playing tricks and confesses. What else could one do? After all, the subject is there alone, a single person relying on memory that, as everyone knows, can be fallible. How much can that count against the growing suspicion of a trained examiner and the scientific evidence of a precise machine, recorded so obviously that even the increasingly distraught subject can see it more clearly with each new chart?

The preceding scenario is likelier to occur in polygraph than in written integrity tests, primarily because the polygraph is used for meticulous interrogations in connection with particular crimes while written tests are used for brief and general checks of the honesty of job applicants who are not under suspicion for any specific misdeed. The following observations concerning the power of lie detection pertain, however, with at least equal force to written integrity tests as to the polygraph.

A Matter of Trust

One ingenious technique to identify a guilty party, reported from India, is to bring all those suspected of a crime together before a tent. They are told that inside is a magic donkey that will bray if a guilty individual pulls its tail but will make no sound if the one administering the tug is innocent. The suspects are then sent into the pitch dark tent one at a time and told to pull the donkey's tail. They are not told that the tail (which is actually attached to no prototype for current models. Keeler went on to become one of the founders of the lie detection profession. Based in Chicago, he utilized his polygraph extensively in criminal investigations during the 1930s and 1940s. Keeler developed some of the formats for lie detector tests that are still in use and founded the first polygraph examiner training institute as well as a company that manufactures polygraph machines.[14]

The polygraph is a device that simultaneously monitors several different physiological processes. The machine is attached to the subject in several ways. An expandable band is placed around the chest (and perhaps a second one around the upper abdomen) to measure breathing patterns. A blood pressure cuff is applied to the upper arm and inflated to about halfway between the diastolic and systolic pressure, to measure fluctuations in blood pressure and pulse rate. A small clip placed on a fingertip measures galvanic skin response (GSR): an electric current, so small that the subject cannot feel it, is passed through the clip, and changes in conductivity reveal variations in the subject's perspiration. Another, similar clip may also be applied to measure pulse and blood volume in the fingertip. Readings from these sensors are recorded by fluctuating pens on a long sheet of graph paper that moves steadily beneath them. During the course of the test, the examiner writes the number of each question on the graph paper as it is asked. This makes it possible, when the chart is analyzed, to connect physiological responses as recorded on the chart with the various questions.

No one (at least, no one since Marston) claims that deception can be measured directly. As with all tests, lie detection deals in representations. In the case of polygraph tests, these representations take the form of a chain of causality leading from prevarication to anxiety or psychological stress and then to physiology. As already noted, the general theory is that emotional stress produces variations in one or more of the physiological functions monitored by the polygraph. One form of stress that may produce such physiological variations is apprehension about being caught in telling a lie. Assuming that other reasons for stress can be ruled out, significant changes in the polygraph tracings that accompany the response to a given question (when a subject donkey at all) had been liberally smeared with lampblack. After the last one emerges from the tent, they are reassembled and ordered to show their hands. The one with clean hands is judged to be the guilty party.[11]

Setting aside the obvious point that this technique could not be used very often because the word would quickly get around, consideration of it reveals one of the prime characteristics of the asymmetrically skewed logic of lie detection. This can be brought out by the question: why should it be expected that only one of the suspects would emerge with clean hands? Any reasonably prudent individual, innocent or guilty, would probably refrain from pulling the tail. After all, why should one trust an ass, no matter how reputedly magic or sage, not to make a mistake? If any suspect should in fact emerge with dirty hands, that person might be judged innocent by the investigators but would also have shown oneself to be a fool.[12]

This vignette reveals a core assumption in the asymmetrical logic of lie detection: innocent or honest test takers are expected to behave completely ingenuously in the test, but the street is one way because the test itself is disingenuous. It is, in this case, a trick based on the lie that the object to be pulled is a genuine donkey's tail. Equivalents of a fake donkey's tail are found everywhere in modern lie detection. One is the interviewer who cajoles an applicant into destructive admissions by framing questions in the spirit of a friendly conspiracy, such as, "You know, Jack, when I have something better to do than go to work, I just call in sick. How about you?" Another is the police who tell a suspect that the case looks very bad and the only way to clear oneself is to take a polygraph test, when in fact the case is so flimsy that the polygraph is used in a final effort to get a confession before dropping the charges. Stanley Abrams, a lie detector advocate, proudly notes that polygraph examiner training schools require students to take a polygraph test to assure that they are of "good moral caliber"[13] and, in the same book, urges these morally straight examiners to deceive subjects (if often for their own good) about the import of test results to make the test sufficiently "meaningful" to them that their responses will not be muted by nonchalance.[14]

Asymmetrical expectations concerning truth are matched or exceeded by asymmetrical expectations about trust. While I have stressed that specific information in these tests flows in one direction only, from test taker to test giver, the very fact that a test is given conveys one unmistakable message in the opposite direction—that the organizations giving the tests do not trust the individuals who must take them. Takers of polygraph or integrity tests, in contrast, are expected to respond to test givers with complete trust and openness. Theoreticians of lie detector tests depict honest persons as peoplewho hold nothing back from public inspection; who, having done nothing wrong, have nothing to hide.[15] They are trusting souls, fully convinced both of the efficacy of modern science (as represented by the polygraph or integrity tests) and of the essential goodwill of others, including (perhaps especially) the test givers.

> This belief that the innocent have in the accuracy of the lie-detector, and that they will be exonerated, is usually shown by their attitude. This attitude is one of genuine confidence in both the machine and the examiner. Because of this confidence they regard the examination as an experience they will want to relate to their family and friends. . . . [They are] at ease, light-hearted, and talkative. However, they are very sincere and their straight-forwardness is displayed when they discuss the case during the interview.[16]

Comments on a questionnaire administered to 220 individuals immediately after taking a routine polygraph test indicated that a number of them left the test with increased respect and confidence in the polygraph, and that they "found the test new, interesting, and enjoyable."[17] The asymmetry is again painfully obvious: these depictions do not explain why honest applicants and employees should extend such confidence to the very persons and organizations that, by requiring a polygraph test, obviously have no confidence in them.

In the minds of test givers, people who do not manifest the total openness in the foregoing profile of the honest individual are suspect from the start. One polygraph examiner told me, quite vehemently, that the only people who complain about lie detector tests are those who have something to hide and that the notion that polygraph tests represent an invasion of privacy is "a bunch of bull brought up by people who can't pass the polygraph." Interviewers are instructed to beware of certain "weasel" words that indicate dishonesty, such as an applicant evasively explaining the departure from a previous job in terms of "personal reasons," "personality conflict," or "I was laid off."

Experienced polygraph examiners often express confidence in their ability to identify guilty subjects quite apart from the test itself. Usually the telltale signs of guilt pertain to deviance from the above depiction of fully frank individuals who, with nothing to hide, compliantly welcome any and all intrusions into their private lives.

> Muscular flexing, or a shifting or lifting of the cuff arm, during the early part of the test questioning, which is ordinarily accompanied by the subject's complaint that the cuff is hurting his arm, is usually indicative of deception. The innocent subject will almost always reserve any such movement or complaint until the latter part or end of the test.[18]

Guilty subjects tend to be late for their test appointments, they appear quite nervous, they will not look the examiner in the eye, they frequently try to convince the examiner that they are deeply religious, they complain that the test is taking too long, and they want to get away as soon as possible, claiming to have another appointment; "when leaving they often quickly shake the examiner's hand and hurry out of the laboratory."[19]

Warren Holmes, one of the most celebrated interrogators and polygraph examiners in the United States, explains some of the intricacies involved in distinguishing between the innocent and the guilty as follows:

> The guilty tell their story in general terms without any specific details. . . . The innocent offer infinite details, and tell their story in such an animated way that you say to yourself, "Damn, nobody could make that up." When you listen to an innocent person, you can sense that he is reliving an actual experience. The innocent sound and look like they're telling the truth.[20]

One wonders if it is quite that simple, however, especially on learning that the general/specific distinction is flatly contradicted by another polygraph expert. For Travis Patterson, it is the liar who refers to specifics, while "the innocent will be general in his remarks."[21]

The notion that honest people gladly take lie detector tests is not easy to establish, because it runs counter to the widespread opinion that people—innocent as well as guilty—are fearful of such tests and do not wish to submit to them. Therefore, to convince both others and themselves, proponents of lie detection devote a good deal of imagination to advancing the proposition that the tests are voluntary. One simple expedient is to tell applicants that a polygraph or written integrity test is a prerequisite for the job and then ask if they are willing to take it. The overwhelming agreement by job applicants to do so is then presented as evidence for the voluntary nature of the test. A protest that applicants agree to take the test only because otherwise they will be dropped from consideration for the job is usually dismissed with the response that the individual is under no compulsion to apply for the job in the first place.

Ratiocinations regarding current employees are similar. My research revealed that if an officer in a metropolitan police department refuses to take a lie detector test in the course of an internal investigation, the chief of police issues a direct order to submit to the test. At that point, the officer who persists in refusing is terminated. It is still maintained that the polygraph test is voluntary, however, because the reason for termination is cited as insubordination to the chief's order, not refusal to take the test.

The zenith of the theory that honest people happily bare themselves to lie detection is represented by a few polygraph examiners and employers who have managed to convince themselves that employees, far from viewing lie detection as a weapon deployed against them, welcome it as promoting their own security and morale. One polygraph examiner explained it to me as follows. Workers in relatively large establishments often do not know each other personally. If the polygraph is used in preemployment screenings, that proves to people that their fellow employees are "decent people." A manager from Zale Corporation, a large jewelry chain that used the polygraph extensively, said, "We explain very carefully to the employee that the best way we know how to make sure the persons working around him are honest, and not stealing, is through polygraphy. . . . Ten percent of our profits, before taxes, goes into an employee profit-sharing plan. It isn't hard to convince the employee that dishonesty costs him personally. Our employees don't want dishonest co-workers around."[22] More than that, the polygraph is transformed into a bulwark of protection for the innocent employee. Each employee of Zale Corporation is told "that if he ever should be suspected or accused of any wrong doing, the polygraph is instantly available as a means of clearing himself."[23]

By now we have disappeared completely into the magic wood, where fake donkey tails hang from every tree. The very instrument of the employer's abiding mistrust of employees is promoted as something not just to be tolerated by those against whom it is directed but actually to be *welcomed* by them as a boost to their morale. The machine—a literal objectification of mistrust—is held up to employees as a certification of their trust in each other. More, the polygraph is redefined as an instrument of solace for those unlucky enough to fall under the shadow of false suspicion, whether in employment or criminal circumstances. Lie detection becomes a helping profession, a fortress for the protection of the innocent. This ideal is enshrined in the Statement of Purpose of the American Polygraph Association:

> Fortunate is he who, being accused or suspected of misconduct, is able to produce credible witnesses to attest to his innocence. Now therefore, and be it known henceforth, it shall be the primary responsibility of the American Polygraph Association to foster and to perpetuate an accurate, reliable and scientific means for the protection of the innocent. To verify the truth—fairly, impartially and objectively—shall be our purpose.[24]

As a step toward putting this principle into practice, in 1960, the APA offered a polygraph test to anyone who claimed wrongful conviction of a capital crime.[25]

Polygraph supporters recognize that these general claims about the positive attitude that honest and innocent subjects adopt toward the test need to be bolstered with empirical evidence. To that end, a number of surveys have been conducted to ask people who have taken polygraph tests if they found them to invade their privacy or to be humiliating or offensive in any other way. Some of these demonstrate a certain concern for objectivity, but others belong to that part of the spectrum far beyond the point where credibility has been strained to the breaking point and snapped. A marvelous example of the latter is the survey conducted in 1978 by the Washoe County Sheriff's Department in Reno, Nevada. Deputy Sheriff and polygraph examiner Richard Putnam resolved to get at the truth of the common accusation that lie detector tests violate people's privacy by conducting a survey among 85 applicants for positions in the Sheriff's Department. The survey document is remarkable and deserves to be reproduced in full.[26]

SURVEY

I, _____ , submitted myself to polygraph examination on _____ at the Washoe County Sheriff's Department, after being advised of my constitutional rights and the fact that the examination was voluntary.

No promise or reward was made to me for answering the following questions:

1. Were you in any manner embarrassed, humiliated, or degraded by any part of the polygraph examination process?

Yes or No _____

2. In your opinion, was there any objectionable or unwarranted invasion of your privacy during the conduct of the polygraph examination?

Yes or No _____

3. Should you be hired, do you believe you will be more secure and comfortable in your work environment knowing that polygraph is used to assist in personnel evaluation?

Yes or No _____

I have answered these questions of my own free will and hereby authorize the release of my answers to these questions to any person or parties having an interest in them.

Signature of Person Examined: _____

Examiner's Signature: _____

Putnam reports with satisfaction that all 85 applicants completed the affidavit even though they were assured that participation in the survey was voluntary. The results were equally gratifying: subjects unanimously affirmed, on question 2, that their privacy had not been violated by the test; 83 of them answered yes to the third question, 1 answered no, and 1 had no opinion. A hint of trouble appeared when 6 applicants responded yes to the first question. But, Putnam hastens to assure us, "five of the six indicated their answer was based solely upon embarrassment caused by information they provided to the examiner which had not been directly solicited by the questions asked."[27] This absolves the examiner from any suspicion of impropriety (while incidentally providing further evidence of the polygraph's capacity to elicit confessions) and cleans up the only place in the survey where the rave reviews of the polygraph drop below 97 percent.

The way in which the questionnaire was administered severely compromises Putnam's survey results. Because they want to be hired, job applicants are highly interested parties in the circumstances of this research. Their primary consideration in completing a questionnaire is not to say what they really think but to say what they think the employer wants to hear and, above all, to avoid saying anything that might dispose the employer against them. Therefore, if research based on a questionnaire is to be credible in these circumstances, it is essential that subjects be convinced that it is impossible to identify who completed what questionnaires. In this case, the form's official-looking stipulations, the required signatures of both subject and examiner, and the authorization of release of the answers to any interested party reduce the whole "study" to a travesty of research. The only surprise is that results were not 100 percent on all three questions.

A survey that initially appears to have been more sensitive to methodological considerations was conducted in 1980 by Toronto polygraph examiner Ben A. Silverberg. He collected questionnaires from 102 job applicants and 118 current employees immediately after they had taken routine polygraph tests. To protect anonymity, subjects were left alone to complete their questionnaires, which they then deposited in a sealed container. The polygraph again passed with flying colors. Responses to questions about fairness of the test, invasion of privacy, willingness to take it on a regular basis, and so on, ranged from 89 to 100 percent favorable to the test.[28]

Silverberg's is one of several surveys, all of which show similar results. As Frank Horvath generalized the results of seven surveys of attitudes of those who have taken preemployment polygraph tests,

> between 85 and 95 percent of the persons who have experienced polygraph examinations said that their examinations were not offensive, objectionable, or an invasion of their privacy. In addition, the overwhelming majority of these people expressed a willingness to take polygraph tests in the future should the situation require it.[29]

A methodological difficulty with these studies, however, is that subjects were asked to complete questionnaires immediately after taking the polygraph test, while still in the examiner's office, and, therefore, before the result of their job application was known. It is possible that they felt their anonymity might not be respected and that their responses might jeopardize their chances of being hired.[30] Further consideration of the Silverberg study suggests that its strategy of leaving subjects alone to complete their questionnaires and drop them in a sealed container was not sufficient to assure anonymity. For one thing, respondents might have realized that their questionnaires could be removed from the container immediately after they left and thus easily linked to them. Further, "each questionnaire instructed the subject to complete a short biographical sketch."[31] It would not be difficult to connect the biographical sketches with information on application forms or employment records to identify respondents to particular questionnaires. Subjects who were concerned about these possibilities had good reason to be, because Silverberg *did* in fact subvert the ostensible anonymity of the study. One of his tables breaks down the responses to the eight questions according to the 185 subjects who were recommended for hiring or retention, the 14 who were given a qualified recommendation, and the 21 who were not recommended.[32] How could he have done that unless he knew who filled out what questionnaires?

To avoid some of these problems, Frank Horvath and Richard Phannenstill conducted a survey in which questionnaires were mailed to respondents well after hiring decisions had been made. Questionnaires were mailed to 596 individuals who had taken preemployment polygraph tests in Milwaukee between 1983 and 1985, and 218 responses were received. Responses were generally positive toward polygraph tests, although less enthusiastically than in the other studies: 72 percent found the test they had taken to be fair, 82 percent said the questions were not objectionable, and 73 percent would take a polygraph test in connection with another job application.[33] A methodological problem may also be detected in this study, however, because "although no identifying information was requested from respondents, each questionnaire was conspicuously identified with a code number."[34] This enabled the researchers to correlate questionnaire responses about attitudes toward the test with information such as admissions of wrongdoing that the individual might have made during the test and whether or not test results warranted recommendation for employment. Research procedures were established which prevented identification of the respondents. Nevertheless, the conspicuous code number on each questionnaire may well have aroused their suspicion that the researchers intended to connect returned questionnaires with the names of individuals to whom they had been sent, and that could have had an effect on the answers.

On the other side of the issue, Lawrence White's psychological experiments and interviews suggest that applicants respond to preemployment polygraph screenings with lowered self-esteem, diminished satisfaction with the job, and increased inclination to steal from the employer.[35] This indicates that lie detection might actually exacerbate the very conditions it aims to curtail. I conducted extended interviews with eight individuals who have taken polygraph tests as preemployment, periodic, or specific investigatory tests. Although my sample is very small, the results correspond much more closely to White's findings than to the studies that report positive attitudes toward polygraph tests on the part of those who take them. Nearly all of my subjects expressed resentment that the sheer circumstances of the test placed them under suspicion of wrongdoing. They judged the test to be embarrassing or uncomfortable and an invasion of their privacy. The test was a particularly unpleasant experience for three of my subjects. One of them, who worked for a janitorial service, was tested under suspicion of theft by what seems to have been an unscrupulous chart roller, who even demanded that she pay for the test herself. She lost her job as a result of the test. Another subject was tested in connection with missing money at the retail store where she worked. She was so humiliated by being suspected and required to take the test that she intended to quit her job as soon as the actual culprit was identified. (She planned to remain until then because she did not want to give the impression that she was quitting because she was guilty.) The third individual was subjected to questions pertaining to her sexual activity and induced to admit to lesbian encounters, although this issue was irrelevant to the ostensible purpose of the test. Nevertheless, this woman took the position that, for all their problems, the tests are still warranted because they contribute to controlling serious social problems such as employee theft and drug use.

Lie Detection and the Disciplinary Technology of Power

A common reaction to lie detector tests is to despise them as unwarranted and humiliating invasions of privacy that, particularly in light of their questionable accuracy, may work a great deal of harm on helpless and innocent people. Certainly, the discussion of the asymmetry of power and trust entailed by lie detection is conducive to a conclusion of this sort. But to reach that conclusion and leave the matter there does not generate a satisfying analysis of lie detection. It does not explain, for example, why some people (certainly fewer than the figures suggested by polygraph proponents but probably a significant number nonetheless) quite willingly submit themselves to lie detector tests. Nor does it encourage exploration of what lie detection can reveal about the nature of contemporary society. A more instructive path is one that delays judgment of lie detection and investigates further the asymmetry that lie detection establishes between potent test givers and impotent test takers, asking what kind of social system it is that succeeds in placing people in such a vulnerable position vis-à-vis the organizations that demand to test them.

The genius of the polygraph test is its promised road to exoneration, which, however, frequently requires the subject to reveal much extraneous information along the way. The examiner may tell the subject that deception is indicated on a relevant question but then suggests that the reason is probably knowledge of the wrongdoing of someone else or spillover from anxiety about some unrelated issue. To clear oneself of suspicion, it then becomes necessary to locate the cause of the problem. Captured by the imperative to get the charts to look right, one may end up pouring out every private, embarrassing, or incriminating fact that memory can locate about oneself or others, until the subject is utterly drained and the chart, finally, runs clear, purged of all indications of deception. And all of this happens because it is time for a periodic test, or the subject happens to work in a department where a crime may have been committed, or is, in all innocence, simply applying for a job.

The necessity to divulge extraneous information is, polygraph examiners insist, just a by-product of the peculiar technology of polygraph tests. It is instructive, however, to imagine that it is not an epiphenomenon at all but the point of the whole process. Then investigations of wrongdoing, periodic checks on employees, and the screening of job applicants emerge as pretexts for getting people into a situation where they are forced to reveal a wide range of potentially damaging information about themselves. From this perspective, lie detection expands immensely in significance to become a technique for maintaining surveillance over people's departures from social norms for some quite general purpose. But what might that purpose be?

A theoretical context in terms of which this expanded view of lie detection makes sense has been developed by social historian and philosopher Michel Foucault. His book, *Discipline and Punish*,[36] is an analysis of the evolution of power in Western civilization. Until about the eighteenth century, power was applied by means of a veritable orgy of violence, examples of which we have encountered in the ordeal and trial by battle. Foucault describes how the bodies of those found guilty of defying the king's justice and power were burned, broken, crushed, cut, or torn asunder in public spectacles of torture and execution designed to terrorize all who might contemplate challenging the established order. In the end, it was, however, an inefficient strategy. Power was applied in sporadic explosions of excess rather than in regular and measured doses. The agony of the victim might attract the crowd's sympathy rather than focusing their attention on the intended lesson that if they did not mind their own behavior, they could well come to a similarly sticky end. If the executioners bungled their job, the ostensibly omnipotent and terrible justice of the king would look foolish and the people might be tempted to confront the king's violence with rebellious violence of their own.[37]

For a brief period at the end of the eighteenth century and the beginning of the nineteenth, the principles of the Enlightenment were applied to the exercise of power and punishment when efforts were made to base conformity to social rules on people's rationality. Criminals had broken the social contract, placing themselves beyond the bounds of society. Punishments should dramatize their status as social exiles and vary appropriately to the specific crimes by which they had defied the social order. Prisons would be open to the public, for the edification of schoolchildren and others, who would observe and learn the inexorably rational connection between breaking the law and paying for it.[38] The appeal to reason seems not to have been an effective means of social control, however, and it was not long before the application of power took yet another form. It shifted toward the development of subjects who were *disciplined* to embody—automatically and unthinkingly—all the proper habits for following authority. This is the disciplinary technology of power, which Foucault describes in terms of the military dream of society:

> Historians of ideas usually attribute the dream of a perfect society
> to the philosophers and jurists of the eighteenth century; but there

was also a military dream of society; its fundamental reference was not to the state of nature, but to the meticulously subordinated cogs of a machine, not to the primal social contract, but to permanent coercions, not to fundamental rights, but to indefinitely progressive forms of training, not to the general will but to automatic docility.[39]

Such a system is especially well suited to the special requirements of industrial and postindustrial society, where individuals must be trained to perform highly specialized tasks and where they must perform them regularly and reliably so as to maintain the proper coordination of the mutually dependent components of the economy and other parts of society.

The disciplinary technology of power requires that people be kept under regular surveillance, in order that deviations from proper behavior might be rapidly detected and immediately redressed. This allows corrective power to be applied sparingly, for small doses are sufficient to curtail small strayings. One instrument designed to facilitate surveillance was Jeremy Bentham's panopticon.[40] Here was an arrangement whereby inmates could be isolated from each other in individual cells and conveniently observed from a central tower. A peculiar advantage of the panopticon in terms of efficient utilization of resources was that as the inmates could not see into the observation tower, an observer did not actually have to be present at all times. Never knowing when they were being observed, inmates would have to behave as if the surveillance were constant. Although Bentham's architectural device has been used primarily in the construction of prisons, the full title of his book makes it clear that he by no means intended it to be limited to penal institutions: "Panopticon; or, the Inspection-House, Containing the Idea of a New Principle of Construction Applicable to any Sort of Establishment, in Which Persons of any Description are to be Kept Under Inspection: and in Particular to Penitentiary-Houses, Prisons, Houses of Industry, Work-Houses, Poor-Houses, Manufactories, Mad-Houses, Lazarettos, Hospitals, and Schools . . ."

A different technique of surveillance was tried for a time by the Ford Motor Company when Henry Ford, concerned by the effect of high turnover rates on productivity, resolved to attract and keep good workers by making them an offer they could not refuse. In 1914, when the going wage for unskilled labor was $2.34 per day, Ford began paying his laborers the unheard-of sum of $5 per day. Ford's primary conditions were that workers justify this munificent wage by "proper living" and that their new affluence neither increase their cupidity nor make them slothful. A "Sociological Department" was formed at Ford to maintain surveillance over employee behavior off the job as well as on it. Its investigators (at the peak of the program, there were 100 of them) would visit employees' homes unannounced to certify that they did not engage in excessive drinking or improper sexual behavior, that no boarders were taken in, and that their houses were kept neat and clean. Employees whose comportment fell short of company standards dropped back to the $2.34 per day wage for a probationary period, but if they mended their ways, they could be reinstated to the $5 day.

Ford's scheme, one of the most dramatic efforts ever adopted by an American company to intervene in the overall lives of its employees, was short-lived. The Sociological Department's surveillance was unpopular, and Ford himself came to hold the opinion that it was better to reward employees for productivity on the job and length of service than for proper living at home. The cost of the program may have contributed to Ford's second thoughts about it. Salaries for the one hundred investigators and other expenses connected with the Sociological Department must have amounted to a considerable sum. And to maintain the premium wage at double the standard wage would require raising the former at twice the rate of the latter, a practice that could become very expensive indeed. As it happened, the daily $5 was not adjusted to keep pace with inflation, so in the years following 1914, it looked less and less extraordinary. Despite its spectacular beginning, the experiment of luring people to hard work and proper living with the inducement of uncommonly high wages faded away after only six years.[41]

If we look at lie detection from the perspective of Foucault's analysis, it may be readily understood as yet another device for surveillance, one that represents a major advance in convenience and economy over both the panopticon and Ford's $5 day. The leap forward achieved by lie detection by polygraph is that it has succeeded in enlisting people as their own watchmen. The central power need simply collect occasional reports of self-surveillance by means of lie detector tests. As the personnel director of the Zale Corporation remarked, "We feel the best place to go to find out the background of a person is to the person himself, and the polygraph is the best way to do this."[42]

The information gathered in this manner should be unrivaled in detail and completeness. Far beyond what can be observed from a central tower or gleaned in occasional visits by company investigators, lie detection achieves the ultimate in surveillance because it taps the constant and undivided attention that constitutes self-awareness—an awareness not only of overt deeds but also of intentions, desires, impulses, and other "inner" phenomena that, but for the test's probing, may never become public. Moreover, lie detector tests operate to control behavior as well as to report on it. The strategic assumption, at any rate, is that people will be deterred from disapproved activities (such as stealing from one's employer) by fear that it will be found out in the next test.

Polygraph tests also represent an advance in the efficiency with which power is applied. Conducted in private, testing avoids the massive expenditure of energy and resources required for public spectacles of torture and execution in the monarchial system of power. Polygraph tests also achieve surveillance over more people more cheaply and conveniently than is possible by means of primitive instruments of a disciplinary technology of power such as the panopticon or Ford's $5 day. Scarcely an hour in duration and requiring only a portable machine and a quiet room, the tests obviate the architectural, construction, and maintenance costs connected with the panopticon, as well as the expense and inconvenience of assembling and confining people for extended periods within its precincts. Ford tried to control employees' behavior with doubled wages and surprise visits by members of the Sociological Department, strategies that required a major financial outlay by the company. Lie detection controls behavior by threatening people with losing the wages they have, and that costs the company very little. Employers seldom go to the trouble and expense of prosecuting those identified by lie detector tests as deceptive or dishonest. Applicants who test deceptive in preemployment tests are not hired; current employees in that unhappy situation may be terminated. This necessitates no legal apparatus to investigate and try cases, nor prisons to hold the offenders. Undesirables are simply excluded from employment. If the measure of efficiency in the application of power is maximum impact at minimum cost, the ratio achieved by lie detection is overwhelming. A procedure requiring small outlay by test givers places test takers at the large risk of not getting, or losing, a job. To the extent that numerous employers apply lie detection, and results of different tests hold constant, some individuals will suffer the cumulative and devastating consequences of losing their ability to earn a livelihood.

The Employee Polygraph Protection Act of 1988 may be thought to have stymied the perfection of this aspect of the disciplinary technology of power when it outlawed mechanical lie detector tests for most purposes in the private sector. Perhaps so, but the antipolygraph law is stimulating phenomenal growth of written integrity tests, and these may prove to be as effective tools of the disciplinary technology of power as the polygraph ever was. To be sure, written tests cannot equal the polygraph's capacity to elicit confessions of past misdeeds of any and all descriptions, and thus they cannot achieve the same meticulous degree of individual surveillance. But since they do not require one-on-one administration, they are considerably cheaper than polygraph tests, and they may conveniently be given to a much larger proportion of the population. Therefore, it may be that the disciplinary technology of power has not in fact retreated before the antipolygraph law but has made a lateral shift preparatory to further growth. What individual surveillance may lose in depth of fine-grained detail it will gain in breadth of application.

Foucault also suggests that the disciplinary technology of power reordered the concept of the individual. Earlier periods of history were marked by what might be termed "ascending individualization": the persons who were known as distinctive individuals were those at the center of power, and/or those who were exalted as heroes or vilified as execrable villains. Information about these exemplary figures flowed to the anonymous beings who composed the masses. There the stories about famous central figures inspired awe (thus helping to maintain the rulers in power) and provided role models for desirable unacceptable behavior. Foucault continues:

> In a disciplinary regime, on the other hand, individualization is "descending": as power becomes more anonymous and more functional, those on whom it is exercised tend to be more strongly individualized; it is exercised by surveillance rather than ceremonies, by observation rather than commemorative accounts.[43]

That is to say, information no longer passes from focal figures to anonymous masses but in the reverse direction: the people who are controlled are known, while those who hold power are anonymous. The asymmetrical, one-way flow of information from those who take lie detector tests to those who give them is an outstanding example of Foucault's descending individualization. But, of course, the examiners who give the tests are not themselves in power. They are only agents of the real power centers. And those centers are so depersonalized that they are likelier to be organizations than persons—corporations, the government, and, ultimately, the total sociocultural system.

The efficient communication of specific information about named and identifiable individuals to anonymous centers of power is accomplished not just by lie detection but by testing of all sorts. An outstanding and very recent addition to the rapidly accumulating set of examples in the contemporary United States is DNA testing or "genetic fingerprinting" of prison inmates. Given a recidivism rate as high as 80 to 90 percent for murder and sex-crime parolees, current inmates are tested and their genetic profiles stored so that they may be readily identified from any body tissue, hair, blood, semen, or saliva that they might leave at the scene of some future crime. By the end of 1991, fifteen states had laws mandating DNA testing of inmates convicted for certain kinds of offenses. Leaders in toughness are Virginia, which tests all felons and which had deposited some 30,000 samples in its data bank in a period of about eighteen months, and South Dakota, where just being arrested leads to DNA testing.[44] With the accelerating development of new technologies and new tests derived from them, Foucault's insights about testing gain in relevance and importance with the passage of time: "The examination is the technique by which power, instead of emitting the signs of its potency, instead of imposing its mark on its subjects, holds them in a mechanism of objectification. . . . We are entering the age of the infinite examination and of compulsory objectification."[45]

There is more. In addition to displaying and fixing the individual as an object of knowledge for the purposes of subjugation, Foucault suggests that the role of testing in bringing about a shift from ascending to descending individualization has contributed to a fundamental redefinition of what the individual is:

> Thanks to the whole apparatus of writing [and now we would add, most emphatically, computer data banks] that accompanied it, the examination opened up . . . the constitution of the individual as a describable, analysable object, not in order to reduce him to "specific" features [those characteristic of the species generally], as did the naturalists in relation to living beings, but in order to maintain him in his individual features, in his particular evolution, in his own aptitudes or abilities, under the gaze of a permanent corpus of knowledge.[46]

Far from being the primal, irreducible, and invariable atom of human society, then, this argument holds that the individual as currently known and conceptualized is a relatively recent invention, an invention generated in large measure by the procedures of testing and serving the disciplinary technology of power.[47] We may not wish to follow Foucault's dark genius to the point of agreeing that the individual was created just in order to be controlled and dominated. Nevertheless, he leads us to the compelling if paradoxical conclusion that the concept of the individual, on which is erected our civilization's particular construction of human freedom and dignity, is itself partly built on testing—perhaps the most pervasive and efficient technique for the application of power and domination to have evolved so far. Lie detection has served as a lens that reveals certain features of testing with great clarity by magnifying or distorting them to the point of caricature. In the following chapters, many of those same characteristics will surface again in other sorts of testing. Their further analysis, and that of numerous other features of testing yet to be analyzed, will afford a better view of the new kind of social order that has evolved over the last two centuries or so and the new kind of individual that has developed with it.

5

TESTING AND THE WAR

ON DRUGS

Let's test these people, to see
if we have a problem.

Candidate for governor of Kansas, 1986,

speaking of all state employees

The *New York Times* of October 31, 1988, reported a subway accident in the city in which a woman had been dragged by a train. In line with the transit authority's normal procedures following accidents, a spokesperson said that "the train involved was taken out of service for inspection and that the driver and conductor will be tested for drugs." So it happens repeatedly in our testing society: when a unit malfunctions, mechanical or human, the response is to remove it from service and test it. The purpose of the test, of course, is to determine if the unit is defective in order that, if so, it might be repaired or replaced. This may be termed the reparative response of testing, the action taken when something goes wrong. As is evident from what happened to the subway driver and conductor, today the most common reparative response to human malfunction is a drug test.

Testing also has an exploratory or preventive side, which takes the form of testing units that have not malfunctioned to discover if they have weaknesses that might cause future failures. Repairing or replacing defective units before they break down is a relatively inexpensive way to prevent major problems. General inspection may reveal signs of stress in certain units, and they are then tested to determine the precise problem. Erratic behavior or excessive absenteeism constitute such signs in employees, and they often lead to drug testing. Again, all units may be routinely tested before being placed in service for the first time, or some method may be adopted to test periodically those units currently in service in the search for defects that have not yet manifested themselves but might cause future problems. These preventive strategies are represented in the world of drug testing by preemployment, periodic, and random tests.

In recent years, proposals for preventive drug testing have reached near-epic proportions. Following 1991 police raids that found drugs in three University of Virginia fraternity houses, Governor Douglas Wilder suggested that all public university students in the state be subject to random drug testing.[1] In 1986, a candidate for governor of Kansas recommended that all state employees be tested for drugs to determine "if we have a problem." Then, if a problem existed, something could be done about it. Attorney General Edwin Meese took much the same attitude when he announced plans to subject government workers to random drug tests in 1987. The aim, explained Meese, was not to fire anyone. Instead, it was to determine the extent of the problem of drug use in the federal work force, to identify who had the problem, and to rehabilitate them.[2] The intention to repair defective units rather than replace them is comforting, but the ultimate sanction of firing those who do not respond successfully to treatment lurks in the background.

But something more is going on here than simply using tests to locate defective parts for the purpose of repairs or preventive maintenance. If that were the entire story, people would be examined for a wide array of physical and emotional problems that could have a negative effect on their job performance. At the present moment in our history, however, the assumption prevails that performance failures of human beings are to be attributed primarily to drug abuse. Hence we test not for a full range of debilitating possibilities but for drugs. So, for example, after a USAir jet skidded into the East River on an aborted takeoff from

LaGuardia Airport in September 1989, one of the first criticisms to be voiced was that the pilot and copilot did not present themselves immediately after the accident for drug and alcohol tests.[3]

Drug abuse, it seems, currently plays a role in American thinking similar to witchcraft a few centuries ago: it is insidious, pervasive, but not easily recognizable, an evil that infuses social life and is responsible for many of the ills that beset us. At the end of the 1980s, before many Americans had even heard of Saddam Hussein, the big war in America was the war on drugs. Drugs were a major issue in the presidential election of 1988. A *New York Times*/CBS News poll in late 1989 found that some 65 percent of Americans considered drugs to be the number one problem facing the nation. Excepting only a time in early 1991 when just over 25 percent pointed to the economy, this is more than triple the number who, in polls taken between 1985 and late 1991, identified any other single issue as America's greatest problem.[4] News reports and public policy debate were preoccupied with the issue. For example, on August 31, 1989—the day that these lines were written in first draft form—of the six items in the 8:00 A.M. news summary on National Public Radio's "Morning Edition," the leading three all dealt with drugs. The first two were "supply side" stories about the drug cartel in Colombia and U.S. accusations against Panama's Manuel Noriega for drug running; the third, on the demand side, reported accusations against the mayor of Washington, D.C., for using crack cocaine. To add some local color, one of the top stories of the summer in my hometown of Lawrence, Kansas, was a proposal that the five elected city commissioners, the city manager, and other top city officials voluntarily present themselves for drug tests. This would have the effect, it was argued, of proclaiming to the world that Lawrence is irrevocably committed to being a drug-free city. Moreover, the public proof that civic leaders are clean would establish them as role models and inspirations to our youth and other ordinary citizens who might be tempted to experiment with drugs. The proposal was defeated by a 3-2 vote, partly because of questions about how "voluntary" a test could be in the light of the suspicion that would probably be directed against those who might choose not to take it. And indeed, those questions were promptly justified by editorial musings in the local newspaper about the motives of those city commissioners who voted against the proposal.[5]

Testing is a major tactic in the war on drugs, and because (as was also the case with witchcraft) one cannot tell if someone is infected with the evil of drug abuse just by looking, much of that testing is of persons who have given no reason to suspect that they use drugs. If the tendency to subject the American people to ever-increasing numbers and types of tests has suffered a setback with the recent restrictions on lie detector tests, its most impressive advance at present lies in the spectacular growth of drug testing. That growth occurred almost entirely during the 1980s, especially in the latter half of the decade.

The first organization to go in for large-scale drug testing was the Department of Defense, particularly the U.S. Navy. In 1981, several developments evoked concern about widespread drug use in the armed services. One survey reported that over half of navy personnel admitted using marijuana weekly or more frequently, while laboratory tests of 160,000 navy personnel, conducted anonymously, revealed traces of marijuana in the urine of 47.8 percent of those tested. On May 26, 1981, an aircraft crashed while attempting a night landing on the aircraft carrier USS *Nimitz*, killing fourteen and wounding forty-two others. Autopsies revealed cannabis in nine of the crew members working on the flight deck.[6] The military decided it was necessary to mount a major campaign against drug use, and, by good fortune, the technological means to undertake large-scale drug testing conveniently and economically became available at just this time, when the Syva Corporation developed a portable kit for urinalysis by a technique known as EMIT.[7] The navy began testing in earnest in 1982, with the highly ambitious intention of subjecting everyone in the navy to unannounced, random tests three times per year. By 1985, the navy was giving nearly 1.5 million tests annually, and the figure rose to over 1.9 million in 1986.[8]

Several wide-circulation magazines and newspapers ran major stories on drugs in the workplace in 1983 and 1984, and many companies began to explore the possibilities of testing programs. By 1985, such programs were being established by large corporations such as GM, IBM, Mobil, and Exxon.[9] The federal government soon became involved. President Ronald Reagan issued the Executive Order on a Drug-Free Federal Workplace in September 1986, mandating drug testing of federal employees in sensitive positions and authorizing testing for applicants and employees connected with accidents or unsafe practices or who are reasonably suspected of using drugs. New U.S. Department of Transportation regulations requiring drug tests of workers in the transportation industry went into effect in December 1989. The rules apply to some four million private sector workers and cost the companies tens of millions of dollars annually. The most controversial aspect of these regulations is that they require random testing at a rate such that each worker has a 50 percent chance of being tested each year. This raises important issues of privacy, for a random selection process subjects workers to testing in the absence of any suspicion that they have used illegal drugs.[10]

The growth of drug testing in the workplace since 1985 amounts to a virtual explosion. Twenty-one percent of 1,090 companies responding to an American Management Association survey in November 1986 reported that they test applicants and/or current employees, and 90 percent of them instituted their programs in 1985 or 1986.[11] Another survey was conducted by the Bureau of Labor Statistics during summer 1988, using a sample of some 7,500 private, nonagricultural business establishments. It revealed that the presence of drug testing programs varies immensely according to establishment size: only about 2 percent of those with fewer than 50 employees have programs, and the incidence of drug testing programs increases steadily with company size, up to 43 percent of the establishments with more than 1,000 employees. Since small businesses vastly outnumber large ones, the proportion of all American companies with drug testing programs is only 3 percent, but they employ some 21 percent of all workers. The survey also found that about 4 percent of all employers without a drug testing program were considering implementing one within the next twelve months.[12] Notice that this figure is larger than the total number of establishments with testing programs currently in place—further testimony to the recent rush toward drug testing programs in the United States.

An April 1987 survey of 2,000 companies by Business and Legal Reports found that 15 percent of responding companies had programs in place for testing current employees and/or applicants, 5 percent intended to implement a program within one year, and an additional 39 percent had a program under consideration.[13] Business and Legal Reports did a followup survey in November 1988, this time receiving 3,192 responses. The growth of drug testing was phenomenal. In the period of just eighteen months between the surveys, the number of companies testing applicants increased from 15 to 25 percent, while those testing current employees more than doubled, from 9 to 19 percent.[14] I conducted a study in 1987–88 of eleven Midwestern organizations with drug testing programs and found that six of the programs had been in force for less than six months.

A curious and fascinating aspect of workplace drug testing is that it seems to be a uniquely American phenomenon. As a visiting professor in Paris in 1989, I found that while an American company (Abbott Laboratories) was attempting to generate interest in drug testing, very few French firms had implemented programs. And a 1988 survey conducted by the Conference Board found that while many companies that test are multinational firms, very few drug testing programs extend outside the United States.[15]

Drug testing programs are now also commonplace in athletics, and they too have experienced spectacular growth, especially in the latter 1980s. The original concern in sport was, however, quite different: to prevent the use of performance-enhancing drugs, particularly anabolic steroids. The death of a European cyclist at the 1960 Olympics who had used amphetamines first drew attention to the problem of drug use in sports. The International Olympic Committee introduced testing in a preliminary way at the 1968 Olympics and then tested comprehensively at the Munich games four years later. It was only at the 1976 Olympics in Montreal, however, that technology became available to test for anabolic steroids. Steroids attracted widespread publicity in the United States in 1983, when a number of athletes were disqualified at the Pan American Games in Caracas and when several members of the U.S. team departed before they had competed and

could be tested.[16] And, of course, immense international publicity was generated when Canadian sprinter Ben Johnson was
stripped of a gold medal at the 1988 Olympics in Seoul because
of a positive test for steroids.

At the collegiate level, the National Collegiate Athletic Association (NCAA) began drug tests at championship events and
football bowl games in 1986. Unlike the International Olympic
Committee's exclusive focus on performance-enhancing drugs,
the NCAA also tests for street drugs such as marijuana and cocaine. This is true also of the testing programs that many colleges
and universities have instituted for athletes on their campuses. In
fact, of the nearly one hundred such programs surveyed by the
NCAA in 1984, all of them were testing student athletes for street
drugs, but only one in four was testing for anabolic steroids. Eric
Zemper believes this is done to convince the public that decisive
steps are being taken to control drug use by athletes, even though
there is no evidence that athletes use street drugs more than others
of the same age group. Nevertheless, public anxieties on that score
were certainly fueled in 1986 by the cocaine-related deaths, a few
days apart, of University of Maryland basketball star Len Bias
and Cleveland Browns football safety Don Rogers.[17]

Evolving public attitudes toward drug tests may be glimpsed
in responses to a rare but interesting arena for testing: schoolchildren. In 1985, it was proposed that all students in a small
high school in New Jersey be subjected to drug tests. The issue
stimulated great controversy, and the plan was immediately challenged in the state courts, which ruled it to be unconstitutional.[18]
Five years later, a parochial school in Chicago, St. Sabina Academy, began a program of random drug testing for students in the
sixth through eighth grades. Unlike the reception that greeted the
earlier proposal in New Jersey, a St. Sabina official told me that
the response of parents and others connected with their school
was overwhelmingly favorable.

Response to the St. Sabina program seems representative of
general public attitudes. Popular support for testing has increased as testing programs themselves have mushroomed during the 1980s. According to a 1986 opinion poll, approval rates for
testing people in various categories were very high: 85 percent for

police, 84 percent for airline pilots, 72 percent for professional athletes, 72 percent for government workers, 64 percent for high school teachers, 60 percent for high school students, 52 percent for entertainment stars, and 50 percent for all other employed persons.[19] Comparable figures from a California poll taken in 1989 showed rates of approval for random testing to be even higher: 89 percent for police and fire fighters, 92 percent for airline pilots, 75 percent for professional athletes, and 78 percent for public school teachers. The California poll also indicated that 83 percent of respondents would be willing to submit to random drug tests themselves, an increase of 6 percent from responses to the same question in a poll taken two years before.[20]

How Drug Testing Works

Numerous techniques are in use for drug testing, and some of them are quite wonderful. One of the latest is an Israeli product known as Drug Alert. It is a spray that anyone can use, and the SherTest Corporation markets it as a way for parents to check up on their children. One simply wipes a piece of white paper on "a surface" (presumably the surface of a child) and then sprays the paper with the product. The color produced on the paper reveals whether the individual on whom it has been wiped has been using drugs. SherTest's Sidney Klein promotes the spray test as a way of enhancing the love and care that should prevail in the family. "It's about breaking down barriers of denial between parent and child," he said.[21]

The National Drug Awareness and Detection Agency of Houston has sensed a potential for profit in the process of breaking down those barriers. The company sends postcards that state, "We have been informed that your children may be using ILLEGAL DRUGS. . . . Please call us IMMEDIATLY [sic]." Some recipients of the card in Lawrence, Kansas, expressed curiosity about how the word on their children made it all the way to Houston, particularly one woman who received the warning and who has no children. Those who call the number on the card are given a lengthy presentation about the dangers of drugs. They are then urged to send $99.95 to purchase a kit that claims to detect drug use by measuring the pupil of a suspect's eye with a "pupilometer."[22]

Setting aside such offbeat techniques, by far the most respectable and common form of drug testing is to look for traces of drugs in an individual's body fluids, and the fluid of overwhelming choice is urine. Of the variety of procedures that have been used, one is gaining acceptance as best satisfying both the concern of containing the cost of testing and the imperative of highly accurate results. Under this procedure, a urine sample is subject to two separate tests. The first of these is called screening, and it is generally conducted by immunoassay (such as EMIT) or thin layer chromatography. Those samples that test negative in the screen (drugs absent or at levels below the designated cutoff point) are not tested further. Samples identified as positive in the screen are subjected to a confirming test by a different method known as GC/MS (gas chromatography/mass spectrometry). This test is extremely sensitive and accurate. Only those samples that are confirmed as positive by this second test are reported back as indicating drug use, and the drug that has been detected is specified. When this procedure is properly applied, the chance that an individual will be mistakenly identified as a drug user is nearly eliminated.[23] Such false positive results are, understandably, a common source of anxiety among those who are subject to testing. The possibility of a false negative result (drugs are actually in the urine but not detected by the test) is greater, because samples that (rightly or wrongly) test negative in the initial screen are not subjected to the more accurate confirming test.

The initial screening test costs about $15, while confirmation by GC/MS, is considerably more expensive, from $40 to $50. However, overall cost is held down because only those samples that test positive on the screen are subject to confirmation. Usually laboratories provide testing for a set fee per sample. The amount depends largely on the anticipated percentage of positive results in the screen, which determines how many of the more expensive confirmation tests will have to be run. Thus, CompuChem Laboratories has a contract to test for the U.S. Department of Transportation at a cost (in 1987) of $26 per urine sample.[24]

Drug testing policies in various organizations stipulate tests in one or a combination of five circumstances. Passing a *preemployment* drug test may be a condition of employment for job applicants. *Periodic* tests are given at set intervals, such as part of regular physical examinations or whenever an employee returns to work from a leave of absence. All individuals who have any connection with an accident that exceeds some specified level of damage may be required to take a *postaccident* test as part of the investigation. *For-cause* tests may be demanded of individuals whose behavior leads supervisors or medical personnel to the reasonable suspicion that they are under the influence of some substance. Finally, *random* tests are given to personnel whenever they are targeted in a drawing or computerized random selection procedure.

A problem with drug testing by urinalysis is that traces of cocaine, heroin, and most other street drugs are detectable for only one to three days following use.[25] This means that drug users (other than hard-core addicts) are often able to survive the testing procedure undetected simply by curtailing their usage for several days prior to the test. This applies, of course, to those situations in which the individual has advance knowledge of the test, most notably, preemployment and periodic tests. Indeed, one argument for random testing is that it closes the loophole provided to users by advance notice. Despite this advantage, random testing is the least common in the workplace, while preemployment testing, although easily defeated because of advance notice, is the most frequent. This is because preemployment testing poses the fewest legal problems and occurs before employees are protected by collective bargaining, while random testing of current employees raises the most serious questions about invasion of privacy and other personal rights and meets the stiffest resistance from unions. (Random testing is more common in athletic organizations, however, as will be discussed below.)

An ironic twist in the detection of drug use by urinalysis pertains to marijuana. Because its active ingredient is stored in body fat, marijuana clears the system much more slowly than other drugs. Precise times depend on amount of use and other individual variables, but marijuana has been detected by urinalysis for as long as one or two months after use, far longer than other drugs.[26] Therefore, the tactic of escaping detection by curtailing use prior to a drug test is much less likely to be successful for marijuana than for other drugs. And there is the irony: the drug that is generally considered to be the least dangerous of the controlled substances is the one that is most likely to show up in drug tests. Combined with the fact that marijuana is the most popular drug, its persistence in the system means that the great majority of positive drug test results are for marijuana. In a study of over 2,500 newly hired employees in the Postal Service in Boston,[27] within the overall rate of 12.2 percent positive drug tests, 7.8 percent were for marijuana alone, and an additional 2.2 percent were for a combination of drugs (and certainly marijuana was often present in the mix). It has been estimated that marijuana may account for up to 90 percent of positive test results.[28]

Beating the Test

Workers and others who must submit urine for drug tests have devised a wide range of techniques to foil them. Abstinence for a few days prior to the test is effective for most drugs, although not for marijuana. Another ploy is substitution: a simple method is to scoop up some water from the toilet bowl and submit that as one's urine sample. Alternatively, one might submit someone else's clean urine in lieu of one's own. It might come from a friend or relative, or, if one is uncertain as to their habits, one can turn to the marketplace. A mini-industry, in fact, is developing for the provision of drug-free urine. Byrd Laboratories of Austin, Texas, advertises clean urine (originating from a senior citizens' home) for mail-order sale at $49.95 per sample. After an unsatisfactory flirtation with freeze-drying, the company developed a dehydration process that reduces the product to a powder for more efficient mailing and handling. According to the instructions, "just add water."[29] The bargain conscious can purchase four ounces of urine guaranteed to be drug- and alcohol-free from The Bladder Man company in Arizona for just $25.[30]

Some people adulterate their urine samples with salt, detergent, or some other substance in an effort to mask drugs. Others try to achieve the masking effect on urine still in the body, attempting to dilute it by drinking huge quantities of water or taking diuretics before being tested or by ingesting various substances that are reputed to mask drugs in the system. In one scheme, no less bizarre than drinking White-Out to confound a lie detector test (see chap. 3), a student athlete I interviewed said that football players from another university apparently acted on the notion that drinking the urine of a pregnant woman would foil the discovery of drugs in their own.

Authorities have adopted various measures to parry such tactics, trying to prevent cheating while attempting to retain some respect for privacy and good taste. Bluing may be added to the toilet bowl water, or samples might be collected in a room where no water is available. The temperature of the sample may be checked, and some organizations also check specific gravity and/or pH (to be sure the sample is acidic). Subjects may be required to strip down to their underwear or completely to prevent them from taking adulterating substances or other people's urine into the stall. The subject may be required to produce the sample under direct observation, a procedure that can occasion considerable embarrassment and resentment. One male athlete described to me how disconcerting it can be when the observer positions his face right next to one's hip, so as to get a close and unobstructed view of the process. Even with such close surveillance, some ploys are extremely difficult to detect. One feminine technique that simultaneously solves problems of stripping, temperature, and anything but the closest observation is to smuggle clean urine (reconstituted, perhaps, from a dehydrated packet purchased from Byrd Laboratories) into the collection room in a balloon or condom inserted into the vagina. This may be opened at the proper time with a sharpened fingernail or a pin.[31] A more radical procedure, available to either sex, is to inject clean urine into one's bladder by means of a catheter and then deposit it in the specimen collection bottle in the normal way.[32]

Possible Futures

Although at present, urine is overwhelmingly the substance of choice for drug testing, other possibilities exist. Some 25 percent of the testing programs in business firms surveyed by the Conference Board in 1988 utilize something else: blood, saliva, or hair.[33] Testing hair has immense potential to open the window of access to drug use considerably wider than is presently possible with urinalysis. Drug molecules are introduced into the blood following use, and as the blood nourishes the hair "roots" or follicles, some drug molecules become permanently trapped among the tightly packed protein strings that form the hair shaft. Thus, a person's hair contains a record of drug use over the entire period that it has been growing: the type of drugs ingested, when, and how much.[34] Werner Baumgartner, who developed the technique of radioimmunoassay of hair (RIAH—which, as he happily notes, is HAIR spelled backward), points out that the possibility of testing hair extends even beyond a lifetime. Thus, a test of the hair of John Keats 165 years after he died revealed that the poet had used opiates, presumably laudanum, to ease the pain of the terminal stages of tuberculosis. And since hair begins growing before birth, testing the hair of newborn infants could reveal the types and amounts of drugs to which they have been exposed while in the uterus.[35]

Although Edward Cone identifies some technical problems that require solution before complete confidence can be placed in testing of hair and its findings will be fully acceptable as scientific evidence in law courts, both he and (especially) Baumgartner extol its potential advantages over urinalysis. The latter test catches only those who have used drugs within a matter of days (or, for marijuana, weeks) prior to the test, and users who have some advance warning can easily escape detection by abstention. Not so with hair testing: a single test every six months to a year would be sufficient to provide a complete record of the subject's substance abuse during that entire period. Hair can be collected, under close supervision, with less intrusion of privacy and embarrassment than urine. More thorough verification is possible because an additional sample pertaining to the same period can easily be obtained by cutting more hair, while urine samples taken even a few days apart are not comparable. Those aiming to beat urinalysis can often do so by acquiring and substituting someone else's "clean" urine or by adulterating their own urine in some way. Substitution would not be possible when the test technician cuts a sample of hair from the subject's head or body. Moreover, before being dissolved for testing, samples are thoroughly washed to remove any chemicals on the surface of hair. This is intended to ensure that only drug molecules trapped in the interior of the hair shaft during growth will be identified by the test. In principle, this would avoid false positive results from traces of drugs that may have been picked up by the hair from someone else's smoke, and it might also foil efforts to avoid detection by chemical treatment of the hair. Absolute control over environmental contamination remains, however, one of the technological issues yet to be resolved in hair testing.[36] Finally, anyone who attempts to foil the test by totally shearing all head and body hair may still not escape, because it is also possible to detect traces of drugs in shavings taken from the nails.[37] In this regard, it is intriguing to recall that for millennia, in societies all over the globe, black magic has been practiced by working spells on the hair and nail clippings of intended victims. Now science can work its own kind of magic on those same substances, penetrating more surely than ever the black magician could to the soul of the targeted individual.

Perhaps partly because it is more difficult to defeat, hair testing results in fewer false negatives—individuals who actually use drugs but are not identified by the test—than urinalysis. Thus, in one study of probationers and parolees, hair analysis detected more drug use than did urinalysis, although unannounced, random urine tests were done on the subjects as often as five times per month.[38] And questions of whether a sample actually comes from a given subject (occasionally a matter of dispute in urinalysis) promise to be definitively resolvable, because DNA fingerprinting techniques hold out the possibility of identifying the owner of even a single strand of hair.

Attitudes toward Drug Testing

Although several surveys have been taken to determine how many companies conduct drug tests and in what circumstances,[39] very little research has been done on the opinions about drug tests held by the people who have to take them. In 1988, I undertook an investigation in an effort to fill this gap.[40] I conducted interviews of managers and workers in eleven organizations that have drug testing policies. In addition, a questionnaire was distributed in three of the organizations. The largest of these was one of the nation's major railroads. The questionnaire was distributed by the company's medical department in August 1988 to 995 engineers, switchmen, brakemen, conductors, and firemen. Letters from me and from the company's medical director explained the purpose of the study. Questionnaires were completed anonymously and mailed, in business reply envelopes with no identifying return address, directly to me at the University of Kansas. Three hundred thirty-three completed questionnaires were returned, a response rate of just over one-third. Space was provided on the questionnaire for additional written comments, and no fewer than 52 percent of the respondents took advantage of this opportunity. The following discussion makes reference to these comments as well as to the statistical results derived from the questionnaire.

Under regulations operative at the time of the survey, the trainmen could be tested in a number of circumstances. The Federal Railroad Administration requires that all crew members and other employees directly connected with any accident exceeding a certain level of damage be tested for drugs. In addition, the company's policy is to include a drug test in all medical examinations. These are required when an employee returns to work after having been placed on leave of absence for any reason and also at periodic intervals of every two years for employees under age 50, annually for employees between 50 and 65, and every six months for those over 65. The company's drug testing policy went into effect at the beginning of 1987, and some 12,000 tests had been given by the time of the study.

Of the 333 respondents, 27 percent reported that they had never been tested for drugs. (Possibly these are individuals who have not had periodic physical exams since the policy went into effect. In some cases, an employee may not have heeded company announcements about drug testing and might not realize that the urine sample taken during a physical exam would be tested for drugs.) Forty-two percent reported being tested once, 19 percent twice, and the remaining 12 percent three or more times. Six percent reported that they were tested in a postaccident situation, while the great bulk of employees (93% of those who had been tested) indicated tests in connection with periodic or return-to-work physical examinations, as mandated by company policy.

How Serious Is the Drug Problem in Industry?

Reports of positive results from drug tests in the workplace vary widely. In a survey conducted by the Bureau of Labor Statistics, establishments that conduct drug tests reported rates of 12 percent positive for applicants and 9 percent positive for current employees.[41] But positive results in some organizations are far lower: some 3,946 New York City police officers were tested in 1988 in connection with promotions or for suspicion of drug use, with less than 1 percent positive results. An additional 8,818 recruits and police academy cadets were tested, yielding a positive rate of about 2 percent.[42]

Of the organizations I studied, the frequency of positives in the seven companies that had administered 200 or more tests ranged from quite high to negligible. Highest was an automobile assembly plant, where 20 percent of the applicants during a large-scale hiring for assembly line jobs had positive test results. An electronic components manufacturer and a transportation company found 14 to 16 percent positives in preemployment testing. The remaining companies had very low positive rates: 2 percent or less in a chemical factory that tests current employees randomly and in a public utility that conducts preemployment testing, while an aviation organization found no positives at all in some 600 preemployment tests and annual tests of current employees.[43] The railroad from which I gathered questionnaires had a 3.5 percent positive rate in its periodic and postaccident tests. This is lower than the 5.6 percent positive rate for current employees reported by transportation industry establishments represented in a recent survey by the Bureau of Labor Statistics.[44]

The questionnaire asked about the respondent's own drug use, with possible responses of (1) never, (2) occasionally (e.g., recreational use on days off only), and (3) more than two times per week, on workdays as well as days off. Only one person in the entire set of 333 responses marked the third possibility. The second option of occasional use was marked by 13 trainmen, representing just under 4 percent of the total, with all other responses being "never." It is interesting that the 4 percent self-reported level of drug use is close to the 3.5 percent positive rate on drug tests. Of course, neither the tests nor a questionnaire (albeit an anonymous one) are likely to identify *all* drug users in the company, so it is probable that actual drug use is somewhat higher than the 4 percent self-reported rate.

Ten of the 174 trainmen who wrote comments stated that alcohol poses a problem as serious as, probably more serious than, drug abuse. This view is shared by most of the personnel managers, EAP (Employee Assistance Program) officials, and union representatives whom I have interviewed from many different organizations.

No clear consensus exists among employees about the effectiveness of testing programs in controlling drug use. Thirty-four percent of the respondents think the program is effective, 23 percent think it is not, and 43 percent do not know. The large number in the "don't know" category may be related to the fact that the program had been in operation for only two years by the time of the study.

When Do Employees Think Drug Testing Is Justified?

Drug tests are typically conducted in the workplace in one or a combination of the following circumstances: preemployment tests, periodic tests, postaccident tests, for-cause tests, and random tests. The questionnaire asked if employees think the tests are justified in each of these circumstances. To provide a wider spectrum of opinion, in addition to data from the trainmen, the following discussion takes account of data from 92 workers from a Midwestern chemical plant who also completed the questionnaire (of 216 to whom it was distributed). In contrasting the responses, it is important to realize that the chemical workers had much less experience with drug testing. At the time of the survey, the chemical company conducted only preemployment testing, in a program that was instituted after most of the respondents were hired. Thus, only 17 percent of these workers reported ever having been tested for drugs, while the corresponding figure for trainmen, who are subject to periodic and postaccident tests, is 73 percent.

Statistical results of the questions about when drug tests are justified are reported in the Appendix, table 1. The only forms that are considered justified by the majority of trainmen and chemical workers are preemployment and for-cause testing. The largest discrepancy between the two groups pertains to random testing, which is considered justifiable by 42 percent of the chemical workers but only 16 percent of the trainmen. After my survey was completed, however, the chemical plant expanded its testing program to include random testing of current employees. While it is difficult to say with any precision how that might affect the attitudes expressed in the table, both management and union officials told me that employees were responding quite negatively to the new policy. It is perhaps significant in itself that when I suggested distributing the same questionnaire to the employees again, with the aim of ascertaining what effect the policy change had had on employee attitudes, management responded that they would prefer to wait until the situation calmed down.

The comments that 174 trainmen and 27 chemical workers added to their questionnaires are especially helpful in understanding why drug tests are approved in some circumstances but not others. A general summary of the comments will be given before we undertake a closer examination of attitudes toward drug testing in various circumstances. Fifty-seven comments expressed support for testing, all for reasons pertaining to safety. The remaining 144 comments were critical of testing. Thirty-nine respondents questioned the accuracy of tests, 38 found tests to be an opportunity for management to harass workers, 38 charged that tests invade privacy and violate constitutional rights, 28 accused testing programs of being discriminatory and demanded that management be tested too, 21 called for tests to be limited to employees who exhibit impaired performance while at work, 17 claimed that urinalysis is humiliating and weakens employee morale, 15 specifically criticized random testing, 13 claimed that alcohol abuse (for which tests are seldom given) is a more serious problem than drug abuse, 9 argued that drug tests are not an effective deterrent because they can be beaten in various ways, and smaller numbers of respondents made still other critical remarks. (These figures add up to more than the total number of commenters because some of them made two or more of the above points.)

Majority approval of both preemployment and for-cause drug testing seems to be rooted primarily in safety considerations. The railroad and chemical employees represented in this study work under conditions of potential danger. As the ones most likely to get hurt in accidents, they are no less concerned about safety than is management. One commenter wrote, "In a hazardous chemical plant I do not want to work with someone who uses drugs." A trainman explained, "We, the people in the operating department, need to be very alert at all times because we are in charge of thousands of tons of equipment and a few tenths of a second of reaction time might save someone's life, maybe their own." Another trainman summed it up bluntly, "I do not work with dopeheads and I approve of tests. . . . Stamp out drugs!!!"

Turning specifically to preemployment testing, reasons for its majority approval do not emerge from the questionnaires because very few respondents specifically addressed this issue in their comments. In a number of interviews I conducted with managers, workers, and union officials from several different industries, however, two points were made frequently. The more substantial one was that workers acknowledge a company's right to demand evidence that an employee will not pose a safety hazard because of drug use. As will become clear in a moment, employees resent drug tests when other means—especially a long record of problem-free employment—are available for this purpose. But they do tend to accept the use of tests in the case of new hires, who have no track record with the company. The other point, more procedural in nature, was that preemployment testing is not a matter for collective bargaining in many companies because union benefits are not available to new employees until the completion of a probationary period.

So far as testing current employees is concerned, safety considerations motivate some people to embrace testing of any and all sorts. (In his questionnaire comments, for example, one trainman advocated random tests monthly or more often for all employees, including supervisors). However, the statistical data, comments on questionnaires, and interviews with workers and human resources managers all indicate that most employees think drug testing of current employees is justified only in cases where there is good reason to believe that a particular employee is under the influence of drugs, and thus poses a safety risk while at work.

Important to the majority opposition to periodic, postaccident, and random testing is that, in these circumstances, the safety issue is not clearly defined. Employees are well aware that drug tests of urine tell only that a substance has been ingested within a certain time prior to the test, varying from two or three days for cocaine or opiates to up to a month or even more for marijuana. Therefore, a worker who has never been under the influence of drugs during working hours—and who therefore is not a hazard on the job—may still have a positive test result from drugs used on weekends or vacation. The results could be destructive: disciplinary action, damage to reputation, and loss of job. Although very few admit to any drug use at all, this characteristic of drug tests violates the principle—fiercely expressed by many employees—that what they do on their own time is none of the company's business.

Postaccident testing is more closely related to safety than periodic or random testing. Although relatively little was said specifically about it in comments and interviews, they did indicate that resentment against these tests is especially strong when the rule is applied so woodenly that those connected with an accident are tested even when the cause obviously lies elsewhere, such as equipment failure. (An example would be testing the crew of the airplane that lost part of its fuselage in flight over Hawaii a few years ago.) A union official I interviewed suggested that a policy of postaccident testing might actually backfire so far as safety is concerned. People in critical jobs such as airplane maintenance might not report an accident because they would then have to take a drug test. The reason might be not that they are on drugs but that they fear a false positive result, or want to avoid the inconvenience of the test and the embarrassment of providing a urine sample under direct observation. The net result, however, is that an accident with potentially hazardous consequences may go unreported.

The most important element of employees' opposition to postaccident, periodic, and random testing has to do with human considerations such as loyalty and trust. These were expressed especially in comments by trainmen. The railroad has done very little hiring in recent years, and all of the respondents save one have worked for the company for seven or more years—two-thirds of them, in fact, for fifteen years or more. Many of them take a great deal of pride in their long and loyal service to the railroad. They want the railroad to reciprocate with equal loyalty and pride in them. Periodic, random, and some cases of postaccident testing are done in the absence of any reason to suspect drug use. Employees resent being subjected to tests in these conditions, where their record of service counts for little beside the demeaning and dehumanizing requirement to provide their urine for chemical analysis. Wrote one,

> I have worked for the railroad for over thirty years. They have never had reason to bitch about my performance. Now suddenly I'm not trusted to run my own life. Yes I am angry about their intrusion into my private life!

According to another,

> I am a faithful and loyal employee. I felt like a common criminal and I didn't even do anything wrong. . . . I happen to have bashful

kidneys. The first time I took a drug test it took me almost 3 hours of water & coffee drinking before I could give a sample. . . . Also I felt as if I was being scrutinized by the nursing staff (they looked at me like I was a criminal). Needless to say I was upset, angry, humiliated, defensive, etc. I HATE DRUG TESTING!

Workers consider drug tests done without reasonable suspicion of drug abuse to be an invasion of privacy that infringes their rights as American citizens. The resentment grows when they perceive the tests to be discriminatory—required of employees in some jobs but not of other workers, supervisors, and management. One trainman commented,

Many men and women have died defending our constitution and now it's being threatened from within by people who are not required to go through this humiliating experience. My feeling can best be described by a quote from Ben Franklin: "Those of us who give up freedom for safety deserve neither freedom nor safety."

Another asserted his determination to fight back: "I, for one, will not hesitate to consult with a lawyer before and after any such test and will not hesitate to sue [the company's] *butt off* if any test shows positive."

Numerous trainmen reported the conviction that the railroad is trying to diminish its work force (or "skinny down," as one of them put it). This produces anxiety about jobs, and in that climate, the present policy of postaccident and periodic drug tests—plus the possibility of future random testing—contributes significantly to low employee morale. The most frequent comment from trainmen, specified by 38 of the 174 who made comments, is suspicion that the company's real interest in drug testing is as a means to harass workers and to fire them.

Evaluations

In chapter 6, the proposition will be developed that drug testing has far broader social significance than just testing for drugs. Any final assessment of the value of testing programs must take those wider considerations into account. It might be useful at this point, however, to consider the relative value of various types of testing programs strictly in the context of the specific goals they are intended to achieve. These have to do primarily with productivity and safety in the workplace. We have shown that there are serious questions about the effectiveness of drug testing by urinalysis as a means to these ends. Both productivity and safety pertain to an individual's on-the-job condition. Drug tests determine only that a substance has been ingested within a certain period of time and provide no information about whether the subject's behavior is currently impaired by it. Probably the vast majority of individuals who test positive are not under the influence of the drug at work, at the time they are tested. And even if one should be under the influence at that moment, the test is of no immediate help. After providing a urine sample, the employee is sent back to work in an impaired condition, and the test result will not be known until a few days later when the report comes back from the laboratory. Moreover, as the following comments from a trainman make clear, urinalysis is unlikely to catch the most serious problems.

> I think it's a waste of time. The frequent users will discover ways to bypass the test, use fresh or clean urine from a clean source. The occasional user will be the only one caught. He will not be as concerned as the frequent user and therefore will not seek expensive or troublesome solutions to hide his recreational use. Therefore the real problem, the frequent users and users of hard drugs, will go undetected while the occasional pot smokers will be the ones that are caught. The result will be that [the railroad] loses a valuable employee, the valuable employee loses his job and reputation, while the real problem continues on endangering everyone.

These considerations indicate that, among the drug testing policies presently in use, the most effective is to limit testing to employees whose behavior arouses reasonable suspicion that they are under the influence of drugs while at work. This policy has the least damaging effect on employee morale because (as is clear from the Appendix, table 1) workers approve of such for-cause testing far more than other types of testing of current employees. To include periodic or random testing in the policy is likely to do more harm than good. It will not ferret out many more drug users, it is costly in terms of the increased number of tests (contracts with laboratories are in the neighborhood of $25 to $35 per test), and it is costlier still in diminished employee morale and the termination of valuable employees who have occasionally used marijuana on their own time. Testing of new hires is less harmful. It might screen out a few addicts who cannot refrain from using cocaine or heroin for even a few days. Since employees tend to think it is justified, such preemployment testing would not seriously depress morale, and it could enhance the company's public image as a good soldier in the war on drugs. It is expensive, however, and it might prevent the hiring of certain people who have used marijuana on occasion but who would have become loyal and efficient employees.

A further advantage of for-cause programs to the employer is their relevance to more problems than just drugs. An employee whose behavior is erratic, whose work is substandard, or who has an inordinately high rate of absenteeism would be sent to the medical department or employee assistance program for evaluation. There the decision would be made to test for drugs or alcohol or to explore the possibility of physical or mental illness, temporary emotional stress, or any other situation that may be adversely affecting work and behavior.

For-cause programs normally rely on the observation of supervisors to determine when an employee should be sent for evaluation. Some companies may not find this to be a workable or desirable arrangement. An alternative would be performance testing: a brief set of tasks done by hand or on a computer to demonstrate that the employee's coordination and reaction times are within the expected range.[45] If they are not, that would constitute cause to send the employee to the medical department for further evaluation. Any form of testing has potential dangers; in the case of performance testing, the outstanding imperatives would be to assure that the tasks demanded on the test are truly representative of the tasks required on the job and to prevent them from being used so frequently that they become a nuisance or harassment to employees and an unreasonable expense for employers. If those requirements were met, then performance testing would be preferable to drug testing by urinalysis as currently practiced. It would be less detrimental to employee morale because it is specifically focused on what virtually everyone, including workers, agrees is the employer's legitimate concern: the ability of employees on the job to perform their assigned duties competently and safely. If given periodically or randomly at the same rates now used for drug testing, performance tests would be less expensive, less time-consuming, and less intrusive than urinalysis. The results would be available immediately, so that if action is necessary, it can be taken when it has definite preventive value—before setting a performance-impaired employee to work.

Athletes and Drug Testing

Drug tests have become an integral part of organized athletics at every level. Most professional sports have testing programs, as do the Olympics and other international amateur athletic events. The NCAA tests student athletes who compete in bowl games, basketball tournaments, and other NCAA-sponsored events. It is now commonplace for colleges and universities to test members of all their intercollegiate athletic teams for drugs, and testing programs for high school athletes (and, in some cases, cheerleaders as well) are beginning to appear.

Drug testing of athletes raises issues and problems quite distinct from those in play in the workplace. One major difference is that safe working conditions and the prevention of accidents—the most frequently cited reasons for testing workers—are only marginally relevant to athletics. One of the few comments pertaining to accident prevention in athletics that I have come across was from a baseball player, who told me that he would not want to bat against a pitcher who throws erratically due to the influence of drugs. Another concern that should probably be classified under safe working conditions is that certain drugs taken by football players are reputed to make them more aggressive, thus raising the risk of injury to themselves and others.

A more popular concern is that athletes who abuse street drugs threaten the integrity of their sport. If they become addicted, a desperate need for drugs may induce them to throw games for bribes, blackmail, or payoffs. Moreover, athletes are often in the public eye, and they are important role models for young people. They therefore have special responsibilities to abide by the law and to maintain untarnished images so as not to disillusion the youth who strive to emulate them or to embarrass the school, team, or city they represent.

Perhaps most important, performance-enhancing drugs are not an issue in employment-related tests, but they are of central importance in athletic drug testing. One such drug is erythropoietin, or EPO, which athletes use for what is known as blood doping. Developed for kidney patients, EPO stimulates the production of red blood cells. This effect materially enhances athletic performance, raising aerobic capacity by an average of 8 percent. However, it may have lethal effects. Since athletes already have a normal red blood cell count, EPO's production of still more red blood cells thickens the blood to the point where, as one hematologist put it, it literally turns to mud. This greatly increases the risk of clotting and strokes, and EPO is suspected in the coronary-related deaths of no fewer than eighteen European cyclists over the last four years. At the present time, no test is capable of detecting EPO.[46]

Blood doping may also be achieved without taking any drugs at all. A pint of blood is taken from the athlete, frozen for storage, and then reintroduced into the veins several weeks later, immediately before competition. During the interval, the body will have replaced the blood that was removed, so introducing the extra blood will provide a surplus of red blood cells, enabling the athlete to experience the same aerobic advantages that accrue from taking EPO.[47]

The best-known performance-enhancing drugs are anabolic steroids. These natural or synthetic derivatives of the male hormone testosterone promote the growth of muscles and may speed their recuperation after strenuous exercise. They are also thought to have the psychological effect of increasing aggressiveness. Many athletes are tempted to use anabolic steroids in their training programs, for any and all of these results may improve performance in athletic events. Although their detrimental impact on health is less clear and immediate than is the case with EPO, steroids may have long-term effects on growth and reproductive capacity and lead to psychoses and kidney and liver disease, including cancer. Steroids may also contribute to heart disease by increasing blood pressure and raising the level of undesirable cholesterol.[48] Using steroids is widely recognized to constitute an unfair advantage over athletes who do not use them. They are banned in athletic competitions, and testing by urinalysis is commonly undertaken to detect them.

To avoid detection, athletes often cycle steroids—using them during training but stopping long enough before a competitive event that they will not be perceptible in the urine when tests are done at the event. Countering that practice, recent developments in the technology of testing have extended the period during which anabolic steroids may be identified. Traditionally, the steroid stanozolol has been difficult to detect, leading athletes to use it up to a few weeks or even days before competition with little fear of drug tests. In 1985, however, it was found that preparing the urine with certain chemicals enables the GC/MS test to identify the drug for up to four weeks after last use. Never used in the Olympics before 1988, this procedure was followed in the test that resulted in Ben Johnson being stripped of his Olympic gold medal when stanozolol was detected in his urine following the 100-meter race. Had this new technique not been used, it is likely that Johnson would not have been undone.[49] It should be added that testing of athletes at the Olympics, at about $200 per urine sample, is much more elaborate and many times more expensive than the techniques used in the workplace.[50]

Steroid-using athletes, however, are not without stratagems of their own. According to a January 16, 1991, report on National Public Radio's "Morning Edition," some athletes escape detection by using testosterone, the naturally occurring male hormone that testers do not consider to constitute a violation until it reaches concentrations of six times the normal level in the urine. It is also likely that testers are not aware of all the performance-enhancing drugs that athletes are using, and some slip through unnoticed. Robert Voy, chief medical officer of the U.S. Olympic Committee, said,

> The athletes are ahead of us and have stuff we don't even know about; I know that for a fact. We are not deterring use at all, as far as anabolic steroids are concerned. We have to come up with better analytical programs and with better technology. We have to catch up and find out what drugs they are using.[51]

As part of my research on attitudes toward drug testing, in 1988, I conducted several interviews and distributed a questionnaire similar to the one used for the railroad and the chemical plant to both men and women from the baseball, swimming, track, and football teams of a large Midwestern university. Questionnaires were completed and returned by 176 student athletes. Twenty-nine of these had not yet taken their first drug test, while the remaining 147 had been tested from one to more than fifteen times. As the high side of these figures indicates, student athletes are subjected to a much more intensive regime of testing than is found in any of the business organizations I have investigated. They are tested at least twice during the school year under a combination of administrative decision (not announced in advance) as to when all members of certain teams will be tested and selection of individuals at random. Given the random component of the program, some individuals may be tested three or more times before everyone is tested twice, giving a total of about 1,100 tests for the 450 student athletes in the program. From 1987 to 1989, the rate of positive results (mostly for marijuana) was about 2 percent. In addition to university-mandated tests, those who participate in bowl games, national tournaments, or other championship events may take additional drug tests mandated by the NCAA.

Of the thirty or so student athletes who responded to my questionnaire's invitation to write additional comments, nine of the ten respondents who identified particular drugs in their comments specified steroids (the tenth specified alcohol). Beyond a rather cynical comment that "nobody cares if they're busted for steroids," all of those who specifically mentioned steroids, and all but three of the other commenters expressed their approval of drug testing. That amounts to an approval rate of about 90 percent of those who commented (as contrasted with 28% of the trainmen and chemical workers who commented). If anything, these student athletes want more and better testing. Eight commenters complained that people are getting away with drug use because the tests are too easy to beat, and several of these called for more rigorous and frequent drug tests. A member of the women's track team wrote, "I think drug testing is very beneficial to those athletes who participate without the use of steroids. If there was no drug testing athletes would be able to use drugs to enhance their performance and if this happened the true meaning of athletics would be lost." The dilemmas and pressures that face those who would compete at the highest level were articulated by a member of the men's track team, who claimed that it is "necessary to prevent steroid abuse on an international level. Competing against those who do use 'roids is unfair, and some feel to keep up is possible only with 'roids."

Two male swimmers distinguished between steroids and other drugs. As one of them put it, "I think testing for steroids is a good idea, but I think testing for drugs that do not directly enhance performance is wrong and an invasion of privacy." This position was also espoused by a member of the men's track team in one of the seven extended interviews I conducted with student athletes, but the others adopted more stringent views. Most approve of random testing; one urged that the programs begin with high school athletes. Others commented that there is no reason to object to testing if one has nothing to hide. One track team member complained in an interview that he is often accused of using steroids because of his build. He said he has seriously thought of wearing a T-shirt to meets which displays the dates of his drug tests and bears the legend, "Give me the cup!"

Continuing to bear in mind that the present comments are limited to the immediate purposes of drug testing, without reference to broader social issues to be developed later, the particular nature of steroids leads us to adopt a position on their detection by urinalysis quite different from that we have recommended for other drugs. Traces of street drugs can be detected in the urine after their behavioral effects have disappeared (in the case of marijuana, several weeks after). Therefore, it is likely that most of those who test positive for such drugs (especially marijuana) on random, periodic, or preemployment tests are not under their influence at the time of the test. Since most positive test results are indeed for marijuana, it follows that, apart from situations where a reasonable suspicion of current impairment exists, urinalysis is not an effective means to identify workers whose on-the-job performance is influenced by drugs. In the case of steroids, however, their effects on body development and athletic performance persist longer than the period during which it is possible to detect them in the urine. Therefore, unannounced and random testing done at any time during training appears to be one of the few effective measures available to prevent athletes from cycling steroid use in such a way that they can realize their advantages while avoiding the risk of detection in preannounced tests done at the time of competition.[52] The problem of steroid use is serious enough in terms of the competitive edge gained by those who use them and their possible long-term detrimental effects on health that a convincing argument in favor of such programs of drug testing of amateur and professional athletes for anabolic steroids can be made.

6

FROM DRUG CONTROL

TO MIND CONTROL

Every form of addiction is bad,

no matter whether the narcotic

be alcohol or morphine or idealism.

Carl Jung,

Memories, Dreams,

Reflections

The explanation that one is most likely to hear for the dramatic increase in the frequency of drug testing since about 1985 is straightforward: drug abuse is increasing in America to an alarming extent and at great social cost, war must be waged on drugs to eradicate them from our society, and testing is an important strategy in that war. While no one would dispute that drugs are responsible for a great deal of personal and social harm, the rest of this explanation does not hold up under scrutiny. Far from growing, drug use is actually *decreasing* in the United States and has been on a downward trend for more than a decade. A series of household surveys undertaken by the National Institute on Drug Abuse at intervals of from one to three years between 1971 and 1991 demonstrates that, for all age groups, drug abuse peaked around 1979 and has been declining ever since. In fact, between 1985 and 1991 the number of current drug users among

Americans aged 12 and over (determined by those surveyed who acknowledged using an illicit drug at least once within the last thirty days) decreased by half.[1] These figures indicate that the explosion in drug testing cannot legitimately be explained as a response to increasing drug abuse. Here I propose the alternative explanation that, as with lie detection, drug testing contributes to more pervasive and efficient surveillance and control of individuals in a disciplinary technology of power.

Testing Athletes

The NIDA household surveys do not address the issue of athletes using anabolic steroids to enhance performance. Therefore, it may be the case that in athletics at least, the increase in drug testing in recent years has come about in an effort to curb increased use of steroids. As with other drugs, however, the evidence indicates that the use of steroids may well have been exaggerated and that if anything it is decreasing rather than increasing.

Estimates of how many athletes use steroids are wildly inconsistent. For example, opinions as to the number of participants in the 1988 Seoul Olympics who used performance-enhancing drugs ranged from 10 to 99.9 percent, with most estimating half or more.[2] It must be stressed, however, that these are educated guesses and not the result of any survey. Those studies that have been done (not, however, of Olympic athletes) indicate a much lower rate. A 1984 questionnaire survey commissioned by the NCAA found that 4 percent of the 2,039 college athletes who responded acknowledged ever using steroids,[3] and a follow-up survey conducted by the same researchers in 1988 found the figure to be 5 percent of 2,282 respondents.[4] A 1985 Big 10 Conference survey was in general agreement, setting steroid use at from 2 to 7 percent.[5] Of the 87 football players at a large Midwestern university who responded to my anonymous questionnaire in 1988, none admitted using steroids, although 7 individuals acknowledged occasional, recreational use of other drugs.

When athletes are tested, the positive results are lower than the findings of these surveys. The Associated Press reported on August 30, 1989, that preseason drug testing for steroids throughout the National Football League (which has about 1,300 players) resulted in just thirteen suspensions (1%), with two additional players suspended for testing positive a second time for other drugs. In 1990, only three individuals were found positive for steroids in preseason testing, and a weekly program of random testing throughout the 1990-91 season identified no steroid users among professional football players.[6] Even with refined techniques that allow the detection of steroids in the urine for up to four weeks after last use, only about thirty urine tests taken at the 1988 Olympics in Seoul were positive, and, of those, just ten were judged unequivocal enough to justify disqualification.[7] Frank Uryasz, Director of Sports Sciences for the NCAA, told me that, as of 1991, the NCAA conducted a total of about 14,000 tests annually. Positive results for all drugs, including marijuana and other street drugs as well as steroids, are less than 1 percent. This represents a significant drop from earlier years. For example, tests at the home campus of each team prior to the 1987 season football bowl games produced 2.8 percent positive results, while later tests conducted on four teams, shortly before the game and at the bowl site, showed a positive rate of 9.4 percent. Uryasz attributes this higher figure to the fact that players did not expect that tests would be given at the bowl sites.

These figures are sharply at odds with the fears expressed by some that steroid use among athletes approaches epidemic proportions. Of course, it is possible that many athletes who use steroids will not acknowledge it even on anonymous surveys and that a number of users who cycle their use carefully or take other evasive tactics are likely to fall through the net of drug testing. Nevertheless, the figures of 2 to 7 percent from survey data—and current positive test results below 1 percent—put a heavy strain on the credibility of estimates that 50 percent or more of Olympic-level athletes use steroids. Perhaps what Gene Upshaw, Executive Director of the NFL Players Association, said about professional football applies to all sports: "The fact that so few players have been suspended for alleged steroid use indicates that the public perception of the steroid problem in the NFL is greatly exaggerated."[8]

If the statistics on declining positive test results in professional football and the NCAA indicate that steroid use has in fact been decreasing rather than increasing over the last few years, an important reason may be that the intended effect of testing programs to deter steroid use is working. If so, that is welcome news. However, the implication of the statistics presented above that levels of steroid use were never very high and have become extremely low recently suggests that deterrence is not sufficient as a complete explanation for the high frequency of drug testing in athletics. An additional component in full account would pertain to public relations. A few highly visible cases have focused intense public attention on drugs in sports. These include the cocaine-related death in 1986 of University of Maryland basketball star Len Bias, and the banning of Washington Redskins defensive end Dexter Manley from professional football in 1989 after a third positive drug test for cocaine. Two famous cases involving steroids are the disqualification of Oklahoma All-American linebacker Brian Bosworth from the Orange Bowl and the stripping of an Olympic gold medal from Canadian sprinter Ben Johnson. Keen apprehension has been voiced about the integrity of sports and the effect of drug use by athlete role models on the attitudes and behavior of young people. In the face of these pressures, it is likely that many universities and amateur and professional sports organizations have instituted tough drug testing programs partly as a public relations tactic to convince people that they view the drug problem in sports as a serious one and are taking decisive steps toward its solution.[9]

Testing Employees

Although the NIDA household surveys indicate that drug use is declining in the United States, that fact has yet to impress itself on public opinion.[10] For example, officials I interviewed from eleven organizations that conduct drug tests all agreed with the general proposition that drug use is a serious—and growing—problem in the American workplace. Interestingly, however, only one of them rated it as a problem in his own organization and then not as a serious problem. This is consistent with some odd statistics in the 1987 Business and Legal Reports survey. Although 59 percent of the approximately 2,000 companies represented already did drug testing, were planning to implement it with a year, or had it under consideration, hardly one in five of them (13% of the total) identified drug abuse as a serious problem in their own company.[11] Again, 68 percent of respondents to the same survey indicated the assumption that the drug problem in other organizations was more serious in 1987 than it was five years previously, but only 36 percent stated that it was more serious in their own organization.[12] All of these facts point to an apparently widespread assumption that drugs constitute a bigger social problem than one's personal experience indicates.

The common perception that drug abuse is on the rise is probably a result of the immense publicity that has been devoted to it by the media and by politicians using it as a major campaign issue. These perceptions might then stimulate organizations to establish drug testing programs in the interests of prevention, even when drug abuse is not a serious problem for them. For example, the New York City Police Department instituted random testing of all police officers in September 1989, despite the rate of only 1 to 2 percent positive results found in previous tests. The rationale: the police force is clean now, and the new program is intended to keep it that way.[13] We might anticipate the claim to be made some years hence that testing is responsible for the low incidence of drug abuse in the department, when very possibly the level would have remained the same whether they tested or not.

If you ask organizations that test workers for drugs why they do so, the most common reason you will be given is safety. A famous accident with possible drug connections occurred in January 1987, when a Conrail freight train driven by an engineer with marijuana in his system went through a switch and collided with an Amtrak passenger train, killing 16 people and injuring 176. A year later, a commuter airliner crashed in Colorado killing 9, and the accident may have been related to cocaine use by the pilot. These events stimulated many companies—particularly those dealing with hazardous equipment or materials—to consider or implement drug testing programs as a means to lessen the probability of accidents. In some cases, the decision is not left up to the companies: the Department of Transportation, the Federal Railroad Administration, and other government agencies mandate drug testing in various circumstances.

Another frequently expressed motive has to do with productivity. Reports have circulated that drug-using employees are more likely to be disciplinary problems and to take more sick leave (as much as sixteen times more) than other employees.[14] A recent study of these matters was conducted in the U.S. Postal Service.[15] Over 2,500 newly hired employees in Boston were tested for drugs, with test results kept secret from postal service authorities for purposes of the study. Some 12 percent tested positive: 7.8 percent for marijuana, 2.2 percent for cocaine, and 2.2 percent for other drugs or combinations of drugs. The study followed the performance of the entire group for over a year. It did reveal some differences in productivity and behavior between those with negative and positive test results. Absentee rates were 7.1 percent for those who had tested positive for marijuana and 9.8 percent for those who tested positive for cocaine, as contrasted with 4 percent for employees whose drug tests were negative. Of those with negative test results, 6.4 percent were fired, while the corresponding figures for those testing positive for marijuana and cocaine are 13.6 and 7.3 percent, respectively (the difference in termination rates between those who tested negative and those who tested positive for cocaine is not statistically significant). Those testing positive for either drug are somewhat more likely to have a compensable accident, and those testing positive for marijuana have slightly higher accident and discipline rates, but a statistically significant difference in these areas was not found between those testing positive and those testing negative for cocaine.[16] Although certain measurable differences in productivity and safety were identified, they are nothing like the vast discrepancies that have been claimed. As the authors conclude, "The findings of this study suggest that many of the claims cited to justify pre-employment drug screening have been exaggerated."[17]

This study, incidentally, was reported in the *Wall Street Journal* under the headline, "Study May Spur Job-Applicant Drug Screening," and with a lead paragraph that reads:

Companies that think their pre-employment drug screening programs are cost-effective will draw comfort from a new study published today. And others may be encouraged to adopt such screening.[18]

This is quite the reverse of the conclusion of the study; only late in the *Wall Street Journal* article, on an inside page, is there reference to a statement by the study's senior author that the findings were less striking than expected. The spin on this story is indicative of the hyperbole that often characterizes media depictions of drug abuse and drug testing. That may partly explain why the American public does not seem to grasp the fact that drug use has been declining in this country for some time, and perhaps also why drug testing programs have been increasing in the workplace.

In the climate of our times, to suggest that drugs are anything other Public Enemy #1 seems irresponsible, even unpatriotic. Nevertheless, a few studies in addition to the one just cited should be noted. Stephen Levy indicates that addicts "not only . . . hold down a wide variety of jobs, but that their drug use goes undetected for long periods of time."[19] David Caplovitz refutes the stereotype of drug use as so debilitating as to make it difficult to lead a normal life.[20] His study of working addicts (mostly heroin users) revealed that even when they took drugs at work, they could successfully accomplish their jobs. White-collar addicts tended to have lower-level jobs than nonaddicts, but the blue-collar addicts he studied tended to have better jobs than nonaddicts.[21] And a Harvard Medical School experiment found that smoking up to three marijuana cigarettes per day has no detrimental effect on one's capacity or motivation to work.[22]

My purpose in mentioning these studies is certainly not to condone drug abuse. Instead, when they are combined with the facts that drug use in general is decreasing and that its detrimental effect on worker productivity, while measurable, is not so massive as commonly thought, these studies engender the strong suspicion that there is something more behind the prevalence and growth of drug testing than just a response to drug abuse.

The Business of Drug Testing

Drug testing generates positive feedback, such that the very existence of testing programs spawns still more of them. This is related, in part, to potential liability. Whatever the reality, the perception is widespread that drugs are a major threat to safety. As more companies conduct drug testing, those who do not may feel pressured to adopt it because failure to test may render them vulnerable to accusations of neglecting to take common, prudent measures to ensure a safe workplace. Moreover, companies that do not test may fear that they will become magnets for unproductive and accident-prone drug users. As this reasoning was expressed by the personnel manager of Lawrence (Kansas) Memorial Hospital in explaining their adoption of a drug testing program, "As it [testing] becomes widespread, drug users may flock to hospitals and other employers that they know don't do testing. Just by not testing, we may be attracting undesirable candidates."[23]

Another aspect of the tendency of testing to spawn more testing has to do with its institutionalization. Drug testing has become a big business. Chemical research and development are necessary to devise and improve the tests; company medical departments are charged with collecting and packing the urine samples; courier firms are engaged to transport them; commercial laboratories contract to evaluate the samples and report the results. One plant I studied which was hiring several thousand workers found it necessary to set up a special telephone line dedicated solely to transmitting test results from the laboratory. In addition to the administration of tests themselves, anxiety about drug abuse and implementation of testing programs have contributed to the development of employee assistance programs to provide preliminary diagnosis and counseling pertaining to drug-related and other problems. Rehabilitation centers have sprung up for outpatient or inpatient treatment of those identified by the tests as drug users. And finally there are the lawyers: lawyers to write drug testing policies, lawyers to review the policies that other lawyers have written, lawyers to represent employees in grievance proceedings stemming from drug tests, and lawyers to defend companies against those grievances. Thus, many wheels are in motion to maintain drug testing; many organizations and individuals derive their business and livelihood from it. They compete for contracts, disseminate information, and sponsor workshops concerning the problem of drugs in the workplace and how testing contributes to its solution. The momentum provided by the institutions that have sprouted to implement drug testing must be counted among the major reasons for its remarkable growth.[24]

Another reason for the growth of drug testing is that some organizations may be interested in fostering an image of themselves as public-spirited citizens who are concerned about the drug problem in America and are taking decisive steps to combat it. I believe this is a major impetus to drug testing in athletic organizations. But in the workplace, I suspect it is essentially cosmetic. In my interviews with human resources executives, at any rate, an altruistic determination to fight on the front lines of society's war on drugs was conspicuously absent. At most, managers expressed the intention to keep their own establishments as free from drugs as possible. Of course, if this attitude is adopted by a great many companies, it will have a general impact on the national situation, but from the point of view of businessmen, that would seem to be only a by-product of more parochial concerns. When I raised this issue specifically with a personnel official from a utility company, he expressed the opinion that while their preemployment testing policy might curtail drug use among their own employees, it could have little effect on the problem in society at large other than shifting it from one social sector to others.

Drug Testing and Social Control

An anthropologist, asked to consider drug testing from the vantage point of a broad, comparative familiarity with human cultures, would identify it as a "mechanism of social control." That term refers to the many customs and practices that operate to direct people toward behavior that is socially acceptable and deflect them from activities that are not. The sanctions that give force to mechanisms of social control may be either positive or negative. Examples of the former are raising salaries or bestowing honorary degrees on estimable employees and citizens; examples of the latter are imprisonment of miscreants by governmental authorities or illness and other misfortunes sent by God, witches, malicious demons, or angry ancestors. Sanctions may also be distinguished according to whether they are public or private. Public sanctions include the presentation of the Nobel Prize and the execution of a criminal in the town square; a letter from one's bank in an unmarked envelope giving notice that a penalty fee is being assessed for bouncing a check belongs to the category of private sanctions.

As with all mechanisms of social control, drug testing carries sanctions. These come in all combinations of positive and negative, public and private, although some of them (especially negative and private) are much more prevalent than others. The rarest form of sanction that I have encountered in drug testing is positive and private. I know of only one example. Princeton Diagnostic Laboratories, Inc., is a firm that conducts biochemical testing of all sorts, including the urinalysis work for the drug testing programs of a number of companies. Speaking at a Columbia University Law School forum on drug testing in October 1988, President and Chief Executive Officer Carlton Turner said that the laboratory subjects its own employees to random drug testing. A unique twist is that each employee who tests drug free under this program is given a cash bonus of $20. Turner reported that this private, positive sanction has made their drug testing program hugely popular with employees, who rejoice in the opportunity to provide urine samples when their numbers come up. (The corresponding, negative sanction is that any employee whose test reveals the presence of drugs is summarily fired.)

Sanctions that are positive and public are also rare in drug testing. Again, Turner (who had been former President Reagan's special advisor on drug policy) mentioned one of the most intriguing of them at the Columbia forum. When the White House drug testing program was established, it was announced that President Reagan would be the first to be tested, followed by

Vice-President Bush and "senior White House staff." This caused employees to tumble over each other in their hopes to be tested early, for this distinction became a badge that marked inclusion in the charmed circle of "senior staff" at the White House.

As a mechanism of social control, drug testing employs negative sanctions far more frequently than positive ones. Public, negative sanctions tend to be most common in athletics. The National Football League tested all players prior to the 1989–90 season and published the names of those players found to have used drugs. Testing at competitive events inevitably leads to public disclosure because those identified by tests as drug users are disqualified. The publicity may become no less than sensational when medals that had been awarded immediately after an event are taken away a day or two later when drug test results become known, as happened to Ben Johnson in the 1988 Olympics. Bringing glasnost into athletics, drug-using Russian athletes discovered under a program of unannounced drug testing conducted jointly with the United States are publicly identified by name, stripped of their medals, and suspended from competition. The Russians, indeed, make findings in this program more public than do their American counterparts.[25]

By far the most common form of sanctions brought on by drug testing, however, is negative and private. Indeed, many drug testing policies lay great stress on the strict confidentiality that surrounds the results of tests and actions taken in response to them. From the perspective of mechanisms of social control worldwide, this is odd. The force behind sanctions is normally supplied by social disapproval, ridicule, and shame, and these can be brought to bear only in public circumstances. On reflection, however, it is quickly apparent that drug testing stings in one of a person's more private parts—the pocketbook. The sanction is severe indeed, because drug testing directly impinges on what in our society is essential for the reasonable satisfaction of one's material needs: the ability to get and keep a job. Moreover, while the results of drug tests and actions taken in response to them are kept strictly confidential, they may nonetheless ultimately have an effect on one's public life. Employment is important to social standing in American society, so it is difficult to establish or maintain public respect (not to mention self-esteem) while unemployed.

The simplest and most common device in drug testing's inventory of negative, private sanctions is denial of employment to job applicants. Most preemployment testing policies specify that securing a job depends on a drug test, and those whose test results reveal drug use are not hired. The whole process is shrouded in confidentiality. Organizations virtually never make it public that certain, named individuals were not hired because of a drug test. Unless specifically asked, often they do not even tell the applicants themselves.

A few organizations apply an equally simple sanction to current employees: they are fired for a single positive drug test. This is the down side to Princeton Diagnostic Laboratories' incentive of a $20 bonus for each negative test result. Immediate termination on the first positive drug test is also the policy of the New York City Police Department.[26] While this policy may appear to be decisive, it may not be economical because it often costs more to locate and train a new employee (especially in a specialized position) than to rehabilitate a current one. In any event, immediate termination is a blunt and ineffective instrument of social control so far as the larger society is concerned. The point of social control, after all, is to induce people to follow acceptable lines of behavior. The most effective forms of social control include provisions for modifying the behavior of those who stray, and termination at the first sign of deviance is not an efficient means to that end.

Most organizations that test current members have adopted a posture that is both more forgiving and more effective in modifying deviant behavior. Its form may be described as "test-intervene-retest." A positive result on a drug test does not immediately provoke termination, but it does act as a signal that behavior modification is required. In response to this signal, the organization begins to intervene in the individual's life. At the beginning, intervention may be relatively mild, such as a single session with a drug counselor for the person who tests positive for the first time. Regardless of the severity of the initial intervention, however, a positive test result usually licenses the employer or other authority to conduct further tests of the individual at will and without warning. Retesting of this sort is normally authorized for a certain period of time, such as a year. If the test results are uniformly negative, at the end of the specified period, the individual returns to the pool of people who are subject only to the normal provisions of the testing policy. But if a positive result is found in the period of retesting, the individual faces more stringent interventions, such as formal rehabilitation on an outpatient or inpatient basis and/or for student athletes, disqualification from participation in games or meets for a certain period. If positive test results persist, the individual is ultimately dropped from the team or terminated from employment.

The regime of test-intervene-retest gets its teeth from the "job jeopardy model." This means that an employee's job (or, similarly, a student athlete's place on the team and, often, retention of a scholarship) is held hostage to successful rehabilitation. "To be totally effective," writes an expert on employee assistance programs, "'job discipline' and 'constructive confrontation' procedures should be an integral function of the program. This approach imposes penalties that ultimately lead to termination if the chemical-dependent employee refuses, discontinues, or does not respond to the EAP's efforts, and fails to maintain a satisfactory job-performance level."[27]

When backed by the sanction of the job jeopardy model, drug testing is a potent mechanism of social control. It assures that, one way or another, the organization will rid itself of the drug use that testing has detected. Either the habit is expunged from the individual's behavior, or, if that should fail, the individual is expunged from the organization. The former solution is the preferred one, partly because it is more humane to the employee, partly because rehabilitating a current employee is often less expensive than hiring and training a new one, and partly because it achieves the general aim of social control to reform deviant behavior. The opportunity for treatment available to current employees under the job jeopardy model is also a more constructive sanction than punishment or ridicule, in that it offers the possibility to overcome dependency on drugs without loss of face or employment.[28]

Drug Testing in the Disciplinary
Technology of Power

The economic sanction of job jeopardy is only part of a larger answer to the question of how drug testing, relying as it does on negative, private sanctions, can be an effective mechanism of social control. The subtler but more fundamental part of the answer pertains to Foucault's theory of the disciplinary technology of power, a method of social domination that relies on constant surveillance to detect individual deviations from expected standards of behavior at an early stage, when they may be quickly and easily rectified. The surveillance is part of "descending individualization," Foucault's term for the general set of circumstances in which increasingly sophisticated techniques allow detailed and comprehensive information about each member of society to be gathered, stored, and easily retrieved.[29] As is true of lie detection, drug testing also constitutes an advance in surveillance techniques over primitive forms such as the panopticon. Particularly with random testing, there is no need to keep people under constant surveillance. They must conform their behavior to expectations even when no one is watching, because they know that they may be called on at any time to provide a urine sample that will reveal what they have been doing.

Drug testing is particularly relevant to Foucault's ideas about how, over the last few centuries, the power to control and coerce people's behavior has operated in collusion with knowledge.[30] Science—especially medicine—has generated immense amounts of knowledge about physical and mental disease, growth and development, deviance, and other human conditions previously known only dimly, if at all. This knowledge took the form of rich new discourse about these conditions: definitions of what they are, methods for identifying them, theories about what produces them, proposals for what might be done about them. In some cases, such as female hysteria and child sexuality, it is likely that the conditions or pathologies did not even exist prior to discourse about their diagnosis and treatment produced by expanding knowledge.[31] Knowledge about human normalities and pathologies enables power to intrude more intimately into people's lives.

It establishes standards or norms for physical, mental, and behavioral conditions of all sorts. It encourages frequent examination of individuals to ascertain if, where, and how they deviate from those norms. It licenses interventions in the individual's body, mind, and behavior for the purpose of maintaining and enhancing those aspects that are decreed to be normal and for treating those that are identified as disorders. These interventions are done to people for their own good, it is claimed, but nevertheless they constitute the exercise of power over them.

Drug testing fits this pattern perfectly. Urinalysis has been developed as a practicable means for gaining knowledge about individuals' drug use habits (and the future promises even better methods, such as testing hair). Drug use has been identified as a serious disorder for the individual and for society—with ample testimony of ruined lives and the violence of criminal drug distribution networks to prove it. This is used to justify the inspection of individuals by means of drug tests and interventions in the form of prevention and treatment (or failing that, exclusion) in the lives of those who test positive. One example is a bill, introduced into the 1992 Kansas legislature, aimed at reducing the number of "crack babies." The bill would require a woman convicted of a felony drug offense to be implanted with a Norplant contraceptive device as a condition of probation. The device would not be removed until random drug tests certified that she had not used drugs for a period of a year. The exercise of power in this particular plan is too blatant for most tastes: critics labeled the bill unconstitutional, discriminatory against women, and ethically repugnant, and it was turned down unanimously in committee.[32] It signals, nonetheless, a possible future.

More successful applications of disciplinary power come in less obviously punitive packages. Foucault stresses that many deviations (mental illness, sexual maladjustment, juvenile delinquency, etc.) are viewed as disorders deserving treatment rather than crimes demanding punishment. He goes on to discuss how the forms of treatment are considered to be helpful interventions that provide individuals with the opportunity to extinguish deviant behaviors that are deleterious to themselves as well as society. Only after strenuous efforts at treatment have failed are incorrigibles excluded from normal society, often by incarceration in an insane asylum or prison.[33]

These attitudes and practices are readily apparent in drug testing programs. Corporate policies (I will quote from one) often stress the company's "caring attitude" toward the well-being of its employees, its "sincere interest in making the workplace as safe as possible and to assist employees to rid themselves of dependency problems." The test-intervene-retest regime is designed to achieve those goals, and officials in employee assistance programs work hard to ensure that the indicated treatment is available and that the troubled employee takes advantage of it. It is also true, however, that drug testing may eventually result in exclusion. Under the job jeopardy model, as discussed already, drug-using employees or athletes who fail at rehabilitation (as demonstrated by a positive drug test after returning to work) are likely to be fired or dropped from the team, and those with positive preemployment test results are not hired. Although each instance of exclusion is from a single organization, it is in principle possible that a drug user might experience a series of rejections based on drug tests from different organizations and eventually be excluded from the employed, self-sufficient sector of society altogether.

Although drug testing displays many of the features that Foucault identifies with the disciplinary technology of power, it appears to deviate in one respect. According to Foucault, the disciplinary technology achieves greater efficiency and economy in the application of power than any previous regime. This is true enough when drug testing is compared with a crude mechanism of surveillance such as the panopticon, but the efficiency of drug testing appears nevertheless to leave much to be desired. Massive numbers are tested, but the rate of positive results hovers around 4 percent. That means that for every individual who faces some sort of action or treatment because of a drug test, some twenty-four others test negative and nothing is done with reference to them. Testing twenty-five to locate one is anything but efficient. Nor is it economical. If an organization with a 4 percent positive rate contracts for drug testing at the rate of, say, $26 per test, the cost per positive test result comes to $650.[34]

But this reasoning stems from the assumption that drug testing is exclusively concerned to identify people who use drugs. In fact, there is much more to it than that. Consider a "for-cause" testing policy (under which individuals are tested if their behavior suggests that they are under the influence of drugs or alcohol). To apply a for-cause policy effectively, it is necessary that supervisors notice abnormal behavior. To this end, they are trained to recognize signs of drug-impaired behavior and admonished to observe workers under their supervision. But such observation extends beyond drug-related issues, because the alert supervisor is likely to notice a variety of deviations from mandated behavior in addition to those possibly caused by drugs. Figure 4, which details how supervisors should proceed in deciding whether to take disciplinary action in any circumstance, is an outstanding example of the emphasis placed on general surveillance in the workplace. Note how the "default mode" of the system is "observe employee behavior." The process begins in that mode, and at every point, whether disciplinary action is taken or not, the system returns to it.

In actuality, employees normally respond more positively to a for-cause testing policy than to periodic or random testing, because it limits testing to situations where the employee's on-the-job behavior provokes reasonable suspicion that something is amiss. I myself endorsed it as the most acceptable form of drug testing, for the same reason: managers and fellow employees certainly have the right to expect that workers will show up for work in a condition to do their jobs competently, especially when considerations of safety are involved. Nevertheless, the stepped-up observation procedures connected with a for-cause policy of drug testing also serve to extend the general surveillance so essential in a disciplinary technology of power. This is one of several examples of how, in testing, discipline and control are ingeniously packaged in forms made palatable to those brought under their sway—and where even an analyst who is generally critical of the expansion of disciplinary power, such as myself, is constrained to condone it.

There is more. Although the low rate of positive results appears to render drug testing an inefficient means of exerting power,

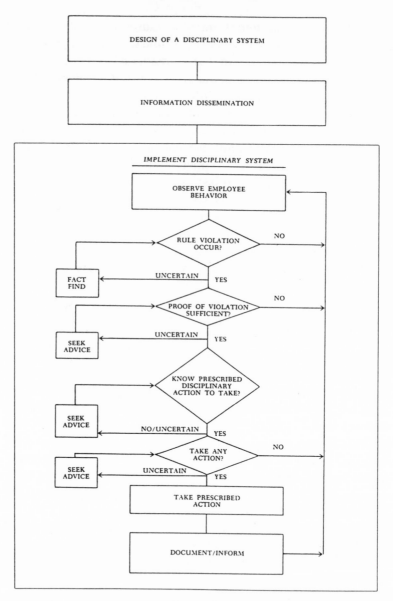

Figure 4.
Steps in the disciplinary process. From McAfee and Chadwick.
"Evaluating an Organization's Disciplinary System,"
Human Resource Management 1 (1981):33.
Reprinted by permission of John Wiley & Sons, Inc.

there may be another way of looking at it. If we attempt something akin to figure-ground reversal, we could imagine drug testing to be oriented as much toward the *negatives* as the positives. That is to say, drug testing might achieve some important result for the 96 percent whose tests do not indicate drug use. If that were the case, our assessment of its efficiency and economy would soar. But what might that result be? It seems that nothing much happens to those with negative test results. If the intention was to hire them, they are hired; if they are already employed, they return to their jobs. Yet I argue that so far as its overall social consequences are concerned, the effect of drug testing is at least as important for those who test negative as for those who test positive.

It has already been indicated that drug testing (particularly random testing) serves to control people's behavior even when they are not under direct surveillance. The possibility that they might be tested at any time is sufficient to prevent some people from using drugs. Therefore, drug testing has a significant impact on them, even when test results show them to be drug-free. More than deterrence is at issue, however, for certainly most people who test negative do not refrain from drug use out of fear that they will be caught by a test. They simply do not want to use drugs and would refrain from using them whether they were subjected to drug tests or not. Does drug testing have any important effect on them?

I think that it does. The reasoning is grounded in Foucault's contention that the disciplinary technology of power produces individuals characterized by "automatic docility." Disciplinary training operates by drill. People are induced to perform specific acts repeatedly, until they do them automatically, by second nature. No effort is made to get them to see the overall picture, to understand the rationale for what they are trained to do. They are conditioned to perform the minute particulars correctly, unthinkingly. If they do that, the resulting totality will come right whether the participants envision it or not. More generally, this type of training develops individuals who are ready to submit without question to new drills that may be handed down. The disciplinary technology of power, that is to say, tends to develop people who are conditioned or disciplined to be automatically docile.[35]

My hypothesis is that drug testing is a disciplinary drill and that those who readily acquiesce—even approve of it—are conditioned to automatic docility. This hypothesis may be applicable to student athletes. It has already been discussed, in chapter 4, how athletes state that they are willing to submit to drug tests because they see it as a means to prevent others from gaining unfair competitive advantage from performance-ehancing drugs. When I discussed possible reasons for the high rate of acceptance of testing among student athletes with a university athletic department official, however, he added another dimension to the issue. He said that coaches make it clear that they must undergo drug testing, and he continued that student athletes do not usually question what they are told to do by their coaches and others in authority. Applying Foucault's terminology, we might say that one reason why student athletes readily accept drug testing is because they have already developed a measure of docility (probably from long experience obeying the commands of coaches in high school, junior high school, little league, etc.). Empirical support for the hypothesis is provided by data from my questionnaire, particularly in the contrasting attitudes expressed by student athletes and trainmen. One question inquired into reactions to one's most recent drug test, the respondent being asked to check possibilities such as "unconcern," "worry," "embarrassment," and "anger." People who submit to drug testing with automatic docility would manifest rather bland attitudes about it; on this question, they would be expected to mark "unconcern" more than the other possibilities. The difference between student athletes and trainmen was considerable: 77 percent of the former reported an attitude of unconcern as opposed to 33 percent of the latter, while the latter much more commonly indicated negative responses such as worry about the possibility of a false positive result (51%, compared with 6% for student athletes) and anger at the distrust implied by testing (trainmen 33%, student athletes 7%). (For full results, see Appendix, table 3). Again, people who are conditioned to submitting to drug testing with automatic docility are likely to express little opposition to the prospect of being tested in the future. The questionnaire asked if experience in an organization that conducts drug tests (as both the railroad and the university do) would make one more opposed, less opposed, or have no effect on one's attitude toward taking future drug tests. The responses again revealed a marked contrast between trainmen and student athletes. Of those who have taken one or more tests, 22 percent of the trainmen but only 4 percent of the student athletes indicated that they would be more opposed to taking future tests, while only 13 percent of the trainmen but 49 percent of the student athletes stated they would be less opposed (see Appendix, tables 6 and 7).[36]

While drug testing acts to reinforce the automatic docility people already have, it can also, more important, be understood as a drill that develops automatic docility. The optimally disciplined and docile population will submit to any demand or directive without seeking to know a rationale or justification for it. Those forms of drug testing that are done in the absence of reasonable suspicion of drug use constitute good training for this. Random testing is particularly apt because its demands are entirely arbitrary: the essence of randomness is that there simply is no rationale for why one number should come up rather than another. In one chemical plant I studied, when the randomizing computer program produces a number, the employee corresponding to it is immediately summoned. The worker is expected to go dutifully to the medical department, and immediately to produce a urine sample. Given the randomness of the system, some employees have been tested several times, while others have yet to be called. This apparent disparity has provoked complaints, but management anticipates that these will subside as people become accustomed to the system. If and when that should occur—if people come to provide a urine sample for testing at the summons of an arbitrary, random selection procedure as readily and unreflectively as they now reveal date of birth and social security number to almost anyone who asks—the development of automatic docility will have taken a great step forward.

In an effort to test this aspect of the hypothesis, the question about attitudes toward drug tests appeared twice in the questionnaire. Subjects were asked to mark any of several responses describing their reactions to their first drug test, and the next question (directed to those who had been tested more than once) was identical except that it referred to the most recent drug test. The hypothesis that drug testing is a means of developing automatic docility would predict that attitudes toward the most recent test would be less intense (more "unconcern" and less "worry," "embarrassment," "anger," or "satisfaction") than those toward the first test. The data from these questions (set out fully in the Appendix, tables 4 and 5) support the hypothesis. For example, although trainmen manifest considerably less docility in the matter of drug testing than do student athletes, a shift in that direction is evident among trainmen as they are tested more frequently. Of the trainmen who have taken three or more drug tests, 25 percent remember facing their first test with unconcern, while those unconcerned about their most recent test swelled to 34 percent; fully half of them were worried about a false positive result when they took their first test, but just 38 percent of them continued to worry about that in their most recent test; 44 percent reacted to their first test with anger that drug tests invade their privacy, while those reporting that feeling at their most recent test dropped to 34 percent. However, the question that asked if the experience of belonging to an organization that conducts drug tests would make one more or less opposed to taking them in the future produced ambiguous results for the hypothesis that repeated testing increases automatic docility (see Appendix, tables 6 and 7).[37]

Interestingly, so far as its contribution to the development of automatic docility is concerned, drug testing has nothing to do with drugs. The important thing is to train people to submit readily to being tested; just what is being tested and the results are beside the point.

The application of disciplinary power increases in economy and efficiency with automatic docility because the more docile the populace, the less the resistance to power. If we examine them from this perspective, certain initially curious drug testing programs and proposals become more intelligible. A case in point is Chicago's St. Sabina Academy, a Catholic school that began random drug testing of all children in grades six through eight in 1990. In an interview, an official of St. Sabina parish told me that drug abuse is not presently a problem in the school. However, it

is a serious problem in the neighborhood and church, and community members have been active in their opposition. They have
exposed drug dealers in the parks and crack houses in the neighborhood, disrupted business in stores that sell drug paraphernalia, organized marches, and in general have taken any grass-
roots action they can think of to rid their community of drugs.

The individual I interviewed is convinced that drug dealers are
beginning to target children as young as eight to eleven, and he
is convinced that steps must be taken to help the children resist
the temptation. His opinion is that children need clearly defined
expectations in terms of which to structure their behavior, and the
drug testing program at St. Sabina Academy is intended to convey
the unequivocal message that drugs will not be tolerated in the
school. Under the program, some 20 to 25 students are selected
at random and tested by urinalysis every quarter. At this rate,
about one-third of the students in grades six through eight will
be tested every year. The testing is intended primarily as a deterrent: not so much to identify students who currently use drugs
(there are few, if any, at present) as to establish a strongly anti-
drug climate in the school that will help children to say no if or
when they are invited to try drugs. The proposal enjoys strong
support in the St. Sabina community. A letter that introduced the
program and requested reaction was sent home to some 350
school families. It drew 210 responses in favor and only 4 against.
Among the most frequent comments from parents was that the
program should not be limited to grades six through eight but
begin in kindergarten.

One can certainly appreciate the concern of the St. Sabina
community to protect their children from drugs. Nevertheless, it
does seem to be a rather extreme move to institute random drug
tests of young children in the school when the evidence is that they
are not using drugs. If drug testing is also understood as a technique for instilling automatic docility, however, the St. Sabina
program makes better sense. People who become habituated to
random drug testing as children are likely to continue to submit
to it without opposition as adults, and they will be conditioned
to accept unquestioningly other disciplinary drills that may from
time to time be imposed on them. In that sense, a program such

as this one diminishes resistance to power and thus contributes to the efficiency and economy of its operation.

Certainly the leaders of the St. Sabina community do not intend this. It was obvious from my interview that they are exclusively motivated by concern for the safety and well-being of their community, especially its children. Nevertheless, institutions have a logic of their own, quite apart from the purposes of the people connected with them. Part of the genius of the disciplinary technology of power is that programs that include among their less obvious consequences the extension and perfection of power also have more visible aspects that people perceive to be in their best interest, and these motivate them to bring those programs into being. Such, I suggest, is the case with the random drug testing program at St. Sabina Academy.

Another remarkably successful tactic of drug testing for lessening resistance to the exercise of power is to generate the pressure to submit to tests from within, from the very people who are to be tested, rather than imposing it from the outside. Such internal motivation is sometimes achieved by offering rewards ("positive reinforcement," in the language of operant conditioning) for taking drug tests. Two examples, discussed already, are the $20 bonus given by Princeton Diagnostic Laboratories to employees for every negative test result and the scramble of officials in Reagan's White House to be among the first tested because that constituted a sign of their inclusion in the select group of "senior White House staff." As with the St. Sabina program, in both of these cases, people are motivated to go along with drug testing because they perceive it to be in their own interest to do so. It is similar with those athletes who are willing and anxious to submit to random testing themselves to prevent others from gaining an unfair competitive advantage through use of steroids.

Again, disciplinary power may ingratiate itself among those under its sway by adopting a friendly face. In addition to urinalysis, the massive antidrug program begun by the navy in 1982 included dogs trained to detect drugs. These would be stationed at gangplanks where they would sniff sailors and their possessions when they returned from shore leave, and they were used to search ships for hidden drug caches. The navy found it most effective to use small dogs for this purpose. Unlike large breeds commonly associated with law enforcement, such as alsatians and dobermans, beagles and other small dogs could more easily investigate cramped places, and their handlers could conveniently hold them aloft to sniff among ceiling pipes. And there were psychological advantages: they "were preferred because they avoided a 'gestapo' image, and . . . the dogs became mascots that the crew protected from mischief or harm."[38] Disciplinary power achieves a high degree of sophistication indeed when its instruments of surveillance and accusation are cute pets that are cuddled and protected by the very population they are used to control.

Peer pressure is another powerful force that moves people to submit to disciplinary techniques such as drug tests. In this case, the motivation may be external to the individual, but it is still internal to the group that is to be tested. As an example, high school students in Bennington, Oklahoma, decided to prove that their school is 100 percent drug-free by having the entire student body of seventy-five voluntarily take drug tests.[39] Of course, the sense of the term "voluntary" is quickly distorted by any formal effort, such as this one, to mandate such tests. A voluntary act is one that may or may not be done, with no external pressure in either direction. Any policy encouraging "voluntary" tests constitutes pressure to take them, and thus they are not voluntary. The pressure can be powerful indeed. In the case of Bennington High School, all seventy-five members of the student body "volunteered" to be tested. The unanimity is not difficult to understand: imagine the kind of suspicion that would have been aroused if one or two students had declined.

Any doubts about the power of community pressure to force people to volunteer for a drug test should be eliminated by a brief dip into the local politics of Lawrence, Kansas. During summer 1989, the fire department was called to rescue a man who had fallen through the hole of an outhouse at a park on the outskirts of town. Apparently the wretch accidentally dropped some money into the offal and fell in while trying to retrieve it. The rumor quickly circulated, however, that it was a member of the City Commission who had been placed in that unfortunate position during the course of a failed drug deal. Although the commissioner in question was in Spain at the time of the incident, the suspicion became sufficiently intense that he took a drug test and eventually had the results published in the local newspaper.[40]

Authenticity Testing and Disciplinary Power

A hallmark of authenticity testing is asymmetry. Whether a test for witchcraft, trial by ordeal or by battle, lie detection, or drug testing, the circumstances of a test provide for information to pass from the test taker to the test giver but never in the opposite direction. Moreover, the test taker has little control over what information is acquired by the test or how it is extracted. The entire situation is set up to enable test givers to exercise power over test takers.

If we raise the analysis one level, however, a somewhat different picture emerges. Here the direction of communication is reversed, because the sheer fact that authenticity tests are given sends a metamessage from test givers to test takers. The significance of that message for power remains the same, however, for it reinforces the dominance of test givers. Regardless of the particular issue in question—commission of a crime, the veracity of what one has set down on a job application form, drug use, suspicion of witchcraft—this message reads: "We don't trust what you say, and we demand that you prove it by taking a test."

On occasion, the distrust embedded in that message is so acute that it departs from the unspoken level of metamessages and becomes an explicit component of the relationship. The following is a passage from *Tally's Corner*, Elliot Liebow's well-known study of urban blacks in Washington, D.C..

> Owners of small retail establishments and other employers frequently anticipate employee stealing and adjust the wage rate accordingly. Tonk's employer explained why he was paying Tonk $35 for a 55-60 hour workweek. These men will all steal, he said. Although he keeps close watch on Tonk, he estimates that Tonk steals from $35 to $40 a week. What he steals, when added to his regular earnings, brings his take-home pay to $70 or $75 per week.

The employer said he did not mind this because Tonk is worth that much to the business.[41]

Tonk's own estimate of what he steals corresponds with his employer's, although Liebow calculates it as a good deal less.[42] Be that as it may, the important point is that expectation of employee dishonesty may become a self-fulfilling prophecy. When the employer takes distrust and the assumption of employee theft so far as to build it into the wages, the employee's only options are to steal (even if initially disinclined to do so) or to be a fool.

Although most employers are not as explicit as Tonk's, the metamessage of distrust conveyed by the demand that employees take authenticity tests is still unmistakable, and it often erodes loyalty and morale. Essentially they are being told, regardless of your record of service, reliability, and safety, you are suspected of theft, dishonesty, or drug use, and that suspicion will be suspended only by your passing this test, and even if you pass, you will be trusted only until the next test. This engenders hostility against the company and may even spur some workers to take steps to confound or subvert the tests purely as a way to maintain a sense of autonomy and dignity in the face of a system that is aimed at systematically humiliating them. Abbie Hoffman's *Steal This Urine Test*,[43] a practical guide to techniques for beating drug tests, is a good example of this reaction. Much more commonly, the metamessage of distrust and lack of consideration conveyed by testing programs and various other employer practices destroys employee motivation to take pride in one's work and perform at a high level and engenders a passive-aggressive response marked by smoldering resentment and diminished productivity. This attitude is clear in the four-page letter that one trainman returned with my questionnaire on attitudes toward drug testing. He was disturbed about a number of things besides the company's drug testing policy, but his letter tells volumes about what can happen to employee morale:

I'm made to work every day without a day off in conditions that I would not force my dog to endure (filthy locomotives, stinking toilets and warm drinking water, etc.). I used to take pride in my work habits. Always on time, prepared and conscientious. For seven years my work record was flawless, but because an industrious trainmaster wanted to shed some light on himself and some glory, I was fired for 45 days for something that was the Dispatchers fault. I went home and bought some marijuana and thanked [the railroad] for the good job they'd given me.

Sir, it has been like that since. I do just enough to get the job done. I don't smoke marijuana on the job nor do I condone the use by fellow employees. I see that the train gets over the road, but if something breaks down or there is something that should be reported, I don't report it, I just look the other way. . . . When I'm done for the day and it's been an unusually long day (which there are many), I'll stop on the way home and have a couple of beers. When I can get some time off of the board [so as not to be "on call"], I'll really unwind and smoke some marijuana as I know a lot of people like myself do. Would you ask if I'm a drug abuser? No, I don't think I am. . . .

As for the [railroad's] testing programs, you should make the [company] Officials be required to have some management and people skills. I'm a hard working, tax paying, Vietnam Veteran and a Registered Voter. I pay my bills, take care and time to love my children and I don't cheat on my wife. I work for the . . . Railroad and until something better comes my way . . . I'll be out here just doing enough to get by.

The typical response to complaints such as these is that the only people who have any reason to fear lie detector or drug tests are those with something to hide. And, indeed, the author of the letter would fall in that category because he admits to smoking marijuana occasionally. But others who do not use drugs at all or have done nothing wrong also express great concern at being subjected to drug, lie detector, or integrity tests. This concern can be articulated on two levels. One argument, on the practical level, has to do with the danger of false positive results due to inadvertent or intentional error in the testing process. As one trainman put it, with specific reference to drug tests,

I cannot describe to you the amount of anger that I feel over this particular issue. Keep in mind that I feel this way and I'm an individual who has no *reason* to be concerned. The very idea that I could lose a job because of someone's incompetence or because of someone's wanting to get back at me for one reason or another is infuriating. This company's attitude that you have nothing to worry about if you've nothing to hide is totally naive and unrealistic.

The second argument, on the level of principle, has to do with the legitimacy of subjecting people to authenticity tests in the absence of any evidence of wrongdoing. Often this is phrased in legal language pertaining to the right to privacy and presumption of innocence. It is more relevant to this work, however, to articulate the point in social theoretical language on the basis of insights put forth by Erving Goffman in *The Presentation of Self in Everyday Life.*[44] To the claim that only those with something to hide need fear drug, lie detector, and other authenticity tests, the proper response is that *everyone has something to hide.* This does not mean that there is a little crook in all of us. It recognizes rather that social interaction consists largely of a series of dramaturgical performances in which people don many masks in an effort to present themselves artfully—concealing certain elements of the self while highlighting and tinting others. The aim is to exercise some control over social situations by influencing others' perception of the self and thereby of the situation. As a family of technologies that extract and reveal information about the self in ways and for purposes that are beyond the control of the self, authenticity testing erodes this distinctive feature of social life. Whether test results are positive or negative is, at this level, irrelevant. The point is that testing opens the self to scrutiny and investigation in ways that the self is powerless to control. So far as the areas of knowledge covered by the tests are concerned, this transforms the person from autonomous subject to passive object.

It might be protested that even if these concerns constitute a potential threat to the self, that threat is never actualized because test results are kept strictly confidential. They are revealed only to the parties who need to know: personnel directors who must review test results before making conditional offers of employment final, EAP and medical personnel involved with counseling, treatment, and rehabilitation, and, perhaps, supervisors. The confidentiality of testing is normally presented as a safeguard for the test taker's reputation, although protecting the organization from legal action is surely of at least equal importance.

However, far from protecting test takers, the confidentiality that shrouds authenticity tests is better analyzed as yet another ingenious and highly effective technique for exercising power and discipline over the individual. In his discussion of the panopticon as an instrument of the disciplinary technology of power, Foucault stressed that it provides for perfect axial visibility while completely obstructing lateral visibility. That is to say, the panopticon's cells are arranged in such a way that their occupants are easily observed from the central tower but they cannot see each other at all. As a result, each inmate faces the representatives of power alone. Their inability to communicate with each other prevents any collusion among them that might constitute a threat to power. As Foucault explains,

> This invisibility is a guarantee of order. If the inmates are convicts, there is no danger of a plot, an attempt at collective escape, the planning of new crimes for the future, bad reciprocal influences; if they are patients, there is no danger of contagion; if they are madmen, there is no risk of their committing violence upon one another; if they are schoolchildren, there is no copying, no noise, no chatter, no waste of time; if they are workers, there are no disorders, no theft, no coalitions, none of those distractions that slow down the rate of work, make it less perfect or cause accidents. The crowd, a compact mass, a locus of multiple exchanges, individualities merging together, a collective effect, is abolished and replaced by a collection of separated individualities.[45]

What was gained by the restriction of lateral visibility in the panopticon is achieved in the contemporary regime of authenticity testing by confidentiality. Although it is advertised as a protective measure for test takers, confidentiality completes the domination of test givers over test takers. It assures that each individual confronts the organizations that mandate testing utterly alone and therefore in the weakest possible state. Here disciplinary power has achieved the remarkable feat of perfecting the domination of people by dividing them and dealing with them singly, all the while convincing them that the arrangement is for their own good.

II

QUALIFYING TESTS

7

THE FOREST OF PENCILS

Examinations, sir, are pure humbug. . . .

If a man is a gentleman he knows quite enough,

and if he is not a gentleman,

whatever he knows is bad for him.

Lord Fermor, in Oscar Wilde's

The Picture of Dorian Gray

Qualifying tests measure aptitude and competency in a variety of abilities as part of the evaluation process for entering, continuing in, or being promoted in schools, occupations, the armed forces, and other organizations. They have a much wider range of application than authenticity tests because the latter are limited to those who are suspected of wrongdoing (sometimes, to be sure, a generalized or diffuse suspicion, as with preemployment drug or integrity tests), whereas modern, industrialized society, with its elaborate division of labor and highly specialized skills and knowledge, has generated an extensive regime of qualifying testing that touches virtually everyone. While people would prefer to avoid authenticity tests whenever possible, they willingly submit themselves to qualifying tests because these unlock the gates to rewards and success in life.

This is not to suggest that everybody likes taking qualifying tests. Some do, but many others are terrified of them. Those who consistently have done poorly on tests cringe at the prospect of yet another demonstration of their inadequacy and limited prospects in life, unless repeated failures in tests and other personal evaluations have put them beyond caring. Others, who have previously done well, shudder at the prospect that this time they may fail—that this test might unmask all the previous ones as mistakes and reveal their true ability to be average or only slightly above. And, of course, there are the few who have always done well on tests and are confident that they always will. They take tests gladly as little pleasures in themselves, reinforcements of their self-image as gifted individuals who gain "A" grades as a matter of course and score above the 95th percentile across the board.

Regardless of people's feelings about them, qualifying tests are a key factor for living successfully in contemporary society. Those who reject the message of personal insufficiency reiterated by poor test performance may turn off on tests, but then the system turns off on them. They are excluded from educational opportunities and good jobs and (just as the tests predicted!) they never are able to accomplish much. The rest continue to take tests, whether they do it happily or under stress, and that has a great deal to do with the niche they find in life. Qualifying tests constitute one of the central conditions of contemporary society. Here I trace how it came to be that way.

The Chinese Civil Service Examination

The distinction of producing the world's first system of qualifying testing unquestionably belongs to imperial China, which predated the West in this area by a thousand years or more. As early as the Chou dynasty (ca. 1122–256 B.C.) some form of tests existed for identifying the talented among the common people, and during the T'ang dynasty (A.D. 618–907) these were developed into a formal system of examinations.[1] But it was from around A.D. 1000, when imperial power rose to near absolutism in the Sung dynasty (960–1279), that the civil service examination was opened to nearly everyone and became the most important avenue to position, power, and prestige in China.[2] The system took its final form during the Ming dynasty (1368–1662) and remained in force until the first decade of the twentieth century.[3] It attracted Western attention as early as the sixteenth century, and the British civil service examinations both in India and at home were influenced by the Chinese examination system.[4]

In a history radically different from the West, the power of hereditary aristocracy in China was largely finished by the time of the Sung dynasty. Thenceforth, the class holding power, wealth, and prestige was composed mainly of administrators and bureaucrats in the emperor's civil service. Membership in this class depended more on passing the civil service examination than on parentage. Persons from certain occupations (and their immediate descendants) were excluded from the examinations: "watchmen, executioners, yamen torturers, labourers, detectives, jailors, coroners, play actors, slaves, beggars, boatpeople, scavengers, musicians and a few others."[5] Still, the great majority of the population was eligible, and the examinations effectively prevented the formation of a hereditary ruling class. For example, the lists of those who passed the highest-level examinations in 1148 and 1256 show that only 40 percent were sons, grandsons, or great-grandsons of civil servants, while the rest came from families with no history in the bureaucracy.[6] Thus, for nearly a thousand years, beneath the overall control of an emperor, China was governed by a meritocratic elite.

It was an elite with distinct privileges. Those who passed the examinations given in the prefectural capitals were designated *sheng-yuan*, or government students. This entitled them to wear a distinctive dress and to courteous treatment from government officials. They were exempted from government labor service and, should they run afoul of the law, from the demeaning punishment of lashing. These perquisites were not perennial, however. Sheng-yuan had to pass the examination each time it was given (every three years) to retain their status.[7] Those who went on to pass higher-level examinations became government officials and enjoyed great privilege, power, and wealth.

Because they constituted the gateways to exalted position, people reputedly spared no exertion to achieve success in examinations. According to C. T. Hu,[8] families with high aspirations for their sons would even commence their education before birth by "requiring expectant mothers to be exposed to books and cultural objects" (a waste of time in this male-dominated system, it would seem, if the baby turned out to be a girl). Aspiring scholars brooked no distractions in their quest for knowledge. When he was young and poor, one famous eighteenth-century poet, scholar, and official "confined himself and two younger brothers in a second floor room without stairs for more than a year at a time, in order not to interrupt their studies."[9] Another is said to have carried his reading into the night by the light of fireflies he kept in a gauze bag. (Some of these stories, however, may have become embellished with retelling. Dubious about the efficacy of fireflies, for example, the K'ang Hsi emperor had his retainers collect hundreds of them and found that he could not read a single character by their light.)[10]

The prefectural examinations were the beginning of a multi-stage process. The number who passed varied with the region, historical period, and needs of the bureaucracy, but the range seems to have been from 1 to 10 percent. Those who passed the prefectural examination were eligible for a further preparatory examination that, if they passed (about half did), qualified them for an examination held every three years in the provincial capital. Successful candidates at the provincial level (again, 1 to 10%) were admitted to the metropolitan examination, also held each three years, in the national capital. Those who passed this examination were summoned to the palace for a final examination conducted by the emperor himself, on the basis of which their final rank on the list of successful candidates was determined. Those who passed all of these examinations were appointed to administrative posts or to the prestigious Hanlin Academy. (Its name translatable as "The Forest of Pencils," or "Brushes," scholars of the Hanlin Academy compiled books and drafted decrees for the emperor.) Lower-level official appointments were often also given to many who qualified for the metropolitan examination but did not pass it.[11]

Masses of candidates would present themselves for examinations—up to 10,000 for prefectural examinations and 20,000 for the provincial examinations in, for example, the southern provincial capital of Chiang-ning-fu. Examinees were crowded into huge, walled compounds that contained thousands of tiny cells. Huddled in his cubicle for three days and two nights, under the scrutiny of guards who prowled the lanes and watched from towers, the candidate would write commentaries on the Confucian classics, compose poetry, and write essays on subjects pertaining to history, politics, and current affairs.[12] No one could enter or leave the compound during an examination, a rule so strictly enforced as to cause certain inconveniences on occasion:

> If a candidate died in the middle of an examination, the officials were presented with an annoying problem. The latch bar on the Great Gate was tightly closed and sealed, and since it was absolutely never opened ahead of the schedule, the beleaguered administrators had no alternative but to wrap the body in straw matting and throw it over the wall.[13]

Numerous stories circulated of candidates going insane during the examination, or being visited by ghosts who would confuse and attack them in retaliation for evildoing, or assist them as a reward for some previous act of kindness.[14] Accounts of miraculous events in examinations dramatized the Buddhist principle of preserving all living things: an examiner finally passed a paper he had twice rejected when, each time he discarded it, three rats brought it back to his desk. It was later ascertained that the candidate's family had not kept cats for three generations. Another candidate received the highest pass after an ant whose life he had saved posed as a missing dot in one of the characters in his essay—a flaw that would have been sufficient for disqualification.[15]

Elaborate measures were taken to safeguard fairness and honesty in the examinations. Candidates were thoroughly scrutinized and searched on entering the examination compound and forbidden to leave while the test was in progress. These precautions were intended to prevent impostors from taking the test in someone's place, smuggling cribs into the examination, or consulting outside materials after the questions were known. Precautions also guarded against collusion or bias by graders. They were cloistered in the compound until all the tests had been evaluated.

Each paper was identified only by number and reproduced by professional copyists to prevent identification of the author by name or distinctive calligraphy. Each one was read independently by two evaluators, their sealed grades being opened and, if necessary, reconciled by a third.[16]

Ingenious strategies were devised to defeat the safeguards and to enlist dishonest means to enhance one's chances of passing the test. Impostors did succeed in taking the examination for their friends or clients, and some clerks and officials were not above accepting bribes. Bookstores did brisk business in tiny printed books of the classics, with characters no larger than a fly's head, that were designed to be smuggled into the examinations.[17] One form of collusion was for a candidate to arrange beforehand with a bribed or friendly grader that a certain character would appear in a specified space and line on the examination paper. This technique enabled the grader to identify his protégé's paper despite precautions of copying papers and identifying them only by number.[18] Such tactics enabled numerous unqualified candidates to pass unscathed through the "thorny gates of learning" that constituted the examination system, such as eight who passed the metropolitan examination in 1156 although they were virtually illiterate.[19]

One reason that crib books and answers smuggled into the examinations could be used with good effect is that the tests placed minimal stress on creativity. By the Ming dynasty, official dogma on the Confucian classics was fixed and allowed no room for individual interpretation. Topics were severely limited, and essays were constrained to such a rigid form that they became "no more than stylistic frippery and literary gyrations."[20] The whole system atrophied. As Miyazaki points out, "Since officials were content as long as there were no serious errors and their fairness was not challenged, and since candidates feared that they would fail if they wrote something too different from the run-of-the-mill sorts of answers, both groups stifled any tendencies toward originality."[21]

As early as the eleventh century (Sung dynasty), the problems attendant on this orientation of the system were recognized. Critics observed that the examination system awarded administrative posts to those who demonstrated an ability to write poetry and to memorize classical texts. They questioned the relevance of these academic skills to the good character and ability to govern that ought to be requisite for civil servants.[22] The weakness of China's bureaucratic system became painfully apparent as China was increasingly exposed to foreign ideas and powers. As Otto Franke wrote in 1905, "Instead of wise and morally outstanding representatives of government authority the system supplied incompetent officials ignorant of the ways of the world; instead of an intellectual aristocracy [it supplied] a class of arrogant and narrow-minded literati."[23] Humiliated by the Boxer Rebellion and the foreign intervention it brought in 1900, the government of the Ch'ing dynasty determined that China must modernize. A new educational system was announced for the entire country in 1901, and the traditional examination system proved to be incompatible with this innovation. The final metropolitan examination was held in 1904, and the system was formally abolished by edict of the empress dowager on September 2, 1905.[24]

When compared with the history of Western institutions, the period of time over which the Chinese civil service examination system functioned is almost unbelievable. Despite its many critics and flaws, it underwent very little change for 500 years prior to its abolition, and it served for nearly 1,000 years as the major device for recruiting civil servants for China's powerful bureaucracy. Given this amazing persistence, together with the central role it played in imperial Chinese society, the Chinese civil service examination must certainly be credited as the most successful system of testing the world has ever known.

Qualifying Tests and the Development of Written Examinations in the West

In the Western world, the earliest qualifying tests were demonstrations of the mastery of skills. Medieval craft guilds regulated advancement to the status of master craftsman through juries that would judge masterpieces submitted by candidates as evidence of their workmanship. It was similar in the medieval and Renaissance universities, where candidates would prove their mastery of a body of knowledge by means of oral examinations, called disputations. Often these took the form of the candidate expounding on an assigned text and then defending his position against the questions and critique of faculty examiners. Compurgators (character witnesses) had their place in universities as well as in medieval law courts (see chap. 2). At Oxford, candidates had to swear that they had read certain books, and nine regent masters were required to testify to their "knowledge" of the candidate's sufficiency and an additional five to their "belief" in his sufficiency.[25]

The first written examination in Europe apparently took place at Trinity College, Cambridge, in 1702.[26] It was a test in mathematics. This seems appropriate, for while theology, morality, or metaphysics lend themselves well to examination by oral disputation, the problem-solving abilities essential to mathematics and the natural sciences are more readily demonstrated in written form. Oxford, which stressed mathematics and the sciences less than Cambridge, was somewhat slower to change. Written examinations were introduced there in 1800,[27] and by 1830, both universities were abandoning oral disputations in favor of written tests.

The earliest record of university examinations in North America is a 1646 requirement that, in oral disputation, the Harvard University degree recipient "prove he could read the Old and New Testament in Latin and 'Resolve them Logically.'"[28] Examinations were not common in colonial times, and in 1762, students at Yale University refused to submit to them other than at the time of graduation.[29] During the first half of the nineteenth century, however, examinations grew both in importance and frequency. Yale's President Woolsey instituted biennial examinations at the close of the second and fourth years of instruction. Following developments at Cambridge and Oxford, they were in written form. For its part, Harvard's first written examination, in mathematics, was given in 1833. Considerable emphasis was laid on examinations at Mount Holyoke, where, in the 1830s, the idea was current that progress through the seminary should be measured not according to the amount of time a student has spent there but according to performance on examinations. The trend continued as the century wore on. Harvard introduced written entrance examinations in 1851, and Yale moved from biennial to annual examinations in 1865.[30]

The frequency and format of examinations in American universities was also greatly affected by important curricular developments during the nineteenth century. The pattern of a uniform, classical curriculum that all students were expected to master lent itself to periodic examinations (annual, biennial, or only at the time of graduation), identical for all students of a given level, and designed, administered, and graded by persons who were not necessarily the students' tutors. Some dissatisfaction with the classical curriculum had been expressed, but the Yale Report of 1828 defended it on the grounds that it developed the mental discipline necessary for the educated person in any walk of life and that any practical or professional training was inappropriate for a college. Although delayed by the Yale Report, elective systems in which students could select among several prescribed curricula, or could design their personalized educational program from a variety of subjects, were introduced at various points in the nineteenth century by the University of Virginia, Brown University, the University of Michigan, Harvard University, Cornell University, and Johns Hopkins University. Early on, these met with varying degrees of success, but they set the trend that after 1900 became established as the rule in American higher education.[31] This development had a significant impact on modes of assessment. Standard examinations based on a common curriculum are obviously inappropriate for students following different programs of study. Much better suited to the elective system is the now-familiar pattern of separate examinations in each course, devised and graded by the instructor.

Soon after their introduction in the colleges, written examinations diffused to the public schools. Boston's elementary and secondary schools had long followed the practice of annual oral examinations conducted by committees of visiting examiners. By the mid-nineteenth century, however, it was becoming impossible for these panels effectively to examine the large number of students involved, particularly in the more populous elementary schools. In 1845, faced with the daunting prospect of examining over 7,000 children in nineteen schools, Boston introduced a written examination. It was probably the first large-scale written test to be used in American public schools. Its goals were well conceptualized:

> It was our wish to have as fair an examination as possible; to give the same advantages to all; to prevent leading questions; to carry away, not loose notes, or vague remembrances of the examination, but positive information, in black and white; to ascertain with certainty what the scholars did not know, as well as what they did know.[32]

There were a few practical wrinkles at the beginning. The same test was given in all schools, and although it was printed, it did not occur to the committee to have it administered in all schools simultaneously. Instead they gave it in the schools one at a time, rushing as quickly as possible from one school to the next in an effort to prevent knowledge of the questions reaching some schools before the test did.[33] Such flaws were soon smoothed out, however, and by the middle of the next decade, written examinations had been adopted by public school systems in nearly all the major cities in the country.[34]

Competitive, written examinations came to exert massive influence, constituting "possibly the single most intrusive and expensive innovation in Western education in the last century."[35] From their origins in the schools, written examinations began in the nineteenth century to proliferate widely throughout the rest of society. A spirit of reform was in the air in Britain as means were sought to improve social policy in ways consistent with the demands of an industrial society and global empire. Beginning around 1850, examinations were settled on as the means to curtail the old patronage system and rationalize personnel selection and appointments in a variety of contexts. The resulting impact of examinations in British life was immense. E. E. Kellett, in his 1936 autobiography, recalls that in his youth, examinations had been "almost the be-all and end-all of school life. . . . If, in fact, I were asked what, in my opinion, was an essential article of the Victorian faith, I should say it was 'I believe in Examinations.'"[36]

The India Act of 1853 introduced competitive examinations for the Indian Civil Service (the first examinations were held in 1855), and new examinations for army commissions followed in 1857–58.[37] By 1870, most positions in the civil service were subject to competitive examination.[38] Examinations also influenced the lives of the lower classes. The Department of Science and Art, a government agency, was founded in 1853 to stimulate British industry by assisting the technical training of artisans. The department operated largely through examinations, inaugurating a test for teachers in 1859 and one for students in 1860. Reluctant to expend its funds on anything other than concrete results, the department established a scheme whereby it paid teachers one pound for each student who achieved a third-class pass, two pounds for a second-class pass, and three pounds for a first-class pass on its examinations.[39]

The flow of written tests from the universities into other sectors of society occurred on a smaller scale in the nineteenth-century United States than in Great Britain. Testing in America, as we will see, flowered in the twentieth century, by which time the technology of testing had undergone significant changes. However, some testing was introduced into the federal bureaucracy during the nineteenth century. It was largely a political matter. The spoils system had become so entrenched that, in the 1860s, the election of a new president brought about a complete change in government employees. The result, of course, was a poorly trained and inefficient civil service. The assassination of President Garfield by a disgruntled office seeker served as the catalyst for the passage of the first step toward reform: the Civil Service Act of 1883. It was a small beginning, bringing just 10 percent of government employees under a system wherein jobs were awarded on the basis of examinations and protected against changes in political administrations. Nevertheless, by 1908, the civil service system had been expanded to cover some 60 percent of the federal work force.[40]

The United States, of course, was founded partly to escape the class privileges of Europe, and the radical democratic spirit that prevailed here fostered a distrust of elites of any sort. This produced an attitude toward civil service examinations very different from that which prevailed in Britain. Government jobs in an egalitarian society, it was held, should be such that anyone would be able to fill them. For this reason, early American civil service examinations were quite simple and stressed practical, job-related skills.[41]

Oral versus Written Examinations

Almost as soon as they were introduced, written examinations became the subject of lively controversy. Their supporters stressed virtues integral to the spirit of positivism, such as precision and efficiency. Written examinations were extolled as superior to oral examinations in objectivity, quantification, impartiality, and economy for administration to large numbers of students.[42] Reflecting on Boston's introduction of written examinations in 1845, Horace Mann claimed for them seven major advantages over the oral format: (1) the same questions being given to students from all schools, it is possible to evaluate the students and their schools impartially (and, indeed, the Boston examiners were at least as interested in using the examination results to measure how well the various schools were fulfilling their mission as they were in assessing individual students—a common use of examinations that persists today); (2) written tests are fairer to students, who have a full hour to arrange their ideas rather than being forced, when a whole class is being examined orally, to display what they know in at most two minutes of questioning; (3) for the same reason, written examinations enable students to express their learning more thoroughly in response to a wider range of questions; (4) teachers are unable to interrupt or offer suggestions to examinees; (5) there is no possibility of favoritism; (6) the development of ideas and connecting of facts invited in more extensive written answers makes it easier to evaluate how competently the children have been taught than is possible with brief, factual oral responses; and (7) "a transcript, a sort of Daguerreotype likeness, as it were, of the state and condition of the pupils' minds is taken and carried away, for general inspection," and this almost photographic image, permanent because written, enables the establishment of objective standards for the accurate comparison of examinees and their schools.[43] Proponents of written tests in England also claimed a wider social advantage of written university entrance examinations to be that they tended to open higher education, formerly the preserve of the aristocracy, to the middle classes.[44]

An important issue in the debate over the relative value of oral and written examinations was the sort of learning they encouraged and, therefore, the sort of minds they tended to produce. Mann's second, third, and sixth arguments (above) supporting written examinations were framed in the context of the Boston public schools where, previously, large numbers of schoolchildren had been examined orally by a visiting committee in a short time. When, however, written examinations were compared with the traditional university oral disputations, in which a single candidate might be questioned by a group of examiners for an hour or more, the opportunities for open-ended development of ideas were obviously greater with the oral format. This was not necessarily a plus for oral examination in the eyes of all interested parties, however. Especially in the late eighteenth and early nineteenth centuries, the very tendency of written examinations to encourage the regurgitation of received wisdom was applauded by some (in language curiously reminiscent of some contemporary critiques of postmodernism) as

> a means of diminishing controversy on subjects potentially injurious to good discipline. This had particularly important implications during the revolutionary years of the late 18th century. An Oxford don rejected the intrusion of French ideas as "that reptile philosophy which would materialise and brutalise the whole intellectual system." The solution was the written examination, with "approved" answers. Writing in 1810, Henry Drummond insisted that it was important to teach "those old and established principles that are beyond the reach of controversy," and Edward Copleston concluded simply that "the scheme of Revelation we think is closed, and we expect no new light on earth to break in upon us." And writing in the late 1870's, Henry Latham recalled that questions about ethics, important in the early 19th century, disappeared as

a Tripos [written examinations at Cambridge] subject because they left too much room for variety of opinion.[45]

Nevertheless, by the 1870s in Britain and the 1880s in the United States, critics had developed a deep suspicion of written tests and used precisely the same arguments as Mann had advanced but in favor of oral examinations. The emphasis in written tests on factual knowledge and questions with preestablished answers tended to stifle imagination and creative thought.[46] They constituted "a system of straitjackets," forcing students with diverse interests and abilities to attempt to satisfy a uniform, stultifying set of expectations and evaluations.[47]

The methodologies connected with written tests were also criticized. Their apparent objectivity is a chimera, it was argued, because graders diverge widely in the marks they give.[48] Grades expressed numerically (e.g., on a scale of 100) are downright misleading, for "in the ultimate analysis he [the grader] is . . . marking by impression and later clothing his impression with a similitude of numerical accuracy."[49] (How the use of oral examinations would solve these problems is not clear.)

Questions were also raised about the possible implications of written examinations for social discrimination, although the concern was apparently more to perpetuate inequalities than to end them. It was argued, for example, that "where both men and women were examined together . . . they [the examinations] caused 'social damage' by leveling the sexes."[50] According to the eleventh (1910) edition of the *Encyclopaedia Britannica,* "Exams have in England mechanically cast the education of women into the same mould as that of men, without reference to the different social functions of the two sexes (the remedy is obvious)."[51] Britons were also alive to the possible effect of written examinations on the class structure, particularly the dangers of opening military and civil service positions that had been traditionally filled by gentlemen to just anyone on the sole basis of an examination. In 1854, no less exalted a personage than Queen Victoria wrote to W. E. Gladstone, an advocate of civil service examinations and then chancellor of the Exchequer, expressing concern that persons who had passed the requisite examination might still lack the qualities of loyalty and character necessary for certain sensitive posts. In his reply, Gladstone expressed the conviviction that the diligence necessary to excel on an examination was simultaneously evidence of good character.[52] In any event, he had little doubt about the capacity of the aristocracy to maintain itself in a system of competitive examinations. He wrote, in 1854,

> I do not hesitate to say that one of the great recommendations of the change (to open competition) in my eyes would be its tendency to strengthen and multiply the ties between the higher classes and the possession of administrative power. . . . I have a strong impression that the aristocracy of this country are even superior in natural gifts, on the average, to the mass; but it is plain that with their acquired advantages their *insensible* education, irrespective of book-learning, they have an immense superiority. This applies in its degree to all those who may be called gentlemen by birth and training.[53]

Nevertheless, even with the extension of qualification by examination to nearly the entire British civil service in 1870, certain posts were exempted. For example, "only a young man whose antecedents and character were thoroughly known could be regarded as 'a fit and proper person to be entrusted with the affairs, often delicate and confidential, of the British Foreign Office.'"[54]

Finally, critics charged that as written examinations became increasingly frequent in the educational system, they tended to focus students' attention on preparation for tests rather than on the subject matter in its own right. Students are then motivated to work for good examination grades rather than for the intrinsic rewards of learning.[55] Examinations also subject teachers to similar pressures. Insofar as teachers and schools are evaluated on the basis of their students' examination results (this was the case, as mentioned above, in the Boston public school system), instructors and school administrators may well attempt to influence the process in their favor by "teaching to the test." Again, the ultimate goal shifts from acquiring knowledge and skills and nurturing the love of learning to successful performance in examinations. Doubtless, an early incentive to teach to the test was provided by the British Department of Science and Art when it adopted the practice of paying teachers for each student who passed its examinations.

Phrenology

The written examinations discussed thus far were largely of an essay format. Although essay examinations were touted as more exact than oral tests, their results were still insufficiently quantifiable or comparable across large numbers of subjects for the examinations to be widely accepted as truly scientific instruments of measurement. Moreover, as with the oral disputations that preceded them, the written examinations that became popular during the nineteenth century were achievement tests. Their gaze was directed to the past, in the sense that they were designed and used to certify that the subject had, at some time prior to the test, mastered a certain body of knowledge or skill. How much more efficient it would be if tests could predict the future, if they could tell in advance whether subjects possessed the aptitude or talent to learn certain skills or perform satisfactorily in some job. Then people could be directed toward goals that they had a high probability of achieving, and palpable benefits would result both for individual fulfillment and the efficiency of society's utilization of its human resources. These dual objectives—to make tests more scientific and to make them future oriented—constitute the positivist program for the development of qualifying tests.

During the nineteenth century, a form of testing that claimed to satisfy both of these objectives with elegant simplicity was enthusiastically put forward under the name of phrenology. It turned out to be both false and pseudoscientific. Nevertheless, phrenology enjoyed a great deal of popularity for a time, and its claim to apply scientific methods to the problem of how to predict future performance on the basis of present information makes it an important and interesting chapter in the history of positivist testing.

The basic principles of phrenology were postulated by Franz Joseph Gall in Vienna at the beginning of the nineteenth century. His starting point was the faculty theory of mind, the notion that the mind is made up of a series of discrete capacities or faculties. Gall identified thirty-seven of them, of which fourteen are "intellective" (including order, language, and time) and twenty-three are "affective" (destructiveness, acquisitiveness, "amativeness" or capacity for love, etc.). He claimed further that a close correlation exists between the various faculties of the mind and the surface of the brain, such that a well-developed mental faculty would be marked by a bulge at the point on the surface of the brain where that faculty is located, while a depression in the brain's surface indicates that the faculty at that cerebral address is underdeveloped. Finally, Gall assumed that the skull fits the brain like a glove, such that the contours of the exterior of the head constitute a faithful map of the shape of the brain within.

None of these propositions is true. Nonetheless, for those who can be convinced of it, the system offers a wonderfully objective and precise means of learning the specific mental qualities of any individual, living or dead. A cranial chart was developed to identify the precise location on the skull corresponding to each mental faculty. Then all that is necessary is to carefully examine the bumps and depressions on an individual's skull and compare them with the standard chart to determine the degree of development of each of the mental faculties.[56] It would be difficult to find a better example of a test, as that term has been defined in this book. The phrenological examination is an outstanding case of intentionally seeking knowledge about someone by collecting information about one thing (the shape of the skull) that is taken to represent another thing (the individual's mind or behavioral propensities).

Phrenology was introduced to the United States in 1832 by Gall's onetime collaborator, Johann Casper Spurzheim. A great popularizer of the technique, Spurzheim's phrenological lectures and demonstrations were an immediate sensation in this country—although his time to give them was limited because, as it happened, he died just six weeks after his arrival. This reverse notwithstanding, phrenology caught the American popular imagination as practitioners, brandishing their motto "Know thyself," promoted themselves as vocational counselors and aids to all who would know better their own nature, the precise combination of their mental faculties. Betrothed couples were urged to consult a phrenologist to ascertain their compatibility. In an early form of preemployment testing, some businesses even began to require phrenological examinations of their applicants. As the profession grew, a number of improvements in the technique for taking phrenological measurements were achieved. Noteworthy among them was the Lavery Electric Phrenometer, a device developed in 1907 and advertised as capable of measuring head bumps "electrically and with scientific precision."[57]

The leading American advocates of phrenology were the brothers Orson and Lorenzo Fowler and their brother-in-law, Samuel Wells. Orson Fowler was unequivocal about the one-to-one mind-brain linkages on which phrenology rested. "The brain," he pronounced, "is composed of as many distinct organs as the mind is of faculties."[58] He expanded somewhat on Gall's analysis of the mental faculties, identifying forty-three in all and classifying them in nine categories: (1) animal propensities, (2) social, (3) aspiring sentiments, (4) moral sentiments, (5) the perfecting group, (6) senses, (7) perceptives, (8) literacy, and (9) reflective faculties. He further organized these into two great classes, the first five being grouped together as feelings and the last four as intellectual faculties. The organs corresponding to the feelings are located in the part of the head covered by hair, while the intellectual organs are found in the forehead.[59]

Fowler claimed to have proved the effect of these faculties 10,000 times by demonstrations on "patients already under magnetized [hypnotic] influence" whose phrenological organs were excited to exaggerated responses when touched with the finger.[60] "Examples: he [the author] never touched Devotion but the patient clasped hands, and manifested the most devout adoration of God in tone, natural language, words, and every other indication of worship. He never touched Kindness but the subject gave away all he could get to give."[61] Proofs provided by Spurzheim during his brief introduction of phrenology to Americans in 1832 were equally convincing: as he would pass a magnet from a subject's area of veneration to that of acquisitiveness, the person would immediately abandon a "worshipful air" and attempt to pick the phrenologist's pocket.[62]

The mental faculties were not to be toyed with by nonprofessionals, however, for abuse could permanently dull their acuity. Such is the sad fate of those who abandon themselves wantonly to the pleasures of sex. Orson Fowler gravely reports that "instances by the hundreds have come under the Author's professional notice, in which a few moments of passioned ecstasy have stricken down the sensory nerves; both killing itself forever after, and along with it their power to enjoy all *other* pleasures of life" (his emphasis).[63]

Typical head shapes vary among groups of mankind, and so, therefore, do their phrenological endowments. Generic portraits of a variety of races (and a few animals, such as the gorilla, thrown in for comparative purposes) are found in Fowler's book, with explanations of their mental capacities.[64] American Indian heads, sad to say, manifest much destructiveness, caution, and quite little in the way of intellectual faculties. Hence, Indians are "little susceptible of becoming civilized, humanized, and educated."[65] What goes for the races also goes for the sexes, and Fowler's comparison finds male heads to be colder, braver, and more reflective, while the female crania show more parental love, religion, and morality.[66] In collusion with his brother Lorenzo, Fowler found that "in females, this faculty [acquisitiveness] is generally weaker than in males, while ideal. [ideality] and approbat. [approbative] are generally much larger, which accounts for the fact, that they spend money so much more freely than men, especially, for ornamental purposes."[67]

In addition to its utility for counseling and self-knowledge, phrenology may be used to improve our understanding of the prominent men of history. "Great men have great brains," wrote Fowler,[68] and that normally means they have big heads. Throughout his book are drawings of the heads of various famous men— Napoleon, Cuvier, Reubens—together with textual explanations of how their peculiar cranial characteristics (pronounced in the drawings) account for their particular accomplishments. At the end of the book, Orson Fowler includes a picture of his own head, with the comment that "the desire to do good is its largest organ."[69] That desire appears to have known no limits, for in this massive tome, Fowler moves beyond the benefits available from phrenology to include a logical argument for the existence of God,[70] a demonstration that we will all be distinct and recognizable individuals in the afterlife, just as we are here,[71] useful advice on how to grind flour properly,[72] and finally, in the closing chapter, "Phrenology Applied," a detailed set of instructions for "How to Make Good Rain Water Cisterns Cheap."[73]

Despite its popular appeal, phrenology was always recognized as a pseudoscience by scholars.[74] The problem, of course, is that phrenology's core assumptions about detailed correlations between faculties of the mind and the brain, as well as between the shape of the brain and the shape of the exterior of the head, are simply false. Ill-founded as it was, however, the *strategy* of phrenology accurately foreshadows the positivist developments in testing that were to come in the twentieth century. Elements of this strategy include the assumption that human faculties can be measured by the techniques of science and that central among those faculties is *aptitude*. This term applies not to what persons have achieved but to what they are likely to achieve, are capable of achieving. The phenomena measured, the means of measuring them, and the rationale behind the measurements have changed, and today the process rests on more secure footing. Nevertheless, in its fundamental spirit of positivism, the development of testing during the twentieth century remains at one with the false start that was phrenology.

The Birth of Scientific Testing

Modern positivist qualifying testing—the program of using scientific methods to measure the differing capacities of individuals with verifiable results—began as an outgrowth of the work of Charles Darwin. Theorists such as Hobbes, Locke, Rousseau, Hegel, and Marx were of the opinion that normal human beings are fundamentally equal, with what individual differences there were in strength or quickness of wit being of minor significance. This view was countered by Darwin's thesis in *Origin of the Species* (1859) that individual differences constituted the raw material on which natural selection works. He reasoned that traits that enable their possessors to survive longer and reproduce more will become more prevalent in the population (while traits conducive to early death and/or diminished reproduction will tend to disappear), and in that way the species evolves. Therefore, Darwin himself and like-minded thinkers formed the opinion that individual differences are of fundamental importance to the present and future state of the human species. This view evolved into the conviction that an applied psychology devoted to the scientific measurement and enlightened cultivation of individual differences could contribute to the progress of civilization as effectively as had engineering.[75] In a nutshell, this captures the vision that has guided positivist qualifying testing ever since.

Francis Galton, Darwin's cousin, was among the first to recognize that if individual differences are fundamental to our understanding of human evolution, they should be identified systematically and studied with scientific precision. To that end, Galton established the Anthropometric Laboratory in connection with the International Health Exhibition held in London in 1884. Adopting the admirable technique of having research subjects contribute to the expense of the project, visitors to the exhibition were measured in a variety of ways for a fee of four pence. Laboratory personnel entered the data in a register and informed subjects of the results, thus enabling them "to obtain timely warning of remediable faults in development, or to learn of their powers."[76] The laboratory continued its work for six years after the Exhibition closed, and in all, over 9,000 individuals were measured according to variables such as keenness of sight, strength, ability to discriminate weights, swiftness of reactions, memory of forms, and ability to discriminate colors. In addition to his pioneering work in human measurements, one of Galton's greatest contributions was to devise the notion of the standard deviation and the statistical concept of correlation, which he found to be useful for the analysis of the large amounts of data his measurements produced.[77]

One of Galton's assistants in the Anthropometric Laboratory was a young American psychologist named James McKeen Cattell. When he became professor of psychology at the University of Pennsylvania (1888–1891) and later at Columbia University, he introduced Galton's style of testing in the United States. In an article published in the British journal *Mind* in 1890, Cattell proposed a test of ten measures, all of which could be readily administered in a laboratory and precisely measured. These were: (1) strongest possible squeeze with the hand; (2) quickest possible movement of the hand and arm; (3) minimum distance between two points of pressure at which they are felt as two; (4) amount of pressure at which it begins to be felt as pain; (5) least notable difference between two weights; (6) minimum reaction time to a sound; (7) minimum time between seeing and naming colors; (8) accuracy of finding the center of a 50-centimeter line; (9) accuracy of judging ten seconds of time; (10) number of random consonants that can be repeated after hearing them once.[78] Clearly Galton's and Cattell's tests were concerned more with physical properties than mental ones. But they believed that physical strength and acuity were indicative of like properties of the mind because, as Cattell put it with reference to the apparently purely physiological character of the strength of the squeeze of the hand, "it is, however, impossible to separate bodily from mental energy."[79] The underlying assumption seems to have been that perception is linked to cognition in such a way that finely developed capacities of sense discrimination (the ability to distinguish colors, weights, or sensations with precision) are signs of intellectual ability. The idea remains embedded in popular attitudes, as when intelligent people are often described as "clear eyed," and physically clumsy individuals are suspected of stupidity.

In his 1869 book, *Hereditary Genius*, Galton argued that human intelligence is largely a matter of inheritance and is distributed unequally among class and racial groupings. His measure was the rate at which different races produce individuals of genius. On this basis, he ranked the Anglo-Saxon inhabitants of his own Britain two grades above Negroes but two grades below the ancient Athenians, whom he took to be the most intelligent race in history.[80] These rankings imply huge racial differences. For example, Galton claimed that a level of intelligence high enough to appear in 1 in every 64 persons among Anglo-Saxons would occur in only 1 of every 4,300 Negroes but 1 in every 6 ancient Athenians.[81] So far as classes are concerned, Galton shared with many others of the day (see the quote from Oscar Wilde's Lord Fermor that serves as epigraph to this chapter) the idea that the aristocracy enjoyed innate superiority over the lower classes. Indeed, that explains why the class differences exist. The Darwinians, interested in the future course of human evolution and hopeful that it would proceed in a beneficial direction, entertained apprehensions about the high birthrate of the lower classes. Herbert Spencer, who blended his Darwinism with a thoroughgoing laissez-faire attitude that it was best to let nature take its course without interference, took comfort in the fact that the high death rate of the lower classes served to weed unfit traits out of the population.[82] Galton, who coined the term "eugenics" in 1883,[83] favored a somewhat more aggressive policy of countering the alarming birthrate of the lower classes by encouraging intelligent people to seek each other out as mates and so improve the mental power of the species.[84] Cattell apparently believed that the best place to start building hereditary lines of intelligence is at home. An already-formed aristocracy being less in evidence in the United States than in Europe, he decided to appeal to the American sense of a good business deal and promised to give $1,000 to any of his children who married the son or daughter of a professor.[85]

Not all earlier thinkers held identical views about the transmission of intelligence. A refreshing alternative was developed by the sixteenth-century Spanish physician, Juan Huarte, whose 1575 book, *Examen de ingenios para las sciencias*, was translated into several languages and ultimately "Englished out of . . . [the] Italian" in 1594 as *Examination of Men's Wits*. Huarte thought that quick and dull wits are indeed a matter of heredity but not in the sense of genius begetting genius. Quite to the contrary, the relationship of intelligence between father and child is, in Huarte's view, inverse. Wise men often have slow children because they do not devote themselves vigorously to the task at hand while copulating, their minds being preoccupied with loftier subjects, and thus their seed is weakened. Duller men, in contrast, "apply themselves affectionately to the carnal act, and are not carried away to any other contemplation," and thus produce strong seed that results in brighter progeny.[86] I must recommend, however, the exercise of some caution in assessing Huarte's conclusions. He seems not to have been an overly exact observer (or else he was in thrall to preconceptions in spite of empirical evidence), for he also reports that the equal ratio of males to females, previously ensured by the fact that all human offspring were brother and sister twins, had been replaced in his own day by single births that produced six or seven females for every male.[87]

Intelligence Testing

Whether clever children are born of dull fathers or (the majority opinion) of clever ones, the question persists of how this differentially distributed intelligence so cherished by Galton, Cattell, and others could be tested. This is a very different proposition from the oral or written tests in education or the civil service. The challenge before intelligence testing is to measure not so much what the subject has already learned as how much the subject is likely to learn in the future, or, better, the subject's ability to learn. Phrenological measurements of the contours of people's heads would have been a marvelous way to ascertain such aptitudes and talents, but unfortunately it did not work. Galton's and Cattell's batteries of anthropomorphic measurements had the merit of precision, but precisely what they told about a person's intelligence was far from clear. A major step in the history of testing was taken when the first successful test of intelligence was developed by the French psychologist, Alfred Binet.

Binet was asked by the French education ministry to develop a test to identify children with learning deficiencies who should be given the benefit of special education. His desire was to measure intelligence apart from any instruction the child may have received. He first did this in 1905 by constructing several series of tasks of increasing difficulty, the test consisting of setting a child to these tasks and noting how far in each series the child was able to go. In 1908, Binet refined the test by deciding at what age a normal child should be able to complete each task successfully. The age level of the most difficult tasks that a child performed successfully was identified as the child's "mental age." Children with mental ages well behind their chronological ages were identified as apt subjects for special education. The relation between mental age and chronological age became IQ (intelligence quotient) when, in 1912, the German psychologist, William Stern, proposed that mental age be divided by chronological age and the result multiplied by 100 (to get rid of the decimal point). Thus, a child with a mental age of 8 and a chronological age of 6 has an IQ of 133, and a mental age of 5 and a chronological age of 7 yields an IQ of 71, while the most perfectly average persons have an IQ of 100 because their mental and chronological ages are identical.[88]

Binet's test was soon translated to America, where it rapidly attracted a great deal of interest. This was partly because its reporting of IQ in numerical form appealed to the positivistic assumptions of many American psychologists that intelligence testing would become truly scientific only when it yielded quantitative results. As educational psychologist E. L. Thorndike wrote,

> In proportion as it becomes definite and exact, this knowledge of educational products and educational purposes must become quantitative, take the form of measurements. Education is one form of human engineering and will profit by measurements of human nature and achievement as mechanical and electrical engineering have profited by using the foot- pound, calorie, volt, and ampere.[89]

Consistent with Binet's own purposes, his test was initially used in the United States to assist in the diagnosis of mental deficiencies.[90] In 1909, Henry H. Goddard, director of research at the Training School for Feeble-minded Girls and Boys in Vineland, New Jersey, applied the test to inmates of his institution and reported that its results squared very well with staff assessments of their mental level.[91] It was, however, Lewis M. Terman who contributed most to the popularity of Binet's test in this country. In 1916, Terman, a psychologist at Stanford University, revised and expanded the test and named it the Stanford-Binet. This has been the model for virtually all American IQ tests ever since.

In addition to its utility for identifying the feeble-minded, Terman was convinced that great social benefits could be reaped by testing the normal population as well. Enunciating the quint-essential positivist creed that the application of science can contribute to the successful and efficient conduct of the affairs of society, he held that intelligence testing would facilitate the placement of people in those educational programs and vocations for which their endowments best suit them.[92] Those with IQs of 75 and below should be channeled into the ranks of unskilled labor, while those of 75 to 85 were appropriate for semiskilled labor. An IQ of at least 100 was necessary for any prestigious and/or financially rewarding profession. Proper training and placement were especially important for those with IQs of 70 to 85. Otherwise, they were likely to fail in school, drop out, "and drift easily into the ranks of the anti-social or join the army of Bolshevik discontents."[93]

Terman's enthusiasm for the efficiency that could result from placement on the basis of predictions provided by intelligence testing was shared by E. L. Thorndike, another strong defender and designer of intelligence tests. He wrote with regard to education, "It is surely unwise to give instruction to students in disregard of their capacities to profit from it, if by enough ingenuity and experimentation, we can secure tests which measure their capacities beforehand."[94] Now at last one could glimpse a possible realization of Saint-Simon's and Comte's utopian visions of the benefits to be realized by applying science to society. It was imagined that testing and judicious placement on the basis of test results could bring about a situation where everybody wins. Society would profit by making optimal use of its human resources, while individual satisfaction would be maximized as everyone finds the niche in which they can contribute most fully and successfully.

The major remaining obstacle to the fulfillment of this positivist dream had to do with the technology of testing. Intelligence tests such as the Stanford-Binet are conducted one on one by trained technicians. Obviously, this technique is too expensive and time-consuming to be used to test the masses. The crucial technological development in test administration was achieved in the context of World War I, mainly through the efforts of Harvard psychologist Robert Yerkes. Sharing the notion with other positivists that mental measurement would become truly scientific only when it became quantitative and standardized against large bodies of data, he concocted a scheme whereby psychology could contribute to the war effort while the war effort contributed to the development of psychology. He proposed that all U.S. Army recruits be given intelligence tests. The results would assist the army in making the most effective use of its manpower, and, simultaneously, psychology would generate a huge body of uniform, quantitative data on which to build its investigations into the nature of intelligence.

The army accepted the proposal, and from May to July 1917, Yerkes, Terman, Goddard, and other major figures in psychology gathered at Goddard's Training School for Feeble-minded Girls and Boys to devise a way that a limited number of psychologists could test the intelligence of massive numbers of subjects in a relatively short time. The crucial technological breakthrough was the multiple-choice question. The first multiple-choice question was devised in 1915 by Frederick J. Kelly (later dean of the School of Education at the University of Kansas) in his Kansas Silent Reading Test for elementary schoolchildren. Arthur Otis, one of Terman's students, had been exploring the potential of Kelly's innovation as a device for testing, and Terman brought the results of that research with him to Vineland.[95] There Yerkes and his group succeeded in fashioning a multiple-choice test that correlated in outcome with one-on-one administrations of the Stanford-Binet. Their test was the Army Alpha, the first written, objective intelligence test and the ancestor of all subsequent tests of that type (often called "aptitude tests") so well known now to every American. A second test, the purely pictorial Army Beta, was devised for illiterate recruits and immigrants who did not know English.

Yerkes and his colleagues certainly got the massive body of data they desired, for in the brief period between the devising of the tests in 1917 and the war's end the following year, 1.75 million men took the Army Alpha or Beta. On the basis of the test results, the psychologists made recommendations such as which recruits were intelligent enough to qualify for officer training and which ones should be assigned to special labor duty or discharged outright on the grounds of mental incompetence. It is unclear to what extent the army actually acted on such recommendations. Nevertheless, some disturbing conclusions emerged from the army testing program. The average mental age of white Americans turned out to be 13 (barely above the level of morons). Test results revealed immigrants to be duller still (the average mental age of Russians being 11.34, Italians 11.01, and Poles 10.74), and Negroes came in last, with an average mental age of 10.41. These findings fueled debates about immigration quotas, segregation, eugenics, and miscegenation for years to come.

But the most lasting effect of the army testing program was that it revolutionized the perception and use of intelligence tests in American society. "The war changed the image of tests and of the tested. Intelligence tests were no longer things given by college professors and resident examiners like Henry H. Goddard to crazy people and imbeciles in psychopathic institutions and homes for the feeble-minded, but legitimate means of making decisions about the aptitudes and achievements of normal people."[96] With the development of written, standardized intelligence tests that could be easily administered to unlimited numbers of subjects, the dream of Terman and other American psychometricians was on its way to realization. Now it would be possible to determine everybody's intelligence and to use that information to channel people in directions where they presumably would both find personal satisfaction and make optimal contributions to society commensurate with their abilities.[97]

CEEB, ETS, and Standardized Testing in Education

The social sector where mass intelligence testing has made its greatest impact is education, particularly in the form of entrance examinations for colleges and universities. Although these tests are often called aptitude tests, the terminological distinction is of little substance. "Aptitude" is used primarily to avoid the political and social volatility of "intelligence," being less freighted with connotations of innate, immutable ability.[98]

The circumstances that eventually resulted in standardized college entrance examinations may be traced back to the immense burgeoning of American secondary education in the decades around the turn of the twentieth century. In 1870, about 80,000 students attended some 500 secondary schools, nearly all of them private. By 1910, the number of secondary school students had grown to 900,000, 90 percent of whom were in public high schools. Between 1890 and 1918, the general population of the United States grew by 68 percent, while the number of high school students over the same period increased by 711 percent.[99] This explosion of the secondary school population of course produced a like increase in higher education: the number of college students grew at a rate nearly five times greater than the general population between 1890 and 1924.[100] The old system of screening college applicants soon proved to be hopelessly inadequate in dealing with the changing circumstances.

To call the old arrangements a system is hardly appropriate, because no coordination existed among the admission procedures followed by the various colleges and universities. Many eastern schools administered written entrance examinations on their own campuses. Faculty committees from some midwestern universities would visit various high schools to evaluate them, and graduates of the schools certified by this process would then be admitted to the university. Other universities assessed applicants on the basis of the performance of previous graduates of their high schools who had attended the university.[101] In an effort to bring order to the chaos, in 1885, the principal of Phillips Andover Academy entered the plea that some organization and standardization be introduced into the preparatory curriculum for college entrance in American secondary schools. Beginning in 1892, the National Education Association formed committees to address this question. Not everyone shared the notion that college entrance requirements should be standardized. Lafayette College president Ethelbert D. Marfield did not look kindly on the prospect of being told by some board whom he should and should not admit. Raising an issue of perennial weight with academic administrators, he insisted that if he wanted to discriminate in favor of the son of a benefactor, he should be able to do so.[102]

Such dissenting voices notwithstanding, a widespread desire to bring some consistency to college entrance procedures and to open admissions to greater geographic and social diversity than was possible under the old system of requiring applicants to take entrance tests on each campus resulted in the formation of the College Entrance Examination Board (CEEB) in 1900. The CEEB was charged to design and administer standard entrance examinations that all member colleges would accept in making their admissions decisions.[103]

In the beginning, the CEEB was composed entirely of eastern colleges, thirty-five of which agreed to accept the board's tests in lieu of their own entrance examinations. The first CEEB examinations—essay tests in chemistry, English, French, German, Greek, history, Latin, mathematics, and physics—were offered during the week of June 17, 1901, at sixty-seven locations in the United States and two in Europe. Columbia University was the dominant influence on the board at its inception: the grading committee met to read the examinations at Columbia's library, and of the 973 persons who took those first examinations, 758 were seeking admission either to Columbia or its sister institution, Barnard College.[104]

The early College Board examinations were achievement tests, intended to measure how well an applicant had mastered Latin, mathematics, and the other specific subjects tested. Aptitude or intelligence testing, which is designed to ascertain an individual's general capacity to learn, was introduced to the college admissions process in 1918. Columbia University again took the lead, this time for dubious reasons pertaining to the changing demographic profile of its student body. Not only did the number of college students vastly increase in the decades around the turn of the twentieth century but immigrants and their children constituted an ever-larger proportion of them. About half of the students in New York City public schools were in this category by 1910. Those who went on to college had for the most part attended City College or New York University. A 1908 change in entrance requirements made Columbia University more accessible to public high school graduates, and during the next decade, the proportion of high school students of immigrant background jumped dramatically. Many of these were Eastern European Jews, whom "many of Columbia's faculty and administration considered . . . [to be] socially backward, clannish, and hostile to upper-middle-class values . . . and scorned as achieving far beyond their native intelligence."[105]

In 1918, Columbia was deluged with applicants of immigrant background for its new Student Army Training Corps class, an officer training program. Given the prevalent belief that immigrants were less intelligent than older American stock, intelligence tests appeared to offer one means of winnowing these unwelcome students without establishing formal quotas. Therefore, in the first use of an intelligence test for college admission, applicants to this program were required to take the Thorndike Tests for Mental Alertness. The following year, Columbia allowed applicants with otherwise acceptable credentials to substitute the Thorndike College Entrance Intelligence Examination for the usual, achievement-type, entrance examinations. This seems to have had the desired effect, for the proportion of out-of-state entrants (most of whom were presumably of suitable social status) increased significantly. The Thorndike test proved also to be a better predictor of first-year college performance than traditional entrance examinations or one's high school record.[106]

In 1919, the CEEB expressed interest in the more general use of intelligence tests for college admissions, but it was not until 1925 that a commission was established under the direction of Princeton psychologist Carl Campbell Brigham to develop one. Brigham had been closely connected with the army testing program during World War I, and the test his commission devised was objective (multiple-choice) in format and heavily influenced by the Army Alpha. One of its major purposes was to test intellectual ability without excessive reliance on any specific subject matter. This would promote the principle of equality of opportunity, in that discrimination against students from inferior secondary schools would be minimized. The new test was dubbed the Scholastic Aptitude Test (SAT). It proved to be remarkably durable, for as late as the 1970s, the SAT was still virtually the same test that Brigham's commission had developed.[107]

The first SAT was taken in 1926 by 8,040 college applicants, but for many years, it remained less popular than the CEEB's traditional essay examinations.[108] That changed in 1942, when war intervened once again in the history of testing in America. In that year Princeton, Harvard, and Yale shifted to a wartime year-round calendar of instruction, with applicants to be informed of admission in early May and freshmen beginning classes in June or early July. CEEB essay examinations were regularly given in June. Since 1937, however, the CEEB had offered a one-day battery of tests in April. These consisted of the SAT and a series of short achievement tests. They were used in scholarship decisions and, from about 1939, by candidates who wanted to learn the fate of their applications before the traditional date in July. The 1942 decision by Harvard, Yale, and Princeton to notify applicants in May directed greatly increased attention to the April tests, so much so that the CEEB decided to cancel the already-announced June essay tests. With that development, the era of essay tests for college admissions abruptly came to an end and the present CEEB arrangement of the SAT plus short achievement tests—all multiple choice in format and to be taken in a single day—was fully established. The enterprise assumed its current form in 1947, when the Educational Testing Service was established as a non-profit, nonstock corporation that took over most of the work of designing and administering tests from the CEEB.[109]

Testing and Learning

A theoretical issue that has remained at the heart of the testing enterprise since its inception has to do with the effect of tests on how and what people learn. By examining applicants on material that is not directly relevant to the positions to which they aspire, qualifying tests have been accused of selecting professionals or functionaries who are ill-suited for the jobs they are supposed to perform. Tests are also criticized for promoting the development of only part of the mind's capacity: encouraging, for example, memorizing disconnected facts and the ability to regurgitate received wisdom at the expense of critical and creative thinking. It is claimed that people—both test givers and test takers—become so engrossed in tests that they become ends in themselves rather than means to the larger end of acquiring knowledge and skill.

These criticisms are perennial. As we have seen, many of them were directed against the Chinese Civil Service Examination nearly a thousand years ago, and they were raised again by both sides in the nineteenth-century debate over the relative merits of oral and written examinations. In our own time, the contended ground has shifted to essay versus multiple-choice test formats, but the basic questions have remained the same.[110] As a result of this debate, the American College Testing Assessment (the ACT, a standardized college entrance examination taken by about one million high school seniors annually) was redesigned in 1989 to place less emphasis on factual material and more on scientific concepts and abstract reading skills. This is the first major revision of the ACT since its inception in 1959. Moreover, the SAT— the nation's other major standardized college entrance exam, taken by some 1.2 million high school seniors each year—will be revamped as of 1994. As with the ACT, changes in the SAT are designed to stress abstract thinking skills. The new SAT will include some math questions with open-ended answers rather than the traditional multiple-choice format and an optional essay question. Serious consideration was given to making the essay mandatory, but the proposal was not adopted because of its potential adverse impact on foreign-born candidates.[111]

A critic who framed the issues of the effect of testing on learning with uncommon clarity was the Reverend Mark Pattison, Rector of Lincoln College, Oxford, from 1861 to 1884. Pattison was an active supporter of the liberal reform movement, which during these years transformed Oxford from a university keyed to preindustrial British society to its modern form. One of the central elements of the reform was selection by merit, as merit was revealed by competitive examinations.[112] Examinations represented a dilemma for Pattison, and the weight of his allegiance shifted from one horn to the other during the course of his career. As a younger don in the 1840s and 1850s, Pattison was favorably impressed by examinations, most notably, their capacity to stimulate otherwise complacent students to harder work. So in 1855 he reckoned that the introduction of written examinations in 1800

> had been the root of the vast improvement in undergraduate study which occurred during the first half of the century; similarly, the opening of scholarships to unrestricted competition [by examination] had not only given "a most powerful impulse" to the schools, but, within the university, had "awakened dormant energies, and stirred the stagnant waters."[113]

Pattison had always recognized that examinations also had severe drawbacks, and by the 1860s and 1870s, the balance of his opinions was swinging against them. The essence of the matter is simple. Examinations are supposed to be a means to an end, that end being learning. But when prizes, scholarships, and prestige are allocated on the basis of performance in examinations, they become transformed from means to ends in themselves. This is destructive to disinterested learning—the greatest good that Pattison knew—because the imperative to excel in examinations dictates precisely what will be studied and prevents students from exploring those areas that have stimulated their curiosity but will not be covered by the tests. Pattison learned this last lesson only too well because, as an Oxford undergraduate himself, he followed his muse into a wider variety of subjects than was prescribed for the degree, with the result that his own performance on examinations was mediocre. Thus a man who became one of the most energetic and effective teachers and scholars in the Oxford of his epoch was for years burdened with a sense of inferiority before those who surpassed him in the examinations. One of the remedies he suggested for these ills was that provision be made for a large proportion of Oxford students to be non-degree-seeking individuals who would come to the university for the pure love of learning and would sit for no examinations at all.[114]

The drive to excel on tests, and thus to get good grades, continues to detract from learning today. Students' intellectual curiosity is eclipsed as they develop proficiency in calculating what material is likely to be covered on tests and studying that exclusively, with little effort to understand or appreciate the subject matter in its own right. Especially when the tests are objective in format, grades depend on students' ability to identify what they have been taught in the precise form that it was presented to them. There is little room or reason to assess material critically, creatively, or synthetically. The all-important measure of success in college is the grade point average.[115] An alarming number of students seem to think that getting good grades is important enough to justify any means to that end. Studies have indicated, for example, that 50 percent or more of college students attempt to improve their grades by cheating.[116]

Probably the most repugnant aspect of the competitive system of testing and grading is that it requires that some fail, if only to identify, by contrast, those who succeed. "Failure is structured into the American system of public education," writes William Bailey. "Losers are essential to the success of winners."[117] The effects of this are psychologically devastating. Donald Holt carried out an experiment in a college course in education by giving failing grades to all students for the first several tests. The reactions were disbelief, anxiety, anger, and, finally, outright rebellion. Although he probably earned the undying enmity of several of the students, at least a few of them eventually got the point of the experiment. "I learned a lesson I will never forget," wrote one, "how it feels to fail."[118]

The stress and threat to self-esteem posed by failure, or the prospect of it, stalk the educational system from start to finish. At the highest level, graduate students endure Ph.D. preliminary examinations that are "extraordinarily stressful and frequently humiliating." "Your whole adequacy depends on them," one student reported. Said another, "It's one of the greatest challenges I have ever been faced with. I will really feel left out if I don't make it. . . . It's the most important thing I've ever come up against. It's either attaining what I've been going for, or not getting there."[119] Failure is no less destructive to young children just entering the educational system who, if they struggle in the classroom, perceive the contrast in teacher attitudes and behavior toward themselves and other children and who lack the power to express their resentment in rebellion. Such children feel guilty and look on themselves as stupid.[120] Eventually their poor performance accumulates in a self-fulfilling prophecy as, over time and with the continued reinforcement of more low grades, the students turn off to education and their learning capacities are curtailed.[121] The impact of this on the future course of their lives—in terms of occupation, income, and social standing—is incalculable.

In concert with Pattison's proposal of nearly a century before, Howard Becker, Blanche Geer, and Everett Hughes suggested on the basis of a 1959–1961 study of university students that the student preoccupation with grades could be refocused on subject matters and the intrinsic rewards of learning if universities would abolish or drastically deemphasize the grading system.[122] Interestingly, about a decade later, a movement along those lines actually caught hold. The University of California at Santa Cruz and Washington's Evergreen State University set aside traditional letter grades in favor of written evaluations of each student's performance by the professor (together, in some cases, with the student's assessment of what he or she gained from the course). Although other universities did not go so far, a widely accepted aim to facilitate learning for its own sake led them to limit grading in many courses to a simple pass or fail, to relax requirements of all types, and to allow students wider latitude in designing their own curricula. But the results of the experiment were disappointing. With a few (far too few) notable exceptions, students lacked the motivation and maturity to enhance their educational experience under a regime of liberalized and minimized requirements. They learned less, not more. Innovations such as one- or two-week study periods between the end of classes and the beginning of final examinations, intended to allow students to explore more deeply the issues touched on in their courses that stimulated their intellectual curiosity, produced more beer parties and ski trips than hours in the library. Recognizing that things were not working out as planned, during the 1980s, American universities moved to restore the requirements that had been relaxed ten to fifteen years previously.

Possibly the experiment was doomed to failure because it took place in the universities. Students came to college after twelve years of primary and secondary education oriented toward grades, and, as Richard Curwin succinctly observed, "Grades motivate students not to learn, but to get good grades."[123] With this sort of background, they may simply not have had the requisite attitudes toward learning, nor have known how to go about it, when they were turned loose on the university campus with the admonition to study for the love of knowledge in its own right. Whatever the reason, after the experiment, we find ourselves very much where we were before it: still caught on the horns of Pattison's dilemma between the capacity of tests and the grading system to stimulate students to work, and their deadening impact on learning.

Further critique of the general practice of grading in the educational system, or of the teacher-devised classroom tests that are central determinants of course grades, is beyond the scope of this study. But standardized intelligence tests are also an important part of the competitive system of success and failure, and they are a matter of central interest here. One of the major items on the agenda of the remaining three chapters is to extend the investigation of when and how intelligence tests are used, the damage they do, and what might be done to control them.

8

WILLING, READY,

AND ABLE:

VOCATIONAL TESTING

A round man cannot be expected
to fit a square hole right away. He must have time
to modify his shape.

Mark Twain,

Following the Equator

The positivist dream of using scientific qualifying tests to identify people's potentials has also taken root in vocational placement. Here the aim is to achieve an optimal match between two sorts of differences: differences in what is required by various jobs in a specialized division of labor and differences in the talents, interests, and other characteristics of the candidates for those jobs. Here I trace how vocational psychology has grown from the desire to intervene in this matching process systematically, even scientifically, and how it has used testing to foster the most effective utilization of human talents and resources in the workplace.

The field may be divided into two orientations according to the primary objective of the intervention. One approach is concerned with selecting the most suitable candidates for jobs or with improving the performance of current occupants of a job. Here the paramount interest in view is that of an organization, and every effort is made to staff it with personnel who can satisfy its needs most efficiently and successfully. This sort of intervention is primarily administered by employing organizations, and the professional field associated with it is usually called organizational psychology. The other approach is designed primarily to help individuals chart life courses that will maximize their personal fulfillment. These interventions tend to take place in schools and counseling centers; the relevant professional field is counseling or guidance.

The idea that it would be a good thing to intervene in people's vocational choices, both for their own good and for that of society, is anything but new. The point could hardly be made more forcefully than it was in the sixteenth century by Huarte. He began the dedication of his *Examination of Men's Wits* to the king of Spain with the following recommendation:

> To the end that Artificers may attaine the perfection requisit for the vse of the commonwealth, me-thinketh (Catholike roiall Maiestie) a law should be enacted, that no carpenter should exercercise [sic] himselfe in any work which appertained to the occupation of an husbandman, nor a tailor to that of an architect, and that the Aduocat should not minister Phisicke, nor the Phisition play the Aduocat, but ecah [sic] one exercise only that art to which he beareth a naturall inclination and let passe the residue. For considering how base and narrowly bounded a mans wit is for one thing and no more, I haue alwaies held it for a matter certaine, That no man can be perfectly seene in two arts, without failing in one of them: now to the end he may not erre in chusing that which fitteth best with his owne nature, there should be deputed in the commonwealth, men of great wisedome and knowledge, who might discouer each ones wit in his tender age, and cause him perforce to studie that science which is agreeable for him, not permitting him to make his owne choice.[1]

Huarte's recommendation to coerce people into the occupations for which they are best suited never, of course, materialized. Instead, for most of history, the most common—and commonsense—means of achieving a good match between human resources and jobs has been by trial and error. From an organization's point of view, of the numerous employees who are hired, those who perform well in the tasks assigned to them are retained and rewarded. From the individual's perspective, one moves from job to job until a satisfying position is found. This method has the advantage of a certain directness, in that the capacity of a person to do a particular job and the satisfaction of the job for the individual are determined from the person's actual experience in the job. However, a good deal of time and productivity are wasted in the "error" side of the trial and error process: those cases where a worker proves not to be cut out for the job, or finds it to be unsatisfying. Moreover, decisions are made by supervisors, and to the considerable extent that different supervisors would evaluate an employee differently, they are subjective and inexact. How much more efficient it would be if one could determine, with precision and in advance, the optimal match between people and jobs! Huarte had proposed sending "men of great wisedome and knowledge" into the population to decide who should do what. Today vocational psychologists fill precisely that role. But they have the advantage of testing—an objective means of measuring human capacities and dispositions—as the keystone of their craft.[2]

The Birth of Vocational Psychology

An early proposal for a special profession devoted to vocational guidance, to be called "vocophy," was advanced in 1881 by Lysander Salmon Richards. Equally skeptical as Huarte about people's ability to select appropriate vocations when left to their own devices, Richards confidently predicted the advent of professional "vocophers" who, "after having studied and gained a thorough knowledge of their profession, should and will in due time, be located in every town and city of importance throughout the civilized world."[3] To be trained as fully and compensated as handsomely as lawyers, vocophers would identify clients' vocational talents by means of a thorough examination of their physiology, phrenology, physiognomy, and mental, moral, and speculative philosophy.[4] Richards's vision was before its time, however, and modern vocational psychology did not begin for another quarter century. In 1908, Frank Parsons opened the Vocational Bureau of Boston and dedicated its work to the principles that have remained at the fulcrum of the guidance-oriented sector of the field ever since: to assist the client to get a clear understanding of the self, to gain knowledge of various vocations, and to match the two. These objectives, and Parsons's methods of pursuing them, were much the same as had been proposed by Richards. Parsons used the tests of sensory acuity, manual dexterity, and memory that were then available, and, for a passing nod to phrenology, he would observe the development of clients' heads before, above, and behind the ears.[5]

If Parsons was a pioneer in the guidance-oriented aspect of vocational psychology, an early contribution to organizational psychology's placement goal of locating the best person for the job is represented by *The Job, the Man, the Boss*. In this book, first published in 1914, Katherine M. H. Blackford and Arthur Newcomb proposed that companies replace haphazard hiring practices with centralized "employment departments" in which trained experts would use scientific methods to select the best-qualified applicants for jobs throughout the company. An intervention of this sort, they argued, would enhance productivity and efficiency, establish uniform policies and standards throughout the organization, and perfect management's control over the firm and its employees.[6] A novel idea at the time, its success may easily be gauged by the ubiquity of personnel (or "human resources") departments in modern corporations.

Any scientific matching of employees to job requirements demands, of course, some means of measuring personal qualities. "After a great deal of study and experimentation," Blackford and Newcomb settled on a method that allowed the assessment of people's "physical, mental, and psychical aptitudes and character" simply by looking at them.[7] The technique required the evaluation of nine variables, including the person's coloring, facial form as seen in profile, degree of fineness or coarseness of hair, skin, nails, hands, feet, general body build, and facial expression. As an example of the procedure, they specify what to look for in a successful salesman. The entire list fills more than a page;[8] it includes (quoting freely) medium color, convex profile, height of

5'6" to 5'10" and weight of 140 to 160 pounds, medium to medium coarse textured hair, elastic flexibility with a medium rigid thumb, medium conical or square hands, fingers that are medium short with broad, smooth, long, pink, clean, fine-textured nails, a clean mouth, eyes that are clear and bright but not too brilliant, no nervous twitchings or unpleasant mannerisms, and cheerfulness as shown by upward curves of the mouth.

Blackford and Newcomb readily admit that numerous exceptions to the values of mind and character that they associate with various physical features will readily spring to mind among the personal acquaintances of any reader. They assure, however, that "exceptions are always merely apparent—never real."[9] The explanation for these apparent exceptions is that in so brief an account, they cannot delve into all of the intricacies of the system, and, in any event, no one could be expected on a single reading to acquire the expertise necessary to apply it. In particular, while it is not difficult to grasp the import of a single variable (a concave facial profile, for example, denotes mildness, absent-mindedness, and "a slow, easy, reliable digestion")[10] to understand how the nine variables conspire together to reflect the complete man is a task best left to trained experts.[11] The scientific skill and precision of these is nothing short of marvelous. Blackford and Newcomb relate how, in one employment department, an assistant walked quickly through one hundred or more applicants to select employees for eighteen jobs, including a boring mill hand, drill press hand, and lathe hand. He sent the men he had selected into the office, "where they were met by the other assistant, who had a duplicate list. In every case the assistant in the office knew for which position each man had been chosen by his team-mate."[12]

Vocational psychology has remained true to Blackford and Newcomb's vision of using scientific methods to match personal characteristics with job requirements. The means of scientific assessment, however, have changed a great deal over the decades. Today, batteries of tests are conjoined with counseling to explore three basic questions about the individual in relation to vocations. One of these concerns the individual's interest in various occupations. The second explores vocational maturity—the extent to which the individual is ready to make vocational decisions and commitments. The third has to do with the person's abilities to do certain sorts of work.

Vocational Interest Testing

If we recollect the distinction made between placement and guidance, it is clear that interest testing is concerned mainly with guidance. Its primary purpose is to help individuals to identify vocations that would be interesting and satisfying to them. Several interest tests are in common use, two of the most popular being the Strong Interest Inventory and the Kuder Occupational Interest Survey. These operate on the assumption that people in a given occupation tend to have a definable pattern of preferences for a variety of activities. These include hobbies and other leisure-time interests as well as activities directly connected with the occupation. Vocational interest tests identify subjects' interests and preferences, in order that they may be matched with standard profiles that have been developed for a variety of occupations by tabulating the preferences expressed by hundreds of people successfully employed in them.[13]

The Strong Interest Inventory and the Self-Directed Search, another popular vocationally oriented test, make use of a general theory developed by John L. Holland of the relation between personality types and occupations. This theory distinguishes six basic personality types and articulates the connections between them in terms of a hexagonal structure, as follows:[14]

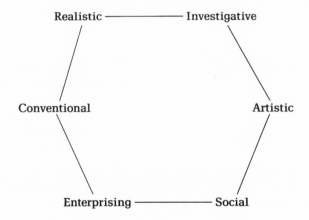

These categories are related, such that adjacent categories (e.g., social and enterprising, or social and artistic) are highly consistent, those at one remove (e.g., enterprising and artistic) are less so, and those occupying opposite positions (e.g., enterprising and investigative) are inconsistent, even contradictory. Each individual's personality may be characterized in terms of one or a combination of these categories. Each occupation is also classified in terms of the same categories. In the guidance process, the makeup of the client's personality is identified on the basis of the Self-Directed Search or the Strong Interest Inventory.[15] The client is then apprised of the various occupations that are congenial to his or her personality type and counseled to give them special consideration in career selection. The classification of occupations is done according to the personality types of people who successfully practice them. Therefore, Holland's theory operates according to the same premises as interest tests such as the Strong Interest Inventory or the Kuder Occupational Interest Survey. All of them seek to match personal traits of clients with personal traits of successful employees in various occupations. The main contribution that Holland's theory adds to this approach is to isolate the six main personality types and specify the degrees of consistency among them according to the hexagon.

Holland states that vocational counseling is least necessary for people whose personalities are clearly classifiable in one or a few adjacent types on the hexagon, with few or no inconsistencies, and where vocational aspirations are highly correlated with the personality type. Those at the opposite extreme require a great deal of counseling, and perhaps psychotherapy, in order to rectify misperceptions of self and the world.[16]

I do not intend to mount a major critique of vocational interest testing. We do need to recognize that it has the potential to do damage to individuals who rely exclusively on its results. Consider, for example, the sad fate of the boy who would be a mortician. This boy was a good student, near the top of his class in all his subjects. His troubles began during the ninth grade, when his parents began to pressure him to select a vocation. Uncertain in his own mind about his chosen career, he asked the school counselor to administer an interest inventory. While the resulting profile was not well defined, it did show him to be in the top 10 percent of the scale for mortician. The boy determined that an undertaker is what he was cut out to be, and he undertook to prepare himself for that calling. Against the advice of the counselor, he rearranged all of his intended high school classes, being sure to take those that constituted the best preparatory track for morticians' school. Once in it, however, he found his new curriculum to be uninteresting. Moreover, it separated him from his friends, and he eventually became alienated from them. He became dissatisfied with school in general, and ultimately he dropped out of high school in his senior year.[17] Miscalculations as blatant as this seem avoidable enough, however, and this boy would have saved himself a great deal of grief if he had heeded the advice of the school counselor. And, on the other side of the coin, vocational interest tests do help many people to get their own interests into clearer focus and to become better informed about the array of occupations available to them and the qualities of various jobs that may or may not be appealing.

One curious—and certainly unintended—consequence of vocational interest testing that should be mentioned is its potentially deleterious effect on social diversity. We live in a society that claims to value diversity. Universities, government agencies, and corporations extol the benefits to be derived from their diverse personnel, while television ads routinely pay obeisance to diversity by ensuring that every group they depict has the appropriate gender and ethnic mix. At first glance, vocational interest testing appears to support the social agenda of promoting diversity. The goal of such testing, after all, is to identify and help apply the client's uniqueness: the particular constellation of abilities and interests that define each one as a distinctive individual. But on further reflection, it becomes clear that the tests lead to the opposite result.

Perhaps the first to recognize this was William H. Whyte, although his reference was to personality tests rather than vocational interest tests per se. In his influential book, *The Organization Man*, Whyte argued that, far from promoting diversity and individuality, the tests widely used for placement purposes following World War II produced conformity among executive employees by consistently rewarding three qualities: extroversion, disinterest in the arts, and cheerful acceptance of the status quo.[18] Whyte vehemently disputed the moral right of organizations to pry into people's psyches. While acknowledging that the threat of not being considered for a job or promotion might make it impossible for an individual to refuse to take a personality test, he reminded, "He can cheat. He must. Let him respect himself."[19]

The tendency to produce conformity out of diversity is clearer still in contemporary vocational interest testing. Consider again how these tests work. The pattern of interests that a client expresses in a diverse array of subjects and activities is compared with the profiles of interests of persons successfully employed in a wide range of occupations. Clients are encouraged to consider those occupations where their patterns of interests match the interests of those already employed in them. Quite obviously, this process works to diminish diversity. Each individual's distinctiveness is identified to place people in precisely those situations where they are *not* distinctive. It follows that to the degree that clients rely on vocational interest tests and the counseling associated with them to select occupations, uniformity among the persons employed in a given occupation increases. This can produce a certain monotony. In the language of information theory, the greater the uniformity in any system, the greater the redundancy, or predictability. Activity in systems characterized by high redundancy tends to be routine, low in interest and creativity. In contrast, systems marked by diversity contain a good deal of information, or unpredictability. That is an important source of interest and imagination.[20]

Most organizations that value diversity do so for the creative cross-fertilization that results from the interaction of people of different interests and backgrounds. This would still emerge from teamwork among people in different specialties—say, among designers, engineers, floor workers, and marketing specialists in a manufacturing enterprise. But when interaction is primarily between people in the same specialty, the intraoccupational uniformity fostered by vocational interest testing may in the long run produce jobs that are less interesting to their occupants in an overall occupational system that becomes sluggish and unproductive of creative innovation.

Vocational Maturity

Beginning with the founding work of Parsons and extending at least through the 1950s, the dominant theoretical orientation in vocational counseling was the "trait and factor" approach. This approach is governed by the assumptions that individuals have certain traits—abilities, interests, personality characteristics— and that various occupations require particular constellations of such traits in those who would pursue them successfully. The counseling process amounts to using tests of various sorts and other techniques to ascertain the client's traits and recommending consideration of occupations for which those particular traits are most appropriate.[21] The trait and factor approach is alive and well in counseling today; for instance, Holland's influential theory of personalities, vocations, and their convergence is rooted in this perspective.[22] Nevertheless, the trait and factor approach has come under fire for relying too heavily on tests and for simply accepting clients' personality traits as givens rather than investigating the psychological and sociological conditions that produce them.

One important reaction to perceived limitations of the trait and factor approach has been increased attention to when and how those personality traits relevant to vocational choices develop. Vocational counselors would identify the unfortunate lad described above, who dropped out of school after a frustrating attempt to pursue a career goal of mortician, as one who had not achieved vocational maturity at the time he took the interest inventory in the ninth grade. He was still in an exploratory phase. Preferences expressed at that time are likely to be unstable, so it is unwise (as it obviously was in this boy's case) to base important decisions and plans on them.[23] Most interest inventories are designed for people of high school age and older, and it is recommended that they not be taken by younger individuals because their interests have not yet stabilized.[24]

Stimulated largely by the pioneering work of Eli Ginzberg and associates[25] and Donald Super,[26] interest in vocational maturity was born in the 1950s and continues to be an important issue in counseling psychology. In a moment of linguistic inspiration, Edwin Herr and Stanley Cramer coined "vocationalization" as the process by which people come to internalize "the values, knowledge, and skills which led [sic? lead?] to effective vocational behavior."[27] The individual who has vocationalized properly comes to define the self to a substantial degree in vocational terms ("I am a musician," or accountant, or bricklayer, etc.). Such people have gained a good understanding of their own abilities and interests and on that basis have selected "occupational careers." This term refers to a vocation that provides the opportunity throughout an entire work life for steady rises to increasing levels of responsibility, prestige, and/or compensation.[28] For those who have vocationalized well, the occupational career is an important part of the meaning they find in life. Among the many occupational careers, a few examples are the academic or military professions (with their well-defined ranks), skilled crafts, management careers in business, and the Catholic priesthood.

For practitioners interested in vocational maturity, one of the major concerns of guidance is to act as midwife to the process of vocationalization. To this end, researchers in counseling have devised tests to measure the level of vocational maturity, for use primarily with adolescents and high school students. Instruments such as the Career Maturity Inventory, the Cognitive Vocational Maturity Test, and the Career Development Inventory measure attitudes toward occupational planning and choice, knowledge of what occupations are available and how to get information about them, and development of decision-making skills.[29]

In a socioeconomic system as complex as our own, vocationalization is a lengthy process that requires extensive shaping of the human raw material to develop in people the specific skills necessary for various occupations and, more profoundly, to dispose them psychologically to include vocation as an important part of their definition of self. In Super's theory, for example, vocational maturity is a process consisting of five stages and

lasting nearly a lifetime. Adolescence is the time for crystalliza-
tion of vocational preferences; identifying a specific career direction and taking initial steps to implement it occurs around
ages 18 to 21; completing necessary training and entering the
relevant occupation occurs around ages 21 to 24; during the
stabilization phase, between ages 25 and 35, the individual set-
tles down in the chosen career; the latter 30s to the mid-40s mark
the consolidation phase, when attention turns to developing se-
niority and security in one's vocation.[30]

If we look at it from the perspective of the socioeconomic system, it is clear that vocationalization is a highly desirable process
because it produces marvelously efficient and devoted workers.
The full significance of this becomes apparent if we compare
vocationalization with Max Weber's thesis in his famous essay,
The Protestant Ethic and the Spirit of Capitalism.[31] There Weber
argued that the industriousness characteristic of capitalists had
its origin in the notion that success in one's worldly calling was
evidence to Protestants that one was among the Elect, destined for
salvation. Hence people strove mightily to succeed so as to prove
to themselves that they were doing God's work and to relieve
anxiety about the fate of their immortal souls. Given its other-
worldly orientation, however, this mind-set could scarcely allow
the successful ones to use the considerable wealth they achieved
for temporal pleasures. They continued to live frugally and valued
self-denial. Even after the religious underpinnings of these attitudes and behaviors passed from the scene, people retained the
habits of industriousness and asceticism, resulting in capitalists
who work not to enjoy the fruits of their labor but as an end in
itself.

I suggest that as a technique for inveigling people to devote
their energy and lives to the growth and efficiency of the socioeconomic system, today's vocationalization is well evolved beyond the situation Weber described. Far from being a hollow shell
left over from former eschatological anxiety, work today has been
positively redefined as a source of satisfaction, happiness, and
meaning in life. For the person who has truly vocationalized, one's
sense of honor, self-worth, and identity is closely tied to career.
Marry this degree of commitment with a program of extensive

training and placement on the basis of the individual's particular abilities and interests, and the result is a corps of workers who serve the system with boundless energy, consummate skill, and unstinting conscientiousness.

At first blush, there seems to be nothing wrong with this, for everybody wins. The socioeconomic system benefits from the attentiveness of its workers, while the workers simultaneously secure material well-being and find meaning in life in the context of an occupational career. Closer scrutiny reveals, however, that such human rewards are by no means invariably forthcoming. Vocationalization theory stresses those factors necessary for success that are dependent on the individual: maturity, ability, motivation, and an appetite for hard work. The theory is silent about external considerations that may impede the determined efforts of even those with high ability and motivation to achieve vocational success. But in reality, factors external to individuals and beyond their control frequently frustrate their career aspirations. In particular, two factors hold the ideal of a satisfying occupational career beyond the reach of many people. The more ancient of the two is denial of equal opportunity because of discrimination. More recent is "corporate restructuring" and the fundamental shift it represents in the organization of employment away from the notion of vocational careers.

Discrimination

The salient issues are embedded in the well-known caricature: when the chairman of the board at General Motors retires, everybody moves up a notch, and they hire an office boy. While the image this evokes plainly depicts an occupational career as a coherent pattern of progress from an entry-level position to retirement through grades of increasing responsibility, respect, and compensation, it reveals two biased assumptions inherent in the whole concept of vocationalization. One is that the process of moving up the career ladder is modeled on the ideal experience of white-collar employees. Workers on the assembly line are not involved. The other is that they hire an office boy, not an office girl. In other words, while vocationalization and an occupational career are held up as ideals for everyone, they are modeled on the stereotyped experience of white, middle-class males.

This bias is built into the concept of vocational maturity at its base.[32] Probably the first explicitly articulated theory of vocational maturation was advanced by Ginzberg and his associates in 1951. The empirical study on which the theory was erected pertained to Anglo-Saxon male adolescents of rather high socioeconomic standing and IQs of 120 or higher.[33] The tests used to measure vocational maturity are similarly skewed. The item construction, selection and validation of two important vocational maturity tests—the Career Maturity Inventory and the Career Development Inventory—was done on the basis of work with middle class subjects.[34] Therefore, the "vocational maturity" that such tests measure may actually be how closely subjects approximate middle-class attitudes toward the world of work.[35] Again, vocational interest tests such as the Strong Interest Inventory and the Kuder Occupational Interest Survey match interests expressed by subjects with those of samples of persons successfully employed in various occupations. Because white middle-class males predominate in the more prestigious and highly compensated occupations, their interests serve as the norm with which subjects' interests are compared. To the extent that interests are conditioned by socioeconomic class, ethnicity, and gender, those of white middle-class male subjects will match better with the norming groups in these higher-level occupations, and therefore test results will show them to be more interested in such occupations than subjects from other social categories.[36]

The tilt toward white middle-class males is apparent in the facts regarding who actually experiences the coherent developmental pattern of an occupational career. Women and minorities have tended disproportionately to hold poorly compensated and less honored jobs. A 1959 study examined what had become of over 1,500 people in their mid-forties who were identified as gifted children (IQ of 135 or higher) in 1921–22. The great majority of the men had achieved prominence in professional and managerial positions, while about 50 percent of the women were full-time housewives.

Of those [women] who were working full time, 21% were teachers in elementary or secondary school, 8% were social workers, 20% were secretaries, and 8% were either librarians or nurses. Only 7% of those working were academicians, 5% were physicians, lawyers, or psychologists, 8% were executives, and 9% were writers, artists, or musicians.[37]

Women's position in the work force has improved since then— but not dramatically. In 1979, women employed full time earned 63 percent of what men earned, while the comparable figure for 1988 was 70 percent. Between 1983 and 1988, the number of women in managerial and professional specialties rose from 41 to 45 percent, but they made no gains in salary, earning 70 percent of male salaries in both years.[38] These figures bear out the wide-spread perception that women's inroads into business and the professions have been largely limited to the lower and middle levels and that a "glass ceiling" continues to bar their ascent to the highest positions.

As for minorities, in the late 1970s, black college graduates were earning about as much as white high school graduates.[39] Since then, the economic condition of black families has actually worsened slightly, for earnings of black families dropped from 72 to 71 percent of those of white families between 1979 and 1988.[40] In 1988, 27 percent of the whites in the work force were employed in managerial and professional positions, while 15 percent of the blacks and 13 percent of the Hispanics held jobs in these categories. Conversely, 23 percent of the blacks and 24 percent of the Hispanics were employed as operators, fabricators, and laborers, while 15 percent of the whites held jobs of these sorts.[41] In sum, minorities are much likelier than whites to hold jobs that are poorly compensated and do not lend themselves to the sorts of challenges, responsibilities, and opportunities for creative growth associated with the notion of an occupational career. "For routine unskilled or semiskilled occupations," writes W. L. Slocum, "the distinctions between occupational steps may be so small and worker turnover so great that it would be difficult to consider that a career line exists at all."[42]

A danger of vocational maturity theory and the practices of guidance derived from it is that it encourages everyone to vocationalize, to place career near the center of their sense of self and the meaning they seek in life. Minorities and the poor who buy into this strategy are likelier than others to be disappointed in their efforts to achieve a successful vocation. Given the emphasis guidance places on internal factors such as ability and motivation, they may well blame the failure on themselves, with resulting damage to their self-esteem. The tragedy is that the responsibility often lies not so much with them as with a system that discriminates against them and denies them equal opportunity. To preserve their psychological well-being, minorities and others who are subjected to discrimination are sometimes driven to a stance totally contrary to that promoted by vocational maturity theory. Far from finding personal fulfillment in work, persons in these circumstances are alienated from their work. They must find ways of convincing themselves that what they do for most of their waking hours has little or nothing to do with what they are as persons.[43]

Charles Ford and Doris Jeffries Ford suggest that this situation calls for a special counseling strategy.[44] They hold that many black workers, recognizing that they face greater obstacles in achieving a successful and satisfying occupational career than do their white counterparts, are not necessarily out to make career an integral part of their self-definition as vocational maturity theory expects. Their lateral movement from one job to another is therefore not "floundering," as it would appear from the perspective of such theories, but "calculated job speculation" designed exclusively to improve their economic position.[45] Clients with this objective may be more effectively served by helping them to develop the most effective strategy for getting the most lucrative and secure job available rather than following the traditional counseling approach of seeking to place them in a vocation in which they might rise over the long term from an entry-level position to the top.[46] Although this may well be an appropriate course for some clients in today's social conditions, it must be acknowledged that implementing it could in certain circumstances be extremely problematic. Imagine the charges of racism that would be forthcoming, for example, if a white counselor encouraged a middle-class white youth to go for his dream of becoming a lawyer while (quite honestly and realistically) informing a lower-class black youth with the same goal that the cards are stacked against success and suggesting that she might want to learn how to become proficient at calculated job speculation.

Even if the utopian day should arrive when there is no more discrimination and equal opportunity is a reality for everyone, many people would still not achieve a satisfying occupational career. That ideal has always been beyond the reach of many, including many white middle-class males. In the mid-1960s, most men did not envision work in terms of a long-term career but made occupational choices according to short-term considerations. Some 70 percent of lower-middle-class men spent less than half their work lives in positions that manifested any sort of orderly career progression.[47] Twenty years later it became apparent that even for the upper middle class, "career development as a process of implementing one's self-concept is a fast eroding dream for many Americans, and not just racial minorities."[48] One thinks, for example, of the executives who must make midlife career changes on losing their jobs in corporate reorganizations, mergers, or takeovers and of the crowd of would-be academics who graduated with Ph.D.'s in the 1970s and 1980s to find no tenure-track faculty jobs awaiting them and who migrated for years from one temporary position to another until many of them left the profession entirely. This brings us to the second external factor that frustrates the ambitions of many people to achieve a satisfying occupational career.

The Demise of Fordism

In about 1973, a fundamental change in the American structure of employment occurred, signaling the end of the "Fordism" that had dominated the scene for the preceding sixty years. With its symbolic beginning in Henry Ford's $5 day (see chap. 4), the Fordist system rested on the proposition that employees be paid sufficiently high wages to enable them to be prime consumers of the ever-increasing quantity of goods produced by industrial capitalism.[49] At its height, this system produced a particular organization of employment.

From World War II through the early 1970s, a growing proportion of American companies organized the division of work and the management of employees within their firms around the key institution of a full-time work force and an "internal labor market." Ordered hierarchies, promotion from within rather than from outside the company whenever possible, the erection of promotion ladders with relatively explicit rules and flexible procedures by which workers would be judged worthy of upgrading—these were the dominant characteristics of this form of corporate bureaucracy.[50]

Note that precisely these are the conditions that foster the vocational experience we have been discussing under the name "occupational career." I suspect, in fact, that the emphasis in vocational guidance on the process of vocationalization and its culmination in an occupational career is an artifact of the Fordist organization of employment. Of course, these conditions were not realized in all companies or for all employees. That is why occupational careers were not available to many workers even at the peak of Fordism. Nevertheless, they did obtain in the largest private and public organizations, and the vocational ideal for everyone was formulated in their terms.

Since about 1973, the Fordist system has been transformed. International markets and competition, fluctuating currency exchange rates, technological innovations, new financial arrangements, and speed of communication favor those companies that can adjust rapidly to changing conditions. In response, many companies are "restructuring" both their blue-collar and white-collar work forces. The core of permanent, full-time employees is reduced ("downsized") and surrounded by a periphery consisting of part-time employees, temporary workers, and subcontractors. This represents considerable savings in labor costs, for peripheral workers are paid lower wages than those in the permanent core and the company does not provide them with health insurance, retirement, and other fringe benefits. Moreover, the company gains flexibility because it can enlarge or diminish the size of its labor force far faster than was possible under the Fordist system by simply adding to or cutting back on its number of subcontractors and part-time and temporary workers.[51]

Under Fordism there was some truth in the adage, "What's good for General Motors is good for the country." But the new system is anything but good for employees, because low-paying part-time or temporary jobs without fringe benefits are replacing Fordist jobs that held out the possibility of increasing responsibility and remuneration in a secure and satisfying occupational career. The transformation has serious implications for the profession of vocational counseling. To the extent that counselors continue to encourage their clients to vocationalize—to prepare themselves for an occupational career and to make it an important element in their self-image—they may be orienting them toward a world that, for many, no longer exists. Today, to make career an integral part of one's concept of self is less advisable than it was even two or three decades ago. In the present circumstances, an employment strategy exclusively focused on economic goals such as calculated job speculation may be relevant to more than just those who suffer from racial or gender discrimination.

Ability Testing

When purchasing steel or any other material used in the manufacturing process, observed H. C. Link in 1919, specifications are set and the material is tested to ensure that it meets them. The human material required by any enterprise ought to be selected with no less care, he argued. Applicants and employees should be extensively tested to ensure that they satisfy the particular specifications set for them.[52] Business has espoused this point of view and regularly tests the abilities of workers before being hired or promoted. When the jobs in question call for physical qualities such as strength, manual dexterity, or hand-foot coordination, the task of stipulating job specifications and designing tests to measure how well people meet them seems to be relatively straightforward. Building in the spirit of Frederick W. Taylor's ideas about scientific management, "methods engineers," as they have been called, have devised a multitude of tests that ingeniously measure motor coordinations and perceptions that are similar to the operations an employee would be expected to perform on the job.[53]

WILLING, READY, AND ABLE

However, these procedures rest on the assumption that a close correlation exists between an individual's ability to perform certain tasks and the efficiency with which one will perform them on a day-to-day basis. That assumption was called into question by the well-known study of Western Electric's Hawthorne works in the 1920s and 1930s. One of the conclusions of that project was that standards of productivity are set by group consensus and tend to be well below what individuals could attain if they worked up to the level of their abilities. To the extent that these findings are correct, they raise serious questions about the value of ability tests for predicting the performance of workers.[54]

More vexed still is the relation between ability tests and the performance of people in management or the professions. The talents here are so elusive that it is difficult to design tests to mirror them. Link's advocacy of testing workers to ascertain their qualifications met a blank wall when it came to managerial positions. Executives themselves do not know what personal qualities contribute to their success, so it is clear that specifications for these jobs have not been defined. In that circumstance, psychologists have little hope of designing tests that can determine to what degree various candidates meet them.[55]

Others have rushed in where Link feared to tread, but professional success has continued to defy explanation in spite of a plethora of theories advanced to account for it. In the nineteenth and early twentieth centuries, the secret was thought to lie in general character traits: proponents of the self-made man extolled thrift and industriousness, phrenologists attributed success in business to well-developed organs of acquisitiveness, and Blackford and Newcomb, in addition to enunciating more specific physical characteristics requisite to particular occupations, stipulated that any worthy employee should possess health, intelligence, honesty, and industry.[56]

Health and honesty continue to be held in high regard, and hiring is frequently contingent on the results of a physical examination and a lie detector test or (in the aftermath of the 1988 legislation controlling mechanical lie detector tests) an integrity test. Aside from gross defects in health or integrity, however, the general trait that has been considered throughout the present century to be most pertinent to occupational success—particularly for professional and managerial positions—is intelligence. Doubtless this is partly due to the notion that intelligence helps people to learn quickly and with retention, to grasp the nuances of situations, and to deal flexibly and imaginatively with new problems—all capacities that would contribute to success as a business executive or professional. Although the drawback has been noted that intelligent people are likely to become bored with routine tasks, a certain degree of intelligence is also useful in less exalted positions because the clever worker can learn a job more rapidly and understand its place in the overall enterprise better than a dull one. The possibility must seriously be entertained, however, that another important reason for the widespread perception of intelligence as important to vocational success is that with the development of intelligence tests, means have been available to *measure* intelligence with greater apparent precision than other general character traits. Moreover, the practice of reporting on intelligence in quantitative terms, such as IQ scores, lends an aura of scientific objectivity to the use of intelligence as a criterion in personnel selection.

It was, in fact, after the development of the first standardized intelligence tests during World War I that psychologists such as W. D. Scott and Hugo Munsterberg devised and promoted intelligence tests for employee selection and placement.[57] By about 1925, however, the keen interest that businesses had originally showed in intelligence testing abated, largely because they did not find the test results to be useful in revealing if candidates had the requisite skills for specific jobs. In conditions of an economic downturn, intelligence testing programs did not generate enough useful information to justify their expense.[58]

The use of intelligence testing for placement purposes has gone through at least two more cycles since the 1920s. With the outbreak of World War II, the armed forces again came to the fore in the history of testing as aptitude tests were used to classify recruits in an elaborate system of categories. Unlike the original Army Alpha and Army Beta used in World War I, which were general intelligence tests, the World War II batteries included aptitude tests for specialized, technical jobs as well as general

intelligence tests.[59] By the war's end, some nine million recruits—five times the number who had taken the army tests during World War I—had taken the Army General Classification Test
and had been sorted by it into five categories of learning ability,
ranging from very rapid to very slow.[60] Personality tests were
also used during the war for purposes of identifying personnel
with submissive or pliable personalities, as well as those who
might be troublemakers or be of liberal or radical political
persuasions.[61]

During the period immediately following World War II, the U.S.
economy experienced a dramatic increase in the need for managerial and professional positions. As had happened after World
War I, a number of firms turned to testing programs modeled on
the military's testing of officer candidates as a means of selecting
the most qualified personnel. By 1950, for example, Sears, Roe-
buck and Co. was testing the intelligence, personality, and vocational interests of some 10,000 employees within the company
as part of the decision-making process for placement and promotions.[62] Further recapitulating developments in the aftermath
of World War I, however, the popularity of testing immediately
following World War II tapered off as the years went by.

One reason was that testing in the workplace was sharply
criticized in works such as Whyte's *The Organization Man*[63] as
unwarranted and insidious intrusions into personal privacy. Another is that intelligence testing came under suspicion in the late
1960s and 1970s as a result of the civil rights movement. The
notion became widespread that intelligence tests are discriminatory because members of minorities and disadvantaged groups
tend to score lower on them than middle-class whites. The bell
curve of general intelligence test scores for blacks, for example,
is about one standard deviation below that for whites.[64] Court
decisions pertaining to Title VII of the Civil Rights Act of 1964
reinforced the perception of intelligence testing as discriminatory. Most important was the 1971 Supreme Court decision in
Griggs v. Duke Power Co., which shifted the notion of employment
discrimination from disparate treatment to disparate impact.[65]
That is to say, whereas discrimination had previously been defined as differential treatment of *individuals* on the basis of race,

sex, religion, and so on, the tendency after *Griggs* was to view a statistical difference in the outcome of employment selection procedures on members of different groups as evidence of discrimination. For example, if whites tend to be hired disproportionately more than blacks because on average the former score higher on intelligence tests, by the disparate impact standard, that is a case of discrimination. This decision led employers to suspend measures such as standardized intelligence tests, because score differences between ethnic groups invited litigation or adverse actions by regulating agencies such as the Equal Employment Opportunity Commission.[66]

In a related development, affirmative action procedures designed specifically to encourage the employment of minorities were introduced. Recognizing that minorities tend on average to score lower than whites on standardized tests, the Equal Employment Opportunity Commission moved to prevent the discrepancy from having a discriminatory effect against minorities by disallowing tests in the employment selection process if they do not recommend members of minority groups for employment at a rate proportional to their representation in the population at large.[67] In response, in the early 1980s, the U.S. Employment Service and many state employment agencies adopted a procedure known as "within-group score conversion" or "race norming." Percentile scores on the Employment Service's General Aptitude Test Battery are calculated by ranking black applicants only with reference to other blacks and Hispanics in comparison to other Hispanics; whites and Asians are lumped together in a third, "other" category. Since blacks and Hispanics tend in general to score considerably lower on the test than whites and Asians, this means that if a black, Hispanic, and white all make the same raw score on the test and that score is sufficient to place the white applicant in the top 40 percent in the "other" category of whites and Asians, the Hispanic would be in the top 25 percent and the black applicant in the top 20 percent of their respective groups. This practice was intended to ensure that some groups are not disproportionately represented in referrals made to employers because of group differences in test scores. However, since usually only the percentile score is reported to them, employers (who are often unaware of the practice) may be misled by within-group score conversion. Returning to our hypothetical three applicants, an employer might easily get the impression that the black did best on the test, the Hispanic next, and the white worst, when in fact raw scores were identical for all three.[68]

Given that the social, legal, and political climate of the time was decidedly critical of testing, John Crites could write in 1983 that although testing had a long and productive history in vocational psychology, current research in the field was not focused in that direction.[69] As if to verify Crites's generalization, an essay from the same year devoted to a review of current theoretical issues in vocational psychology made almost no mention of testing.[70] What little theoretical attention testing received during this period tended to be of a critical nature, as, for example, Lee Cronbach's assessment of the Armed Services Vocational Aptitude Battery (ASVAB). Its primary purpose is to enable the armed services to identify potential recruits, but many school districts use it for the more general purpose of assisting high school seniors to identify vocations commensurate with their abilities. A unique feature of the ASVAB is that the military administers the test, scores it, and reports the results free of charge. This incentive has so much appeal to budget-conscious school districts that the ASVAB is one of the most prevalent tests in America, taken by over one million high school seniors annually. It would seem that everyone benefits. The schools can provide vocational testing at no charge, and the armed forces have access to information about large numbers of young people among whom they can identify potential recruits. The only losers may be the students who take the test. Cronbach argued that its reporting techniques and the research into its reliability and validity were inadequate. Although it may be of help in conjunction with other tests and when interpreted by a trained counselor, a student who makes important vocational decisions alone or in consultation with a military recruiter solely on the basis of ASVAB results may be seriously misled. This is especially true for females, because the test is oriented toward typically male interests and activities.[71] Cronbach's critique led to a revision of the ASVAB, although its utility as a vocational guide is still questionable because it is oriented more toward general rather than specific abilities.[72]

Now the worm is turning again. The shift to the political right in America in the 1980s has muffled civil rights concerns about ethnic and class bias in testing and reinvigorated interest in testing—at least, intelligence testing—for vocational purposes. The possibility that different racial groups really do differ in intelligence is being raised again as people notice that Great Society programs seem to be doing little to reduce the discrepancies in intelligence test scores between different groups. One response was to maintain that intelligence is not so important to many jobs after all and to relax employment requirements. But, according to Linda Gottfredson, this represented wishful thinking and resulted in diminished performance and productivity.[73] Now many vocational psychologists are resurrecting the notion that intelligence is a significant factor in job performance and argue that testing is a valuable tool for successful vocational placement. Two special issues of the *Journal of Vocational Behavior* have been devoted to issues of intelligence testing in vocational psychology (one in 1986 and the other in 1988), and nearly all contributors adopt a positive stance toward testing. For example, John Hawk of the U.S. Employment Service holds that general intelligence is so crucial to performance in all human activities that other tests of specific aptitudes are largely redundant. In his mind, the most effective vocational counseling amounts to advising individuals about the probabilities of success in different vocational levels on the basis of general intelligence tests.[74] Today some employers require that college graduates applying for jobs submit SAT scores as part of their application materials. It may seem curious to demand that people who are on the verge of graduating from college (or have already graduated) submit results of a test that they took in high school, a test used primarily to predict how well they would do in college (and especially in the first year of college). However, employers who require it may recognize that the SAT is basically an intelligence test, and they may use it as a convenient way to gain information about the general intelligence of their applicants without having to go to the trouble and expense of giving them a new test.[75]

The contemporary move toward intelligence testing in the workplace is part of a general effort to curtail affirmative action programs, which in some quarters have even been branded as detrimental to the very groups they were designed to assist. It has been suggested, for example, that blacks are well aware that they may be hired because of preferential treatment rather than individual merit, and this undermines their confidence and self-esteem.[76] Arguments such as these have brought within-group score conversion on the General Aptitude Test Battery (whereby, as discussed above, scores for blacks and Hispanics are adjusted upward relative to scores for whites and Asians) under fire in 1991 as a quota measure. It is probably no accident that the matter was brought to the public's attention at a particularly sensitive time, just when Congress was trying to craft a civil rights bill that could not be construed as demanding racial quotas in hiring and promotions. No one seems prepared to defend within-group score conversion, which appears to be a blatant case of preferential treatment for minorities, so federal and state employment agencies are fast discontinuing the practice.[77]

Parallel developments are occurring on the legal front. Authors such as Clint Bolick[78] and James Sharf[79] argue that the doctrine of disparate impact stemming from the *Griggs* decision is counter to the spirit of Title VII of the Civil Rights Act of 1964, which they claim is oriented toward protecting the rights of individuals rather than groups. This is not a unanimous opinion, for Richard Seymour claims that Congress *did* intend to control disparate impact as well as disparate treatment in Title VII.[80] In any event, Sharf perceives in the 1988 decision on *Watson v. Fort Worth Bank & Trust* an indication that the present Supreme Court may be willing to reconsider *Griggs* and is adopting a more tolerant attitude toward the use of standardized testing in employment decisions.[81]

The Supreme Court's 1988 *Watson* plurality decision is likely to be viewed in years to come as the turning point in the *Griggs* disparate impact definition of discrimination. . . . Refocusing on objective employment standards will likely have the salutary effect of returning individual merit to its rightful place as the touchstone of opportunity. Objective standards are coming back into focus in both education and employment, personnel measurement is "in," and the rising of competence cannot be far behind.[82]

Its use in the context of vocational placement marks the second place where we have encountered intelligence testing in the course of this book. The other is in the educational system, as described in chapter 7. As our review of recent history indicates, intelligence testing has provoked an immense amount of controversy. Most of the points of contention are equally relevant to its role in vocational and educational placement. Thus, it will be convenient to consider the social effects of intelligence testing in these two areas together. The issues are sufficiently numerous and complex that chapter 9 is devoted entirely to them.

9

"ARTIFICIAL"

INTELLIGENCE

*The decisive moment was at hand
when the hopes reposed in Sapo were to be fulfilled,
or dashed to the ground. . . . Mrs. Saposcat, whose piety grew
warm in times of crisis, prayed for his success. . . . Oh God grant he
pass, grant he pass, grant he scrape through!*

Samuel Beckett,

Malone Dies

This chapter is a critique of intelligence testing; more, it is a critique of the conventional concept of intelligence. After some preliminary remarks about the relation between intelligence testing and the principle of equality of opportunity, an effort will be made to define "intelligence" as it is conceptualized by the general public. I identify a number of unfortunate consequences of the conventional concept of intelligence and suggest that it came into being largely as a result of intelligence tests. "Intelligence" is not some preexisting quality waiting to be measured by intelligence tests but is rather defined and fabricated by them. Hence the title of the chapter: the intelligence of the human mind is no less "artificial" than the intelligence associated with computers.

249

Intelligence, Equality, and Inequality

In 1928, the state of Wisconsin established the Committee on Cooperation to explore ways of predicting who, among the rapidly growing high school population, could be expected to succeed in college. The intent was to lessen "the serious tragedy of student mortality" by discouraging those who are doomed to fail in college from matriculating in the first place. Positioning itself to grapple with its charge, the committee adopted the following as its guiding philosophy:

> That educational opportunity shall be viewed as a broad highway extending from kindergarten to college graduation and that every child has a right to travel this highway as far as his native interest, capacity and endowment will permit. If this philosophy is sound then the committee felt that it must think of its problem, not in terms of that democratic principle which insists upon the political equality of human beings but in terms of the principle of biological *inequality* of human beings. While the committee subscribed completely to the principle of equality of opportunity it recognized just as completely that equality of opportunity means, not identity of opportunity but diversity of opportunity.[1]

With these words, the Wisconsin committee enunciated the tacit assumption that underlies essentially all intelligence testing. That assumption marries two propositions, one having to do with inequality and the other with equality.

The first proposition holds that human beings are created unequal. In classical antiquity, Plato distinguished among men of gold, silver, and brass. The first category contains the leaders and decision makers of society, the second of their administrators and henchmen, and the third the farmers and ordinary workers. The assumption of human inequality is still nearly universally affirmed, although the metaphor is no longer metallurgical and the tripartite division has been replaced with a smoother slope of finely graded distinctions. The second proposition is of more recent vintage. As articulated in eighteenth-century documents such as the Declaration of Independence, it holds that all men (today, human beings) are created equal. This in no way contradicts the first proposition, for the one acknowledges that individuals differ in their interests, talents, and motivations, while the other stipulates that all have (or should have) identical civil rights and equal opportunity. The two principles are actually complementary. The principle of equal opportunity makes it possible for the unequal talents and qualities of different individuals to be recognized and appreciated. "The argument for democracy," Thorndike wrote, "is not that it gives power to all men without distinction, but that it gives greater freedom for ability and character to attain power."[2]

The United States was the first Western nation to wed the assumptions of equal opportunity and unequal endowments. It was argued, particularly before social reforms moved Europe in the same direction, that equal opportunity and the social mobility that inevitably stems from it assured America's success in competition with the class-ridden countries of the Old World. Even with roughly equal populations, the United States would have a larger pool from which to draw human talent because important positions were available to everyone rather than reserved for members of the upper social stratum.

> There was an explicit rejection of the classic conservative assumption that virtue could be concentrated in an elite social class and transmitted by blood over generations. The mobility ideology rested on the equalitarian premise that talent was distributed at random throughout the population. This made the repeated running of the race conducive to progress; the open society could tap the energies of all its members by allowing all to compete freely.[3]

A Positivist Meritocracy

It is difficult to imagine a more efficient, rational social order than one in which all persons are placed in the positions for which their particular talents are most suited. Such a social order is often called meritocracy. The concept becomes all the more compelling when positivism serves as its midwife, when the powerful techniques of science are enlisted to achieve the goal of the optimal utilization of human resources. The positivist meritocracy shines as a utopian state in which want, waste, and conflict will be replaced by prosperity, efficiency, personal satisfaction, and social tranquility. People looked especially to psychology as the science that would lead the way to the meritocratic utopia, and American psychologists of the era during and after World War I eagerly anticipated the "prediction and control," "human engineering," and "social efficiency" that would be realized from applications of their science.[4] These attitudes persist in some sectors of psychology today, particularly in behaviorism and in psychometrics, the branch of psychology concerned with measurement and testing.

The essence of positivist meritocracy is scientific placement of persons according to ability: political heads would be those with the greatest leadership and decision-making abilities, scholars would manifest the most highly developed cognitive skills, captains of industry would have uncommon ability in matters pertaining to economics and management, and artists and artisans would be talented in manipulating material of various kinds, while unskilled laborers would be those who lack sufficient abilities to suit them for anything else. A meritocracy grounded in equal opportunity requires that the race be run repeatedly in order that the unequal talents of people from all social strata might be identified and put to optimal use. What form should the race take? According to a blue ribbon committee convened in the late 1970s by the National Research Council,

> One tool that appeared particularly promising in organizing society—and one that was promoted particularly aggressively by its practitioners—was the new technique of educational and mental testing, which emerged at the turn of the century. Enthusiasts claimed that testing could bring order and efficiency to schools, to industry, and to society as a whole by providing the raw data on individual abilities necessary to the efficient marshaling of human talents.[5]

Testing was considered to be a no-lose instrument of meritocracy, because the public benefits to be realized from the most efficacious placement of people would be matched by the advantages to be reaped by each individual, whose peculiar interests and capacities would be identified by testing and then nurtured and developed by education. So even John Dewey, a strong proponent of education for the development of the individual and no great friend of testing, pointed early to its potential service to both the individual and society in "My Pedagogic Creed" of 1897: "Examinations are of use only so far as they test the child's fitness for social life and reveal the place in which he can be of most service and where he can receive the most help."[6]

The way testing is used, however, is strangely at odds with certain core features of modern society. If there is anything that characterizes the modern socioeconomic system, it is complexity. The jobs that need to be done to keep the multifaceted system going require a multitude of different skills. The abilities with which people are assumed to be unequally endowed are great in number and diversity. If, then, a meritocratic selection technique is to achieve the optimal placement of persons in social positions, certainly it should measure their capacities along many different dimensions. Curiously, one ability soon came to stand above the others as most likely to ensure success in any and all endeavors. This is mental ability, or general intelligence.[7] I suggest that an important reason for the ascendancy of intelligence as the premier candidate for meritocratic selection is because it became technologically practicable to *test* intelligence on a massive scale. The first mass test was an intelligence test. Thanks to the technological breakthrough of the multiple-choice question, the Army Alpha of 1917 became an instrument that could evaluate millions of individuals cheaply and quickly. Additional refinements such as machine grading further perfected the efficiency of the Army Alpha's descendants to the point that, particularly in the last half century, standardized intelligence tests have been applied repeatedly to virtually everyone in our society.

Of course, the perpetuation and expansion of the huge and lucrative enterprise of intelligence testing required it to be commonly accepted that what intelligence tests measure is something of importance. Among many others, psychologists from H. H. Goddard, Lewis Terman, and E. L. Thorndike at the dawn of the era of mass testing to Arthur Jensen, Richard Herrnstein, Linda Gottfredson, and John Hawk of the present day have vigorously promoted the notion that level of intelligence is a crucial variable for success in virtually every undertaking.

What Is Intelligence?

Despite the immense importance claimed for it, precisely what intelligence is has been the subject of a great deal of uncertainty and debate. This may relate to a certain disinterest in theory that has characterized testing. The intellectual center of testing lies in the branch of psychology known as psychometrics, a term that means simply the measurement of mental phenomena. Several psychologists have remarked on a gap that has opened up between psychometrics and another major branch of the discipline, cognitive psychology. Cognitivists, who trace their pedigree from Wilhelm Wundt, have been interested in determining the basic processes of mind and behavior in general. Differences between individuals are of marginal interest in this research program. Psychometricians, however, descend intellectually from biologists—especially Darwin—via Galton. Their attention has been directed precisely to individual differences, originally in an effort to trace the operation of natural selection in the evolutionary development of our own species.[8] But this theoretical orientation waned as psychometricians increasingly concentrated their attention on the practical applications of testing. A number of psychologists have criticized this development, claiming that psychometricians have accommodated themselves to demands from the public for simple solutions to complex problems by developing tests that claim to predict who is likely to succeed in various educational programs, military assignments, jobs, and so on. The result has been a profusion of tests with little substantial grounding in psychological theory.[9] The situation has become serious enough that Oscar Buros, who founded the *Mental Measurements Yearbook* as a means of reviewing and providing some quality control for the multitude of mental tests now available, stated in both the 1972 and 1978 editions that "at least half of the tests currently on the market should never have been published."[10]

In 1923, Harvard psychologist Edwin Boring set out to cut the Gordian knot over what intelligence really is by calling it simply the human capacity that is measured by intelligence tests. This is termed an "operational" definition—the practice of defining something in terms of the procedures used to measure it. "Intelligence," as Boring put it, "is what the tests test."[11] This definition has been reiterated several times since.[12]

At first blush, the concept of intelligence held by the general public seems quite different from the operational definition. The popular view, seldom precisely articulated, focuses on general mental ability; perhaps it is best stated as the ability to learn. This is fleshed out by associating the general ability called "intelligence" with three attributes: (1) it is a single thing; (2) it comes in varying quantities, and different people have different amounts of it; and (3) the amount of intelligence possessed by each individual is fixed for life. Although the popular or conventional concept of intelligence does not have the classic form of an operational definition ("intelligence is what intelligence tests test"), I argue that it nevertheless is operational in essence because the attributes commonly associated with intelligence stem from testing practices. First, the idea that intelligence is a single thing is rooted in the fact that the results of intelligence tests are often expressed on a single scale, such as IQ, even when the test itself consists of several distinct parts. Where there is a single score, it is widely assumed that some single thing must exist to which that score refers. The second attribute—that intelligence is quantitative, and that some people have more of it than others— derives from the practice of reporting intelligence test scores on numerical scales. Only quantitative phenomena may be expressed in numbers. And when those numbers vary from one person to another, so must the amount of intelligence that the numbers represent. Finally, the notion that the amount of intelligence possessed by each individual is fixed for life stems from the belief that intelligence tests measure not what one already knows but one's *ability* to learn. It is commonly believed that how much an individual actually learns depends on opportunity, motivation, and ability. Opportunity and motivation may vary at different times in the individual's life, but sheer ability to learn is generally considered to be a constant. It is hard-wired in the person. Hence each individual's intelligence is considered to be fixed by heredity.[13]

This conventional or popular notion of intelligence has achieved the status of a bedrock assumption. It is taken by most people in our society to describe a simple fact of nature. I wish to dispute that point of view. I have just argued that the popular concept of intelligence results from intelligence testing. And I argued earlier (chap. 2) that all testing traffics in representations and that any representation is not a given in nature but is a product of cultural conventions. By this reasoning, the "intelligence" that is represented in intelligence tests is not some independently existing natural phenomenon but a reality as construed by culture. It could very well be—and in fact is—conceptualized differently in other cultural traditions.[14]

An important reason why the particular concept of intelligence that reigns in our society has gained ascendancy is that intelligence tests have made it possible to measure, evaluate, and make a variety of selections among the masses conveniently and economically. Nevertheless, as I will attempt to demonstrate, that notion of intelligence has been responsible for a great deal of confused thinking, unjust policies, and human damage.

Eugenics

The most blatantly noxious social policy spawned by the conventional concept of intelligence goes by the name eugenics. This is the policy of strategically governing human reproduction so as to maximize the most desirable traits (and eradicate the undesirable ones) in future generations. Seizing on the notion that intelligence is fixed for life and determined by heredity, eugenicists placed it at the top of the list of traits to be manipulated by selective breeding. When Thorndike enumerated things humanity could do do improve its future, his first recommendation was "better genes." "A world in which all men will equal the top ten percent of present men" is within reach if the "able and good" will assiduously propagate. Meanwhile, for the good of the future, the "one sure service (about the only one) which the inferior and vicious can perform is to prevent their genes from survival."[15]

Thorndike's conjoining of "able" and "good" is not serendipitous. The assumption was widespread that moral fiber varies directly with intelligence. According to Terman, "all feeble-minded are at least potential criminals. That every feeble-minded woman is a potential prostitute would hardly be disputed by anyone. Moral judgment, like business judgment, social judgment or any other kind of higher thought process, is a function of intelligence."[16]

Terman and others concerned about the moral deficiency of the feeble-minded encouraged the use of intelligence testing to identify them. Goddard used the test particularly to ferret out morons, a term he coined to refer to those "high-grade defectives" (well above idiots and imbeciles) with a mental age of from eight to twelve. Goddard wrote, "The idiot is not our greatest problem. He is indeed loathsome; he is somewhat difficult to take care of; nevertheless, he lives his life and is done. He does not continue the race with a line of children like himself. . . . It is the moron type that makes for us our great problem."[17] Given the presumed link between intelligence and morality, Goddard was persuaded that the ranks of criminals, prostitutes, and ne'er-do-wells of all sorts contained disproportionate numbers of morons. It was impossible to ameliorate their condition, for, he believed, it was the unalterable result of heredity. It was unrealistic to expect them voluntarily to refrain from multiplying, for their dull mentality and deficient morality would hardly enable them either to grasp or to embrace their civic responsibility. Society could, however, take steps to prevent them from reproducing. Sterilization could do the job, but Goddard had misgivings about using it until more perfect understanding of the laws of human inheritance had been achieved. His solution of choice was "colonization:" morons should be confined in institutions (perhaps on the model of Goddard's own Training School for Feeble-minded Girls and Boys) where society could minister to their inadequacy, control their immorality, and curtail their sexuality. Whatever financial burden such institutions might place on the public treasury would be more than offset by reduced needs for almshouses and prisons.[18]

So much for the morons already here. Goddard was also concerned to prevent more from entering the country. Beginning in 1912, he directed efforts to identify possible morons among the new arrivals at Ellis Island. As a first sort, he used women who, he claimed, could pick out likely morons simply by looking at them. The candidates they selected were then subjected to Binet's intelligence test. Resulting IQs were appallingly low, leading him to conclude that immigrants of that time were the dregs of Europe. Thanks largely to Goddard's efforts, numerous immigrants were deported for mental deficiency in 1913 and 1914.[19]

Notwithstanding Goddard's misgivings about its social palatability, sterilization was for a time practiced as a more aggressive treatment for those whose inferior and vicious genes were to be extirpated. A proposal at the First National Conference on Race Betterment in 1914 called for a total of about five million Americans to be sterilized between 1915 and 1955.[20] An organization rejoicing in the name of the Committee to Study and Report on the Best Practical Means of Cutting Off the Defective Germ-Plasm in the American Population took the position that "'society must look upon germ-plasm as belonging to society and not solely to the individual who carries it' . . . and advocated segregation, sterilization, and education in the facts of heredity as the chief means of reducing defective germ-plasm" in the 10 percent of the American population who carry it. Committee chairman H. H. Laughlin targeted for sterilization "the feebleminded, insane, criminalistic ('including the delinquent and wayward'), epileptic, inebriate, diseased, blind, deaf, deformed and dependent ('including orphans, ne'er-do-wells, the homeless, tramps, and paupers')."[21] While such grandiose plans were never realized, some 8,500 people were sterilized between 1907 and 1928 in the twenty-one states that enacted sterilization laws.[22]

In eugenics, the conventional concept of intelligence leads to a particularly vicious form of injustice and discrimination because it encourages the privileged and the powerful to vilify the moral character of society's most defenseless members and sanctions the use of violence (such as enforced sterilization and confinement) against them. Mercifully, the most blatant cries for eugenics are in the past, although occasional apparitions prove that some elements of the mind-set are still alive. For example, the tacit assumption that "germ-plasm" belongs to society and not solely to individuals carrying it underlies the (ultimately unsuccessful) proposal set before the 1991 Kansas State Legislature that unmarried female welfare recipients be paid $500 to allow a contraceptive device to be implanted under their skin, as well as the 1991 stipulation by a judge in California that a woman sentenced for child beating use a similar device during three years of probation (the order is currently under appeal).

Race, Class, Gender, and Affirmative Action

While it is doubtless true that human abilities are to some extent inherited, numerous unfortunate consequences are spawned when the notion of heredity joins with the conventional idea of intelligence as a single thing that is possessed in a fixed amount for life. An offspring of this union that has done incalculable social damage is the idea that intelligence varies among different ethnic groups. If intelligence is inherited, so the reasoning goes, groups that marry and breed primarily within themselves might differ from each other in amount of intelligence just as they do in other inherited traits such as skin color or color and texture of hair. Those who are persuaded by this reasoning find evidence for it in the palpable differences in average intelligence test scores achieved by different ethnic groups. An example discussed earlier is the differences found between immigrants from different countries in the Army Alpha examination administered to army recruits during World War I. Similar discrepancies persist today. Jews and Japanese Americans tend to score higher than whites on intelligence tests, while blacks on average score about one standard deviation below whites.[23] That is to say, the bell curve for blacks on an IQ scale is about 15 points lower than that for whites.

This situation is relevant to public policy because intelligence tests are often among the criteria used for hiring, school admissions, and other important selective decisions made about people. The difference in test scores means, of course, that Jews, Asian Americans, and whites are likelier to be recommended for selection than blacks or other minorities with lower average test scores. Civil rights advocates would identify the systematic discrepancy in test scores and the decisions made on that basis as an example of institutional racism. So, as Seymour has pointed out, "The use of tests and similar instruments can be an engine of exclusion of minorities far more efficient than any individual's personal intent."[24]

The engine slowed down for a while from the late 1960s to the early 1980s, when the general political climate favored steps to compensate for disadvantages suffered by minorities through affirmative action. These included quotas of various sorts and within-group score conversion. As explained, this procedure involves upward adjustments in the percentile scores for blacks and Hispanics on the U.S. Employment Service's General Aptitude Test Battery to assure that members of ethnic groups were not recommended for jobs in numbers different from the proportion of that group in the population at large.

Since the latter 1980s, however, many affirmative action practices have come under fire as contradictions of the basic American principle that people be judged solely according to their individual merits. The basic issues pertaining to affirmative action had been crystallized in the late 1970s by the Bakke case, which concerned the admission of some members of minority groups to a medical school even though they had credentials that were inferior to those of some white males who were rejected. Within-group score conversion, in use since the early 1980s, was catapulted into the public spotlight during congressional debate over civil rights in 1991. The practice was widely condemned as a particularly blatant quota measure that adulterates individual merit with considerations of group membership. A scramble to do away with it ensued, and it was explicitly outlawed by the Civil Rights Act of 1991.

Rolling back affirmative action measures does not answer the question of what should be done about the fact that minorities tend on average to score lower than whites on standardized tests and therefore tend to lose out when vocational selection is made on the basis of them. Gottfredson's response is to accept the message conveyed by test scores at face value and to deal with it forthrightly: "We do not have a testing problem so much as we have a social problem brought on by real differences in the job-related capacities that tests measure,"[25] primary among them being a real difference in general intelligence between ethnic groups.[26] It is a long-term social problem, she goes on to say, that can eventually be solved only if it is addressed in a nonpatronizing, nondefensive, and nonpolitical manner.[27] She does not go deeply into the form that such solutions might take. However, one certainly nonpatronizing and nondefensive (but hardly nonpolitical) course of action that Gottfredson foresees even in the shorter run has to do with supposed differences in intelligence between blacks and whites of equal education. Reasoning from the facts that blacks on average score lower than whites on both the precollege SAT and the pregraduate school GRE and fail professional licensing examinations more frequently, she concludes that the mean IQ of blacks is lower than that of whites of equal education. Out of a conviction that job performance varies directly with intelligence, she continues, "Black-white differences in intelligence at equivalent educational levels suggest that if employers rely heavily and equally on educational credentials when selecting black and white workers, then the blacks they select can be expected to be less productive on the average than the whites they select."[28] Presumably, the antidote to the unwelcome consequences that stem from relying equally on educational credentials is to rely on them unequally. Employers who are mindful of Gottfredson's warning, that is to say, may favor white applicants over black ones with equivalent educational credentials, or they may "replace educational credentials with more valid selection criteria."[29] Confronted with an argument such as this, one wonders what blacks can possibly do to get ahead. Just when they begin to acquire the education that has always been held up to them as the key to success, the rules change and equal education turns out not to assure equal opportunity after all.

Because Gottfredson's conclusion and the action it seems to recommend are likely to dismay those who favor affirmative action for minorities, it is worth unpacking the logic of her argument. It begins with the principle that people should be evaluated exclusively on their merits and abilities as individuals. In line with the conventional concept of it, general intelligence is taken to be a single, largely inherited thing—a very important thing because it is closely related to job performance and productivity. It is noticed, however, that minority group members on average score lower than whites on intelligence tests. Because general intelligence is thought to be accurately measured by the tests, the difference in test scores must mean that members of these minority groups are, on average, less intelligent than whites. Now comes an important twist in the argument: people are supposed to be considered purely as individuals rather than as members of groups, but now it develops that group membership *is* relevant to intelligence because members of some groups, on average, have less of it than members of other groups. People then allow this group-related consideration to affect their treatment of individuals. Given the average difference in general intelligence between members of different groups, when evaluating individuals from different groups who present equal credentials, the safer course is to select candidates from the more intelligent group.

Notice how this line of reasoning has culminated in a position precisely opposite from where it started. Beginning with the insistence that persons be assessed purely as individuals, we end up with the conclusion that they will be evaluated partly as members of groups. This involves no less bias on the basis of group membership than affirmative action policies are accused of, but with this difference: while affirmative action normally seeks to redress injustice by favoring groups that have traditionally suffered from discrimination, this is a form of affirmative action that works to perpetuate the privileges of the already advantaged. It is not a matter, as in the Bakke case, of selecting blacks over whites who have superior credentials. It is selecting whites over blacks who have equal credentials.

Lloyd Humphreys applauds Gottfredson's candid confrontation of the black-white difference in intelligence and wishes she had gone even further.[30] Presumably the next step he desires is to add a class component to considerations of ethnicity. He points out that tested intelligence is correlated more strongly with so-cioeconomic status than with race,[31] and the conclusion he draws from this seems less to be that a disadvantaged social position is responsible for lower tested intelligence than vice versa. So, in terms reminiscent of the link that Thorndike, Terman, and God-dard forged between intelligence, morality, and social value, Humphreys claims that the "cognitive deficits" measured by intelligence tests "are part of a complex that includes the development of the underclass, teen pregnancy, female-headed families, crime, drugs, and AFDC." Adopting a stance not remote from eugenics, he rues the fact that the possibility of dealing with these problems through the "constructive social action" of liberalized abortion has sadly been curtailed by religious and other pro-life groups.[32]

The remark about abortion makes it clear that Humphreys too evaluates individuals on other than purely individual criteria. If there were some way of knowing *which* unborn fetuses were going to be cognitively deficient and turn into criminals, teen mothers, female heads of families, or welfare recipients, so that only they would be aborted, then, unpalatable as it may still appear to some, at least this final solution to our social problems would rest on individual considerations. But of course such foreknowledge is impossible, so the judgment as to what abortions are salutary must be made according to group-based and other criteria, of which the socioeconomic class and marital status of the mother would appear to be paramount. As it did with Gottfredson, the conventional concept of intelligence and the assumption that it is accurately measured by tests has led Humphreys a long way from the hallowed American value that people be assessed solely as individuals.

Humphreys is certainly correct that intelligence test scores vary systematically by socioeconomic status as well as by race. As table 2 demonstrates, the correlation between average SAT scores and family income is perfect. Of course, this information is not entirely independent from the relation already discussed between race and intelligence test scores, because ethnic minorities such as blacks and Hispanics are disproportionately represented in the lower class. Thus, Terman combined class and

TABLE 2
Average SAT Scores by Family Income

Family Income	Combined Verbal/Math SAT Score
Over $50,000	998
$40,000–$49,999	968
$30,000–$39,999	947
$24,000–$29,999	927
$18,000–$23,999	900
$12,000–$17,999	877
$6000–$11,999	824
Under $6000	771

Source: Data released by FairTest in 1985 and reprinted here from Fallows (1989:164)

ethnicity when he raised the alarm about the consequences of the reproductive rates of desirable and undesirable stocks:

> The fecundity of the family stocks from which our gifted children come appears to be definitely on the wane. It has been figured that if the present differential birth rate continues, 1,000 Harvard graduates will at the end of 200 years have but 50 descendants, while in the same period 1,000 South Italians will have multiplied to 100,000.[33]

Herrnstein is among those who in our own day have rushed to man the rampart formerly guarded by Terman. In "IQ and Falling Birth Rates," an article that appeared in the *Atlantic Monthly* just at graduation time (May 1989),[34] he berated commencement speakers who encourage intelligent female graduates to enter business and the professions for doing scant service to society. Herrnstein notes with some alarm that women of lower socioeconomic status produce more children per capita than those of higher classes. According to measures such as intelligence tests, the prolific proletarians tend to be mentally inferior to their wealthier, better educated, but reproductively reticent counterparts. Persuaded that intelligence is largely a matter of inheritance, Herrnstein, echoing Terman, anticipates that the discrepant fecundity among the classes will result in a general lowering of intelligence in future generations. His suggested antidote is to reaffirm the value of motherhood in the eyes of intelligent young women, in the hope that they will be fruitful and multiply for the sake of the nation.

If one is inclined to detect group bias in Herrnstein's argument, one would see it as directed most explicitly against the lower socioeconomic class. It is also possible, however, to discern a subtler sexism. It is, of course, yet another example of men telling women what to do with their bodies, but there is more. Herrnstein does not address the question of *why* it would be a good thing to prevent the general level of intelligence in the population from declining, but certainly the answer is self-evident: the more intelligent the people, the more effective the conduct of social, economic, and political affairs—of, indeed, all human activities. But who is to manage those affairs? Herrnstein's thesis is that today's bright young women should not be overly encouraged in that direction, for fear that it would divert their attention from motherhood and thus compromise the quality of the next generation. So the enlightened conduct of human affairs falls, by default if nothing else, to the men. What of the next generation? What roles does he envision for the children conceived from the happy mating of wealthy, well-educated, intelligent parents? What, specifically, would he have those children do if they happen to be daughters? Because they are likely to grow up, as their mothers, to be wealthy, well-educated, intelligent young women, presumably they should do the same thing that their mothers are supposed to do—reproduce. The enlightened management of human affairs would have to be left largely in the next generation, as in this one, to their brothers. And so it would go indefinitely: bright women should bear sons to run the world and daughters to bear sons to run the world and daughters to bear sons. . . .

Obviously, one effect of this arrangement would be to quash the competition for lucrative and prestigious positions that males (who have traditionally held them) have recently experienced from upstart females. Herrnstein's proposals thus boil down to yet another case of affirmative action that favors an already-advantaged group. Females cheeky enough to venture into the masculine world of work would be vulnerable to public condemnation for charting a selfish life course that threatens the well-being of future generations.

Arguments such as those by Gottfredson, Humphreys, and Herrnstein typically begin with the premise that people should be evaluated entirely on their individual merits, among which are the scores they achieve on intelligence tests. Then, by a convoluted logical transit, they end up judging people in terms of gender, class, or ethnic group membership. Now I want to suggest that a similar situation obtains the other way around—that what initially appears to be assessment on the basis of group membership turns out to be grounded in the principle that the sole relevant criterion for evaluating persons should be individual ability.

Let us develop the argument through an analysis of within-group score conversion on intelligence tests. This looks like a group-based procedure if ever there was one, because the percentile score that is reported for any individual depends not only on the raw score achieved but also on the person's ethnic group. We need to ask, however, *why* scores are converted. As we have seen, it stems from the purely individualistic assumption lying at the heart of the American creed of social mobility and equal opportunity: ability is not correlated with group membership. If this assumption is correct, then average intelligence test scores would be identical for all groups. That this is not the case indicates that factors other than intelligence must be influencing the performance on tests by members of different groups. These factors are usually identified with inequalities of opportunity, such as differences in home environment and educational preparation stemming from socioeconomic status, and cultural bias in the tests themselves.[35] So, for example, IQ scores of Australian aboriginal children rise as their contact with whites is greater. This is one of several facts that "should not be hard to explain considering the tests were designed by and for Northwestern Europeans."[36] When one controls for socioeconomic status, health, and the attitudes and motivations connected with home and school background, the differences in average test scores achieved by members of different ethnic groups in the United States drop to insignificant levels.[37]

Within-group score conversion may be understood as a measure to screen out the effect of these extraneous factors on intelligence test scores. Therefore, while it initially appears to assess people according to group membership, in fact within-group score conversion turns out to have the precise opposite effect of *doing away with* group-related privileges and disadvantages. The scores after conversion reveal what the distribution of intelligence would look like if those tested were assessed exclusively according to individual abilities in circumstances of truly equal opportunity.

The final proposition in this argument is that within-group score conversion is a temporary measure. The assumption that group membership is not a determining factor in the distribution of ability generates the anticipation that if and when differences in opportunity produced by social conditions such as discrimination and poverty are ended, group-related differences in intelligence test scores will disappear. At that point, within-group score conversion and other affirmative action measures will no longer be necessary.

Having attempted to unravel the tangled premises and consequences of the arguments about whether intelligence testing entails individual or group-related assessments, let me now spell out my own position on the issue. Of the two positions we have considered, I much prefer the one that accepts affirmative action policies because it avoids the racist, classist, and sexist implications that we detected in the alternative. In the last analysis, however, I think that *both* of these stances are untenable. The culprit beneath the entire debate is the conventional concept of intelligence. Specifically, both of the positions are built on the notion that intelligence is a single thing that is measurable by intelligence tests. The salient difference between them is that one accepts current testing as an accurate measure of intelligence, while the other claims that test results at present are adulterated by extraneous considerations. I do not accept the assumption that intelligence is singular and measurable by intelligence tests. In fact, my purpose in exploring these arguments about possible group differences in intelligence and affirmative action has been to point out how the conventional notion of intelligence is responsible for a great deal of confused thinking and unwieldy if not downright destructive social policies. In the concluding section of this chapter, I will present the quite different concept of intelligence that is much preferable to the conventional one. Our exploration of the deleterious consequences of the conventional concept is not quite finished, however. Having looked at some of its sociocultural consequences, we must now say a few words about its psychological effect on individuals.

Self-Definition and Self-Esteem

A few years ago, students at a prestigious women's college began wearing T-shirts with the inscription, "I'm a 1600. What are you?" Few methods of presenting the self are more popular today than messages written on T-shirts and sweatshirts. These announce one's allegiance to a university or professional athletic team; declare, rebuslike, affection for a city ("I ♡ New York"); broadcast political causes ("It will be a great day when our schools get all the money they need and the air force has to hold a bake sale to buy a bomber"); or, all other subjects having been exhausted, display information about themselves ("My parents had a fantastic vacation in New Orleans and all I got was this dumb T-shirt"). Students who wear the slogan, "I'm a 1600. What are you?" simultaneously boast about their own intelligence—1600 is the top score on the SAT—and issue a challenge to others. Most important, the students *define themselves* in terms of the test score. (It is, however, a fanciful or idealized self-definition, because those who actually achieve 1600 on the SAT are extremely rare.)

Likewise, people are defined by others in terms of tests. Byron Hollinshead answers the question posed in the title of his 1952 book *Who Should Go to College?* largely in terms of intelligence tests. It is in the interest of society at large, he argues, that its best talent be identified and developed. Therefore, "we believe that all students in the upper quarter in ability of the age group should be given a certificate which so states and that society should find ways of financing those who want a college education if they need assistance."[38] Those to receive the certificate and all the rights and privileges thereunto appertaining are to be identified by IQ tests, high school record (special consideration should be given to performance in mathematics and language classes), and teacher recommendations, with special school committees making the decisions in borderline cases.[39]

How Hollinshead conceptualizes and evaluates persons is obvious from several little fictional vignettes that he presents to dramatize his ideas about what society owes to, and can expect from, individuals of various ability levels. It is worth reproducing a few of them in full:

John is a high school graduate with an I.Q. of 143. Most of the youngsters in his block think he is a little queer, since he spends much of his spare time fiddling with radio sets. He graduated on the honor roll in high school, but his parents think they cannot afford to send him to college. If he goes to college, the chances that he will do well and graduate are about five to one. In peacetime or wartime, he will be such an asset that society cannot afford not to send him. Furthermore, he is a good risk to spend college endowment on, and his parents are justified in sacrificing for him.

Mary has an average high school record and only average perseverance. She has an I.Q. of 110. This would give her a low rating in a first-rate college, where her chances of success are poor. In a mediocre college she has about one chance in two of success. Society might take a chance on her, though the risk is great. A first-rate college which would have to support her partially by endowment would scarcely be justified in admitting her. Her parents might take the chance if it does not involve sacrifices on their part.

Alice is a lovely girl, with many friends. She tried hard in high school, but did not do well in any courses except typing and homemaking. Her I.Q. is 102. She played in the band and was a cheerleader. She would do well in a community-college course in cosmetology or secretarial work, although she would have trouble with shorthand. Her chances for success in a four-year college of even mediocre standards are poor. Alice's parents are scarcely justified in making many sacrifices for her education. If society provides the opportunity of a community college, it has done its share.[40]

The benefits to be realized by society from keeping students in the top quartile in school are so great, Hollinshead holds, that where necessary, the community should provide the necessary financial support. If such a student is forced by economic necessity to consider dropping out of high school, for example, he recommends that friends and local organizations such as parent-teacher associations provide the needed funds.[41] (It is amusing to imagine parents participating enthusiastically in bake sales and other fund-raisers to keep someone else's child in high school while their own children receive no special support because they failed to qualify for the magical top 25%.)

Defining persons—both the self and others—in terms of intelligence blends immediately and imperceptibly into evaluating them on the same grounds. This produces preoccupation with personal limitations. While people have been expected since biblical times to make the most of their God-given talents, it has also always been believed that God gives a good deal more in the way of talents to some people than to others. The discrepancy can produce a sense of inferiority among the less endowed and superiority among the gifted. The same considerations apply to intelligence, and for most of us, the precise location of the upper limit of our abilities (as revealed by intelligence tests) is a matter of supreme importance for our sense of self. I remember one summer day in 1959 when a high school friend and I compared our IQs as tested years before in grade school. Everything about the incident is vivid in my mind: we were in a swimming pool, and we splashed each other with playful anxiety as we counted up the scale one point at a time until our scores were reached. I especially recall the slight stab of dismay I felt when I learned that his IQ was (is now, and ever will be!) one point higher than mine. Now I knew why, a year or two previously, he had scored higher on the PSAT than I did. Would I never, I wondered, be able to aspire to quite the same heights as he?

Walter Kirn captures the painful self-assessment brought on by intelligence tests with humor and pathos in his short story, "A

Satisfying Ride in the Country."[42] Paul, the story's protagonist, found that he no longer had to work hard in school after a childhood IQ test showed him to be a genius (by 2 points). His teachers assumed he was brilliant and graded him accordingly even when he did not complete his assignments. The idea that he was a genius became a crucial component of Paul's self-image, and he decided to take another intelligence test as an adult. His curiosity about whether he still had the genius IQ was tempered with anxiety, leading him to adopt various delaying tactics before he finally sat down to take the test. When he did, his worst fears were confirmed, and the effect was devastating. As he tried to come to terms with the score, "I sat there, shaking. I faced the wall. . . . The drop was of a mere six points, of course, but that is a lot when you are alone and have only two to spare."[43]

For those near the bottom of the heap, the irremediable character of the news that one's intelligence has been measured and found to be insufficient for anything but the lowliest of social and occupational positions can be devastating to self-esteem. In his fanciful history, *The Rise of the Meritocracy, 1870-2033*, Michael Young claims that those who occupy the lower rungs of the social ladder are particularly abject in a meritocracy since they know they are there because of their own inferiority.[44] Gardner made the point unequivocally:

It must never be forgotten that a person born to low status in a rigidly stratified society has a far more acceptable self-image than the person who lost out in our free competition of talent. In an older society, the humble member of society can attribute his lowly status to God's will, to the ancient order of things, or to a corrupt and tyrannous government. But if a society sorts people out efficiently and fairly according to their gifts, the loser knows that the true reason for his lowly status is that he is not capable of better. That is a bitter pill for any man.[45]

The assault on self-esteem produced by the perception of low intelligence is not evenly distributed throughout society because test scores that indicate low intelligence are disproportionately represented among ethnic minorities and the lower class. Gottfredson's discussion of personal development suggests that these connections between social status and intelligence are established during childhood. Children develop a sense of social class and personal ability during the stage of orientation to social valuation, which typically occurs between the ages of nine and thirteen. This phase of development largely sets the prestige and ability level of the vocations they are willing to entertain as possibilities for themselves.[46] Linkages are forged such that high ability and high prestige occur together, as do low ability and low prestige. This is clear from Gottfredson's references to "lower-level" and "high-level" jobs,[47] locutions that combine both ability and prestige levels. In another essay, she explicitly develops the proposition that the hierarchy of occupations is related to general intelligence. As the relationship between job levels and the intelligence of their occupants is more perfectly actualized, overall economic productivity increases.[48]

Gottfredson's theory is supported by popular assumptions. It is widely believed (at least in the middle and upper classes) that lower-class people tend to be of limited intelligence and should fill low-level jobs (so defined in terms of both prestige and ability), while middle- and upper-class people are more intelligent and should fill the high-level jobs. This opinion obviously works at cross purposes with the notion that equality of opportunity can and should result in a high degree of social mobility. It fosters instead a stultifying notion of limitations, including psychological limitations that mark the child's developing image of self. The linkage of class membership with intelligence not only conditions the expectations and promises that society holds out for various categories of people but also colors the expectations and prospects that individuals imagine for themselves.

The conventional concept of intelligence and its measurement by intelligence tests are deeply implicated in this unfortunate situation. The notion that intelligence is inherited bolsters the idea that different classes, as largely in-marrying groups, may have different average levels of intelligence. Testing supports this point of view because, as we have seen already (table 2), intelligence test scores are highly correlated with socioeconomic status. Therefore, to use such tests as qualifiers for higher-level jobs will assure that those positions, with their higher levels of compensation, continue to be reserved for the higher classes. As for the more psychological issue of self-esteem that is our primary focus now, the correlation between socioeconomic status and test scores means that testing the intelligence of children in the schools likewise reinforces the association they develop in their perceptions of self between the class to which they belong and the amount of intelligence that they imagine they have. Thus, general intelligence testing *perpetuates* the problem rather than contributing to its solution.

The root of these social evils, I have claimed, is the conventional concept of intelligence as a single, innate mental capacity that varies considerably between individuals but remains fixed in each individual throughout life. We turn now to a critical examination of the merits of that concept.

Is Intelligence Fixed?

Consider first the notion that the amount of intelligence possessed by each individual is immutable. The source of that idea doubtless stems from the common view that intelligence has to do not with what a person has learned but with the ability to learn. That is not an achievement but a capacity or talent, and those are commonly thought to be part of a person's genetic makeup. No one denies that inheritance has something to do with human intelligence, but precisely what is not presently possible to isolate. If intelligence were a simple biological trait such as blood type or eye color, it would be meaningful to talk about it in terms of heredity and immutability. But intelligence is a *behavioral* trait (or, as will be argued shortly, a complex of different behavioral traits), and it is extremely difficult to deal with behavioral characteristics in terms of hereditary biology.[49] As Anne Anastasi put it, the individual inherits not intelligence "but certain chemical substances which, after innumerable interactions with each other and with environmental factors, lead eventually to different degrees of intelligent behavior. . . . It should be obvious that the relation between the intellectual quality of the individual's behavior at any one time and his heredity is extremely indirect and remote."[50]

As already mentioned, intelligence is commonly conceptualized as the ability to learn, as distinguished from what one has actually learned. That distinction is often framed in terms of the difference between achievement and aptitude tests. Achievement tests are designed to measure how much the subject knows about a given subject matter, so that one might speak of achievement tests in calculus, or music theory, or the history of seventeenth-century France. Aptitude tests aim to measure not so much what the person has learned in particular but rather one's ability to learn in general (sometimes broken down into a few broad divisions of knowledge, for example, quantitative and verbal). This ability is commonly thought to constitute intelligence, so intelligence tests such as the pioneering Army Alpha and Beta tests developed during World War I, the Stanford-Binet and Wechsler Intelligence Scales, and the SAT and ACT college entrance examinations are all aptitude tests.

It is essential to recognize, however, that no aptitude test *directly* measures the ability or capacity to learn. That is an inference drawn from a sampling of what people have already learned. Therefore, the difference between aptitude and achievement tests is much less than is commonly recognized by the general public.

It is now widely accepted [by psychologists] that all cognitive tests measure *developed abilities*, which reflect the individual's learning history. Instruments traditionally labeled as aptitude tests assess learning that is broadly applicable, relatively uncontrolled, and loosely specified. Such learning occurs both in and out of school. Instruments traditionally labeled as achievement tests, on the other hand, assess learning that occurred under relatively controlled conditions, as in a specific course of study or standardized training program; and each test covers a clearly defined and relatively narrow knowledge domain."[51]

For Anastasi, all mental ability tests may be located along a continuum in terms of the degree of specificity or generality of experiential background that they presuppose. To call some of them "aptitude tests" and others "achievement tests" may be confusing and lead to the misuse of test results.[52]

Sternberg goes even further than Anastasi in discounting the distinction between aptitude (or intelligence) tests and achievement tests:

> If one examines the contents of the major intelligence tests currently in use, one will find that most of them measure intelligence as last year's (or the year before's, or the year before that's) achievement. What is an intelligence test for children of a given age would be an achievement test for children a few years younger. In some test items, like vocabulary, the achievement loading is obvious. In others, like verbal analogies and arithmetic problems, it is disguised. But virtually all tests commonly used for the assessment of intelligence place heavy achievement demands upon the individuals tested.[53]

Intelligence tests have been concerned to measure previous learning from the very beginning. Binet, author of the first intelligence test, aimed to measure intelligence as something distinct from any instruction a child had received. Nevertheless, Robert Schweiker's synopsis of what Binet actually did makes it plain that his intelligence test was also, as Sternberg would put it, last year's (or the year before that's) achievement test:

> First grade teachers told Binet that most children had opportunity to learn many things before starting school. Those children who had learned many of those things, later learned well in school. Binet made a test of many of those things-which-most-children-had-opportunity-to-learn, and found that the test gave a fair prediction of success in school.[54]

In other words, the logic of Binet's test, as with all subsequent intelligence tests, is that the probability of learning things in the future is directly proportional to what one has learned in the past. But once this logic is made explicit, it immediately becomes obvious that even if the individual is endowed with a fixed amount of innate mental ability, that can be only one of several variables responsible for one's past learning and, therefore, one's performance on intelligence tests. Important among the others are the person's opportunities and motivation to learn. These are complex phenomena, turning on matters such as what rewards and encouragements the individual has received for learning, personal relationships with parents and teachers, if and when the individual was exposed to subject matters that stimulated interest, how much time and how many scarce or expensive facilities, books, instruments and other resources have been available for learning, and so on.[55] These factors may increase or decrease with time, and one's intelligence, as measured by intelligence tests, will change accordingly.

Binet was explicit that the intelligence possessed by an individual is not permanently fixed.[56] His main purpose was, in fact, precisely to increase the intelligence of those children who, for one reason or another, were developing slowly. Binet's test was intended to identify such children, so that they might be placed in special education classes where they could learn better habits of work, attention, and self-control and thus assimilate information more successfully.[57] His notion of special education, that is to say, focused on metalearning, or learning to learn. And that involves a change in the individual's intelligence. Binet wrote,

> It is in this practical sense, the only one accessible to us, that we say these children's intelligence can be increased. We have increased what constitutes the intelligence of a student, his capacity to learn and to assimilate instruction.[58]

Many contemporary theorists agree that intelligence can be increased. Sternberg, for example, argues that "intelligence is malleable rather than fixed,"[59] and he is one of several psychologists who have developed programs for increasing intelligence.[60] To conclude, that part of the conventional notion of intelligence which holds that each person's intelligence is fixed for life at a certain level is untenable.

Is Intelligence a Single Thing?

The popular notion that intelligence is a single thing stems largely from our habit of referring to it by a singular noun and the practice of reporting the amount of it that an individual has in terms of a single number: IQ, composite SAT score, and so on. Quite clearly, this is an example of the fallacy of misplaced concreteness. This is the error of assuming that where there is a name—in this case, "intelligence"—and a number, there must be some unique, preexisting phenomenon to which the name and number refer.

The fallacy of misplaced concreteness escalates to the point of absurdity under the operational strategy of defining intelligence (as Boring and several more recent psychologists cited above have done) as that which is measured by intelligence tests.[61] Consider, for example, the effect of this definition on efforts to improve intelligence tests, such as the changes that are currently being made in the ACT and the SAT. If intelligence is nothing more or less than that which is measured by intelligence tests, it is nonsense to say that changes in a test could produce more accurate measurements of it. The "improved" test, being different from its predecessor, would not measure the same thing better but must measure something *else*. The addition of an essay section on a college entrance examination, for example, quite obviously brings skills into play that are different from those involved in answering multiple-choice questions. Therefore, the operational definition leads to the conclusion that there are as many "intelligences" as there are different tests to measure it. To imagine that for every intelligence test that ever has been or will be devised there is a real, unitary phenomenon waiting to be measured by it is to be absurdly mired in the fallacy of misplaced concreteness.

Throughout the history of theorizing about intelligence, scholars such as Alfred Binet, E. L. Thorndike, L. L. Thurstone, and J. P. Guilford have recognized this problem and have suggested that what we call "intelligence" is really a variety of different abilities, some of them possibly only distantly related to others.[62] Different intelligence tests tap different combinations of these abilities and place different emphasis on them. The notion of intelligence as multifaceted continues to be fruitfully developed today, particularly by Howard Gardner and Robert J. Sternberg. Gardner's theory of multiple intelligences stipulates several quite distinct kinds of intelligence: linguistic, musical, logical-mathematical, spatial, bodily-kinesthetic, and "the personal intelligences" (capacities to deal effectively with one's inner feelings and social relationships).[63] Sternberg's "triarchic" theory distinguishes three aspects of intelligence: components (the nature of the thinking process); experience (learning from and reasoning on the basis of experience); and context (adapting to and shaping the environment).[64]

Gardner and Sternberg agree that present intelligence tests are woefully inadequate measures of the full range of intelligence. Gardner contends that they are focused primarily on linguistic and logical-mathematical abilities and are especially deficient in providing information about the musical, bodily-kinesthetic, and personal intelligences.[65] Sternberg's opinion is that current tests pertain to scarcely one-third of intelligence's triarchy, being limited essentially to certain parts of its componential aspect.[66]

So long as intelligence is viewed from a purely psychological perspective, as a property of individual minds and behavior, the view of it as plural or multifaceted appears to be entirely accurate and highly useful. But things change dramatically when we look at intelligence from a sociocultural perspective— as a product of social institutions rather than a property of the individual. From that point of view, intelligence emerges again as a single thing. Moreover, both the definition of what intelligence is and the amount of it empirically possessed by any individual are, from the sociocultural perspective, determined by intelligence tests. Curiously, this brings us to a position quite close to the absurd outcome of the operational definition, that for every possible intelligence test there is an "intelligence" waiting out there to be measured by it. The main difference is that a sociocultural view denies the preexistence of intelligence; it takes intelligence to be constructed by the test instead of somehow discovered by it. So the formulation becomes that for every possible intelligence test, there is an "intelligence" out there that is fabricated by it. This does not diminish the reality of intelligence, for artificial things are no less real than natural ones. Nor, although I will argue for its validity, do I wish to imply that the sociocultural concept of intelligence as a single thing is any less absurd than the operational view. There are, after all, no guarantees that the human condition is free from absurdity.

The sociocultural perspective on intelligence can be developed most clearly if we engage in the thought experiment of constructing a new test and imagining its consequences. Let us call it, simply, the New Intelligence Test, or NIT. It is intended especially to excel current tests by paying more attention to the practical aspects of intelligence used in everyday life and to sample more widely from the scope of intelligence as conceptualized by proponents of the multifaceted view. Hence, the NIT consists of nine sections.

1. A name recall scale tests ability to remember the names of persons to whom the subject has just been introduced.

2. A mathematics section tests the subject's ability to do problems of arithmetic and algebra.

3. The first impression scale invites a panel of ordinary people to evaluate the personableness of subjects by simply looking at them.

4. In the exposition of ideas section, the subject is given five minutes to read a page from Rousseau describing his distinction between self-love (*amour de soi*) and selfishness (*amour-propre*) and thirty minutes to present a clear and accurate written account of it, with original examples. (To avoid subjects learning of this problem in advance and studying for it, different forms of the test will feature other, analogous tasks in this section.)

5. The small talk scale evaluates subjects' ability to carry on an interesting conversation with someone they have never met.

6. A bullshitting scale assesses skill at participating in a discussion with two other people on a topic about which the subject knows nothing.

7. In the follow-the-directions scale, the subject is told once, at the speed of ordinary conversation, to do a task that consists of six distinct steps and is evaluated on how well the task is accomplished.

8. The adult sports scale evaluates the subject's ability to play golf or tennis, with suitable adjustments for male and female subjects.

9. Finally, the SES scale is a simple rating of subjects according to parental socioeconomic status.

A composite score is generated from the results of the NIT's nine sections. What ability or human capacity is tested by the NIT? A good operational response would be that it tests the skills or wits used in taking the NIT, no more and no less. This is certainly nothing inconsequential, for were the appropriate studies to be done, it would doubtless turn out that high NIT scores correlate positively (probably more positively than IQ scores) with desirable social outcomes such as success in the university, high income, and election to public office. But it is also obvious that what the NIT tests is not a single quality or capacity of persons. It is rather a set of distinct qualities, which have been measured by the several sections of the NIT and combined into a single score for convenience in reporting NIT results. In that sense our thought experiment is in line with the view of intelligence as multifaceted.

But assume now that the NIT were to catch on in a big way—that it came, for example, to be widely used for college and graduate admissions and for hiring and promotion purposes by law firms, government, and corporations. In such an event, the composite of different abilities measured by the NIT would not remain static. People would spare no effort in preparing for the test, in the hope of achieving the rewards awaiting those who excel on it. They would review arithmetic and algebra, they would master techniques for remembering the names of strangers, they would practice bullshitting, they would take golf and tennis lessons, they would groom themselves to appear more likable on first sight. High school and college curricula would shift in the direction of more training in the areas covered by the NIT (if they did not, irate parents would demand to know why their children were not being taught something useful). Kaplan and Princeton Review would explode into the marketplace with courses that promise dramatic improvement in one's NIT scores. (One side effect would swell the public treasury as people report inflated income to improve their children's showing on the NIT/SES scale—and then have to pay taxes on it.)

All of this dedicated effort would have a palpable effect. Although the NIT obviously measures several quite different abilities, people would knit them together as they strive to improve them all in order to raise their NIT scores. They would begin to imagine these several abilities to be one. They would name it, perhaps, "NITwit." Given its importance for success in life, it would be valued as a thing of great significance. People would worry about how much of it they possess; they would envy evidence of its abundance in their contemporaries and look for promising signs of it in their children.

Not only would a new mental category swim into the social consciousness. The empirical amount of it possessed by individuals would literally increase as, in preparing for the NIT, they hone their skills at following directions, expounding on ideas, small talk, and the rest of it. And, of course, as individuals increase these skills, NIT scores would go up. There would be rejoicing in the land as today's average NIT scores exceed those achieved in the past or by test takers in other countries—until, perhaps, an apogee were passed, and then national consternation about declining NIT scores would set in. Given all these transformations and developments, it is fair to say that NITwit would become a new, singular personal trait, an objective reality literally constructed by NIT testing. Perhaps the ultimate development (and the ultimate absurdity, but it unquestionably would happen) would be when rival tests are marketed that claim to test it faster, cheaper, or more accurately than the NIT.

What happened in our thought experiment has been the experience of "intelligence" in the real world. Because of intelligence tests, a variety of disparate abilities (to do mathematical problems, to comprehend texts, to compare shapes, to sort ideas or objects into classes, to define words, to remember historical events, and to do all of these things rapidly) have been lumped together to form a new, unitary mental characteristic called "intelligence." It is a quality considered to be of great importance because intelligence tests serve as the basis for offering or denying educational and career opportunities and other social rewards. Given this importance, intelligence has become a target for special effort and training, with the result that people increase their overall proficiency in it. Precisely as with NITwit in our hypothetical example, intelligence has been fashioned into an objectively real personal trait by the practice of intelligence testing.

From this perspective, intelligence seems to belong to a wonderland where everything gets absurdly turned around. If we examine the form of representation that is involved in intelligence testing, in principle, it is clear that IQ scores and other intelligence test results are supposed to be signifiers of certain abilities and capacities. That is to say, intelligence (the signified) comes first as a thing in itself, and test results are signifiers or representations of it. But this analysis has demonstrated that the tests come first, that those abilities and capacities constituting "intelligence" have been formulated by society and developed in individuals on the basis of the tests that measure it. Thus the absurd situation emerges in which the process of signification does not so much *represent* the signified as *produce* it. From this point of view, it is appropriate to refer to all intelligence—the human kind as well as that developed in machines—as "artificial" intelligence.

This issue will be developed further later. For the moment, I want to suggest that absurdities of this sort are not particularly rare. They are, indeed, so common that the term "absurd" may not be appropriate for them. For the most part, human beings regulate their affairs in terms of conventions or agreements they have established among themselves (often tacitly) rather than according to the dictates of external reality. Constitutions and codes of law, religions, money, hierarchical systems of rank and privilege are all cases in point. Indeed, what external reality is understood to be and appropriate methods for knowing it are themselves matters of social convention.[67] The concept of intelligence that has been analyzed and criticized in the preceding pages is conventional not only because it is commonplace but also in the sense that it is one example of a social convention or tacit agreement in terms of which human affairs are regulated. In a society such as ours, it is important to have *some* means of evaluating people for the purpose of allocating scarce rewards and opportunities, and "intelligence" as a socially constituted phenomenon has come to be an important criterion in that process.

To explain something is not, however, to justify it. The burden of this chapter has been that the conventional concept of intelligence has done a great deal of mischief by closing opportunities and damaging self-esteem for millions. It has created and justified eugenic programs of selective mating, immigration quotas, sterilization, and other blatant and insidious forms of racial, class, and gender discrimination. If this concept of intelligence is the product of social convention, however, it stands to reason that it can be changed by social convention. How that might be accomplished is one of the topics to be addressed next.

10

CONCLUSION:

MAN THE MEASURED

Thomas Gradgrind, sir. A man of realities.
A man of facts and calculations. . . . With a rule and a pair of scales
. . . always in his pocket, sir, ready to weigh and measure any parcel
of human nature, and tell you exactly what it comes to.

Charles Dickens,

Hard Times

This book's sociocultural perspective on testing has generated two basic theses. One is that tests do not simply report on preexisting facts but, more important, they actually produce or fabricate the traits and capacities that they supposedly measure. The other is that tests act as techniques for surveillance and control of the individual in a disciplinary technology of power. This concluding chapter extends the analysis and critique of these two properties of tests and offers some suggestions as to what might be done about them.

PRODUCTION

The Efficiency of Representation

If people were left to their own devices, they would identify their interests and talents by introspection and select training programs and occupations accordingly. The only way of knowing whether they had chosen well would be to assess their performance after they had actually entered the program or had been working for some time on the job. From the point of view of a positivist agenda to manage social affairs scientifically, that process of trial and error is utterly wasteful. People with insufficient understanding of their own inclinations and abilities are likely to choose inappropriate goals and thus misdirect their efforts. Their mistakes will be revealed only after they, the training programs, or their employers had wasted much time, effort, and money in false starts and failed projects. The most visible waste is represented by those who aim too high or drastically in the wrong direction and who fail after perhaps years of frustration and futile effort. Less evident but no less wasteful are the missed opportunities of those who aim too low or only somewhat askew. They do reasonably well in their chosen vocation but would have attained loftier heights and made greater contributions had their aspirations been better targeted.

Testing offers a solution to this problem because it is designed to identify who will do well in what parts of the race before it is run. The reason, of course, is that much testing is concerned to assess not so much what one has done already but one's aptitude or potential to do it. This stems from the representational nature of all tests. The information collected by any test is important not in itself but only as it represents *other* information about the subject (what we have called the target information). When the target information pertains to events that will happen (or will probably happen) after the test is given, those tests may be termed future oriented. An example is using the SAT to predict how a high school senior is likely to perform in college.

In principle, future-oriented testing slices through the inefficiency associated with placement by trial and error. No longer need people spend months or years in a particular vocation to discover whether they are really cut out for it. Aptitude tests measure their ability against what is required in that vocation; interest inventories reveal whether they are likely to enjoy it; drug and integrity tests reveal if they have the requisite moral qualifications. All of these matters can be discovered not only prior to

entering a vocation but even before entering a training or education program that prepares one for it.

So, at least, goes the propaganda promoting the efficiency of
testing. In reality, testing delivers less than it promises, and it
brings a number of unsavory side effects in tow. The typical stress
in aptitude tests on verbal and quantitative skills is so narrow that
these tests are often imperfect indicators of who is best suited for
certain jobs or educational opportunities; especially are they silent on such critical matters as motivation and emotional sta-
bility. Moreover, although future-oriented tests are designed to
predict performance, they accomplish this with reasonable success only in the short term. For example, Naomi Stewart's findings
indicate a positive correlation between IQ and prestige level of
occupation among thousands of army recruits in World War II.[1]
Her study, however, correlated intelligence as measured by the
Army General Classification Test taken on induction with occupation held immediately prior to induction. When research is
extended over the long term, a different picture emerges. Another
study of World War II servicemen found no correlation at all
between the predictions based on a one-and-one-half-day battery
of aptitude tests taken by 10,000 recruits aged about 20 and their
occupational success twelve years later.[2] Also relevant is the longitudinal study of men who attended public schools in Kalamazoo,
Michigan, between 1928 and 1950 and who were interviewed in
1973 and 1974, when they ranged in age from 35 to 59.[3] When
comparing their first jobs with scores on intelligence tests taken
as youths, the correlation of high scores with top jobs was indeed
visible. In subsequent years, however, the pattern changed as men
with low intelligence test scores began to find their way into
prestigious occupations. The percentages of those with childhood
IQ scores of 100 or below rose from 26 percent of the professionals
and 36 percent of those who held managerial positions in their first
jobs to 31 percent of the professionals and 42 percent of the managers in their current jobs. Thus, the value of intelligence test
scores for predicting occupational success diminishes over time,
and it is especially unwarranted to imagine that those with low
scores will not succeed in top-level occupations. The results of
these studies underline how erroneous and destructive it is to

discount the future prospects of people who happen to have done poorly on intelligence tests as children or youths.[4]

The Priority of Potential Over Performance

It could be argued that the poor capacity of future-oriented tests to predict in the long range is ultimately a practical shortcoming that will eventually be overcome with improvements in testing theory and technology. Be that as it may, certain other consequences inevitably accompany testing because they are embedded in the tests systemically, or in principle.

Some of these consequences stem from the peculiar nature of tests as representational devices. I have demonstrated that in intelligence testing, the relation between signifier and signified gets turned around. Now I want to extend that argument to cover all future-oriented testing.[5] Normally signifiers follow signifieds in time and are in one way or another modeled on them. For example, an Elvis look-alike is a signifier of Elvis Presley. The look-alike comes after the original Elvis and resembles the original Elvis in appearance. In future-oriented testing, the signifier precedes the signified. The signifier is the test result: a present or previous state of affairs measured by the test. The signified is the target information: a future state of affairs that the test result is used to predict. Consider drug tests. The signifier concerns whether the subject has used drugs during some period prior to the test. This is what the test directly measures. But, especially in the preemployment situation, the ultimate point of a drug test is not to gain information about what the subject has done in the past. It is to use that information to indicate something about what the individual is likely to do in the future, as an employee of the company. That prediction is the signified. Therefore, in urinalysis, particularly when used in the preemployment context, the signifier (the test result) precedes the signified (the subject's future behavior). The case is even clearer with qualifying tests such as the SAT and ACT. Obviously, the test measures what the student knows at the time of taking it. Nevertheless, the explicit purpose of the test is to use its result to predict (to signify) how well the student will do in college. Again the signifier comes first because, of course, the individual takes the test before entering college.

We have noted that in the usual form of representation when the signifier follows the signified, the signifier is modeled on the signified. But when the signifier precedes the signified, this modeling relation is also reversed. Consider some other cases of representation where the signifier precedes rather than follows the signified: a recipe is a signifier of the dish that is made from it, a blueprint signifies the building to be constructed according to its specifications, and a particular structure articulated in DNA is a signifier of the plant, animal, or human being having that genotype. Notice that in each of these examples it is not simply the case that the signifier precedes the signified. The signifier also acts as a *code* that is used to *produce* the signified. This is also true of most testing, and it is of critical importance for the fabricating quality of tests. Usually tests do not simply measure things in a purely neutral and nonintrusive manner, as calipers might be used to measure the length of a skull or the width of a nose. Tests often change or condition that which they purport to measure. It is essential to recognize this property, because many of the unintended and often unrecognized social consequences of testing flow directly from it. The fabricating process works according to what may be called the priority of potential over performance. Because tests act as gate-keepers to many educational and training programs, occupations, and other sectors of social activity, the likelihood that someone will be able to do something, as determined by tests, becomes more important than one's actually doing it. People are allowed to enter these programs, occupations, and activities only if they first demonstrate sufficient potential as measured by tests. The result of this, I argue, is that to pass through the gates guarded by testing is to undergo metamorphosis. The process works in two ways: by selection and by transformation.

Selection

The selective power of testing may be introduced by considering contemporary authenticity tests. An employer who wants to avoid hiring people who might use drugs, steal, embezzle, or engage in industrial espionage or other disapproved behavior may make the appointment contingent on a drug, integrity, or (until they were outlawed in the private sector in 1988) lie detector test. These tests use past behavior as the basis for prediction of future behavior. Drug testing by urinalysis in particular is a crude instrument because it reveals drug use during only a short period prior to the test. From the employer's point of view, it would represent an advance if authenticity tests were more purely future oriented, revealing the probability that people will engage in certain kinds of behavior in the future even if they have never behaved in that way before. To draw out the logic of this situation, imagine that a genetic tendency to drug abuse or crime had been identified. It would then be possible to base employment decisions on genetic tests, with employers declining to hire individuals who fit the troublesome genetic profile. Of course, it is not likely that such tests would predict future behavior with absolute certainty. Some who would have made perfectly honest and reliable employees will be excluded, while others who seem to be a safe bet on genetic grounds will turn out to be bad apples. Nonetheless, it would serve the interests of employers to use the genetic test in employment decisions because it would reduce the statistical incidence of undesirable behavior in the workplace.

Notice, however, what would happen if such practices were put into effect. The goal is to avoid hiring drug users, criminals, and troublemakers of various sorts. But the end actually achieved is to avoid hiring anyone who is identified by a test as fitting a certain profile that has a probability of such behaviors. This is how testing, as a selective gate-keeping device, results in the priority of potential over performance. Decisions are made about people not on the basis of what they have done, or even what they certainly will do, but in terms of what they might do.

All this is more than the dream of the positivist social planner or the nightmare of the civil libertarian. Some actual forms of testing fit this description precisely. One of them is preemployment integrity testing. These are past oriented to a degree, in that they normally include a section that invites the subject to divulge any previous wrongdoing, and those admissions are taken into account as possible indicators of future behavior. But the tests also include questions that probe general attitudes and opinions with the purely future-oriented purpose of revealing general dispositions that are thought to have a probability of producing unacceptable behavior, quite apart from any past record. Employers make hiring decisions on the basis of this information, and those decisions exemplify the priority of potential over performance in the same way as the imaginary example of genetic testing described above. As a result, integrity tests utilize selection to modify that which they are intended to measure, for a work force hired with the aid of integrity testing tends to manifest a certain personality profile. Thus, as was reported in chapter 3, the proprietor of a fast food chain in Texas said, "We used written honesty tests for a while but quit when we found that the people we were hiring were just *too weird.*"

Potential predominates over performance even more in qualifying tests than in authenticity tests. Aptitude and placement tests of all sorts stand as gate-keepers to select who shall be admitted to and promoted in various educational programs from nursery school through graduate school, vocations, professions, and positions of influence and responsibility. It is impossible to receive awards such as a National Merit Scholarship or a National Science Foundation Graduate Fellowship—and nearly impossible to be admitted to a prestigious college or graduate or professional school—without achieving high scores on one or another standardized aptitude test such as the PSAT, SAT, ACT, GRE, MCAT, GMAT, or LSAT. Duke University sponsors a Talent Identification Program that provides a special summer course of enriched study for junior high school students. The sole qualification for this program is a sufficiently high score on the SAT or the ACT, taken in the seventh grade. As with the authenticity tests considered a moment ago, these qualifying tests mold, by systematic bias of selection, the intellectual and personality characteristics of award recipients, student bodies, and members of professions.

Aptitude tests often become ends in themselves rather than means to an end. High school seniors are pictured in local newspapers because their scores on entrance examinations result in

National Merit Scholarships, but their progress through college is not given the same attention. This is part of a general tendency in contemporary society to place more emphasis on qualifying to do something than actually doing it. In academia, scholars may be more honored for receiving contracts and grants to conduct research than for successfully completing the work and publishing significant results. In the world of work, it is often harder to get a job than to keep it. Union contracts, various forms of tenure, and the Equal Employment Opportunity Commission and other regulating agencies make it onerous to remove someone from a job for mediocre or minimal performance of duties. Illegal or flagrantly immoral behavior will normally suffice as grounds for dismissal, but charges of gross incompetence may or may not stand up against protests and hearings, while mere inadequacy is often a nonstarter. Thus, potential is again prior to performance, because after people have succeeded (often by tests) in demonstrating the potential necessary to get hired, it is not likely that they will be dismissed from it merely because that potential is not realized on the job.

Finally, the power of tests to select, and therefore to create that which they profess to measure, is so great that they sometimes determine life chances in the most literal sense. Parents use amniocentesis to identify the gender of fetuses, and in some cases, they couple the procedure with abortion if the gender is not to their liking. This may have a dramatic impact on the sex of fetuses that are carried to term. Philadelphia medical geneticist Laird Jackson reports that "virtually all of the babies ultimately born to his [East] Indian patients are males. For other patients, the relation of males to females is about 50-50."[6] There can be no more vivid or disturbing example than this of how future-oriented tests, as gate-keepers, may exercise a determining effect on those who are allowed to pass through.[7]

The case of amniocentesis highlights the crucial mechanism whereby selection operates in tests. The effect is in the aggregate: amniocentesis does not change the sex of any particular fetus, but selective abortion based on test results can have a dramatic impact on the sex ratio of babies that are ultimately born. Similarly, integrity or intelligence tests use a screening process to exercise a determining effect on the aggregate personality, cognition, and other characteristics of people who pass through their gates to be hired or promoted, awarded a scholarship, admitted to a prestigious college or graduate program, and so on.

Transformation

It also happens that tests bring about the transformation of individual subjects. The sheer act of measuring something may change it. In physics, the Heisenberg uncertainty principle holds that the outcome of experiments on subatomic particles is affected by the experiments themselves, and probably everyone has had the experience of blood pressure rising simply because it is being taken. A similar effect, albeit subtler and more pervasive, often occurs with the various kinds of tests that we have been examining.

One transforming capacity of tests is played out in the negative, in that tests prevent changes or developments in individuals that would otherwise take place. In schools, tests enable teachers to identify deviations in learning early, making it possible to correct them with small interventions. One thinks of Nancy Cole's image of the ideal classroom of the future—a sort of constant examination where the work of each student (done on a computer) is subject at every moment to observation, analysis, and correction by the teacher.[8] This is an outstanding example of Foucault's notion, discussed especially in chapter 4, that constant surveillance enables power to be applied with maximum efficiency.[9] Just as in the political realm dissidents, detected early by constant surveillance, can be nipped in the bud, so in the realm of thought, regular testing enables early identification and correction of deviant or independent thinking. One must not, of course, ignore the beneficial results of this. It enhances the learning process by identifying things that students do not understand and preventing them from going off on unproductive tangents. Nevertheless, it is also a marvelously efficient means of thought control, and it comes at a price. Often, it is not possible to be certain in advance that a tangent will be unproductive. In all areas of social life— political, artistic, intellectual, technological, economic—as well as in biological evolution, change often originates in minor deviations that, if allowed to develop, may open up hitherto unrealized potentials. By inhibiting aleatory exploration in thinking, testing encourages stagnation of the status quo and impedes the process of change.[10]

Among transformations in individuals that testing produces rather than prevents, test scores redefine the person in the eyes of others and in one's own eyes as well. Such was the case with Victor Serbriakoff, who transformed himself from a school dropout working as a day laborer to the author of books and president of the International Mensa Society after an intelligence test reported his IQ to be 161. The other side of the issue is less inspiring: low intelligence test scores have caused untold numbers to be treated as stupid by their teachers, lose opportunities, lower their aspirations, and suffer lingering injury to self-esteem. And, as was explained in chapter 4, polygraph tests have the capacity to redefine people in their own eyes by convincing them that they are guilty of misdeeds that they did not in fact commit.

The transforming capacity of tests works on individuals before taking them as well as after. Because people covet the rewards that are available to those who pass through the gates guarded by tests, many spare no effort to remake themselves in ways that will improve their test performance. An outstanding example is the ancient Chinese civil service examination. Ambitious Chinese youths and men spared no effort over years and even decades of arduous study to acquire the knowledge and skills that would be tested. Thus, they literally transformed themselves to mirror the expectations embodied in the examination. The remarkable capacity of the Chinese civil service examination to mold human material was summarized by Wolfgang Franke: "For over 500 years the traditional Chinese system achieved harmoniously and smoothly, with almost no resort to force, a degree of intellectual homogeneity eagerly sought, but so far scarcely attained, by the most totalitarian systems."[11]

People also transform themselves for the sake of doing well on tests in our own society. For many students, learning is less a matter of acquiring the information covered in their courses than becoming skillful at cramming and other techniques to get high grades on tests. Kaplan courses and the Princeton Review are designed explicitly and exclusively to raise scores on standardized tests. Nor are students the only ones who put test performance ahead of the acquisition of knowledge. Teachers often "teach to the test" with the goal that their students' performance on aptitude and minimum competency tests will make them (the *teachers*) and their school look good. Jacques Barzun has suggested that the preoccupation with doing well on standardized tests has literally conditioned the way young people in America think.[12] They have better-developed cognitive abilities to recognize random facts than to construct patterns or think systematically, he argues, because the former skill is favored and rewarded by the multiple-choice format of standardized tests. In all of these ways, tests create that which they purport to measure by transforming the person.

In some cases, the transformation may be quite unintended and even counterproductive. Integrity tests, for example, do not seem to be conducive to integrity. Those who take them are job applicants who enter the situation not as disinterested and compliant subjects (as is usually the case, for example, with tests given in the context of psychological experiments) but as deeply interested parties who are out to get hired. In responding to questions about their attitudes and opinions, their answers are likely to be what they believe will produce the most favorable result rather than what they actually think. Therefore, a test that is intended to measure an applicant's honesty actually diminishes the honesty that the subject manifests while taking it. This may also have a persistent effect. Some employees may see little reason to extend loyalty and respect to employers who trust them so little as to demand integrity tests, and so the likelihood that such employees will steal or cheat if given the opportunity might actually increase.[13]

Tests, I have claimed, transform people by assigning them to various categories (genius, slow learner, drug-free, etc.), where they are then treated, act, and come to think of themselves according to the expectations associated with those categories. But tests do more. As with recipes, blueprints, or codes articulated in DNA, they also define or act as constitutive codes for the categories themselves. It was argued in chapter 2 that in sixteenth-and seventeenth-century Europe, tests for witchcraft (and the fact that numerous suspects were revealed by them to be witches) served as important wedges for inserting the belief in witches into the public mind. The process works by a reversal of logic. Ostensibly the reasoning proceeds deductively: there are witches; witches have teats; this individual has teats; therefore, this individual is a witch. In actuality, however, the logic runs in the opposite direction: this individual has teats; teats are associated with witches; therefore, this individual is a witch; therefore, witches exist.

The capacity of tests to act as constitutive codes for social beliefs and categories remains in evidence today. As one important example, for the last three-quarters of a century or more, the idea has been abroad in the land that intelligence is a single thing that is possessed in significantly different amounts by different people, who on that basis may be classified on a scale of categories ranging from idiot to genius. As was discussed in chapter 9, the source of that complex of beliefs and categories is our widespread use of tests that report the intelligence of individuals on simple, quantitative scales such as IQ. The same reversal of logic that operated centuries ago for witchcraft is in play today with reference to intelligence. The apparent structure is deductive: intelligence is a single thing differently distributed among individuals; intelligence is measured by IQ tests; these individuals made certain scores on an IQ test; therefore, each one has the amount of intelligence corresponding to his or her score. But in fact, the premise about intelligence that starts the deductive chain is the *conclusion* that emerges when the argument runs in the opposite, inductive direction: these individuals made certain scores on an IQ test; IQ tests measure intelligence; therefore, each one has the amount of intelligence corresponding to his or her score; therefore, intelligence is a single thing differently distributed among individuals.

Still more subtly, as part of a process that has been taking place since at least the Industrial Revolution, testing has contributed to a general transformation in the way in which the person is known. As occupational specialization has become widespread, the various roles that an individual plays in social life have become increasingly disparate. In small hunting-and-gathering, herding, or farming communities, the same people interact with each other in a wide variety of contexts—familial, religious, economic, political. The result is that people are known to each other as complete persons, in all their roles. They know each other's skills, preferences, sense of humor, mannerisms, temper, general state of health, and so on.

Family members, friends, and close work associates still know each other in much the same way. But with increasing social complexity and division of labor, the individual tends to interact with different groups of people in different roles and thus is known to most other people only as a partial person: as a relative to some, a church member to others, a co-worker to others, a community volunteer to still others, and so on indefinitely. This has produced a certain fragmentation in the person as socially known, and possibly the different constituencies and rules that operate in the distinct spheres of the individual's life are conducive to disarticulation of the person even as known to oneself.

Testing is a major contributor to this general transformation of the person or self. Because of all the testing presently done, more knowledge has been accumulated about individuals in our society than at any previous time in history. It is a sort of knowledge, however, that probes deep into each particular but does little to connect them. The knowledge is stored in records kept in different places and used for different purposes. Physicians, dentists, optometrists, psychologists, and psychiatrists have records of tests pertaining to the individual's state of health; schools and universities keep records of academic tests; each employer has records of integrity and drug tests and tests of aptitude or skills taken in connection with a job; and the police may have records of lie detector, drug, or forensic tests taken in connection with criminal investigations. Officials in each of these spheres normally have little interest in the records of tests held in another, and even if they did, rules protecting privacy and confidentiality prevent transmission of the information. For example, a previous employer will not share an individual's test and other work records with a subsequent employer, for fear of grievances or lawsuits.

The result of all this is that individuals are known not in the round but piecemeal—different fragments for different circumstances. Therefore, while testing has indeed produced an explosion of knowledge about persons, it is an explosion in the literal sense of blowing the person apart. It scatters discrete bits of information to diverse points on a vast grid of disparate purposes and interests. The consequence is that the self as a coherent, integrated whole is vanishing. In its place this dissecting way of knowing produces a self as *coincidence*—a chance intersection of scores, measurements and records in standardized schemes of classification.[14]

These remarks apply not only to how the person is known to others but also to oneself. As we have seen, a polygraph test has the disconcerting capacity to divide the self and set the parts against each other, for the body betrays the mind to the polygraph machine. Another consequence of testing for self-knowledge may be drawn from George Herbert Mead's insight that "the individual experiences himself . . . not directly, but only indirectly, from the particular standpoints of other individual members of the same social group or from the generalized standpoint of the social group as a whole."[15] If (as argued above) others know a person not in the round but in fragments, and if the person knows oneself through the eyes of others, then the self will know itself as fragmented rather than as a coherent whole. This implies that the decentered knowledge of persons (self as well as others) that stems from testing may be partly responsible for the widespread malaise about the self and the contemporary orientation of popular psychology and psychotherapy toward knowing or "getting in touch with" oneself to become an integrated or "put together" individual. Given the role of testing at the source of the fragmentation of the self, it is ironic that one of the most common methods to get in touch with oneself is through still more tests, either various personality tests administered by professional counselors and psychotherapists or the myriad ten-question tests promising insights into the self that abound in popular magazines.

The piecemeal notion of the person that results from testing should be related, finally, to a general fragmentation that has been identified by social theorists as an important characteristic of postmodern society. As the modernist anchors in absolute truth, fixed reality, and integrative meaning tear loose, the beliefs and institutions of society become disengaged both from firm foundations and from each other. The result is not unlike the disarticulated, coincidental self described above: a collection of loosely connected parts that constantly rearrange their associations as they slide in and out of contact with each other in unstable, varying patterns.[16]

The Hyperreality of Testing

Testing produces the priority of potential over performance because decisions are made and actions are taken on the basis of test results rather than on more direct knowledge of the target information that they supposedly signify. Positivist proponents of testing perceive this as an efficient means of ascertaining how well someone can do something without expending time and resources in a trial period of actually doing it. At least as important, however, it is easier and safer to act on test results because they are "hyperreal."[17] As the term is used here, a situation is hyperreal when a signifier so dominates or enhances the process of representation that it (the signifier) becomes more impressive, memorable, actionable, and therefore more real than what it signifies. A radio baseball commentator described "what might have been the greatest catch I ever saw." He qualified it thus because he saw it in a minor league stadium that lacked a huge screen that could flash instant replays of the catch, reproducing it several times, stopping the action at critical junctures, displaying it from various angles. Instant replays are, of course, representations or signifiers of actual events. But they are hyperreal because they allow richer experience of events than mere observation of the real thing. So deeply have these representations become embedded in our expectations that the commentator remarked how, having seen the catch only once, as it actually happened, it did not seem quite real.

Test results are also hyperreal. Unlike the more complex and nebulous target information they presumably signify, test results are distinct, explicit, and durable. Partly, this is because they are written down: concrete records that are storable, retrievable, and consultable. They bear the same relation to the aptitude, ability, or other personal qualities they report on that the instant replay bears to the catch in baseball. The one is a signifier or representation of the other, but it is more palpable and scrutable than a fleeting event or an abstract, immaterial quality. The signifier therefore takes on a greater reality than the signified. Test results are unlike instant replays, however, in that the difference between signified and signifier in tests is greater. Test results are expressed in a form that is different—and drastically pared down—from what they signify. Consider, for example, the compression and transformation that is necessary to get from the rich complexity of an intelligence to the single number IQ score that supposedly represents it.

Perhaps most important, test results take on a greater importance and more palpable reality than what they signify because test results are *actionable*. The abbreviation of test results constitutes an operational advantage when, as commonly happens in contemporary society, many people vie for limited rewards, and those charged with making the selection have no extensive knowledge of the candidates and time only for a rapid review of their credentials. Decision makers for scholarships or fellowships, admission to selective colleges, or other competitive programs often know the candidates only as the bearers of certain academic and extracurricular records, test scores, and assessments in letters of recommendation. Their work would be vastly complicated and perhaps unmanageable if all the applicants were to present themselves as complete human beings with full and nuanced ranges of interests, talents, penchants, and problems. In evaluating people for a position in which intelligence is deemed to be an important criterion, for example, it is faster and simpler to make a decision between two candidates when told that one has an IQ of 125 and the other 115 than when given detailed, richly textured accounts of their respective cognitive capabilities. Nor should we overlook the security factor involved. Resting decisions on explicit and readily comparable test scores makes it possible to claim that the best selection was made on the basis of the information available, should decisions work out badly or there be troublesome protests or lawsuits.

The Problem of Intelligence

One of the most harmful instances of hyperreality that is spawned by testing is the peculiar notion of intelligence that holds sway in America. A grossly abbreviated and distorted signifier of the complex and varied capacities of the mind, the components of this notion are that intelligence is a single entity, that it is unequally distributed in the population such that some people have considerably more of it than others, that each person's allotment of it is fixed throughout life, and that it has a great deal to do with the vocations to which people might aspire and the success they can expect to achieve in them. In some of its forms, "intelligence" has additional, particularly destructive corollaries, such as that it is differentially distributed by gender or among ethnic groups.

Numerous theorists and studies reviewed earlier recommend a viewpoint quite contrary to this notion of intelligence. Gardner and Sternberg promote views of intelligence as multifaceted. Binet held that an individual's intelligence is not fixed but can improve. Varying profiles on intelligence test scores achieved by different ethnic groups can be attributed to differences in culture and socioeconomic variables rather than differing amounts of something called innate intelligence. Longitudinal studies have found little if any correlation between results on intelligence tests taken in childhood or youth and occupational success later in life. And yet the conventional notion of intelligence persists. In its name, rewards and opportunities are extended to some, while others are dismissed as having too little potential to justify investments to develop it. Because intelligence is generally accepted as a preeminently important capacity, those who are considered to be deficient in it are viewed both by others and themselves as inferior, while those who are thought to richly endowed with it receive social adulation and develop a bloated sense of self-worth (often accompanied by neurotic fragility born of anxiety that perhaps they are not really as intelligent as everyone thinks they are). In sum, the notion of intelligence that abides in America is both erroneous and detrimental, and it should be changed.

The burden of my argument has been that the conventional concept of intelligence has its source in the abundance of intelligence *tests* that are routinely given in today's society. If this is true, then a useful way of undoing the popular concept of intelligence would be to do away with intelligence tests. This would be a step of considerable magnitude. It would mean terminating one-on-one tests that style themselves as intelligence or IQ tests, such as the Stanford-Binet and the Wechsler Intelligence Scales. But much more important, also slated for extinction would be the myriad standardized so-called aptitude tests given at all levels in elementary and secondary school, the SAT, ACT, and ASVAB for high school seniors, the GRE, MCAT, LSAT, and GMAT for applicants to graduate or professional schools, and the GATB for applicants who seek jobs through the U.S. Employment Service.

Massive as the prospect may be, such a development is not inconceivable. It may already have begun. Although the trend is still toward increasing emphasis on admissions tests, in recent years, a reaction against them has sprouted. Antioch, Bard, Hampshire, and Union colleges, together with some two dozen others, no longer require applicants to submit SAT or ACT scores, and Harvard Business School has dropped the GMAT (Graduate Management Aptitude Test) as an application requirement.[18] These institutions make their selections on the basis of academic records, written statements by applicants, and letters of recommendation, and they manage to operate their admissions programs effectively without intelligence tests.

If intelligence tests were abolished, it would not be long before the conventional notion of intelligence as a single, quantifiable entity would change. People would distinguish more clearly among a variety of abilities, and these might be demonstrated, as

CONCLUSION

Howard Gardner suggests, by evidence of an individual's accomplishments in linguistic, musical, logical-mathematical, spatial, bodily-kinesthetic, and personal intelligences.[19] This would not signal the end of all qualifying tests. In addition to other evidence of accomplishments, tests would continue to play a role in decisions about school promotions and graduation as well as competition among aspirants for scholarships, admission to selective colleges and training programs, or employment in desirable jobs. The tests, however, would be strictly past oriented. They would be concerned to measure how well individuals had succeeded in mastering knowledge or skills that had been presented to them in academic courses or technical or artistic training programs. Different individuals would, of course, perform at different levels on these tests, and this would be taken into account along with other accomplishments in deciding who will receive scarce rewards and opportunities.

To develop these practices and attitudes is not unthinkable. They are already well established in some sectors. Consider how evaluation works in a typical American college course. Depending on the discipline, students are usually graded on the basis of some combination of the following: problems or questions to be completed and handed in at regular intervals, laboratory reports, term papers, performance in discussion groups, and tests. Far from being future-oriented intelligence tests, the tests are strictly based on material covered in the course. (To include anything else, as every professor knows, is sure to provoke students to rise up in rebellion.) The notion of general intelligence plays almost no role in the process. When students do not perform adequately and one wishes to understand why, the first questions have to do with how much interest they have in the subject matter and how much effort they put into it. If it is clear that they are interested and are trying hard, investigation turns next to their preparation. Have they developed good study habits? Do they have the requisite background for this course? Have they learned the particular modes of thinking and analysis that are used in this discipline? Academic advisers account for the great majority of cases of unsuccessful course performance in terms of one or another of these lines of investigation. Only for the few cases that remain does the question of sheer ability or "intelligence" come up. And even then, the matter is posed in terms of the particular abilities appropriate for a specific subject matter (ability to do mathematics, to draw, to interpret poetry, etc.) rather than general intelligence.[20]

If the attitudes represented in this process were to become commonplace, it is likely that we would lose the habit of thinking of intelligence as an all-important, single thing that is distributed unequally among the population. Instead, we would evaluate quality of performance in terms of a variety of factors, only one of which is native ability in that particular area. Such a change in thinking would drastically curtail the destructive view that some people are irredeemably inferior to others by birth, perhaps even by race. It would place primary responsibility for achievement squarely on the individual's effort and hold out the promise that if given a fair opportunity, the degree of one's own determination is the major factor in achieving one's goals.

The most important discontinuity in applying the model of procedures in a college classroom to larger evaluation programs has to do with equal opportunity. It is a given that all of the students enrolled in a single course have the opportunity to receive the same instruction, but this, of course, does not hold if large numbers from different localities and backgrounds are being assessed. The applicants will have been exposed to a variety of different experiences and curricula in schools that are anything but uniform in the quality of education they provide. The question is how to achieve a fair evaluation of how well people have acquired academic, technical, artistic, or other skills when some of them have had much richer opportunities to acquire them than others. This is no new problem. It also plagues the present system, for, as we have seen, a direct correlation exists between intelligence test scores and family income. Sad to say, the present proposal offers no magic bullet for solving this most intransigent dilemma in our system of education and mass evaluation. Probably no simple solution exists. In the short range, admissions committees and other evaluators will need to continue, as they do now, to factor variables of previous opportunity into their decisions. But this is a difficult process at best, and some decision makers are less adept at it or take it less seriously than others. The only satisfactory long-range solution is the obvious one of making a massive commitment to provide all primary and secondary school children with equal educational opportunities. And that, of course, will require much more than just fixing the schools. It also involves fostering supportive home environments, and that will be realized only when the larger social problems of poverty and discrimination are successfully resolved.

DOMINATION

From Seduction to Pornography

If some of the most important social consequences of tests flow from their representational character, others stem from the fact that they are devices of power. Testing is an outstanding example of the collusion and mutual extension of power and knowledge (expounded on by Foucault in nearly all his works), because testing as a technique for acquiring knowledge about people has simultaneously operated as a means to extend power over them. How this comes about is, in the most general terms, signaled in the clause of our definition stating that tests are applied by an agency to an individual with the intention of gathering information. Test givers are nearly always organizations, while test takers are individuals. Organizations are richer and stronger than individuals, so a power differential is established at the start.[21] The asymmetrical relation of power is further evident from the total control that the test-giving agency exercises over the situation. The individual is required to submit passively while the agency extracts the information it wants in order to use it for its own purposes.

Compare this situation with how persons are otherwise known. In *The Presentation of Self in Everyday Life*, Erving Goffman examined how the person seeks to manipulate the impressions that others form of oneself and thereby to exert some measure of control over the social situations in which one participates through a process of creative and selective masking and revelation of the self.[22] The self so presented is typically a nuanced character, evincing a unique pattern of abilities, temperament, and preferences. It is also variable, for depending on the circumstances and ends in view, one may present a self that is forthright and businesslike, or playful, or vindictive, or seductive, or enigmatic, and so on.

The capacity of the self to adopt such a rich variety of roles in social life is grounded in "privileged access." This term refers to the idea that other people have no direct knowledge of what is going on in someone's mind—one's thoughts, desires, daydreams, fantasies, jealousies, and hidden agendas. The notion that the self can exclude all others from this inner sanctum (except, in some religious persuasions, God) ensures the ultimate uncertainty or mystery that the self can parlay into selective, creative, and variable presentations in the social world. Obviously, if this mystery were dispelled and all one's inner states were transparent to others, one's ability to mold one's public image would be drastically curtailed.

The effect of testing is precisely to dispel that mystery. Testing thwarts privileged access, intruding unchaperoned into the private realm formerly controlled by the self as gatekeeper and monitor of information. We have seen in earlier chapters how such intrusion is the explicit goal of lie detection, but it also occurs in somewhat subtler forms in all kinds of testing. Intelligence tests probe one's cognitive faculties, personality tests profile one's temperamental and emotional state, and drug tests provide information about possible private habits, proclivities, and activities. Production and presentation of knowledge about the self comes under the control of test givers. The self is no longer able, in a test situation, to temper or embellish it. Whatever tempering and embellishing takes place now stems from the tests themselves, which, as we have seen, regularly redefine or even fabricate the qualities they are intended to measure. If the artful presentation of Goffman's self is seductive, what happens in testing is, to borrow a simile from Jean Baudrillard, pornographic.[23] Pornography differs from seduction in that the individual fixed by the pornographic gaze is powerless to conceal, control, or nuance anything. She or he is displayed for the observer's inspection, recreation, probing, and penetration in whatever way satisfies his or her purely selfish purposes.

The development of testing is an outstanding example of Foucault's thesis that power has been evolving in the direction of increasing efficiency, subtlety, and scope. Tests are applied ever more frequently for an expanding array of purposes. Especially remarkable is that people have increasingly found themselves in the position where they feel their only recourse is to ask, even to insist, that they undergo the pornographic scrutiny of tests. Power has become refined indeed when people demand that they be subjected to it.

In medieval times, this was limited to circumstances in which a person was suspected or accused of some wrongdoing and would demand trial by ordeal or by battle as a means of exoneration. A similar situation exists today when people under investigation by law enforcement agencies or employers, or who feel the need to lend credence to some important statement they have made, demand a lie detector test in an effort to bolster their veracity. The polygraphing of Anita Hill in connection with her accusation of sexual harassment against Supreme Court nominee Clarence Thomas during his confirmation hearings in 1991 is a case in point. People also request or demand drug tests in circumstances of individualized suspicion. An example occurred in 1990 when a Northwest Airlines pilot was called in at the last minute as a substitute to take a flight from Detroit to Atlanta. While they were waiting for him, a woman (recollecting an incident that had occurred six weeks earlier, when three Northwest Airlines pilots were arrested on charges of drunkenness after they landed a plane in Minneapolis) speculated to the other passengers that the delay was probably due to his being drunk or partying. Learning of her statements, the pilot refused to take off until blood and urine tests proved that he was not under the influence of drugs or alcohol.[24]

While people still demand to be exonerated by authenticity tests, as they did centuries ago, modern lie detector and drug tests are much less violent than ordeal by water or hot iron, they involve less expenditure of public resources, and they are used in a wider range of circumstances. This is in line with Foucault's claim that power has developed in the direction of lighter, more efficient, and more pervasive application. Most important in this regard, contemporary authenticity testing advanced beyond the medieval forms when it burst the limitations of individualized suspicion. No one would demand trial by ordeal or by battle unless they had been accused of some specific misdeed. But with the development of preemployment, periodic, and random lie detection and drug testing, the pool of potential test takers expanded to include people in general, who are suspected of having committed some as yet undiscovered wrongdoing. The advance from individualized to generalized suspicion as grounds for tests vastly increased the number of people who are subject to them and who, therefore, are brought under the exercise of power.

The law has supported the expansion of drug testing to cover those under generalized suspicion, with a number of recent court decisions sustaining random testing. And if testing of hair should become popular, it would constitute an advance beyond urinalysis and blood tests both in efficiency and simplicity in procedures for sample collection and in the period over which drug use could be monitored. In contrast, mechanical lie detector testing in circumstances of generalized suspicion was drastically cut back by the federal antipolygraph law of 1988. Although this deflected the growth trajectory of authenticity testing, it did not stop it. Written integrity tests are filling the breach created by the curtailment of polygraph testing,[25] and the result is likely to be a net gain for authenticity testing. While written tests are largely limited to preemployment testing,[26] from the perspective of efficiency and economy, they are far superior to polygraph tests. The latter require an hour or more of one-on-one contact between examiner and subject, while the standardized format of written tests allows them to be given to subjects either individually or in groups of any size. This, together with the fact that they can be machine graded in a matter of seconds, makes written integrity tests much cheaper than polygraph tests (often under $10 per test as opposed to $50 to $100). Hence they have a growth potential considerably beyond that ever enjoyed by polygraph testing.

If one were to imagine the next step in the perfection of power by testing, it would be for people to *request* that they be tested in circumstances of generalized suspicion, as they already ask to be tested when they are under individualized suspicion. At first glance, such a development seems preposterous. Why would anyone demand a test to prove that they are not doing something that nobody accuses or specifically suspects them of doing in the first place? To bring this about would mark a truly ingenious extension of power.

Claims for it have actually been made on behalf of lie detection, but they are not convincing. A high-ranking police officer who manages lie detection in a metropolitan department told me that the police welcome the polygraph screen they all must pass as part of their training, because it bolsters the esprit de corps of the force as a fraternity of outstanding individuals, honest and true. But when I raised this possibility with one of the lower-ranking members of this police fraternity—who was more on the receiving than the giving end of polygraph tests—his answer was a terse and unequivocal, "Bullshit." Again, Zales jewelry chain has argued that polygraph tests boost employee morale because they assure that one's co-workers, superiors and subordinates, are honest people. This is welcome news to employees because it eliminates worry that company profits (and, therefore, one's benefits from the employee profit sharing plan) are being ripped off by unscrupulous fellow workers.[27] But this information comes from the personnel director at Zales rather than from employees themselves. And even if this were a correct characterization of employee attitudes, at most it would mean that they approve a policy of lie detector tests on the basis of individualized suspicion. There is no suggestion that Zales employees make specific requests to be tested unless they are identified as suspects.

It falls to drug testing actually to achieve this next step in the extension of power: getting people positively to endorse—on occasion, even specifically to request—tests of themselves even when no suspicion has been directed against them. One case in point has to do with the use of steroids by athletes. It is widely recognized that steroids enhance performance in many events. Athletes who observe the ban against steroids in their own training are deeply concerned that their competitors who use steroids gain an unfair advantage. The several college athletes whom I interviewed on this issue expressed the opinion that the only way to be sure that no athletes use steroids is to test all of them. One individual stressed the importance of dealing with this issue early and recommended that the testing begin in high school. The strategy to deter steroid use by testing athletes universally or at random is currently in effect for the Olympics, NCAA events, and as part of the policies governing intercollegiate athletics at many universities. Most important for the present analysis, many if not most athletes approve that strategy although it requires that they themselves submit to testing. In this case, then, the level of power has been achieved where people gladly submit themselves to testing in the absence of individualized suspicion.

Moving to street drugs, the students of Oklahoma's Bennington High School enlisted in the war on drugs with such fervor that they decided to make themselves an example of a school that is 100 percent drug free. To prove it, the entire student body (all seventy-five of them) voluntarily took drug tests. They all passed, and as evidence of their continuing commitment, 10 percent of them selected at random are to be tested again each month. Here is a situation in which people who are under no individualized suspicion of drug use positively *ask* to be tested. The students proudly wear black T-shirts that proclaim, "Drug Free Youth"; 15-year-old sophomore Christie Wilson gushed, "I just hope that they start doing this drug test all over."[28]

There are some signs of her wish coming true. As discussed above, Chicago's St. Sabina Academy conducts random drug tests of sixth through eighth graders, although drugs have not been a problem within the school. Parents welcomed the move. Their most common response when the program was proposed was, why not begin in kindergarten?

How can we analyze people's willingness to display themselves to the scrutiny of drug tests when they are not suspected of using drugs? In cases of individualized suspicion, a person is already in some degree of trouble, and the offer to take a test is made as an effort to clear oneself. The individual submits to the application of power represented by the test, that is to say, to escape from a present threat. Someone who volunteers to take a test when not under individual suspicion would seem to be under far less compulsion. That is not the case, however. Power works more subtly here, but no less insistently. What is not a present threat may quickly become one. After a policy has been adopted for voluntary testing of a group, any member of that group (e.g., a student at Bennington High School) who declines to "volunteer" for the test is immediately suspected of having something to hide. The choices become either to submit to the test now in order to avoid being brought under individualized suspicion or to submit to it later in an effort to clear oneself of individualized suspicion.

This reasoning does not account for those who take the lead in movements to encourage voluntary testing or for individuals who are anxious to submit to testing when they do not belong to a group that brings pressure on them to do so. Probably some of them are ingenuous. The gravity of the drug problem, the imperative to win the war on drugs, impresses itself on them so overwhelmingly that they believe extraordinary measures are necessary in the face of a monstrous threat. Hence they willingly open themselves to the power of testing and work to get others to do the same in the name of a great cause that justifies compromising the control they exercise over the collection and promulgation of information about themselves. Others may be more cynical and perceive the war on drugs as an opportunity for self-advancement. A political figure who calls for voluntary drug testing can garner publicity and gain the reputation as a diligent and fearless public servant who demands decisive action against the evil lurking at our very doorsteps. Moreover, the tactic is politically safe. Voluntary drug testing does not call for a significant outlay of funds, and it plays on the acute anxiety about drug abuse that has dominated the media and public opinion in recent years. It is not difficult to dismiss the civil libertarians who carp about invasion of privacy as being soft on drugs and pointedly ask why they should oppose voluntary testing unless they have something to hide.

Authenticity testing has been unmasked here as a technique for maintaining people under surveillance and insidiously transforming them into docile and unwitting subjects of an expanding disciplinary technology of power. What steps can be taken to curtail this threat to the autonomy and dignity of the individual?

I have argued that the expansion of surveillance and coercion exercised by authenticity testing has largely been a story of the increasing application of the tests to people who are under generalized rather than individualized suspicion. It follows that the harmful effects of these tests would be greatly reduced if that development were reversed. Quite simply, then, my suggestion is that authenticity tests be strictly limited to circumstances of individualized suspicion.

One effect of this proposal would be to extend the provisions of the Employee Polygraph Protection Act of 1988 (EPPA). That act outlaws most lie detector tests by polygraph and other mechanical devices in the private sector. It should be expanded to cover the few private industries now exempted. Most important, governmental agencies should be brought under the act, for at present it does not apply to them, and local, state, and federal agencies may use lie detector tests in any way they wish.

In the wake of the EPPA, integrity tests given in written and other forms have flourished in the private sector. These too would be eliminated by my proposal. Some preliminary steps have already been taken in that direction, but efforts to control integrity tests by legislation crafted along the lines of the EPPA are complicated by the fact that it is difficult to construct a watertight definition of them.[29] The EPPA uses a technological definition, proscribing tests that use a mechanical device such as a polygraph machine or psychological stress evaluator. A technological definition is problematic for integrity tests because some of them are taken in written form, others at a computer terminal, and still others orally either by direct interview or over the telephone. The publishers of many of them do not even acknowledge that they are tests, choosing instead to designate them by a wide variety of terms such as "survey," "inventory," or "audit." The policy recommended here that authenticity testing be limited to cases of individualized suspicion avoids this definitional problem because it focuses not on what the tests are but on how and when they are used. It would virtually terminate integrity tests, because they are used almost exclusively in circumstances of generalized suspicion, most especially preemployment testing.

CONCLUSION

Adoption of this proposal would also bring about drastic reductions in drug testing. Preemployment, periodic, and random tests would be eliminated, for these are all conducted on the basis of generalized rather than individualized suspicion. The only legitimate circumstance for a drug test would be for cause: when there is good reason to suspect from an individual's behavior that the person is under the influence of drugs.[30] There are certain encouraging developments in this direction. As of July 1991, fourteen states had enacted legislation regulating drug testing by private employers. So far as current employees are concerned, a trend toward rejecting testing on the basis of generalized suspicion is visible:

> Most of the statutes provide that before requiring drug testing of an employee, the employer must have a reasonable suspicion that the employee is impaired to the point of affecting job performance.[31]

The statutes allow drug tests of job applicants without individualized suspicion, but Montana, at least, restricts such preemployment tests to those applying for jobs involving security, public safety, a hazardous work environment, or fiduciary responsibility.[32]

Implementation of my recommendation would dramatically change the landscape of authenticity testing, and energetic opposition would inevitably be forthcoming from a coalition of interests committed to it. Those with an economic stake are the people and organizations that conduct and market the tests. Politicians who play on public fears about crime and drugs and who use outspoken support for testing as a way to draw attention to themselves and to obtain votes have a political interest in perpetuating authenticity testing. Those with an ideological commitment may be divided into two categories. One is composed of social scientists and others imbued with a positivistic creed that any and all means of acquiring and applying scientific information about people and society should be encouraged as contributions to social progress. The other includes persons of an authoritarian turn of mind who explicitly or implicitly operate on the assumption that people in general are not to be trusted and that society is best served by firm controls that keep human impulses and liberty in check.

Although the opposition would be formidable, with sufficient resolve, a policy to restrict authenticity testing to cases of individualized suspicion could be implemented in the short term. The reason is that authenticity testing is not yet inextricably woven into the fabric of society. Few other institutions are dependent on it, and therefore it could be drastically reduced with minimal effect on the social structure. Drug testing, for example, is a recent phenomenon. The socioeconomic system got along without it quite adequately some ten years ago, when drug use was actually more prevalent in the United States than it is today. A general policy shift prohibiting preemployment, periodic, and random drug tests would have little effect on hiring and promotion practices, other than to make them less complicated and less expensive. Lie detection by polygraph was never massively practiced in the workplace, and its demise with the passage of the EPPA has not brought private business to its knees. Integrity testing has only been practiced in the last few years, and there has not been time for other business institutions to become systemically dependent on it. Terminating it before it becomes established would not produce major disruptions in personnel practices except, again, to save business the time and expense of giving the tests.

Implementing the policy would, however, require some explicit state or even national commitment in the form of a general agreement among employers or legislation. Organizations are reluctant to cease (or not to commence) authenticity testing in preemployment and other circumstances of generalized suspicion for several reasons. As has been demonstrated, they get the notion that they have to test because otherwise, with everyone else testing, drug abusers and criminals would flock to them. Again, if some organizations routinely conduct preemployment, periodic, and random tests for drugs and/or integrity, those that do not test feel vulnerable in case of accidents or losses to lawsuits claiming that they did not take reasonable precautions. That is, one of the strongest reasons organizations test is the fact that others do. They conclude that they must expend the time and money to conduct authenticity tests out of generalized suspicion not because they anticipate any particular benefits in productivity but in self-defense. General consensus or legislation on the policy to restrict authenticity testing to cases of individualized suspicion would defang that incentive.

Testing and the Birth of the Individual

I have argued that several forms of authenticity and intelligence testing pose a threat to the autonomy and dignity of the individual, and my suggestion for countering that threat has been to do away with many of the most offensive tests. This should not be taken as a recommendation that we return to some earlier time when tests were fewer and the individual was freer. No such time ever existed, because the human individual as we know it is a relatively recent creation and one that to a significant extent has been produced by testing.

In probably the most perceptive analysis of testing yet written, Foucault has argued that the contemporary concept of the individual is a product of the development and extension of examinations in the seventeenth and eighteenth centuries.[33] He does not mean, of course, that prior to that time there were no individuals. Obviously, there were, for people had individual names, they could tell each other apart, and it was possible to identify an individual as the same person on encounters at different times or in different places. Foucault is referring instead to the concept of the individual as a complex, dynamic being with specified physical, mental, political, and other properties. He means the individual as an object of study and detailed knowledge, for whom it is possible to define ranges of the normal along various physical and psychological dimensions, to explain the nature and processes of normal development and behavior, to diagnose deviations from the normal, and to intervene with the aim of correcting or treating those deviations. Obviously, all of this requires that there be a rich corpus of knowledge about individuals, and prior to the seventeenth and eighteenth centuries so little information about individual persons was systematically gathered and recorded that discourse about the properties, development, and pathologies of the human individual was not possible. This changed with more systematic examination of patients in hospitals and students in schools and with the keeping of retrievable records of those examinations and of information about individuals gathered in other contexts such as the military. These developments enabled "the constitution of the individual as a describable, analyzable object."[34] Because Foucault views examinations and record-keeping as disciplinary devices, he regards the individual as both constituted and dominated by the disciplinary technology of power.[35]

If the individual as an object susceptible of description, analysis, and treatment was born with the testing practices of the seventeenth and eighteenth centuries, this study suggests that its mature form is largely a product of the testing practices of the twentieth century. Today's individual is much more richly textured and fine grained than its ancestor of two and three centuries ago, a being with normalities and pathologies then undreamed. If, as Foucault maintains, power is exercised over the individual by interventions licensed by knowledge (guidance, treatment, punishment, rehabilitation, etc.), the contemporary individual is subject to even more coercion than its predecessors. As we have seen at every point in this study, the rich panoply of tests that are routinely deployed to probe all aspects of our physical and mental makeup, the decisions and interventions that are taken on the basis of test results, and the asymmetrical relation of power between test givers and test takers conspire to produce an individual who is suspended within an increasingly total network of surveillance and control.

Although "individual" implies singularity and unity, the sheer number and diversity of tests to which people are subjected has a corrosive effect on the integrity of both the concrete reality and the concept of the individual. As different constituencies limit their interest to only some of its tested parts, the twentieth-century individual tends to become a fragmented being. The complete individual is known and treated less as a unique entity than as a coincidental intersection of scores and measurements on a broad array of standardized classifications. And finally, particularly in the mental sphere, contemporary tests are future oriented to a degree far surpassing previous ones. This too has its effect on the person of the late twentieth century. It creates an individual who is less real than hyperreal: not so much a present as a potential or deferred being, defined less by what it is than by what it is likely to become. As the mapping of the human genome proceeds and new genetic tests are developed, we can expect the twenty-first century to bring with it an extension of future-oriented testing into the physical realm. The individual will increasingly be known in terms of the diseases it is likely to contract, how and when the feebleness of old age will set in, and so on.

When combined with Foucault's path-breaking work and other studies, this analysis of the social consequences of testing indicates that the accumulation and storage of information about the individual has been steadily increasing. The process has accelerated in the twentieth century and shows every sign of continuing in the future. It is not possible to turn the clock back. Nor should we want to, because if the growth of knowledge about the individual has enhanced coercion, it has also encouraged human liberation. As Foucault has pointed out,[36] the seventeenth and eighteenth centuries produced both the military dream of society that leads to the disciplinary technology of power and also a liberal dream of individual rights, freedom, and dignity based on the social contract and enshrined in documents such as the American Declaration of Independence and Constitution and the French Declaration of the Rights of Man. It follows that by fostering both domination and autonomy, the historical development of the individual is laced with contradictions and tensions. The contradictions offer us, as participants in the formation of our own destiny, toeholds for intervening in the process. If we seek to stimulate the growth of personal autonomy and to slow the spread of coercion, it is not so much an effort to reverse the course of history as to influence the trajectory of the individual's and society's future development. To control testing is one positive intervention that is well within our grasp.

APPENDIX:

DRUG-TESTING TABLES

Tables 1 and 2

The most important point of comparison among these tables is that the category with the highest rate of approval for student athletes is random testing, while of the five sorts of testing, limited random testing is in third place with chemical workers and a poor fifth place with trainmen. Although periodic and for-cause testing seems to be less approved by student athletes than by employees, I fear this difference may be largely an artifact of how people responded to the questionnaire. Although they were invited to mark more than one possibility, employees actually made multiple selections considerably more than student athletes. For example, while 33 student athletes marked "anytime, as with random testing," only 7 of them also marked any of the other possibilities. It may be that they assumed the "anytime" in the random option covered most or all of the other options automatically. Thus, I think it is possible that student athlete approval of the other forms of testing is higher than appears in table 2.

The 41 percent approval rate of random testing by football players is almost identical to the 42 percent of chemical workers who also consider random testing to be justified, as reported in table 1. These figures may not be directly comparable, however, because these people have very different experiences of drug testing. Only 27 percent of the chemical workers who approve random testing had ever been tested themselves, none of them under a random program, while 74 percent of the football players who judge random testing to be justified have been tested under the university's policy of random and unannounced testing.

Tables 4 and 5

Responses to the two questions about attitudes toward most recent and first drug tests are combined in these tables. I have cross-tabulated this information with data from another part of the questionnaire to break the responses down according to the total number of drug tests each individual has taken. The presence of several variables makes these tables somewhat difficult to read. Perhaps the most important figures are found in the far right-hand column. Looking at table 4, they indicate that of the student athletes who have taken six or more drug tests, 64 percent remember facing their first test with unconcern, while those unconcerned about their most recent test rose to 76 percent; at the time of their first test, 16 percent worried about a false positive result when they took their first test, but just 4 percent continued to worry about that in their most recent test, and so on down the table. The data presented in tables 4 and 5 do support the hypothesis that attitudes toward drug tests become less intense with repeated testing (and therefore repeated testing contributes to the development of automatic docility), with the pattern for trainmen being somewhat more marked and consistent than that for student athletes. (Possibly the discussion in chapter 6 of how student athletes tend to be docile even before coming under the university's testing program is relevant to the difference between the patterns in tables 4 and 5.)

Tables 6 and 7

Another questionnaire item pertinent to the hypothesis about repeated testing as a means of establishing automatic docility asked whether experience of being subject to testing in one's current position would make one more opposed, less opposed, or have no affect on one's attitude to being tested in the future. Results are given in tables 6 and 7. At first blush, the hypothesis that testing develops automatic docility would seem to predict that individuals who have taken several tests would be less opposed to future testing than individuals who have taken few or no tests. From this perspective, the data in table 6 from student athletes support the hypothesis, but those in table 7 from trainmen are more problematic. Although a modest increase does occur in the "less opposed" category, as the hypothesis would predict, the percentage of "more opposed" responses also increases and much more noticeably. That finding would seem to refute the hypothesis.

My phrasing is so conditional because I have become suspicious of the utility of this question. The experience of a chemical company I studied indicates that the true situation is much more complex than a straight line development of attitudes as one is subjected to more tests. When the company limited testing to new hires, current employees were quite accepting of the idea of drug testing, including even the concept of random testing of current employees (their attitudes are tabulated in table 1). But when the company actually instituted random testing of current employees, a good deal of opposition emerged. (Precisely how much I do not know, because the company was unwilling for me to distribute a questionnaire until the furor had died down.) Thus, I think the actual pattern of opposition to testing is probably a curve that begins relatively low when one contemplates the issue in the abstract, rises as testing programs are introduced into one's own workplace, and diminishes again as people become accustomed to testing and automatic docility sets in. What I do not know is at what point in a person's experience of testing the opposition lessens; certainly it is different for different people. These considerations may also have an effect on the data presented in tables 4 and 5.

Tables 8 and 9

These tables are derived from questions about student athletes' attitudes toward their first and most recent drug tests. The aim is to ascertain to what extent student athlete approval of drug tests can be attributed to the belief that drug tests will prevent competitors from gaining unfair advantages through the use of steroids. Thus, these tables record how many respondents expressed satisfaction that testing would prevent others from taking drugs. Table 8 reports on members of the men's track and football teams (where steroids are most likely to be a problem), and table 9 pertains to other teams. As is argued in chapter 6, these figures give scant support to the hypothesis that athletes approve of drug tests out of the conviction that they deter steroid use.

TABLE 1
Opinions of When Drug Testing Is Justified

	Trainmen	Chemical Workers
Upon being hired (preemployment testing)	63	82
Anytime, as with random testing	16	42
Periodically, as upon returning to work or in regular physical exams	46	39
Whenever an employee has been involved in an accident	31	30
When an employee on the job appears to be under the influence of drugs	62	72
Never	12	4
No opinion	2	1

Note: 312 responses from trainmen, 92 from chemical workers. All figures are given in percentages. Percentages add up to more than 100 because respondents were invited to mark more than one option.

TABLE 2
Student Athlete Attitudes toward Testing

When do you think it is justifiable to require student athletes to take a drug test? (Mark as many as apply.)

Anytime, as with random testing	41
Periodically, as in regular physical exams	26
When a student athlete appears to be under the influence of drugs at times other than practice and games	21
When a student athlete appears to be under the influence of drugs during practice or games	21
Never	13
No opinion	6

Note: All figures are given in percentages. Responses from 80 football players. Percentages add to more than 100 because respondents were invited to mark more than one option.

TABLE 3
Trainman and Student Athlete Attitudes toward Most
Recent Drug Tests

Answer only if you have been tested more than once: What was your attitude as you took your most recent drug test? (Mark as many as apply.)

	Trainmen	Student Athletes
Unconcern	33	77
Worry that the test would wrongly identify you as having used drugs	51	6
Worry that the test would rightly identify you as having used drugs	2	0
Embarrassment that you might be observed as you urinated for the test	27	9
Anger that your privacy would be violated	41	14
Anger because you were not trusted to refrain from using drugs without being tested	33	7
Satisfaction because testing would prove you don't use drugs	33	20
Satisfaction because testing would discourage other people from using drugs	24	15

Note: All figures are given in percentages. Responses: 91 trainmen, 125 student athletes.

TABLE 4
Student Athlete Attitudes toward First and Most Recent Drug Tests

What was your attitude as you prepared to take your first drug test? Your most recent drug test? (Mark as many as apply.)

	Number of Tests Taken			
	One	Two	Three to five	Six or more
Unconcern				
first test	76	76	69	64
most recent test		78	76	76
Worry that the test would wrongly identify you as having used drugs				
first test	5	10	10	16
most recent test		7	7	4
Worry that the test would rightly identify you as having used drugs				
first test	0	0	0	0
most recent test		0	0	0
Embarrassment that you might be observed as you urinated for the test				
first test	5	15	20	8
most recent test		7	10	8
Anger that your privacy would be violated				
first test	10	5	27	16
most recent test		5	20	16
Anger because you were not trusted to refrain from using drugs without being tested				
first test	5	10	17	4
most recent test		7	7	8
Satisfaction because testing would prove you don't use drugs				
first test	14	20	25	12
most recent test		12	27	16
Satisfaction because testing would discourage other people from using drugs				
first test	10	22	19	8
most recent test		22	14	8

Note: All figures are given in percentages. Responses: 21 for one test, 41 for two tests, 59 for three to five tests, and 25 for six or more tests. Columns do not add to 100 because respondents were invited to mark as many options as they wished.

APPENDIX

TABLE 5
Trainman Attitudes toward First and Most Recent Drug Tests

What was your attitude as you took a drug test for the first time? Toward your most recent drug test? (Mark as many as apply.)

	Number of Tests Taken		
	One	Two	Three or more
Unconcern			
first test	25	27	25
most recent test		25	34
Worry that the test would wrongly identify you as having used drugs			
first test	61	59	50
most recent test		54	38
Worry that the test would rightly identify you as having used drugs			
first test	2	0	0
most recent test		2	0
Embarrassment that you might be observed as you urinated for the test			
first test	32	37	28
most recent test		29	19
Anger that your privacy would be violated			
first test	46	40	44
most recent test		37	34
Anger because you were not trusted to refrain from using drugs without being tested			
first test	36	29	33
most recent test		29	34
Satisfaction because testing would prove you don't use drugs			
first test	31	25	44
most recent test		22	47
Satisfaction because testing would discourage other people from using drugs			
first test	27	24	25
Most recent test		25	19

Note: All figures are given in percentages. Responses for one test: 139; 2 tests responding on first test: 63; 2 tests responding on most recent test: 59; 3 or more tests responding on first test: 36; 3 or more tests responding on most recent test: 32.

TABLE 6
Student Athlete Attitudes toward Taking Future Drug Tests

In the future, if an employer should require you to take drug tests in order to get or keep a job, do you think your experience with the university's drug testing program will make you:

| | Number of Tests Taken | | |
	None	One or two	Three or more
Less opposed to taking future drug tests	38	49	49
More opposed to taking future drug tests	14	2	6
My experience with the university's program will probably not influence my attitude one way or the other toward taking drug tests in the future	48	49	45

Note: Figures are percentages. Responses: 21 for no tests, 57 for one or two tests, 82 for three or more.

TABLE 7
Trainman Attitudes toward Taking Future Drug Tests

In the future, if an employer should require you to take drug tests in order to get or keep a job, do you think your experience of working for a company that requires drug testing will make you:

| | Number of Tests Taken | | |
	None	One or two	Three or more
Less opposed to taking future drug tests	9	13	14
More opposed to taking future drug tests	15	21	29
My experience working for this railroad will probably not influence my attitude one way or the other toward taking drug tests in the future	77	66	57

Note: Figures are percentages. Responses: 82 for no tests, 196 for one or two tests, 35 for three or more.

TABLE 8

Football and Male Track Team Attitudes toward Deterrent Effect of Drug Tests, by First and Most Recent Tests

What was your attitude as you prepared to take your first drug test? Your most recent drug test?

	Number of Tests Taken			
	One	Two	Three to five	Six or more
Satisfaction because testing would discourage other people from using drugs				
first test	10	17	11	12
most recent test		13	8	6

Note: All figures are given in percentages. Responses: 21 for one test, 23 for two tests, 37 for three to five tests, and 17 for six or more tests.

TABLE 9

Student Athlete (Other than Football and Men's Track) Attitudes toward Deterrent Effect of Drug Tests, by First and Most Recent Tests

What was your attitude as you prepared to take your first drug test? Your most recent drug test?

	Number of Tests Taken			
	One	Two	Three to five	Six or more
Satisfaction because testing would discourage other people from using drugs				
first test	—	39	32	0
most recent test		50	23	13

Note: All figures are given in percentages. Responses: No responses for one test, 18 for two tests, 22 for three to five tests, and 8 for six or more tests.

NOTES

1. Introduction: Infinite Examination

1. See Nelkin and Tancredi (1989) for a full-scale discussion of the social consequences of medical tests.

2. For a full presentation of the theory and method of institutional analysis, see Hanson (1975).

3. Brodkey 1988:221.

4. McGarvey 1989:37.

5. Fallows 1989:164, 228–229.

6. *New York Times,* September 29, 1988, A18; Leisner 1989.

7. Sternberg 1985:313–314.

8. Kolata 1992.

9. *New York Times,* October 28, 1988, B1.

10. Woodard 1990:31.

11. Sweetland and Keyser 1986.

12. The purpose of this test is to identify those persons whose test scores might be affected by test anxiety. One wonders, however, if the result of the Test Anxiety Behavior Scale might itself not be skewed by the anxiety of some subjects who take it. If so, would it be possible to devise still another test, say, a Test Anxiety Scale Anxiety Scale? Infinite regress threatens, and the mind boggles.

13. Medina and Neill 1990:3.

14. Clines 1990.

15. Payer 1988:141.

16. Austin 1912:801.

17. Rizzo 1991.

18. Angier 1991:4.

19. Durkheim 1962:191.

20. Hanson 1973.

21. Actually Rapans did not claim ignorance about their age but tended to reply "thirty-three" to that question. The first person I interviewed gave that answer, and apparently the word got around that I seemed satisfied with it.

22. It does occasionally happen that people take tests to learn something about themselves: readers voluntarily take the self-tests that are found in popular magazines, people test their own blood pressure by means of machines in supermarkets and drugstores, students go over tests given previously in a course as part of their preparation for the tests they must take, and people might decide to take intelligence tests out of curiosity about their own IQs. In all these cases, however, the tests themselves (questions, scoring keys, technology of blood pressure tests, etc.) are devised by agencies other than the test takers, who are individuals. In that sense, at least, the distinction between test givers and test takers holds even for self-testing.

23. The civil service examination in imperial China, a qualifying test of great importance in a preindustrial society, represents an exception to these generalizations.

2. Before Science: The Early History of Authenticity Testing

1. Thompson 1956:372–373.
2. Ibid.:374.
3. Ibid.
4. Vance 1955:22–23.
5. See Grey 1956:73; Grey 1971:30. The erotic parts appear only in the Maori version.
6. Thompson 1956:375.
7. Briggs 1971 2:129.
8. Ashliman 1987:175.
9. Rotunda 1942:23–24.
10. Num. 5:11–31.
11. Briggs 1970 2:168.
12. Baughman 1966:298; Briggs 1970 2:497; Rotunda 1942:29.
13. Ashliman 1987:187.
14. Kings 3:16–28.
15. Ashliman 1987:248.
16. Lea 1968:28.
17. Ibid.:41.

18. Ibid.:36–37.
19. Quoted in Bartlett 1986:109.
20. Ibid.:135.
21. Ibid.:136.
22. 1 Sam. 17:1–54.
23. Lea 1968:93.
24. Ibid.:174.
25. Ibid.:174–181.
26. Bartlett 1986:122.
27. Lea 1968:195–199.
28. Ibid.:101–105.
29. Bartlett 1986:115.
30. Lea 1968:119–127.
31. Ibid.:120.
32. Kay 1978:167.
33. Lea 1968:111.
34. Ibid.
35. Ibid.:135.
36. Ibid.:117.
37. Ibid.:118.
38. See Bartlett 1986:125.
39. Ibid.:4.
40. Ibid.:9–11, 34.
41. Quoted in Bartlett 1986:88.
42. Dan. 3:19–30.
43. Exod. 3:1–3.
44. Gen. 19:23–29.
45. See Bartlett 1986:21–22; Guazzo 1929:158; Lea 1968:226, 231.
46. Bartlett 1968:1.
47. Ibid.:13
48. Ibid.:17–18.
49. Guazzo 1929:158.
50. Lea 1968:250.
51. Bartlett 1986:23.
52. Ibid.:34.
53. Ibid.:53, 81–89, 100.
54. Lea 1968:257–258.
55. Deacon 1976:121.
56. Lea 1968:257.
57. Midelfort 1972:76–77.
58. Bartlett 1986:151.

59. Ibid.:145. Although the devil sometimes protected his own, he was a capricious master who would often turn on his minions, for example, inciting them to suicide (and therefore to eternal damnation) to escape further torture or being burned at the stake (Guazzo 1929:129–132). In 1605, a demon played a particularly foul trick on a ninety-year-old witch named John. John had undone the serenity of the Serene Duke John William of the Duchies of Cleve and Julich, bewitching him with madness, fear, and panic. The demon came to John with the news that the duke was about to summon him about the matter and warned that it would be dangerous to go. It must be acknowledged that John's response was curt, but surely not such as to deserve what follows:

> The sorcerer answered: "What is that to you? I shall go where I wish." Hearing this, the demon said no more but, as the witch himself told, pulled down his breeches (for he had taken the form of a nobleman with an attendant servant) and, turning his bum to him, let fly a fart of such an intolerable stink that the sorcerer could not be rid of that stench for three days, although he fumigated the house with incense and other rare perfumes.

As it turned out, there had indeed been something to the demon's warning, for John went when summoned, confessed his witchcraft, and was condemned to burn at the stake (130).

60. Deacon 1976:93.

61. Ibid.:93, 109, 121–123; Guazzo 1929:15, 55–57; Midelfort 1972:104; Taylor 1908:42–44.

62. Deacon 1976:111, 132; Guazzo 1929:15; Hopkins 1647:52–54.

63. Taylor 1908:124.

64. Ibid.:131–133.

65. Evans-Pritchard 1937:22, 40–49.

66. Schieffelin 1976:78–79.

67. Bartlett 1986:135.

68. Ibid.:142.

69. Guazzo 1929:124–126.

70. Ibid.:55–57, 130; Midelfort 1972:27.

71. Bartlett 1986:145.

72. Guazzo 1929:130.

73. Lienhardt 1961:257.

74. If one were to get precious, it would be necessary to say that the image on the neon sign is a *depiction* of a martini glass, which it therefore signifies by metaphor, and the glass so depicted is in turn a metonymic signifier of the concept "cocktail lounge." Such intricacies, however, are not at issue here.

75. The disinclination of a son to shoot arrows at his father's body may seem more "natural" than the other more arbitrary examples given. But among the Hua and Fore of Papua New Guinea, corpses of beloved husbands and fathers were eaten by widows and children (Lindenbaum 1979:19–28; Meigs 1984:40, 101), and our own custom of burning them to a crisp may not be viewed in all quarters as an act of filial piety.

76. Bartlett 1986:145.

77. Foucault 1979.

78. Hirst 1985:99–100.

79. The latter would qualify as a test, by our definition, only if someone had put the hair in his bedding (or used its accidental presence there) for the purpose of gaining information about him. That point is not addressed in Thompson's (1956:375) listing of the motif.

80. See Hanson and Hanson (1981) for a much more detailed analysis of the logic of situations such as this. It must be remembered, of course, that other stories convey different, even contradictory messages. Cinderlad (of "The Princess on the Glass Hill") and the clever peasant girl who becomes the king's wife suggest that nobility may sometimes be a matter of personal character instead of birth. Folk literature is no more constrained to be consistent than, for example, proverbial sayings: "Absence makes the heart grow fonder"; "Out of sight, out of mind."

81. One might wish to read this as a parable about an individual's ideal relationship to God. Be that as it may, it would not detract from the story's relevance to the proper relationship between classes in this world.

82. Hopkins 1647:50–51.

83. Ibid.:53, 55–58.

84. Ibid.:58.

85. See Bartlett 1986:145.

86. This is similar to Winston's realization, at the end of George Orwell's *1984*, that he loves Big Brother.

3. Lie Detection

1. Abrams 1977:153.

2. Lykken 1981:40.

3. Ryle 1949.

4. Defoe 1731:34.

5. Holmes 1977:325.

6. Ferguson 1971:103, 105; Inbau and Reid 1953:21–22.

7. Durkheim 1962:191.

8. Abrams 1977:154.
9. Ferguson 1971: chap. 4.
10. Ferguson 1971:220.
11. Inbau and Reid 1953:113.
12. Lykken 1981:26–28; Munsterberg 1908.
13. Lykken 1981:28.
14. Keeler 1984; Lykken 1981:30–31.
15. Abrams 1977.
16. Ibid.:48.
17. Ibid.:5.
18. Ibid.
19. Smith 1977:407.
20. HR Report 1987:3.
21. Rapoport 1973.
22. Chass 1987.
23. Gwertzman 1985.
24. HR Report 1987:8.
25. Ibid.:7, Meinsma 1985:35; Nagle 1985:13; Sosnowski 1985; Sullenberger 1985:44.
26. HR Report 1987:7–8.
27. Ibid.:3.
28. Prior 1985.
29. Putnam 1978:261.
30. Great Britain 1985:71–72.
31. Price n.d.:63
32. Patterson 1979:57–58.
33. Abrams 1977:66.
34. Inbau and Reid 1953:15.
35. Ibid.:12.
36. See Abrams 1978; Barland 1978.
37. See Davis and McKenzie-Rundle 1984:193; Lykken 1981:22.
38. Abrams 1977:76; Inbau and Reid 1953:19–22.
One would think that if the subject answers control questions honestly, it could jeopardize the interpretation of test results. It might be claimed, however, that even if the subject answers honestly, the emotional stress associated with recalling a past misdeed would produce physiological responses similar to a deceptive answer. Another criticism of the method is that it seems entirely possible that an innocent subject could well be more threatened by being suspected of committing a serious crime than about a minor misdeed from childhood. In that event, the reaction to the relevant questions would be stronger than that to the

control questions, leading to the erroneous test result that the subject is deceptive—and guilty.

39. Davis and McKenzie-Rundle 1984:189–190.

40. Inbau and Reid 1953:113. It is interesting how, in this passage, the authors assume the subject to be guilty. Was that determination made before the test was given or, perhaps, on the basis of the first chart?

41. See Lykken 1981:38–39.

42. Abrams 1977:70.

43. See Iacono 1985; Lykken 1981:249–307.

44. Keeler 1984:59–60.

45. Ibid.:76.

46. Davis and McKenzie-Rundle 1984:195.

47. Lykken 1981:238–239.

48. HR Report 1987:7.

49. Rapoport 1973.

50. Ferguson and Gugas 1984:29.

51. Lykken 1981:184.

52. Ferguson 1971:197.

53. Lykken 1981:184, 194.

54. *New York Times,* December 28, 1988, A13.

55. HR Report 1987:5, 8.

56. Ibid.:4.

57. See ibid.:16, 18–19.

58. Isikoff 1991.

59. HR Report 100–659, 12.

60. HR Report 100–659, 13.

61. Ceol 1991.

62. Isikoff 1991.

63. But see Tolchin 1991.

64. O'Bannon, Goldinger, and Appleby 1989:8.

65. Ibid.:2, 9.

66. HR Report 1987:3.

67. O'Bannon, Goldinger, and Appleby 1989:34, 137, 159.

68. See ibid.:121–290.

69. Moree and Clouse 1984.

70. Lykken 1981:199; O'Bannon, Goldinger, and Appleby 1989:117; Sackett, Burris, and Callahan 1989:496; Sackett and Harris 1984:222.

71. Sackett, Burris, and Callahan 1989:421.

72. OTA 1990:8.

73. Ibid.:78.

74. Goldberg et al. 1991:19–25.

75. OTA 1990:7.
76. Ibid.:26.
77. Litvan 1990; Sackett, Burris, and Callahan 1989:498.
78. OTA 1990:16, 18, 37.
79. Hanson 1991:529.
80. Hartshorne and May 1928:411, 414.
81. Rushton 1980:63–64.
82. Sackett, Burris, and Callahan 1989:519.
83. Ibid.:494.
84. Lykken 1981:200.
85. Ibid.:201.
86. Sackett, Burris, and Callahan 1989:518.
87. Lykken 1981:201.
88. Kovach 1986:47.
89. See Hanson 1991:528.

4. No Sanctuary

1. Foucault 1979.
2. Ferguson 1971:103.
3. Ibid.:106–107.
4. Ibid.:113.
5. Ibid.:49.
6. In my investigation of lie detection, I have come across reference to only two female polygraph examiners. Hence the masculine pronoun is appropriate in this case.
7. Reali 1978:281.
8. Inbau and Reid 1953:19–22.
9. Lykken 1981:206.
10. Nagle 1985:10.
11. Price n.d.:6.
12. Unless one thought about the matter more deeply. A clever suspect may doubt the whole rigmarole about the donkey, divine a trick, and pull the tail. Guilty or innocent, that one's hands would be as dirty as those of any innocent but foolish one who pulled the tail in all ingenuousness.
13. Abrams 1977:144.
14. Ibid.:3.
15. Ferguson and Gugas 1984:4.
16. Inbau and Reid 1953:108.
17. Silverberg 1980:168. Silverberg does not specify how many subjects made these comments, but, as will be discussed below, the statis-

tical results from his questionnaire were overwhelmingly favorable toward polygraph testing.

18. Inbau and Reid 1953:86.

19. Ibid.:107–108. Note the bid for the scientific status of the polygraph by the reference to the examining room as a "laboratory." This is especially interesting because it is embedded in a review of utterly subjective criteria for distinguishing the innocent from the guilty.

20. Holmes 1977:332.

21. Patterson 1979:96.

22. Ferguson 1971:146–148.

23. Ibid.:147.

24. Reproduced in Abrams 1977:28.

25. Ferguson 1971:44–45.

26. From Putnam 1978:262.

27. Ibid.:259.

28. Silverberg 1980.

29. Horvath 1985:45.

30. Horvath and Phannenstill 1987:19.

31. Silverberg 1980:163.

32. Ibid.:168.

33. Horvath and Phannenstill 1987:23.

34. Ibid.:21.

35. White 1984:371.

36. Foucault 1979.

37. Ibid.:60–64, 73.

38. Ibid.:111, 113–114.

39. Ibid.:168.

40. Ibid.:195–231.

41. Baritz 1960:33–34; Levin 1927a, 1927b.

42. Ferguson 1971:147.

43. Foucault 1979:193.

44. Stafford 1991.

45. Foucault 1979:187, 189.

46. Ibid.:190.

47. Ibid.:194, see also Foucault 1973:386–387.

5. Testing and the War on Drugs

1. Baker 1991.

2. The most dramatic proposals are probably designed primarily to attract political attention. The Virginia and Kansas schemes were never

put into effect. The federal program, however, was implemented. Attorney General Meese's statement is reported in the *Daily Labor Report* 34, February 23, 1987, A8.

3. Associated Press, September 25, 1989.
4. Kagay 1991.
5. *Lawrence Journal-World,* June 7, 1989, 1, 4.
6. Mulloy 1991:93, 94; Walsh and Trumble 1991:26.
7. Walsh and Trumble 1991:27.
8. Mulloy 1991:97, 100, 102.
9. Walsh and Trumble 1991:28–30.
10. *New York Times,* December 18, 1989, 36.
11. AMA 1987:14–20.
12. BLS 1989:2–3.
13. BLR 1987.
14. BLR 1989.
15. Axel 1991:142.
16. Zemper 1991:114–118.
17. Ibid.:118–119.
18. Walsh and Trumble 1991:31.
19. Miners, Nykodym, and Samerdyke-Traband 1987:94.
20. Walsh and Trumble 1991:45–46.
21. Aig 1990.
22. Kahler 1990.

23. The greatest problem with GC/MS is human error, because it is sometimes difficult to find technicians with sufficient skill and experience to realize the full potential of GC/MS technology. This is especially so in athletic testing, where great expertise is required to identify the complex metabolites of anabolic steroids (Zemper 1991:127).

24. The information in the preceding two paragraphs is taken from Miike and Hewitt 1988. Readers wishing more technical information about urinalysis are referred to their readable and highly informative account.

25. Miike and Hewitt 1988:642.
26. Ibid.:642–643, 648.
27. Zwerling, Ryan, and Orav 1990.
28. Miike and Hewitt 1988:658.
29. AMA 1987:35; Hoffman 1987:218–219.

30. *Employment Testing: Biweekly Reporter,* February 15, 1987. In the semiotic terminology introduced in chapter 2, any substitution for one's own urine is a metaphoric representation of it. The water scooped up from the toilet or clean urine borrowed from a friend or purchased from

the Bladder Man company metaphorically stands for one's own urine in the same way that a cucumber stands for an ox on certain occasions when the Dinka are called on to offer a sacrifice, or a champion stands for a damsel in medieval trial by battle. It may be a measure of how far society has come from the time idealized in *Ivanhoe* that then the champion was a knight in shining armor, while today's champion is a packet of dehydrated drug-free urine.

31. Hoffman 1987:238.

32. Zemper 1991:125–126.

33. Axel 1991:151.

34. Cone 1989.

35. Baumgartner 1989.

36. Baumgartner 1989:443; Cone 1989:440.

37. Baumgartner 1989:446.

38. Ibid.

39. AMA 1987; BLR 1987, 1989; BLS 1989.

40. Some of the following information on employee attitudes toward drug tests has been previously published in Hanson 1990.

41. BLS 1989:9.

42. McKinley 1989.

43. Differing frequencies in drug use may not be the only reason for the remarkable variation in rates of positive test results. The drug most commonly detected is marijuana, and one factor in the variation may be the amount of the drug that must be present for the result to be judged positive. The thresholds adopted by various companies differ, and the percentage of positive results varies accordingly. Another variable is testing technology. The 20 percent positive preemployment tests reported above from an automobile assembly plant were confirmed, but the confirming test was a repeat of the inexpensive initial screen rather than the much more accurate (and expensive) GC/MS procedure. Therefore, the 20 percent figure may be inflated by failure of the confirming test to catch a number of false positives. Working in the opposite direction, all organizations use relatively inexpensive tests as the initial screen and do not run a confirming test on the negatives. Thus, it is possible for a number of individuals who actually did have drugs in their urine to slip through the screen as false negatives, and they would not be identified by a confirming test.

44. BLS 1989:9.

45. See *Personnel Journal,* July–August 1987, 144.

46. Starkman 1991.

47. Zemper 1991:136.

48. Ibid.:121; Altman 1988b.
49. Altman 1988a.
50. Janofsky and Alfano 1988.
51. Quoted in ibid.
52. Zemper 1991:127.

6. From Drug Control to Mind Control

1. NIDA 1989a, 1989b, 1990; Sullivan and Martinez 1991.
2. Janofsky and Alfano 1988.
3. Anderson and McKeag 1985:3.
4. Cited in Zemper 1991:129–130.
5. Rose and Girard 1988:789.
6. National Public Radio, "Morning Edition," March 6 and 7, 1991.
7. Janofsky and Alfano 1988.
8. Associated Press, August 30, 1989.
9. See Zemper 1991:119.
10. It must be noted that cocaine use does not show the same steady decline in NIDA household surveys as is visible for other drugs. The number of those who reported using cocaine during the last month diminished by half (from 5.8 million to 2.9 million) between 1985 and 1988, declined sharply again to 1.6 million in 1990, but then rose to 1.9 million in 1991. Those who use it *weekly* or more increased from 647,000 in 1985 to 862,000 in 1988, then dropped to 662,000 in 1990, and increased again to 855,000 in 1991 (NIDA 1989a, 1989b, 1991; Massing 1992:42; Sullivan and Martinez 1991). These figures are certainly correlated with the growing association of cocaine with violent crime: mentions of cocaine in hospital emergency room cases have risen dramatically in recent years, from 8,831 in 1984 to 46,020 in 1988 to 25,400 in just the second quarter of 1991 (NIDA 1989a, Sullivan and Martinez 1991). But employee drug testing is not the best tool for grappling with this particular problem, because cocaine use is shifting out of the workplace. Drug Czar Robert Martinez has stated that the war on drugs is making far less progress among unemployed users (particularly those who are minority, inner-city dwellers) than among the employed (Sullivan and Martinez 1991, see also Massing 1992). The percentage of cocaine users in the United States who are unemployed jumped from 16 to 54 percent between 1983 and 1987 (Washington State Substance Abuse Coalition, as reported in the September 1989 issue of *Health-*

Quest, a newsletter of the Kansas State Employees Health Care Commission). Therefore, attempting to ferret out frequent cocaine users by means of employee testing boils down to looking for them where they are not.

11. BLR 1987:27.
12. Ibid.:26.
13. McKinley 1989.
14. Winslow 1990:B4.
15. Zwerling, Ryan, and Orav 1990.
16. Ibid.:2642.
17. Ibid.:2643.
18. Winslow 1990.
19. Levy 1972:13.
20. Caplovitz 1976.
21. Ibid.:316, 314.
22. *Human Behavior,* May 1977, 53.
23. Dunham 1987; see also Axel 1991:147; Winslow 1990:B4.
24. See Walsh and Trumble 1991:39–40.
25. Clines 1990.
26. *New York Times,* September 6, 1989, 16.
27. Scanlon 1986:37–38.
28. One unintended consequence of the job jeopardy model should, however, be mentioned. The Rehabilitation Act of 1973 prohibits employers from discriminating against employees (and that includes, of course, firing them) on the basis of a handicap, and drug addiction is defined within the provisions of the act as a handicap. While several other conditions must also be satisfied, an employee with a positive drug test result from, say, smoking marijuana on an occasional weekend may be able to avoid being fired by claiming to be an addict and thus protected under the Rehabilitation Act (Hebert 1988:848). The ironic upshot is that drug testing programs, when juxtaposed with the Rehabilitation Act, may have the effect of making addiction appear more widespread than it really is.

29. Foucault 1979:193–194.
30. Foucault 1980.
31. Foucault 1978:146–147.
32. Jones 1992.
33. Foucault 1965, 1979.
34. This is the rate that CompuChem Laboratories charged in 1987 for each urine sample tested for the U.S. Department of Transportation (Miike and Hewitt 1988:658).

35. Foucault 1979:149–156.

36. It might be argued that student athletes react to drug testing more positively than trainmen do not out of automatic docility but because they think testing will help prevent their competitors from gaining an unfair advantage from performance-enhancing steroids—an issue that is not present in workplace testing. Indeed, precisely this point was repeatedly made by student athletes in comments on questionnaires and in interviews, Curiously, however, it is not supported by statistical data from the questionnaires. One of the possible attitudes toward testing presented on the questionnaire was "satisfaction because testing would discourage other people from using drugs." If the primary reason for athletes' approval of drug tests is to prevent competitors from using steroids, a large proportion of them (considerably more than trainmen) would have checked that option. In fact, student athletes selected this option at a *lower* rate than trainmen, by a margin of 15 to 24 percent (see Appendix, table 3).

Another curiosity is that when broken down according to the number of tests a student athlete has taken, the profile of responses to this question indicates that the deterrent effect of testing is not widely recognized by those who are starting their college athletic careers, gains in significance for those who have been tested from two to five times (who have probably been in the program one or two years), but drops to a meager 8 percent among those who have been tested six or more times (see Appendix, table 4). Since this last category would presumably include those with the greatest experience of intercollegiate competition, they are precisely the ones that one would think would be the *most* interested in this aspect of this issue, not the least interested.

There is still another puzzling aspect to these figures. The sports in which anabolic steroids are most pertinent to performance enhancement are football and men's track. It would seem to follow that participants in those sports would be the most concerned about the unfair advantage that steroids could provide for their competitors. Therefore, one would expect them to be likeliest to welcome drug tests as a means of preventing others from using steroids. Again the facts are contrary to expectations: student athletes from other sports acknowledged satisfaction with the deterrent effect of tests on drug use by others at rates two to three times higher than did members of the football and men's track team (see Appendix, tables 8 and 9).

37. The results in Appendix tables 6 and 7 may be mitigated by a complex transformation of attitudes that might be expected to occur as

one is tested more frequently. See the Appendix for a discussion of this matter.

38. Mulloy 1991:105.
39. Kramer 1990.
40. *Lawrence Journal-World,* April 27, 1990.
41. Liebow 1967:37.
42. Ibid.:37.
43. Hoffman 1987.
44. Goffman 1973.
45. Foucault 1979:200–201.

7. The Forest of Pencils

1. Lai 1970:1.
2. Franke 1960:1–7.
3. Ibid.:8. During its immensely long history, the civil service examination underwent numerous changes. Given our concern to set out its fundamental principles, this account is a somewhat generalized description of the system since the Sung dynasty.
4. Franke 1960:15.
5. Lai 1970:1.
6. Kracke 1953:69.
7. Franke 1960:9–10.
8. Hu 1984:14–15.
9. Ibid.:15.
10. Ibid.
11. Ibid.:10–11; Kracke 1953:65–66; Miyazaki 1976:59, 100–101; Morris 1961:3.
12. Franke 1960:4–6; Miyazaki 1976:41–44.
13. Miyazaki 1976:42.
14. Ibid.:46–50.
15. Hu 1984:17.
16. Kracke 1953:67; Miyazaki 1976:27–30, 43–45, 51–56.
17. Chaffee 1985:113–114; Miyazaki 1976:21.
18. Miyazaki 1976:62.
19. Chaffee 1985:114.
20. Hu 1984:1.
21. Miyazaki 1976:22.
22. Franke 1960:16–26; Miyazaki 1976:124–125.

23. Quoted in Franke 1960:26.
24. Franke 1960:48–71; Miyazaki 1976:125.
25. Rashdall 1936 3:142.
26. Morris 1961:30.
27. Nimmo 1982:155.
28. Smallwood 1935:8.
29. Ibid.:35.
30. Ibid.:15–35.
31. Dressel 1963:1–9.
32. Quoted in Kandel 1936:25.
33. Ibid.:26.
34. Ibid.:27.
35. MacLeod 1982:16.
36. Quoted in Roach 1961:3.
37. Ibid.:24; Hearl 1982:114–118.
38. Roach 1961:210–211.
39. Butterworth 1982:28–31.
40. Wigdor and Garner 1982 1:83–84.
41. Ibid.
42. MacLeod 1982:6.
43. Kandel 1936:26.
44. MacLeod 1982:7, 15.
45. Ibid.:6.
46. Ibid.:9–11.
47. Kandel 1936:27.
48. Ibid.:27–28.
49. Petch 1961:59.
50. MacLeod 1982:11.
51. Quoted in ibid.:22.
52. Roach 1961:30–31.
53. Ibid.:193.
54. Ibid.:211.
55. Kandel 1936:27–29; MacLeod 1982:8–11.
56. Hothersall 1984:62–63.
57. Ibid.:63–65; see also Wyllie 1954:38–39.
58. Fowler 1873:158.
59. Ibid.:28–30.
60. Ibid.:204.
61. Ibid.:205.
62. Hothersall 1984:64.
63. Fowler 1873:156.

64. Ibid.:180–190.
65. Ibid.:180.
66. Ibid.:186.
67. Fowler and Fowler 1839:95.
68. Fowler 1873:169.
69. Ibid.:1199.
70. Ibid.:792–793.
71. Ibid.:887–891.
72. Ibid.:441.
73. Ibid.:1168–1173.
74. Hothersall 1984:65–66. Curiously, as late as 1989, of symbols for the various sciences that appeared on the brochure for the prestigious National Science Foundation Graduate Fellowship program, the one representing the social sciences was nothing other than the phrenologist's chart of the cranium!
75. Hale 1982:8–9.
76. Quoted in DuBois 1970:13.
77. DuBois 1970:12–14; Goslin 1963:22–24; Gould 1981:76.
78. Cattell 1890.
79. Ibid.:374.
80. Galton 1978 [1869]:338–342.
81. Ibid.:34.
82. Vroon 1980:14–15.
83. Gould 1981:75.
84. Vroon 1980:18–20.
85. Ibid.:19.
86. Huarte 1594:286.
87. Ibid.:289.
88. Gould 1981:149–150. The age ratio means of calculating IQ has a number of drawbacks, such as poor applicability to adults. The Wechsler-Bellevue test (published in 1939) reported IQ scores based on means and standard deviations, and that practice was adopted for the revised Stanford-Binet in 1972 (Cunningham 1986:74).
89. Thorndike 1922:1.
90. The story of the development of intelligence testing in the United States through Yerkes and the army tests has been masterfully told by Stephen Jay Gould (1981:158–233). Where other citations are not given, the summary in the following paragraphs is based on Gould's book.
91. Zenderland 1987.
92. Minton 1987:105–106.
93. Gould 1981:182; Terman 1919:285.

94. Thorndike 1922:7.
95. Samelson 1987:118–120.
96. Reed 1987:76.
97. Gould 1981:195.
98. Garner 1982:316.
99. Resnick 1982:187; Wigdor and Garner 1982 1:85–86.
100. Crouse and Trusheim 1988:19.
101. Resnick 1982:187.
102. Rudolph 1962:436–437.
103. Crouse and Trusheim 1988:17.
104. Ibid.:17–18.
105. Ibid.:19.
106. Ibid.:20–22; Kandel 1936:95.
107. Crouse and Trusheim 1988:22–25; Sternberg 1988:3.
108. Crouse and Trusheim 1988:22–25.
109. Ibid.:25–27.
110. See, e.g., Barzun 1988; Hoffmann 1962; Hotyat 1969:357; Kandel 1936:80–87.
111. DePalma 1990; Fiske 1989; Greenberg 1991.
112. Nimmo 1982:153–154.
113. Ibid.:155.
114. Ibid.:158–160.
115. Becker, Geer, and Hughes 1968.
116. Evans 1976:43–44.
117. Baily 1976:75.
118. Holt 1976:13.
119. Mechanic 1978:xxix, 23, 25.
120. Napier 1976:24.
121. Curwin 1976:140.
122. Becker, Geer, and Hughes 1968:138–147.
123. Curwin 1976:141.1

8. Willing, Ready, and Able: Vocational Testing

1. Huarte 1594.
2. Zytowski and Borgen 1983:5.
3. Richards 1881:50.
4. It is refreshing to find, in a book written over a century ago, a remarkable sensitivity to sexism in language and in the workplace:

In using the pronoun HE throughout the work, we do not use it with any thought of male superiority or adaptation. No distinction of sex is generally intended in these pages, but convenience prompted the use of HE, instead of HE AND SHE. If any female possesses or can gain the necessary requirements demanded in any honorable trade, profession or occupation, through at present solely followed by man, there can be no objection, whether morally or religiously considered, to her following it. (Richards 1881:iii)

5. Brewer 1942:59–64, 304.
6. Blackford and Newcomb 1921:33–39.
7. Ibid.:119–120.
8. Ibid.:72–73.
9. Ibid.:161.
10. Ibid.:159.
11. Ibid.:178–183.
12. Ibid.:74.
13. Brown 1983:384–399.
14. Holland 1985:29.
15. The Self-Directed Search identifies personality types on the basis of interests, abilities, and values. The Strong Interest Inventory is limited to interests but nevertheless is used to make inferences about the client's personality in terms of Holland's hexagonal theory.
16. Holland 1985:139.
17. Cody 1968:38–39.
18. Whyte 1956:196.
19. Ibid.:201.
20. Moles 1966:133, 162, 196–197.
21. Herr and Cramer 1972:30.
22. Zytowski and Borgen 1983:8.
23. See Campbell 1973:36; Jordaan and Heyde 1979:172; Osipow 1983:168; Ryan and Gaier 1967.
24. Brown 1983:386.
25. Ginsberg et al. 1951.
26. Super 1953.
27. Herr and Cramer 1972:29.
28. Slocum 1965:858.
29. Super et al. 1974.
30. Osipow 1983:157–158.
31. Weber 1958.
32. Herr and Cramer 1972:54.
33. LoCasio 1967:32.

34. LoCasio 1974:127–129.
35. Smith 1983:190; Williams 1979:177.
36. G. Smith 1980:21. It should be noted, however, that steps have been taken to control for this bias so far as systematic differences in interests between the sexes are concerned (Cunningham 1986:330–331).
37. Fitzgerald and Betz 1983:87.
38. *Handbook of Labor Statistics* 1989:162, 169, 194.
39. Ford and Ford 1978:54.
40. *Handbook of Labor Statistics* 1989:200.
41. Ibid.:78.
42. Slocum 1965:859.
43. Smith 1983:189; see also Harmon 1974:82–83.
44. Ford and Ford 1978.
45. Ibid.:53.
46. Ibid.:55–56.
47. Slocum 1965:862; see also Gross 1967:418.
48. Smith 1983:189.
49. Harvey 1989:125–126.
50. Harrison and Bluestone 1988:43–44.
51. Ibid.:44–45; Harvey 1989:147–171.
52. Link 1919:111.
53. See Drake 1942.
54. Baritz 1960:94–96.
55. Link 1919:189–190.
56. Blackford and Newcomb 1921:28.
57. Brewer 1942:207; Kornhauser and Kingsbury 1924:82–97, 107–111, 128–129, 156.
58. Baritz 1960:67–74; Borow 1944:71–72; Brewer 1942:207–208.
59. Borow 1944:74–75.
60. Hale 1982:23.
61. Baritz 1960:159.
62. Hale 1982:28–29.
63. Whyte 1956.
64. Gottfredson 1986:403–405.
65. Sharf 1988:263.
66. Allen 1988:367; Bolick 1988:325–326; Sharf 1988:263.
67. Wigdor and Garner 1982 1:98, 100.
68. Bolick 1988:326; Holmes 1991; Miller 1991.
69. Crites 1983:311.
70. Harmon and Farmer 1983.
71. Cronbach 1979:232–236.

72. Cunningham 1986:303–307.
73. Gottfredson 1986:403–405.
74. Hawk 1986:411–412; see also Hunter 1986:360.
75. The legitimacy of this practice depends on whether there is such a thing as general intelligence and the relation of that concept to intelligence tests. These issues will be discussed critically in chapter 9.
76. Bolick 1988:327; see also Gottfredson 1988:316–317.
77. Barrett 1991; Holmes 1991; Miller 1991.
78. Bolick 1988:326.
79. Sharf 1988:263.
80. Seymour 1988:338–339.
81. Sharf 1988:246–247.
82. Ibid.:263.

9. "Artificial" Intelligence

1. Quoted in Kandel 1936:113.
2. Thorndike 1920:235.
3. Thernstrom 1970:64.
4. Minton 1987:106.
5. Wigdor and Garner 1982:I, 82.
6. Dewey 1940:9.
7. Brewer 1942:207.
8. Vroon 1980:40–41.
9. See Anastasi 1967:297, 302; Anastasi 1968:549; Glass 1986: 10–13.
10. Buros 1972:xxvii; Buros 1978:xxxi.
11. Boring 1923:36.
12. See, e.g., Eysenck 1979:10–11, 78; Herrnstein 1973:107; Jensen 1972:75–76.
13. Howard Gardner (1983:7, 320), Carl Milofsky (1989:184–185), and Robert J. Sternberg (1988:8–9) describe the commonly held view of intelligence (which they all reject) in terms of essentially the same attributes.
14. For example, instead of thinking of intelligence as something distributed quite unequally among the population, in a bell curve within which each individual is endowed with a numerically specifiable amount, James Fallows reports that the Japanese conceive of it as something akin to how we think of health or patriotism. It is not considered to vary sig-

nificantly from one individual to the next; with a few exceptions, everyone has "enough" (Fallows 1989:155).

15. Thorndike 1940:957.
16. Terman 1916:11.
17. Goddard 1912:101–102.
18. Ibid.:105–109, 117.
19. Gould 1981:158–168.
20. Karier 1976:371.
21. Haller 1963:133.
22. Karier 1976:345.
23. Gottfredson 1988:297, 298. For a specific example, in 1985–86 and again in 1987–88, mean scores on the Graduate Record Examination General Test were about 1.3 standard deviations lower for blacks than for whites (ETS 1987:74; ETS 1991:11). However, slight increases in scores of blacks relative to those of whites occurred on the SAT and ACT in 1987 (Schmidt 1988:288).
24. Seymour 1988:333.
25. Gottfredson 1988:294.
26. Ibid.:297–298.
27. Gottfredson 1986:406–407; Gottfredson 1988:316–317; see also Bolick 1988:326–329; Schmidt 1988:287–288.
28. Gottfredson 1986:404.
29. Ibid.:404.
30. Humphreys 1986:432.
31. Ibid.:431.
32. Ibid.:432.
33. Terman 1924:363.
34. Herrnstein 1989.
35. See Wigdor and Garner 1982 1:121.
36. Molnar 1992:273.
37. Ibid.:275–277.
38. Hollinshead 1952:83.
39. Ibid.:14–15, 85–86.
40. Ibid.:120–123.
41. Ibid.:77–78.
42. Kirn 1990.
43. Ibid.:123.
44. Young 1959:86–87.
45. Gardner 1961:71–72.
46. Gottfredson 1981:549, 560–565.
47. Ibid.:576.

48. Gottfredson 1986:396–397.
49. Molnar 1992:278.
50. Anastasi 1967:301.
51. Anastasi 1985:xxix. Her emphasis.
52. Anastasi 1982:394–396.
53. Sternberg 1985:306. Sternberg's observation points to an interesting irony in mental testing. Achievement tests are past oriented, in that they are explicitly intended to measure what subjects have already learned. Intelligence tests—expecially when they go by the name of aptitude tests—are future oriented in the sense that they are used as indicators of how much or how well subjects will learn in the future. That is why these tests are used as predictive measures in making admissions decisions for college and postgraduate study. The irony is that as last year's achievement tests, the supposedly future-oriented aptitude tests actually focus on a more remote past than do explicitly past-oriented achievement tests!
54. Schweiker 1968:718.
55. See Binet 1984:104.
56. Ibid.:105–106.
57. Ibid.:108.
58. Ibid.:109.
59. Sternberg 1988:71.
60. Ibid.:9–11.
61. See Block and Dworkin 1976a:415–416.
62. Binet 1984:107, 164–203; Block and Dworkin 1976a:462–466; Cunningham 1986:245; Kandel 1936:76–77, 129.
63. Gardner 1983.
64. Sternberg 1988:58–70.
65. Gardner 1983:321; Gardner 1987.
66. Sternberg 1985:299–314; Sternberg 1988:70.
67. See, e.g., Berger and Luckmann 1966; Hanson 1979.

10. Conclusion: Man the Measured

1. Stewart 1947.
2. Herr and Cramer 1972:255.
3. Olneck and Crouse 1978:9.
4. See Fallows 1989:156–158.
5. The following discussion of varying relations between signifiers and signifieds is theoretically informed by Jean Baudrillard's insightful analysis of the three orders of simulacra (1976:78–93).

6. Kolata 1988:38.

7. Even though amniocentesis is a biological test, incidentally, the effect of cultural conventions and in the constitutive role of testing is especially clear in this example, for the test drastically skewed the gender birthrate among Dr. Jackson's patients of one ethnic group but not others.

8. Cole 1986.

9. Foucault 1979:195–228.

10. This resembles the point made in chapter 8 that by encouraging people to enter occupations inhabited by others very much like them, vocational interest testing can dull interest and creativity in the workplace.

11. Franke 1960:13.

12. Barzun 1991:32–37; *New York Times,* October 11, 1988.

13. White's research (1984:371) indicates similar effects of preemployment polygraph screening.

14. See Finkelstein 1991:171.

15. Mead 1964:202.

16. Derrida 1978:280; Lyotard 1984.

17. Baudrillard 1981; Eco 1986.

18. Deutsch 1988:4.

19. Gardner 1983.

20. Becker, Geer, and Hughes nuance this point somewhat: faculty attribute academic performance to a combination of student motivation and ability, while students see it exclusively in terms of the effort they put into a course. "We," they go on to say, "tend to agree more with students than with faculty" (1968:39).

21. See Coleman 1982.

22. Goffman 1973.

23. Baudrillard 1985.

24. Incidentally, the woman who voiced the speculations received "quite a bit of verbal abuse" from the other passengers, and when the plane finally left, she and her husband were not on board, electing to take a later flight (*New York Times,* April 22, 1990, 20).

25. Roel 1990.

26. I am aware of only one case in which a written integrity test was used to investigate a specific crime. A foreman was nearly killed from rat poison in his coffee, and a Stanton honesty test consisting of yes-no questions and short essays was given to the thirty-eight suspects. The test results pointed to one of them, and that individual subsequently confessed (Kovach 1986:46).

27. Ferguson 1971:147.

28. Kramer 1990.

29. Hanson 1991:529; OTA 1990:16, 18.

30. Polygraph tests of persons reasonably suspected of wrongdoing would also be permitted under the letter of this policy, but I would hope that they might be curtailed on other grounds, such as problem with their accuracy. One exception to the policy that may actually be desirable in present circumstances pertains to steroid use by atheletes. As was discussed at the end of chapter 5, the increased strength and endurance produced by steroids persist after the drugs can be detected by tests. Therefore, athletes can cycle steroid use in such a way that tests taken at contests or meets will be negative while they will still realize their performance-enhancing benefits. It would be helpful if observable symptoms of steroid use could be identified, so that only those who are reasonably suspected would be subject to testing. Until then, however, about the only effective measure available to prevent athletes from using steroids is to make all of them susceptible to tests on generalized suspicion and to conduct unannounced tests at any time during training.

31. Berlin 1991:21.

32. Ibid.:20.

33. Foucault 1979:184–194. Foucault's is one of several recent insightful analyses of the development of the individual. For Karl Weintraub (1975:838–847), the idea of individuality became fully developed in the late eighteenth century, when Justus Moeser and the young Herder stressed historical diversity—local peculiarities and the unique value and experience of each *Volk*—over the singular view of history as the unfolding of God's plan or the development of natural law. This perspective on history reinforced and perfected the notion, originating in the Renaissance, of the human individual as a unique, unrepeatable being. Joanne Finkelstein, on the other hand, relies on Lionel Trilling (1972) to develop the argument that the concept of the individual as a distinct, unique being dates from the sixteenth century, when dissimulation, mistaken identity, and individual nuances of character (visible, for example, in Shakespeare's plays) became topics of widespread fascination (Finkelstein 1991:157–162). For a sensitive development of this point, see Daniel Vigne's film *Le retour de Martin Guerre.*

34. Foucault 1979:190.

35. Ibid.:194.

36. Ibid.:169.

REFERENCES

Abrams, Stanley
   1977   *A Polygraph Handbook for Attorneys*. Lexington, Mass: Lexington Books.
   1978   The Utilization and Effectiveness of the Stimulation Test. *Polygraph* 7:178–181.
Aig, Marlene
   1990   The Latest in Drug Detection: Simply Rub, Spray and Wait. *Lawrence Journal-World*, August 15, 1990. (Associated Press.)
Allen, W. B.
   1988   Rhodes Handicapping, or Slowing the Pace of Integration. *Journal of Vocational Behavior* 33:3653–3678.
Altman, Lawrence K.
   1988a   New Olympic Drug Test Foiled Sprinter. *New York Times*, October 4, 1988, A1.
   1988b   New Breakfast of Champions: A Recipe for Victory or Disaster? *New York Times*, November 20, 1988, 1.
AMA (American Management Association)
   1987   *Drug Abuse: The Workplace Issues*. New York: American Management Association.
Anastasi, Anne
   1967   Psychology, Psychologists, and Psychological Testing. *American Psychologist* 22:297–306.
   1968   *Psychological Testing* 3d ed. London: Macmillan.
   1982   *Psychological Testing* 5th ed. New York: Macmillan.
   1985   Mental Measurement: Some Emerging Trends. In *The Ninth Mental Measurements Yearbook*, ed. James V. Mitchell, Jr. Pp. xxiii–xxix. Lincoln, Neb: The Buros Institute of Mental Measurement.
Anderson, William A., and Douglas B. McKeag (project directors)
   1985   *The Substance Use and Abuse Habits of College Student-Athletes. Research Paper #2: General Findings*. Michigan State University, College of Human Medicine.

REFERENCES

Angier, Natalie
1991   The Biology of What It Means to Be Gay. *New York Times,* September 1, 1991, E1.
Ashliman, D. L.
1987   *A Guide to Folktales in the English Language.* New York: Greenwood.
Austin, Cecil Kent
1912   Medical Impressions of America. *Boston Medical and Surgical Journal* 166:799–804.
Axel, Helen
1991   Drug Testing in Private Industry. Pp. 140–154 in Coombs and West 1991.
Bailey, William J.
1976   A Case Study: Performance Evaluation at Concord Senior High School. Pp. 74–82 in Simon and Bellanca 1976.
Baker, Peter
1991   Reaction Seen for Wilder's Drug Plan. *Washington Post,* June 28, 1991, p. B5.
Baritz, Loren
1960   *Servants of Power: A History of the Use of Social Science in American Industry.* Middletown, Conn: Wesleyan University Press.
Barland, Gordon H.
1978   An Introduction to the Number Test. *Polygraph* 7:173–175.
Barrett, Laurence I.
1991   Cheating on the Tests. *Time,* June 3, 1991, 57.
Bartlett, Robert
1986   *Trial by Fire and Water: The Medieval Ordeal.* Oxford: Clarendon Press.
Barzun, Jacques
1988   Multiple Choice Flunks Out. *New York Times,* October 11, 1988, A31.
1991   *Begin Here: The Forgotten Conditions of Teaching and Learning.* Chicago: University of Chicago Press.
Baudrillard, Jean
1976   *L'echange symbolique et la mort.* Paris: Gallimard.
1981   *Simulacres et simulations.* Paris: Editions Galilee.
1985   The Ecstasy of Communication. Pp. 126–134 in Foster 1985.
Baughman, Ernest W.
1966   *Type and Motif-Index of the Folktales of England and North America.* Indiana University Folklore Series no. 20. The Hague: Mouton.
Baumgartner, Werner A.
1989   Hair Analysis for Drugs of Abuse. *Employment Testing Biweekly Reporter* 3:442–443, 446.

REFERENCES

Becker, Howard S., Blanche Geer, and Everett C. Hughes
1968   *Making the Grade: The Academic Side of College Life.* New York: Wiley.

Berger, Henry L., and Thomas Luckmann
1966   *The Social Construction of Reality.* Garden City, N.Y.: Doubleday.

Berlin, Philip E.
1991   More State Laws Now Regulate Drug Testing in the Workplace. *National Law Journal,* July 8, 1991, 19–21.

Binet, Alfred
1984   *Modern Ideas About Children.* N.p.: Suzanne Heisler. Trans. Suzanne Heisler.

Blackford, Katherine M. H., and Arthur Newcomb
1921   *The Job, the Man, the Boss.* New York: Doubleday, Page & Co.
[1914]

Block, N. J., and Gerald Dworkin
1976a   IQ, Heritability, and Inequality. Pp. 410–540 in Block and Dworkin 1976b.

1976b   *The IQ Controversy: Critical Readings.* New York: Pantheon.

BLR (Business and Legal Reports)
1987   *1987 Survey of Drug Testing in the Workplace.* Madison, Conn.: Business and Legal Reports, Inc.

1989   Survey Documents Dramatic Rise in Drug Testing. *Personnel Manager's Legal Reporter,* February 1989, 7–8.

BLS (Bureau of Labor Statistics)
1989   *Survey of Employer Anti-drug Programs.* Bureau of Labor Statistics, U.S. Department of Labor, Report 760, January 1989.

Bolick, Clint
1988   Legal and Policy Aspects of Testing. *Journal of Vocational Behavior* 33:320–330.

Boring, Edwin G.
1923   Intelligence as the Tests Test It. *New Republic,* June 6, 1923, 35–37.

Borow, Henry C.
1944   The Growth and Present Status of Occupational Testing. *Journal of Consulting Psychology* 8:70–79.

Brewer, John M.
1942   *History of Vocational Guidance: Origins and Early Development.* New York: Harper & Brothers.

Briggs, Katharine Mary
1970   *A Dictionary of British Folk-Tales, Part A.* London: Routledge & Kegan Paul. 2 vols.

1971   *A Dictionary of British Folk-Tales, Part B.* London: Routledge & Kegan Paul. 2 vols.

REFERENCES

Brodkey, Harold
1988   Stories in an Almost Classical Mode. New York: Knopf.
Brown, Frederick G.
1983   Principles of Educational and Psychological Testing. 3d ed. New York: Holt, Rinehart and Winston.
Buros, Oscar Krisen, ed.
1972   The Seventh Mental Measurements Yearbook. Highland Park, N.J.: Gryphon. 2 vols.
1978   The Eighth Mental Measurements Yearbook. Highland Park, N.J.: Gryphon, 2 vols.
Butterworth, Harry
1982   The Science and Art Department Examinations: Origins and Achievements. Pp. 27–44 in MacLeod 1982b.
Campbell, David P.
1973   The Strong Vocational Interest Blank for Men. Pp. 20–57 in Zytowski 1973.
Caplovitz, David
1976   The Working Addict. Journal of Psychedelic Drugs 8:313–316.
Cattell, J. McK.
1890   Mental Tests and Measurements. Mind 15:373–380.
Ceol, Dawn
1991   Thomas Will Not "Cry Uncle." Washington Times, October 13, 1991, A1.
Chaffee, John W.
1985   The Thorny Gates of Learning in Sung China: A Social History of Examinations. Cambridge: Cambridge University Press.
Chass, Murray
1987   Yank Lie-Detector Test Won Few Friends for Steinbrenner. New York Times, January 11, 1987, Y17.
Clines, Francis X.
1990   Soviet Drug Testing: Full Disclosure Is the Rule. New York Times, December 9, 1990, Y28.
Cody, John J.
1968   Appraisal of Disadvantaged Youth. In Counseling the Disadvantaged Youth, ed. William E. Amos and Jean Dresden Grambs, pp. 30–53. Englewood Cliffs, N.J.: Prentice-Hall.
Cole, Nancy S.
1986   Future Directions for Educational Achievement and Ability Testing. Pp. 73–88 in Plake and Witt 1986.
Coleman, James S.
1982   The Asymmetric Society. Syracuse: Syracuse University Press.
Cone, Edward J.
1989   Hair Testing for Drugs: Developments in an Infant Science. Employment Testing Biweekly Reporter 3:439–441, 446.

REFERENCES

Coombs, Robert H., and Louis Jolyon West, eds.
1991   *Drug Testing: Issues and Options.* New York: Oxford University Press.

Crites, John O.
1983   Research Methods in Vocational Psychology. Pp. 305–353 in Walsh and Osipow 1983. Vol. 1.

Cronbach, Lee J.
1979   The Armed Services Vocational Aptitude Battery—a Test Battery in Transition. *Personnel and Guidance Journal* 57:232–237.

Crouse, James, and Dale Trusheim
1988   *The Case Against the SAT.* Chicago: University of Chicago Press.

Cunningham, George K.
1986   *Educational and Psychological Measurement.* New York: Macmillan.

Curwin, Richard L.
1976   In Conclusion: Dispelling the Grading Myths. Pp. 138–145 in Simon and Bellanca 1976.

Davis, Phillip W., and Pamela McKenzie-Rundle
1984   The Social Organization of Lie-Detector Tests. *Urban Life* 13: 177–205.

Deacon, Richard
1976   *Mathew Hopkins: Witch Finder General.* London: Frederick Muller.

Defoe, Daniel
1731   *An Effectual Scheme for the Immediate Preventing of Street Robberies and Suppressing all other Disorders of the Night.* London: J. Wilford.

DePalma, Anthony
1990   Revisions Adopted in College Entrance Tests. *New York Times,* November 1, 1990, A1, A9.

Derrida, Jacques
1978   *Writing and Difference.* Chicago: University of Chicago Press.

Deutsch, Claudia H.
1988   A Mania for Testing Spells Money. *New York Times,* October 16, 1988, sec. 3, 4.

Dewey, John
1940   *Education Today.* New York: G. P. Putnam's Sons.

Drake, Charles A.
1942   *Personnel Selection by Standard Job Tests.* New York: McGraw-Hill.

Dressel, Paul L.
1963   *The Undergraduate Curriculum in Higher Education.* Washington, D.C.: Center for Applied Research in Education.

REFERENCES

DuBois, Philip H.
1970   *A History of Psychological Testing.* Boston: Allyn & Bacon.
Dunham, Bonnie
1987   LMH Policy to Institute Drug Tests. *Lawrence Journal-World,*
        October 21, 1987, 1.
Durkheim, Emile
1962   *Socialism.* New York: Collier Books.
Eco, Umberto
1986   *Travels in Hyperreality: Essays.* San Diego: Harcourt Brace
        Jovanovich.
ETS (Educational Testing Service)
1987   *A Summary of Data Collected from Graduate Record Exami-
        nations.* Princeton, N.J.: Educational Testing Service.
1991   *Sex, Race, Ethnicity, and Performance on the GRE General
        Test: A Technical Report.* Princeton, N.J.: Published for the
        Graduate Record Examinations Board by Educational Testing
        Service.
Evans, Francis B.
1976   What Research Says about Grading. Pp. 30–50 in Simon and
        Bellanca 1976.
Evans-Pritchard, E. E.
1937   *Witchcraft, Oracles and Magic Among the Azande.* Oxford:
        Clarendon Press.
Eysenck, Hans J.
1979   *The Structure and Measurement of Intelligence.* Berlin:
        Springer-Verlag.
Fallows, James
1989   *More Like Us: Making America Great Again.* Boston: Hough-
        ton Mifflin.
Ferguson, Robert J., Jr.
1971   *The Scientific Informer.* Springfield, Ill.: Charles C. Thomas.
Ferguson, Robert J., Jr., and Chris Gugas
1984   *Preemployment Polygraphy.* Springfield, Ill.: Charles C.
        Thomas.
Finkelstein, Joanne
1991   *The Fashioned Self.* Philadelphia: Temple University Press.
Fiske, Edward B.
1989   Changes Planned in Entrance Tests Used by Colleges. *New
        York Times,* January 3, 1989, A1.
Fitzgerald, Louise F., and Nancy E. Betz
1983   Issues in the Vocational Psychology of Women. Pp. 83–159 in
        Walsh and Osipow 1983, vol. 1.
Ford, Charles, and Doris Jeffries Ford
1978   Is Career Counseling for Black People? *Journal of Non-White
        Concerns in Personnel and Guidance* 6:53–62.

Foster, Hal, ed.
1985   *Postmodern Culture.* London: Pluto Press.
Foucault, Michel
1965   *Madness and Civilization: A History of Insanity in the Age of Reason.* New York: Vintage.
1973   *The Order of Things: An Archaeology of the Human Sciences.* New York: Vintage.
1978   *The History of Sexuality. I: An Introduction.* New York: Vintage.
1979   *Discipline and Punish: The Birth of the Prison.* New York: Vintage.
1980   *Power/Knowledge: Selected Interviews and Other Writings, 1972–1977.* New York: Pantheon Books.
Fowler, O. S.
1873   *Human Science: or, Phrenology.* . . . Philadelphia: National Publishing Company.
Fowler, O. S., and L. N. Fowler
1839   *Phrenology Proved, Illustrated, and Applied.* . . . 4th ed. Philadelphia: Fowler & Brevoort.
Franke, Wolfgang
1960   *The Reform and Abolition of the Traditional Chinese Examination System.* Harvard East Asian Monographs 10. Cambridge: East Asian Research Center, Harvard University.
Galton, Francis
1978   *Hereditary Genius: An Inquiry into Its Laws and Conse-*
[1869] *quences.* London: Friedmann.
Gardner, Howard
1983   *Frames of Mind: The Theory of Multiple Intelligences.* New York: Basic Books.
1987   Beyond the IQ: Education and Human Development. *Harvard Educational Review* 57(2):187–193.
Gardner, John W.
1961   *Excellence: Can We Be Equal and Excellent Too?* New York: Harper.
Garner, Eric
1982   Some Aspects of the Use and Misuse of Standardized Aptitude and Achievement Tests. Pp. 315–332 in Wigdor and Garner 1982, Pt. II.
Ginzberg, Eli, Sol W. Ginsburg, Sidney Axelrad, and John L. Herma
1951   *Occupational Choice: An Approach to a General Theory.* New York: Columbia University Press.
Glass, Gene V.
1986   Testing Old, Testing New: Schoolboy Psychology and the Allocation of Professional Resources. Pp. 9–27 in Plake and Witt 1986.

REFERENCES

Goddard, Henry H.
1912   *The Kallikak Family: A Study in the Heredity of Feeble-Mindedness*. New York: Macmillan.
Goffman, Erving
1973   *The Presentation of Self in Everyday Life*. Woodstock, N.Y.:
[1959] Overlook Press.
Goldberg, Lewis R., Julia Ramos Grenier, Robert M. Guion et al.
1991   *Questionnaires Used in the Prediction of Trustworthiness in Pre-Employment Decisions: An A.P.A. Task Force Report*. Washington, D.C.: Scientific Directorate, American Psychological Association.
Goslin, David A.
1963   *The Search for Ability: Standardized Testing in Social Perspective*. New York: Russell Sage Foundation.
Gottfredson, Linda S.
1981   Circumscription and Compromise: A Developmental Theory of Vocational Aspirations. *Journal of Counseling Psychology* 28:545–579.
1986   Societal Consequences of the g Factor in Employment. *Journal of Vocational Behavior* 29:379–410.
1988   Reconsidering Fairness: A Matter of Social and Ethical Priorities. *Journal of Vocational Behavior* 33:293–319.
Gould, Stephen Jay
1981   *The Mismeasure of Man*. New York: Norton.
Great Britain
1985   House of Commons Report on the Polygraph. *Polygraph* 14: 43–78.
Greenberg, Karen L.
1991   The Vote Against an Essay on the Scholastic Aptitude Test Sets the Wrong Example for Writing Teachers at All Levels. *The Chronicle of Higher Education*, January 16, 1991, B1, B3.
Grey, Sir George.
1956   *Polynesian Mythology, and Ancient Traditional Life of the Maori*. . . . Christchurch: Whitcombe & Tombs. (English translation of Grey 1971, first published 1855.)
1971   *Nga Mahi a Nga Tupuna*. 4th ed. Wellington: Reed.
Gross, Edward
1967   A Sociological Approach to the Analysis of Preparation for Work Life. *Personnel and Guidance Journal* 45:416–423.
Guazzo, Br. Francesco Maria
1929   *Compendium Maleficarum*. London: John Rodker.
Gwertzman, Bernard
1985   This Time, Shultz Has the Last Word. *New York Times*, December 22, 1985, E1.

REFERENCES

Hale, Matthew
1982   History of Employment Testing. Pp. 3–38 in Wigdor and Garner 1982, pt. 2.
Haller, M. H.
1963   *Eugenics*. New Brunswick: Rutgers University Press.
Handbook of Labor Statistics
1989   U.S. Department of Labor, Bureau of Labor Statistics, bull. 2340.
Hanson, F. Allan
1973   Political Change in Tahiti and Samoa: An Exercise in Experimental Anthropology. *Ethnology* 12:1–13.
1975   *Meaning in Culture*. London: Routledge & Kegan Paul.
1979   Does God Have a Body? Truth, Reality and Cultural Relativism. *Man* 14:515–529.
1990   What Employees Say about Drug Tests. *Personnel*, July 1990, pp. 32–36.
Hanson, F. Allan, and Louise Hanson
1981   The Cybernetics of Cultural Communication. In *Semiotic Themes*, ed. Richard T. DeGeorge, pp. 251–273. Lawrence: University of Kansas Publications, Humanistic Studies 53.
Hanson, George Allan
1991   To Catch a Thief: The Legal and Policy Implications of Honesty Testing in the Workplace. *Law and Inequality* 9:497–531.
Harmon, Lenore W.
1974   Problems in Measuring Vocational Maturity: A Counseling Perspective. Pp. 81–86 in Super et al. 1974.
Harmon, Lenore W., and Helen S. Farmer
1983   Current Theoretical Issues in Vocational Psychology. Pp. 39–77 in Walsh and Osipow 1983.
Harrison, Bennett, and Barry Bluestone
1988   *The Great U-Turn: Corporate Restructuring and the Polarizing of America*. New York: Basic Books.
Hartshorne, Hugh, and Mark A. May
1928   *Studies in Deceit. Bk I: General Methods and Results*. Vol. I of Studies in the Nature of Character, by the Character Education Inquiry, Teachers College, Columbia University. New York: Macmillan.
Harvey, David
1989   *The Condition of Postmodernity*. Oxford: Basil Blackwell.
Hawk, John
1986   Real World Implications of g. *Journal of Vocational Behavior* 29:411–414.
Hearl, Trevor
1982   Military Examinations and the Teaching of Science, 1857–1870. Pp. 109–149 in MacLeod 1982*b*.

REFERENCES

Hebert, L. Camille
1988   Private Sector Drug Testing: Employer Rights, Risks, and Responsibilities. *University of Kansas Law Review* 36:823–868.

Herr, Edwin L., and Stanley H. Cramer
1972   *Vocational Guidance and Career Development in the Schools: Toward a Systems Approach.* Boston: Houghton Mifflin.

Herrnstein, R. J.
1971   IQ. *Atlantic Monthly*, September 1971, 43–64.
1973   *I.Q. in the Meritocracy.* Boston: Little, Brown.
1989   IQ and Falling Birth Rates. *Atlantic Monthly*, May 1989, 73–79.

Hirst, Paul
1985   Is It Rational to Reject Relativism? In *Reason and Morality*, ed. Joanna Overing, pp. 85–103. London: Tavistock.

Hoffman, Abbie (with Jonathan Silvers)
1987   *Steal This Urine Test.* New York: Penguin Books.

Hoffmann, Banesh
1962   *The Tyranny of Testing.* New York: Crowell-Collier.

Holland, John L.
1985   *Making Vocational Choices: A Theory of Vocational Personalities and Work Environments.* 2d ed. Englewood Cliffs, N.J.: Prentice-Hall.

Hollinshead, Byron S.
1952   *Who Should Go to College?* Published for the Commission on Financing Higher Education. New York: Columbia University Press.

Holmes, Steven A.
1991   Test Score Issue Inflames Rights Debate. *New York Times*, May 17, 1991, A10.

Holmes, Warren D.
1977   How the Guilty Reveal Themselves. *Polygraph* 6:325–336.

Holt, Donald D.
1976   An Experience with Failure. Pp. 10–13 in Simon and Bellanca 1976.

Hopkins, Matthew
1647   *The Discovery of Witches.* London: R. Royston.

Horvath, Frank
1985   Job Screening. *Society* 22(6):43–46.

Horvath, Frank, and Richard J. Phannenstill
1987   Preemployment Polygraph Testing: The Attitudes of Applicants and Their Relationship to Personal Characteristics. *Polygraph* 16:18–32.

Hothersall, David
1984   *History of Psychology.* Philadelphia: Temple University Press.

REFERENCES

Hotyat, F.
1969   Examinations and Educational Objectives. Pp. 355–359 in Lauwerys and Scanlon 1969.
HR Report
1987   *Employee Polygraph Protection Act: Report.* House of Representatives Report 100–208.
1988   *Employee Polygraph Protection Act of 1988: Conference Report.* House of Representatives Report 100–659.
Hu, C. T.
1984   The Historical Background: Examinations and Control in Pre-Modern China. *Comparative Education* 20:7–26.
Huarte, John [Juan]
1594   *Examen de Ingenios—The Examination of Men's Wits.* Trans. M. Camillo Camilli, Englished out of his Italian by R. C[arew], esq. London: Adam Islip.
Human Behavior
1977   Working While Stoned. *Human Behavior* 6 (May 1977): 53.
Humphreys, Lloyd G.
1986   Commentary. *Journal of Vocational Behavior* 29:421–437.
Hunter, John E.
1986   Cognitive Ability, Cognitive Aptitudes, Job Knowledge, and Job Performance. *Journal of Vocational Behavior* 29:340–362.
Iacono, William G.
1985   Guilty Knowledge. *Society* 22(6):52–54.
Inbau, Fred E., and John F. Reid
1953   *Lie Detection and Criminal Interrogation.* 3d ed. Baltimore: Williams & Wilkins.
Isikoff, Michael
1991   Hill's Story Said to Pass Polygraph Examination. *Washington Post*, October 14, 1991, A1.
Janofsky, Michael, with Peter Alfano
1988   System Accused of Failing Test Posed by Drugs. *New York Times*, November 17, 1988, A1.
Jensen, Arthur R.
1972   *Genetics and Education.* New York: Harper & Row.
Jones, Christopher B.
1992   Panel Rejects Plan to Implant Women with Contraceptive. *Kansas City Star*, February 28, 1992, C2.
Jordaan, Jean Pierre, and Martha Bennett Heyde
1979   *Vocational Maturity During the High School Years.* New York: Teachers College Press.
Kagay, Michael R.
1991   As Candidates Hunt the Big Issue, Polls Can Give Them a Few Clues. *New York Times*, October 20, 1991, E3.

REFERENCES

Kahler, Kirk
1990   Postcard's Claims about Drug Abuse Prompt Local Alert. *Lawrence Journal-World*, February 6, 1990.

Kandel, I. L.
1936   *Examinations and Their Substitutes in the United States.* New York: Carnegie Foundation for the Advancement of Teaching, bull. 28.

Karier, Clarence J.
1976   Testing for Order and Control in the Corporate Liberal State. Pp. 339–373 in Block and Dworkin 1976b.

Kay, Richard
1978   *Dante's Swift and Strong: Essays on Inferno XV.* Lawrence: Regents Press of Kansas.

Keeler, Eloise
1984   *Lie Detector Man: The Career and Cases of Leonarde Keeler.* N.p.: Telshare

Kirn, Walter
1990   A Satisfying Ride in the Country. In Walter Kirn, *My Hard Bargain: Stories*, 115–123. New York: Knopf.

Kolata, Gina
1988   Fetal Sex Test Used as Step to Abortion. *New York Times*, December 25, 1988, A1, 38.
1992   Track Federation Urges End to Gene Test for Femaleness. *New York Times*, February 12, 1992, A1, B11.

Kornhauser, Arthur W., and Forrest A. Kingsbury
1924   *Psychological Tests in Business.* Chicago: University of Chicago Press.

Kovach, Jeffrey L.
1986   Psychological Testing Is Fair: True or False? *Industry Week*, January 20, 1986, 44–47.

Kracke, E. A., Jr.
1953   *Civil Service in Early Sung China, 960–1067.* Harvard-Yenching Institute Monographs 13. Cambridge: Harvard University Press.

Kramer, Farrell
1990   Students at Oklahoma High School 100 Percent Drug Free. *Lawrence Journal-World*, March 5, 1990, 10B.

Kuvlesky, William P., and Rumaldo Z. Juarez
1975   Mexican American Youth and the American Dream. Pp. 241–296 in Picou and Campbell 1975.

Lai, T. C.
1970   *A Scholar in Imperial China.* Hong Kong: Kelly & Walsh.

Lauwerys, Joseph A., and David G. Scanlon, eds.
1969   *Examinations.* The World Year Book of Education, 1969. London: Evans Bros.

REFERENCES

Lea, Henry C.
1968 *Superstition and Force: Essays on the Wager of Law, the Wager*
[1870] *of Battle, the Ordeal, Torture.* 2d rev. ed. New York: Greenwood Press.

Leisner, Pat
1989 Genetic Tests Prove Girl's Parentage: Biological Parents Win Visiting Rights. *Lawrence Journal-World*, November 20, 1989. (Associated Press.)

Levin, Samuel M.
1927a Ford Profit Sharing, 1914–1920. I. The Growth of the Plan. *Personnel Journal* 6:75–86.
1927b The End of Ford Profit Sharing. *Personnel Journal* 6:161–170.

Levy, Stephen J.
1972 Drug Abuse in Business: Telling It Like It Is. *Personnel*, September-October 1972, 8–14.

Liebow, Elliot
1967 *Tally's Corner.* Boston: Little, Brown.

Lienhardt, Godfrey
1961 *Divinity and Experience.* Oxford: Clarendon Press.

Lindenbaum, Shirley
1979 *Kuru Sorcery: Disease and Danger in the New Guinea Highlands.* Palo Alto: Mayfield Publishing Co.

Link, H. C.
1919 *Employment Psychology: The Application of Scientific Methods to the Selection, Training and Grading of Employees.* New York: Macmillan.

Litvan, Laura M.
1990 Study Distrusts Pre-Employment Tests. *The Washington Times*, September 27, 1990, C1.

LoCasio, Ralph
1967 Continuity and Discontinuity in Vocational Development Theory. *Personnel and Guidance Journal* 46:32–36.
1974 The Vocational Maturity of Diverse Groups: Theory and Measurement. Pp. 123–133 in Super et al. 1974.

Lykken, David Toresen
1981 *A Tremor in the Blood: Uses and Abuses of the Lie Detector.* New York: McGraw-Hill.

Lyotard, Jean François
1984 *The Postmodern Condition: A Report on Knowledge.* Minneapolis: University of Minnesota Press.

McGarvey, Robert
1989 Confidence Pays. *USAir*, June 1989, 34–38.

McKinley, James C.
1989 In New York, New Drug Tests Set for Police. *New York Times*, September 6, 1989, 16.

REFERENCES

MacLeod, Roy
1982a Introduction: Science and Examinations in Victorian England. Pp. 3–23 in MacLeod 1982b.
1982b *Days of Judgement: Science, Examinations and the Organization of Knowledge in Late Victorian England.* Driffield, N. Humberside: Nafferton.

Massing, Michael
1992 What Ever Happened to the "War on Drugs"? *New York Review of Books,* June 11, 1992, pp. 42–46.

Mead, George Herbert
1964 *On Social Psychology: Selected Papers.* Ed. Anselm Straus. Chicago: University of Chicago Press.

Mechanic, David
1978 *Students Under Stress: A Study in the Social Psychology of Adaptation.* Madison: University of Wisconsin Press.

Medina, N. J., and D. Monty Neill
1990 *Fallout from the Testing Explosion: How 100 Million Standardized Exams Undermine Equity and Excellence in America's Public Schools.* 3d rev. ed. Cambridge, Mass.: FairTest.

Meigs, Anna
1984 *Food, Sex, and Pollution: A New Guinea Religion.* New Brunswick, N.J.: Rutgers University Press.

Meinsma, Gloria
1985 Thou Shalt Not Steal: Employee Theft—Why It Happens and Where It Occurs. *Security Management,* December 1985, 35–37.

Midelfort, H. C. Erik
1972 *Witch Hunting in Southwestern Germany, 1562–1684: The Social and Intellectual Foundations.* Stanford: Stanford University Press.

Miike, Lawrence, and Maria Hewitt
1988 Accuracy and Reliability of Urine Drug Tests. *University of Kansas Law Review* 36:641–811.

Miller, Andrew C.
1991 Job Test Scores Spur Civil Rights Dispute. *Kansas City Star,* May 28, 1991, 1.

Milofsky, Carl
1989 *Testers and Testing: The Sociology of School Psychology.* New Brunswick, N.J.: Rutgers University Press.

Miners, Ian A., Nick Nykodym, and Diane M. Samerdyke-Traband
1987 Put Drug Detection to the Test. *Personnel Journal,* August 1987, 90–97.

Minton, Henry L.
1987 Lewis M. Terman and Mental Testing: In Search of the Democratic Ideal. Pp. 95–112 in Sokal 1987.

REFERENCES

Miyazaki, Ichisada
1976   *China's Examination Hell: The Civil Service Examinations of Imperial China*. Trans. and intro. by Conrad Schirokauer. New York: Weatherhill.

Moles, Abraham
1966   *Information Theory and Esthetic Perception*. Urbana: University of Illinois Press.

Molnar, Stephen
1992   *Human Variation: Races, Types, and Ethnic Groups*. 3d ed. Englewood Cliffs, N.J.: Prentice-Hall.

Moree, James E., Sr., and William Robert Clouse
1984   A New Touch to Employee Screening: Testing by Telephone Can Eliminate Bias. *Security Management*, September 1984, 102–105.

Morris, Norman
1961   An Historian's View of Examinations. Pp. 1–43 in Wiseman 1961.

Mulloy, Paul J.
1991   Winning the War on Drugs in the Military. Pp. 92–112 in Coombs and West 1991.

Munsterberg, Hugo
1908   *On the Witness Stand: Essays on Psychology and Crime*. New York: McClure.

Nagle, David E.
1985   The Polygraph in Employment: Applications and Legal Considerations. *Polygraph* 14:1–33.

Napier, Sandra Folzer
1976   Grading and Young Children. Pp. 23–27 in Simon and Bellanca 1976.

Nelkin, Dorothy, and Laurence Tancredi
1989   *Dangerous Diagnostics: The Social Power of Biological Information*. New York: Basic Books.

NIDA (National Institute on Drug Abuse)
1989a   *Highlights of the 1988 National Household Survey on Drug Abuse*. NIDA Capsules (rev. August 1989).

1989b   *Use and Consequences of Cocaine*. NIDA Capsules (rev. August 1989).

1990   *National Household Survey on Drug Abuse: Highlights 1988*. National Institute on Drug Abuse, DHHS Publication (ADM)90-1681.

1991   *National Household Survey on Drug Abuse: Highlights 1990*. National Institute on Drug Abuse, DHHS Publication (ADM)1789-91.

REFERENCES

Nimmo, D. B.
  1982   Mark Pattison and the Dilemma of University Examinations. Pp. 153–167 in MacLeod 1982b.
O'Bannon, R. Michael, Linda A. Goldinger, and Gavis S. Appleby
  1989   *Honesty and Integrity Testing: A Practical Guide.* Atlanta: Applied Information Resources.
Olneck, Michael, and James Crouse
  1978   *Myths of the Meritocracy: Cognitive Skills and Adult Success in the United States.* Madison: University of Wisconsin, Institute for Research on Poverty Discussion Papers 485–478.
Osipow, Samuel H.
  1983   *Theories of Career Development.* 3d ed. Englewood Cliffs, N.J.: Prentice-Hall.
OTA (U.S. Congress, Office of Technology Assessment)
  1990   *The Use of Integrity Tests for Pre-Employment Screening.* OTA-SET-442. Washington, D.C.: Government Printing Office.
Patterson, Travis B.
  1979   *Lie Detection via the Polygraph.* South Lake Tahoe: Marmaduke.
Payer, Lynn
  1988   *Medicine and Culture: Varieties of Treatment in the United States, England, West Germany, and France.* New York: Henry Holt.
Petch, J. A.
  1961   Examinations and the Grammar School. Pp. 44–61 in Wiseman 1961.
Picou, J. Steven, and Robert E. Campbell, eds.
  1975   *Career Behavior of Special Groups.* Columbus, Ohio: Merrill.
Plake, Barbara S., and Joseph C. Witt, eds.
  1986   *The Future of Testing: Buros-Nebraska Symposium on Measurement and Testing.* Vol. 2. Hillsdale, N.J.: Lawrence Erlbaum Associates.
Price, Carroll S.
  n.d.   *The Truth Detector.* Unpublished manuscript.
Prior, Leroy E.
  1985   Polygraph Testing of Vermont State Police Applicants. *Polygraph* 14:256–257.
Putnam, Richard L.
  1978   Polygraph Screening of Police Applicants: Necessity or Abuse? *Polygraph* 7:257–262.
Rapoport, D.
  1973   The Greening of the Lie Detector. *Washington Post*, April 15, 1973.

Rashdall, Hastings.
1936   *The Universities of Europe in the Middle Ages*. Oxford: Clarendon Press. 3 vols.
Reali, Sylvestro F.
1978   Reali's Positive Control Technique: A New Concept of Polygraph Procedure. *Polygraph* 7:281–285.
Reed, James
1987   Robert M. Yerkes and the Mental Testing Movement. Pp. 75–94 in Sokal 1987.
Resnick, Daniel
1982   History of Educational Testing. Pp. 173–194 in Wigdor and Garner 1982, Pt. II.
Richards, Lysander Salmon
1881   *Vocaphy: The New Profession*. Marlboro, Mass: Pratt Brothers.
Rizzo, Tony
1991   High-Tech Tests Are Focus of Suit on Wrongful Birth. *Kansas City Star*, December 3, 1991, A1.
Roach, John
1961   *Public Examinations in England, 1850–1900*. Cambridge: Cambridge University Press.
Roel, Ronald E.
1990   Study Doubts Honesty Tests Are. *Newsday*, October 14, 1990.
Rose, Laurence M., and Timothy H. Girard
1988   Drug Testing in Professional and College Sports. *University of Kansas Law Review* 36:787–821.
Rotunda, D. P.
1942   *Motif-Index of the Italian Novella in Prose*. Bloomington: Indiana University Press.
Rudolph, Frederick
1962   *The American College and University: A History*. New York: Knopf.
Rushton, J. Philippe
1980   *Altruism, Socialization, and Society*. Englewood Cliffs, N.J.: Prentice-Hall.
Ryan, Doris W., and Eugene L. Gaier
1967   Interest Inventories and the Developmental Framework. *Personnel and Guidance Journal* 46:37–41.
Ryle, Gilbert
1949   *The Concept of Mind*. London: Hutchinson.
Sackett, Paul R., Laura R. Burris, and Christine Callahan
1989   Integrity Testing for Personnel Selection: An Update. *Personnel Psychology* 42:491–529.
Sackett, Paul R., and Michael M. Harris
1984   Honesty Testing for Personnel Selection: A Review and Critique. *Personnel Psychology* 37:221–245.

REFERENCES

Samelson, Franz

1987   Was Early Mental Testing (a) Racist Inspired, (b) Objective Science, (c) A Technology for Democracy, (d) The Origin of Multiple Choice Exams, (e) None of the Above? (Mark the RIGHT Answer). Pp. 113–127 in Sokal 1987.

Scanlon, Walter F.

1986   *Alcoholism and Drug Abuse in the Workplace: Employee Assistance Programs.* New York: Praeger.

Schieffelin, Edward

1976   *The Sorrow of the Lonely and the Burning of the Dancers.* New York: St. Martins.

Schmidt, Frank L.

1988   The Problem of Group Differences in Ability Test Scores in Employment Selection. *Journal of Vocational Behavior* 33: 272–292.

Schweiker, Robert

1968   Discard the Semantic Confusion Related to "Intelligence": A Comment on "Social Class, Race, and Genetics: Implications for Education." *American Educational Research Journal* 5: 717–721.

Seymour, Richard T.

1988   Why Plaintiffs' Counsel Challenge Tests, and How They Can Successfully Challenge the Theory of "Validity Generalization." *Journal of Vocational Behavior* 33:331–364.

Sharf, James C.

1988   Litigating Personnel Measurement Policy. *Journal of Vocational Behavior* 33:272–292.

Silverberg, Ben A.

1980   Attitudes of Job Applicants and Employees Toward the Polygraph. *Polygraph* 9:162–169.

Simon, Sidney B., and James A. Bellanca, eds.

1976   *Degrading the Grading Myths: A Primer of Alternatives to Grades and Marks.* Washington, D.C.: Association for Supervision and Curriculum Development.

Slocum, W. L.

1965   Occupational Careers in Organizations: A Sociological Perspective. *Personnel and Guidance Journal* 43:858–866.

Smallwood, Helen

1935   *An Historical Study of Examinations and Grading Systems in Early American Universities.* Cambridge: Harvard University Press.

Smith, Elsie J.

1980   Career Development of Minorities in Nontraditional Fields. *Journal of Non-White Concerns in Personnel and Guidance* 8:141–156.

1983   Issues in Racial Minorities' Career Behavior. Pp. 161–222 in
        Walsh and Osipow 1983, Vol. I.
Smith, Gloria S.
1980   Developing Career Cognizance, Goals and Choices in Minor-
        ities. *Journal of Non-White Concerns in Personnel and Guid-
        ance* 9:19–22.
Smith, Robert Ellis
1977   Statement of Robert Ellis Smith, Publisher, Privacy Journal.
        Polygraph 6:401–408.
Sokal, Michael M., ed.
1987   *Psychological Testing and American Society, 1890–1930.* New
        Brunswick, N.J.: Rutgers University Press.
Sosnowski, Daniel E.
1985   Curbing Employee Theft—How Firms Do It. *Security Manage-
        ment,* September 1985, 109–112.
Stafford, Diane.
1991   Inmates Undergo First DNA Testing. *Kansas City Star,* No-
        vember 28, 1991, C19.
Starkman, Randy
1991   New Wonder Drug May Speed Athletes to the Killing Fields.
        Toronto Star, April 17, 1991, B1.
Sternberg, Robert J.
1985   *Beyond IQ: A Triarchic Theory of Human Intelligence.* Cam-
        bridge: Cambridge University Press.
1988   *The Triarchic Mind: A New Theory of Human Intelligence.*
        New York: Viking.
Stewart, Naomi
1947   A.G.C.T. Scores of Army Personnel Grouped by Occupation.
        Occupations 26:5–41.
Sullenberger, Tom E.
1985   Is the Polygraph Suited to Pre-Employment Screening? *Secu-
        rity Management,* August 1985, 44–48.
Sullivan, Louis, and Robert Martinez
1991   News Conference, December 19, 1991. Federal Information
        Systems Corporation, Federal News Service.
Super, Donald E.
1953   A Theory of Vocational Development. *American Psychologist*
        8:185–190.
Super, Donald E., et al.
1974   *Measuring Vocational Maturity for Counseling and Evalua-
        tion.* N.p.: National Vocational Guidance Association.
Sweetland, Richard C., and David J. Keyser, eds.
1986   *Tests: A Comprehensive Reference for Assessment in Psychol-
        ogy, Education, and Business.* 2d ed. Kansas City: Test Cor-
        poration of America.

REFERENCES

Taylor, John M.
1908   *The Witchcraft Delusion in Colonial Connecticut, 1647–1697.*
        New York: Grafton Press.
Terman, Lewis M.
1916   *The Measurement of Intelligence.* Boston: Houghton Mif-
        flin.
1919   *The Intelligence of School Children.* Boston: Houghton Mif-
        flin.
1924   The Conservation of Talent. *School and Society* 19:359–
        364.
Thernstrom, Stephan
1970   *Poverty and Progress: Social Mobility in a Nineteenth-Century
        City.* New York: Atheneum.
Thompson, Stith
1956   *Motif-Index of Folk-Literature.* Vol. 3. Bloomington: Indiana
        University Press.
Thorndike, E. L.
1920   Intelligence and Its Uses. *Harper's Magazine* 140:227–
        235.
1922   Measurement in Education. Pp. 1–9 in Whipple 1922.
1940   *Human Nature and the Social Order.* New York: Macmillan.
Tolchin, Martin
1991   Professor Passes a Polygraph Test. *New York Times,* October
        14, 1991, A10.
Trilling, Lionel
1972   *Sincerity and Authenticity.* Cambridge: Harvard University
        Press.
Vance, Randolph
1955   *The Devil's Pretty Daughter and Other Ozark Folk Tales.* New
        York: Columbia University Press.
Vroon, Pieter A.
1980   *Intelligence: On Myths and Measurement.* Advances in Psy-
        chology, 3. Amsterdam: North Holland Publishing Co.
Walsh, J. Michael, and Jeanne G. Trumble
1991   The Politics of Drug Testing. Pp. 22–49 in Coombs and West
        1991.
Walsh, W. Bruce, and Samuel H. Osipow, eds.
1983   *Handbook of Vocational Psychology,* Hillsdale, N.J.: Erlbaum.
        2 vols.
Weber, Max
1958   *The Protestant Ethic and the Spirit of Capitalism.* New York:
        Charles Scribner's Sons.
Weintraub, Karl J.
1975   Autobiography and Historical Consciousness. *Critical In-
        quiry* 1:821–848.

REFERENCES

Whipple, Guy Montrose, ed.
1922   *Intelligence Tests and Their Uses.* National Society for the
        Study of Education. Twenty-first Yearbook. Bloomington, Ill:
        Public School Publishing Company.
White, Lawrence T.
1984   Attitudinal Consequences of the Preemployment Polygraph
        Examination. *Journal of Applied Social Psychology* 14:364–
        373.
Whyte, William H., Jr.
1956   *The Organization Man.* New York: Simon and Schuster.
Wigdor, Alexandra K., and Wendell R. Garner, eds.
1982   *Ability Testing: Uses, Consequences, and Controversies.* 2 pts.
        Washington, D.C.: National Academy Press.
Williams, James H.
1979   Career Counseling for the Minority Student: Should It Be Dif-
        ferent? *Journal of Non-White Concerns in Personnel and Guid-
        ance* 7:176–182.
Winslow, Ron
1990   Study May Spur Job-Applicant Drug Screening. *Wall Street
        Journal*, November 28, 1990.
Wiseman, Stephen, ed.
1961   *Examinations and English Education.* Manchester: Manches-
        ter University Press.
Woodard, Bill
1990   Measure for Measure. *Kansas Alumni Magazine*, June 1990,
        pp. 30–35.
Wyllie, Irvin G.
1954   *The Self-Made Man in America: The Myth of Rags to Riches.*
        New Brunswick, N.J.: Rutgers University Press.
Young, Michael
1959   *The Rise of the Meritocracy, 1870–2033: The New Elite of Our
        Social Revolution.* New York: Random House.
Zemper, Eric D.
1992   Drug Testing in Athletics. Pp. 113–139 in Coombs and West
        1991.
Zenderland, Leila
1987   The Debate Over Diagnosis: Henry Herbert Goddard and the
        Medical Acceptance of Intelligence Testing. Pp. 46–74 in
        Sokal 1987.
Zwerling, Craig, James Ryan, and Endel John Orav
1990   The Efficacy of Preemployment Drug Screening for Marijuana
        and Cocaine in Predicting Employment Outcome. *Journal of
        the American Medical Association*, November 28, 1990, 2639–
        2643.

REFERENCES

Zytowski, Donald G., ed.
   1973   *Contemporary Approaches to Interest Measurement*. Minneapolis: University of Minnesota Press.
Zytowski, Donald G., and Fred M. Borgen
   1983   Assessment. Pp. 5–40 in Walsh and Osipow 1983, vol. 2.

INDEX

Compositor: Braun-Brumfield, Inc.
Text: 10/13 Auriga
Display: Eurostile Bold Extended
Printer: Braun-Brumfield, Inc.
Binder: Braun-Brumfield, Inc.